PRENTICE HALL
FOUNDATIONS OF MODERN SOCIOLOGY SERIES

Alex Inkeles, Editor

SO-BPI-470

INDUSTRIAL SOCIOLOGY
Ivar Berg

INTRODUCTION TO SOCIAL RESEARCH, Second Edition
Ann Bonar Blalock/Hubert M. Blalock, Jr.

RACE AND ETHNIC RELATIONS
Hubert M. Blalock, Jr.

THE LIFE COURSE: A Sociological Perspective
John A. Clausen

DEVIANCE AND CONTROL
Albert K. Cohen

MODERN ORGANIZATIONS
Amitai Etzioni

SOCIAL PROBLEMS
Amitai Etzioni

AGING AND OLD AGE: New Perspectives
Anne Foner

THE SOCIOLOGY OF MEDICINE: A Participant Observer's View
Renée C. Fox

LAW AND SOCIETY: An Introduction
Lawrence M. Friedman

THE FAMILY, Second Edition
William J. Goode

GENDER ROLES AND POWER
Jean Lipman-Blumen

THE SOCIOLOGY OF SMALL GROUPS, Second Edition
Theodore M. Mills

THE SOCIOLOGY OF RELIGION, Second Edition
Thomas F. O'Dea/Janet Aviad

A SOCIOLOGICAL PERSPECTIVE ON POLITICS
Mildred A. Schwartz

DELINQUENCY AND SOCIETY
James F. Short

THE EVOLUTION OF SOCIETIES
Talcott Parsons

SOCIAL STRATIFICATION: The Forms and Functions of Inequality,
Second Edition
Melvin M. Tumin

DELINQUENCY AND SOCIETY

A15042 031622

JAMES F. SHORT

Washington State University

HV
9104
.S449
1990
WEST

Prentice Hall, Englewood Cliffs, New Jersey 07632

Library of Congress Cataloging-in-Publication Data

Short, James F.
  Delinquency and society / James F. Short.
     p.   cm. -- (Prentice Hall foundations of modern sociology
  series)
  Bibliography: p.
  Includes index.
  ISBN 0-13-199258-9
  1. Juvenile delinquency--United States. I. Title. II. Series.
HV9104.S449 1990
364.3'6'0973--dc19   89-31334
                                                      CIP

Editorial/production supervision and
  interior design: Merrill Peterson
Manufacturing buyer: Carol Bystrom

 © 1990 by Prentice-Hall, Inc.
A Division of Simon & Schuster
Englewood Cliffs, New Jersey 07632

All rights reserved. No part of this book may be
reproduced, in any form or by any means,
without permission in writing from the publisher.

Printed in the United States of America

10 9 8 7 6 5 4 3 2 1

ISBN 0-13-199258-9

Prentice-Hall International (UK) Limited, *London*
Prentice-Hall of Australia Pty. Limited, *Sydney*
Prentice-Hall Canada Inc., *Toronto*
Prentice-Hall Hispanoamericana, S.A., *Mexico*
Prentice-Hall of India Private Limited, *New Delhi*
Prentice-Hall of Japan, Inc., *Tokyo*
Simon & Schuster Asia Pte. Ltd., *Singapore*
Editora Prentice-Hall do Brasil, Ltda., *Rio de Janeiro*

CONTENTS

CHAPTER   **3**

PROCEDURAL REFORM   44

CHAPTER   **4**

**BEHAVIORAL CONTEXTS OF JUVENILE DELINQUENCY:
POLICE AND JUVENILE COURTS   61**

CHAPTER   7

MACROSOCIAL FORCES AND PRINCIPLES   133

CHAPTER 8

CHAPTER 9

CHAPTER 10

DELINQUENCY AND SOCIETY 209

PREFACE

This volume is the culmination of four decades of study and research, of working with delinquents and thinking about juvenile delinquency. It is embarrassing to report that it is nearly three decades since I first undertook to write a book on the topic. That first effort floundered, despite the encouragement and goodwill of Arnold Rose, who had pressed the project on me. Research and other commitments, which seemed to be more fun, always seemed to interfere with the writing of that first book, and so the years have passed by.

In addition to a well-developed sense of guilt over the incompletion of that first book, this present book is motivated by my conviction that the study of juvenile delinquency ought to become part of the mainstream of the social and behavioral sciences. In this book I try to relate the special theories of criminology to the more general theories of human behavior. The book is also my most ambitious attempt to integrate much of my own research into the work of others who have studied juvenile delinquency. In doing this, the book is selective, rather than exhaustive; focused, rather than encyclopedic.

I have organized the study of juvenile delinquency in this book somewhat differently from what is usually done in traditional texts. The institutions and agencies of law enforcement are treated, as I believe they must be, as part of the social setting, and, therefore, as part of the etiology of juvenile delinquency. The special recognition given them is due solely to their special missions and functions. The *ideal* role of law enforcement institutions has always been to reflect and to reinforce community values, and also a variety of special interests, found in communities. Those values and special interests are manifest, and they operate, both through institutions and interpersonal relationships. The treatment of institutions as behavioral settings for delinquent behavior is selective and illustrative, rather than exhaustive.

Two other features of the book deserve mention. Except for the treatment of law enforcement institutions noted previously, little attention is given the vast machinery of juvenile justice and the other efforts used to control delinquency. Correctional institutions, probation, and parole are treated extensively elsewhere, and space and time considerations have precluded their detailed consideration in this volume.

Finally, it should be noted that the book draws almost entirely from work published in English. In addition, except for the excellent work of David Farrington, at the Institute of Criminology, Cambridge, and the work of a few other British scholars, the literature review comes largely from the United States. This is necessitated by my inadequacy in other languages and by my despair at the prospect of taking into account the very large literature on juvenile delinquency from other societies and cultures. The major exceptions to these limitations are in Chapter 2, which discusses historical aspects, and in Chapter 7, which treats macrosocial theories and research.

ACKNOWLEDGMENTS

When Alex Inkeles first asked me to write a volume on juvenile delinquency for the Foundations of Sociology series, I accepted with some trepidation, based on my earlier experience. Were it not for his patience and unfailing support, and his always attentive and helpful editing, this volume would never have been completed. I am grateful beyond the telling for all the ways in which he has helped me bring the book to completion.

I am grateful, also, to collaborators, beginning with Andy Henry, from whom, over the years, I have learned so much. Albert Cohen and Fred Strodtbeck deserve special mention. I thank Al for our early collaboration on chapters for the Merton and Nisbet edited text, *Contemporary Social Problems*, and for his continued friendship and support over the years. I thank Fred for his collaborative role in the Chicago gang research. Special acknowledgment must be made also of Washington State University, which has provided a stimulating and comfortable setting in which to work and a variety of support services. I wish to thank the faculty and student colleagues at the university who have supported me in other ways, both professionally and personally. The critiques of the entire manuscript by Bob Meier and Mark Stafford have been especially helpful.

Finally, to my wife, Kelma, and to our children and grandchildren this book is lovingly and humbly dedicated.

CHAPTER 1
DEFINING, STUDYING, AND EXPLAINING JUVENILE DELINQUENCY

This book is about juvenile delinquency and the young people we call juvenile delinquents. By one definition, juvenile delinquents are persons so defined by the law. While that definition is accurate insofar as the *legal* status of a "juvenile delinquent" is concerned, it is unsatisfactory and inaccurate in other respects. We shall see, for example, that behavior *legally* defined as delinquent is so varied that knowing a young person is legally delinquent tells us very little about him or her, or about his or her *behavior*. In addition, many less serious forms of juvenile delinquency occur almost universally among adolescents, yet most adolescents do not become officially delinquent in a legal sense. What, then, is juvenile delinquency, and who are the juvenile delinquents?

THE NATURE OF JUVENILE DELINQUENCY

At one level, juvenile delinquency is defined by a large number of laws, institutions, and beliefs regarding children and their behavior, and it is defined by the legal machinery and institutions developed to control behavior considered delinquent and to cope in other ways with youth problems. None of these elements is static, and, therefore, social change further complicates problems of analysis and understanding.

At another level, juvenile delinquency is *behavior*: the behavior of young people, their families, peers, and others who are involved in the behavioral settings out of which delinquent behavior emerges. These settings, too, change continuously.

Some delinquent behavior is serious, challenging personal or institutional values; some is trivial, posing no threat to such values, but sufficiently offensive to the sensitivities of others that the law is, at times, mobilized. Crimes are also delinquencies when they are committed by minors. But there are exceptions to this, as when a crime is committed by someone too young to be considered responsible for such an act. In addition, some acts are unlawful *only* when committed by minors. These *status offenses*—so termed because the age and status of the minors defines them as illegal—include many behaviors which are highly valued and even encouraged in most societies, for example, the freedom to work, to marry, to move, and to consume alcohol. We will want to understand how and why these restrictions on youthful behavior are proscribed under the law.

Other matters under the jurisdiction of juvenile courts focus on the behavior of parents or other guardians, and on certain *living conditions* of juveniles. These matters include child neglect, dependency, and abuse. Dependency entails no legal fault on the part of parents or guardians, only the inability to care for a child. Neglect and abuse generally imply legal fault, the former for inadequate care, the latter for willful injury to a child. While our chief concern is with delinquent behavior, many of the same historical and contemporary issues that relate to delinquency also relate to these other types of behavior.

This first chapter has a dual purpose: to engage the reader in thinking about the major issues to be addressed in the book, and to outline the presentation of these issues.

JUVENILE DELINQUENCY AS A SOCIAL PROBLEM

The first issue concerns the description and analysis of juvenile delinquency as a social problem. This is no simple task. As noted previously, juvenile delinquency is composed of many elements. It is a social construction of enormous complexity.[1] Chapters 2 and 3 examine the historical circumstances and the legal heritage out of which that social construction emerged. Fundamental changes in relations between parents and children, and between families and the larger society, were necessary before juvenile delinquency as a social problem could even exist. Religious, political, and economic changes were critical aspects of this history, and they continue to influence the nature of juvenile delinquency.

Chapters 4 and 5 explore the equally complex behavior of juveniles and others—on the street, in schools, in police stations, in courts, in families, and in communities—through which juvenile behavior becomes juvenile delinquency, and through which juveniles become juvenile delinquents. The emphasis in these chapters is less historical and more contemporary than in the two previous chapters.

Identification of delinquent acts and youngsters as delinquent involves interaction among people, and it involves many *decisions:* for the *juvenile* (whether or not to act in a particular way), for the *victim* (whether or not to report the act to the police and file a complaint), for the *police* (whether or not to settle the matter by reprimand or by arrest). And decisions are made up the line through the offices of prosecutors, court officials, judges, and others involved in the juvenile justice system. Prior to these interactions and decisions, political decisions are involved (with all the interactions these entail) as laws are passed and enforcement policies determined. At every juncture decisions are made, and at several points records are entered, in police and court files, on correctional institution rosters, and often in other institutional settings.

MEASURING JUVENILE DELINQUENCY: SOME PROBLEMS AND SOLUTIONS

At what point do we "identify" delinquents? At what point do we "measure" delinquency? Whose behavior are we identifying, and what is being measured? The answers to these questions are the subject of much controversy. They have consequences for juveniles and for those whose actions produce the official records. The answers to these questions influence public understanding and public policy with respect to delinquency as a social problem. They are important, as well, for social scientists who study the nature of delinquency as a social problem.

What are we to make of reports of rising (or falling) numbers of arrests or convictions, or of changing prison or juvenile institution populations? As must be clear from previous remarks, behavioral events provide many opportunities for counting and for the accumulation of statistics. What is counted varies greatly from one jurisdiction to another, depending on policies and practices of those doing the counting—depending also on the behavior of juveniles and on such matters as complainant preferences. A broad range of evidence on the amount and types of violative behavior, and its distribution among categories of people, will be presented in Chapter 6. In this first chapter, however, we consider a few general problems and principles associated with measuring delinquency and delinquents.

A major problem with all sources of data concerning both delinquency and delinquents—that is, data about the extent and nature of the behavior we call delinquency, and the children we define as delinquents—is *representativeness*. How representative of the total problem, or of some aspect of it, are data available from official records or other sources? Representativeness is critical to the reliability (the extent to which repeated measures provide data that are not biased) and validity (the fit between data and the reality of phenomena to which data refer) of statements about the extent and the nature of juvenile delinquency and about those who become delinquent.

OFFICIAL RECORDS

Agencies which report official statistics are public bodies, responsible to some executive or judicial branch of government. They are, therefore, subject to pressures from the constituencies of those branches of government, and they are concerned that reports of their activities should not reflect badly on their job performance. Many efforts have been made to improve the quality of official statistics, and great improvements have been made. But we should never forget that the recording of delinquent acts, and of delinquent youth, for official purposes is always the result of official decision making.

More than half a century ago, *three general principles* or *criteria* were enunciated as guidelines for the recording of law violations by the authorities:

1. *Measures of behavior are more representative if they are close to the events being reported, in time, place, or in the relationship of the observer to the event.* Conversely, the further away measures are from the actual commission of delinquent acts, the less reliable are records of those acts.
2. Crimes, in order to be reliably reported, must be *serious enough to ensure that they will be brought to the attention of authorities* by the victims or by others.
3. *There must be an injured party* who knows he or she has been offended against.

The most widely utilized reports of crime in the United States are the Uniform Crime Reports (UCR), compiled annually by the Federal Bureau of Investigation. These reports are based on these three principles.

Criteria 2 and 3 are important because crime comes to the attention of social control institutions (i.e., the police and the courts) primarily as a result of the activities of other people—victims, witnesses, or other concerned citizens. For the most part, as we shall see in greater detail in Chapter 4, the police and the courts "discover" crimes and other "problems" by means of reports from citizens. Even when police act "proactively," as in the case of "stake outs," they do so largely in response to citizen reports and concerns.

Criteria 2 and 3 are especially troublesome with respect to juvenile delinquency, since so much delinquent behavior is of minor seriousness. Many delinquent acts (including most status offenses) do not involve an injured party who is likely to report the offense, since the "victim" is often also the "offender" in such cases.

Police data satisfy the first of these criteria better than data gathered at other points in the juvenile and criminal justice systems, but much behavior that comes to the attention of the police does not meet the standards of the other two criteria (a crime of seriousness and a knowing victim). By these criteria even the broadest police data are inadequate with respect to the vast numbers of vaguely described behaviors that appear under the laws defining juvenile delinquency. Note, also, that *crimes* known to the police provide no information about *persons* committing crimes.

Juvenile (and criminal) court data are even further removed from the actual behavior of juveniles, and institutional records even further removed. Neither provide good measures of delinquency in the general population because they comprise samples of *unknown representativeness* of children who engage in delinquent behavior.

The argument has been made that court records represent a *lower bound* of *severity* for purposes of defining the delinquent and for assessing delinquency in society. Robert A. Gordon has shown that participation in delinquency based on this criterion demonstrates consistency over a variety of conditions.[2] Much juvenile delinquency that comes to the attention of both the police and the courts consists of less serious behavior, however. In addition, youth at any stage of processing in the juvenile justice system are influenced in a variety of ways by their experiences in that system, experiences which are themselves the basis for the statistics of the system. Because we are interested in the nature of such experiences, and their effects on young people, we will examine data gathered by a variety of methods in order to identify and study delinquents and to measure delinquency.

ALTERNATIVE METHODS

It may be helpful to conceptualize the behavior of juvenile delinquents as falling on a continuum of *inclusiveness*. One end of the continuum is represented by those who are incarcerated—for all practical purposes, the most extreme official action. Juveniles, as we shall see, are incarcerated only after multiple screenings. Incarcerated delinquents are therefore the least representative of juveniles who break the law, though they are very likely more representative of the most serious offenders. At the other end of the continuum is the delinquent *behavior* of juveniles, some portion of which becomes known to others, who may or may not bring it to the attention of officials. At this most inclusive end of the continuum—inclusive of both persons and acts of a delinquent nature—are reports by respondents to surveys of their own behavior, commonly referred to as *self-reports*. In between these extremes lie other sources of data concerning delinquency and delinquents.

Investigators have been quite inventive in pursuit of information about the extent and nature of delinquent behavior and about the juveniles who engage in such behaviors. Some data have come from *clinical reports* from agencies that treat cases that have been referred to them not only by the police and the courts but also by schools and social agencies. Some data have come from *observational studies* in schools, in gang hangouts, and other settings where delinquent behavior often occurs. Other data are available from a variety of *surveys*.

We have learned much from these studies. Some are rich in detail, and the best of them speak to questions of causation and control in ways which official records and large scale surveys cannot. Like official statistics, however, most of these methods are of unknown representativeness. How representative—and, therefore, how generalizable—are studies of a single school or school system, for example? Similarly, it is impossible to judge precisely the generalizability of findings from observational studies, for example, studies based on the observation of particular gangs in relation to other gangs. Similar problems attend studies based on the reports of clinics to which problem youth are referred.

Questions such as these cannot be answered solely on the basis of representativeness, as problematic as that may be. At issue, also, are problems related to the objectivity of investigators and what they have been trained to see and to overlook. It has often been noted that ways of seeing are also ways of not seeing. The *ways* in which we are trained to observe the world about us do not equip us to observe many significant features of social life. In addition, the *things* or *features* we are trained to observe may cause us to miss things of significance. A psychologist may neglect to observe what is considered most important to a sociologist or an economist, for example. *Assumptions* made by one discipline may be regarded as problematic and important by another discipline. Problems such as these become most important when we try to understand what *causes* something. These problems are important, also, in influencing the accuracy of a description. The following example from research on youth gangs in Chicago illustrates these problems:[3]

> Throughout the project we placed graduate research assistants in the field with detached workers (so-called because they worked with gang members on the gang's turf, rather than in institutional buildings and through conventional programs). One evening early in the project, a graduate research assistant was observing a group on Chicago's near South Side in their pool hall hangout. He knew most of the boys, and they knew him, and he thought he knew what was happening...The pool hall was a place where young and old met and socialized but where outsiders, unless they were under "legitimate" sponsorship as was our observer because he was sponsored by a detached worker, were decidedly unwelcome. About the middle of the evening the detached worker asked the observer if he had noted the drug transactions going on. He had not, though it was happening literally in front of his eyes. He had noted that an attractive girl occasionally took the pool cue from one of the boys who was playing, but this boy's actions appeared little different from those of others in the group. In fact they were, for this boy, nicknamed "Smack-Daddy" or "Slap-Daddy" for his heroin habit, was pushing drugs. The girl was a prostitute who also pushed drugs, leaving the more dangerous part of the task, carrying and transferring drugs to the customer, to the gang boy. The latter was carried out with considerable sophistication, since no direct contact ever was made between buyer and seller.
>
> The point is not so much that our research assistant's observations would have been inaccurate, but they would have been incomplete in important respects without the greater knowledge and sophistication provided by the detached worker. In other respects, particularly concerning sensitivity to types of data which are important conceptually, the detached workers lacked the sophistication of research assistants. Both were important to the project.

These observations were part of a carefully designed research program that employed a variety of research methodologies involving close collaboration between behavioral scientists, trained graduate students, and "streetwise" youth workers. Malcolm Klein and Cheryl Maxson note that the mid-1960s was a period during which street work programs and gang research reached high levels of sophistication.[4] Much has changed since that period. Street work declined in popularity after the 1960s, as did research on gangs.[5] In contrast, police organization and intelligence with respect to gangs has increased dramatically in many cities since the 1960s. Correspondingly, Klein and Maxson suggest, the sophistication of police information concerning gang activity has increased. It is important to note, however, that police information is collected *for police purposes* and not for scientific research purposes. The usefulness of police data for the study of crime causation (etiology) is, therefore, limited.

The richest descriptions of delinquent behavior are based on systematic observations of individuals and groups, or on delinquents' own descriptions of their behavior. These observations have often been the basis for hypotheses concerning the etiology of delinquent behavior and the nature of delinquency as a social problem. When observational descriptions are added to data gathered by other means *on more general populations,* it is possible to construct a more complete portrayal of the extent and the nature of delinquent behavior.

Two principle strategies have been used to gather data on more general populations: (1) self-reports, and (2) victimization reports. Both employ standard survey research techniques.[6] Samples are drawn from a city, state, or nation. Respondents are asked to complete a questionnaire or they are interviewed concerning (1) their involvement in a list of behaviors, including delinquent behaviors, and (2) their behavior as the victim of a criminal act. The number and types of acts studied vary greatly, as do the methods employed to elicit the information. Evaluation of data generated by both of these research strategies is presented in Chapter 6.

THEORETICAL PERSPECTIVES ON DELINQUENTS AND DELINQUENCY

In the course of a study of police encounters with juveniles in three midwestern and western cities, a well-developed rationale concerning the nature of the juvenile delinquency problem emerged from field observations and unstructured interviews. This "theory" of why delinquency occurs and why delinquents behave as they do is captured in the following comments by some of the police officers interviewed:[7]

> The classic violations come from this (lower-class) group...Boys from broken homes, father left, mother works, seem to have more difficulty with police and commit more serious crimes.
> ...the problem is with the parents' supervision. Lack of this can be a result of too much time at work, both parents working or a lack of interest in the rest of the family. I also feel when there is a lack of interest in the family you will find a lack of gainful employment.
> You see these (lower-class) kids out all the time running around. Their parents don't care. The kids live on the streets. They're street-wise. And their parents could care less. They don't give them any values.
> These kids have no supervision. Their parents let them get away with murder...If the parents would do their job we'd have a lot less problems. It's respect for adults, most of all their parents. That's what they lack.
> In 90 percent of the cases I handle the cause is found back in the first five years of the child's life. The home! It's due to the way a person is brought up. If they cannot be taught to respect other people and their property, it is the fault of the folks.
> For this kind (of lower-class boys) parental contacts are important— mother frequently works, father is tired, frustrated when he gets home. He (the lower-class boy) has the lower-class physical strength, daring which causes more of a disrespectful attitude toward the police.

The linkage of social class, parental neglect, and delinquency by these police officers is an example of a crude theory of delinquency. Theories are attempts to explain types of phenomena, for example, types of behavior, types of people engaging in the behavior, and types of *relationships* which may help to explain the behavior. Note the language used to describe the behavior and the youngsters involved in delinquency. References are made to "the classic violations," to "90 percent of the cases I handle," to "this kind" [of lower-class boy]. The explanations for this behavior are also generalized in such phrases as "broken homes," "parents' supervision," and "their parents don't care."

These generalizations are based on the beliefs and experiences of the police studied. The theory is crude not because it emanates from the police, but because it is not formally derived and based on a systematic examination of evidence or stated in testable terms. The opinions expressed by the police respondents in this study are little more than *descriptions* of the *common experiences* of these men and women. In the language of the social sciences, these experiences represent a restricted sampling of the relevant data. If, as often is the case in high-delinquency neighborhoods, a large proportion of *all* homes are "broken" by separation, divorce, or out-of-wedlock births, then "broken homes" can hardly be the sole *cause* of delinquent behavior. Instead, the question must be asked, what is it about the homes of delinquents, intact as well as broken, that leads to delinquent behavior?

The experiences shared by police men and women are important influences on the values and beliefs they bring to their work, and on their relationships with the public, including juveniles. The nature of these influences will be examined in later chapters.

Why should we be interested in theories at all? Why not simply "stick to the facts"? One reason is that it is extremely difficult to ascertain precisely what the facts *are,* or even to determine which facts are *relevant* to a knowledge of the extent and nature of juvenile delinquency. Description is critical to explanation in that it specifies what is to be explained, *but description does not explain.* Explanation is the province of theory. Neither the descriptive accounts of delinquency nor the statistics of social distribution can explain. But both descriptive accounts and statistics *require* explanation. Facts do not "speak for themselves."

An attempt is made, in Chapters 2 and 3, to explain the "invention of delinquency," its emergence as a social problem and its present and changing character. The explanation proceeds by reference to relevant historical evidence concerning the *creation* of the phenomena so loosely grouped under the term "juvenile delinquency." This historical evidence and its interpretation continue to be disputed, as new evidence is discovered and new interpretations are made.

Interpretation involves theories, implicitly or explicitly. There is also much dispute regarding theories. We turn now to a few of these disputes and to theories concerning the etiology, or causation, of delinquency and of delinquent behavior.

A NOTE ON THE LOGIC OF CAUSAL THINKING

The notion of *cause* has a variety of meanings. Lest there be any confusion, I mean that to the extent that "determining influences" can be ascertained, we may properly speak of *cause. Theories* of causation propose interpretations of the determining influences of phenomena. Theories interpret what is known, or thought to be known, about phenomena.

In the behavioral sciences, causal imputation is extraordinarily difficult for a variety of reasons. The subject matter is, to begin with, extremely complex and continually changing. Often we cannot even be certain that the factors which appear to be causal existed *prior* to the behavior or condition we wish to explain—and this is the most elementary requirement of causal analysis. In addition, many of the causal factors and processes of which our theories consist *interact* with the phenomena to be explained rather than being related in a simple and direct manner to them. Consider parent-child relations, which are demonstrably associated with much delinquent behavior. We know, for example, that parental rejection is associated with aggressive behavior by their children. The most common inference, supported by much evidence, is that parental rejection causes the aggressive behavior of their children. It is also the case, however, that parental rejection may *result from* the aggressive behavior of their children. Causation in this case may, therefore, go both ways; that is, the variables may be causes *and* effects of one another.

The point is more general: The causes of most human behavior involve interaction among variables. Human behavior *develops out of interaction*, rather than simply and directly in response to a specific stimulus or condition.

The complexity of phenomena is related to other characteristics of the sciences of human behavior: *Different aspects of behavior* are the focus of different social and behavioral sciences and professions. A further consequence of this division of labor is that *different sorts of questions* are asked regarding the behavior to be explained. Different hypotheses (and answers) are, of course, derived from different questions. Hypotheses differ in many ways—in the assumptions they make and in the causal processes or conditions they regard as most important. Healthy competition of ideas concerning behavior, conditions, and their relation to one another results from asking different questions. However, the resulting welter of questions and answers is often confusing, to specialists and nonspecialists alike.

Sciences and their practitioners tend to be specialized and parochial. As a general rule, the more advanced the science, the higher the degree of specialization of the subject matter, the theory, and the research methods of the science. This principle extends to specializations within, as well as between, disciplines. As a result of such differences, scientists of a particular stripe (e.g., geneticists, psychologists, sociologists, and the specialists within each of these disciplines) are often unacquainted with even the questions posed by other sciences, and little concerned with the answers provided by them.[8] Problems of understanding and communication between and within disciplines are compounded because critical review of theory and evidence is a hallmark of scientific disciplines. Disputes within, as well as between, disciplines therefore are frequent and often heated and confusing.

Some of the confusion which results from specialization (perhaps even parochialism) and criticism occurs because theories address different *levels of explanation.* The notion of levels of explanation is common in scientific discourse. Disciplines are identified with the levels of explanation to which they address questions, as when reference is made to biological, psychological, and sociological theories of behavior. Distinctions also are made within disciplines, for example, with respect to the psychobiological and the cognitive levels of explanation within psychology, or the situational levels within both psychology and sociology.

Explanation of any complex phenomenon, such as human behavior, may be sought in the operation of a variety of components and processes, not one of which is likely to be complete in its explanatory power. Disciplines and subdisciplines tend toward specialization in the components and processes they choose to study, and in their methods and techniques of study. What most clearly distinguishes social sciences from other sciences is that human beings are *active agents* in a sense quite different from the objects of study of the other sciences, even those sciences that deal with the behavior of other animals.

THE NATURE OF HUMAN NATURE

Not all theories of human behavior are in agreement with the previous statement. Disagreements most often focus on age-old questions as to whether or not, or the extent to which, human nature is aggressive or benign. Is human nature driven by innate drives, or is it plastic, a *tabula rasa* that can be shaped or determined in any manner? Or is it possessed of free will? Conceptions of the nature of human nature[9] embodied in various theories will be noted as seems appropriate throughout the book. We begin, however, with a brief discussion of the view that is adopted in this book. This view is widely (though not universally) shared within both scientific and philosophical communities. The reader may thus be forewarned as to whatever biases may be present in the discussions to follow.

Most contemporary scientific and philosophical statements reject the extreme positions regarding human nature as noted previously. Rather, they agree that human nature is neither aggressive nor benign, neither innately driven nor plastic, per se. One implication of this position is that it makes good sense to ask both what motivates and what controls delinquent acts; that is, "Why do they do it?" and "Why don't they do it?"

Albert Bandura's discussion of "distinctive human capabilities" captures the special sense in which human beings are active agents in their own behavior. Bandura stresses humans' "remarkable capacity to use symbols" that underlies the capability of "forethought," "the capacity to learn by observation" ("vicarious capability"), the "self-regulatory capability," and the "self-reflective capability."[10] Human nature, he concludes "is characterized by a vast potentiality that can be fashioned by direct and observational experience into a variety of forms within biological limits."[11] This "social cognitive" perspective will be more fully developed in Chapter 8.

Scientific conceptions of human nature are often posed, and opposed, in terms of the concept of determinism versus the concept of free will. Bandura notes that the social cognitive view of human nature is not incompatible with freedom. Indeed, "because self-influence operates deterministically on action...some measure of freedom is possible."[12] Similarly, determinism is not incompatible with personal responsibility. Behavior necessitates choices from among alternatives present in any situation, and self-influences on those choices are important determinants of action. Self-influence, the essence of personal responsibility, will be further examined in Chapter 8.

LEVELS OF EXPLANATION

Levels of explanation are distinguished by the questions they ask. Theories often differ, not so much because they disagree as to the answers, but because they ask different questions to begin with.

Much of this book is organized around three levels of explanation: the individual, the macrosocial, and the microsocial. These are not the only levels of explanation, and others may prove to be equally convincing or more powerful. Given the present state of knowledge, however, these three levels serve the useful purpose of organizing what is known about the kinds of questions that have been asked about delinquency and delinquents. These questions, and the conceptual distinctions they imply, may be described briefly as follows:[13]

1. *The individual level of explanation* inquires as to characteristics of *individuals* that explain delinquent behavior. It is to this level that most theories about delinquents and their behavior have been directed, both historically and in contemporary thinking. Data directed to questions posed at this level typically describe individuals and their behavior. Most delinquency control policies attempt to change individuals or to prevent individuals from committing crimes or from taking part in further delinquent behaviors.

2. *The macrosocial level (or simply the macro-level) of explanation* asks what it is about *social systems, social structures, and cultures* that produces different *rates* of delinquency and different views and laws defining what is considered criminal or delinquent.[14] The focus of theory and research at this level is on social systems, structures, and cultures, rather than on individuals. And it focuses on rates of behavior and differences in law and societal reaction, rather than on individuals who violate the law.

3. *The microsocial level (or micro-level)* focuses on *events*, rather than on individuals or social systems and structures. Attention is directed to the unfolding of events, to the interaction of parties involved in events—interaction which shapes their behavior. This level of explanation asks the following question: How did this *event* occur, and especially, what was the nature of the interaction among event participants which led to the outcome of this event? Note that as the term is being used in this book, microsocial does not refer to smallness. Micro-level questions may be addressed to events occurring in large or small groups, or in crowds, in institutional settings (such as school classrooms), or on city streets. This level focuses on *how human activity develops*, whatever the setting.

Most studies, and most theories, are focused on the individual and on the macrosocial levels of explanation. Traditional disciplines tend to be organized around either the individual or the macrosocial level. For example, psychology is concerned primarily with the individual level, whereas sociology divides its attention between the two. The micro-level, in contrast, has no such agreed upon usage among the disciplines. For example, the focus of micro-economics is on smaller economic systems; and sociologists' studies of small groups sometimes are referred to as "micro." As we use this term, however, the size of a group within which behavior occurs is *not* the focus of the microsocial level. Rather, it is on *ongoing action* within any setting, whether it is a large or a small group, a milling crowd, a structured situation, such as a school classroom, or a gathering on the street. A great deal of delinquency, as we shall see, develops out of the spontaneous interaction of participants. The microsocial level looks for explanatory principles in that interaction.

Problems posed by differing levels of explanation are dealt with in a variety of ways by scholars, as well as others. Some continue to urge either environmental determinism or the determinism of internal dispositions. Evidence of the importance of both types of influences, and of their interaction, has also led to "one-sided interactionism" in which behavior is conceptualized as passively determined. In contrast, the social cognitive model regards "behavior, cognitive and other personal factors, and environmental influences…as interlocking determinants that affect each other…"[15] The patterning and strength of mutual influences in this model are neither fixed nor immutable. Instead, the "relative influence exerted by the three sources of interlocking determinants will vary for different activities, different individuals, and different circumstances."[16] Sorting out these influences will be a major task of the chapters to follow.

Sociological criminologists have approached this task by employing a variety of classification systems. Donald R. Cressey, for example, distinguishes between "situational" ("mechanistic" or "dynamic") theories which focus on "processes which are operating at the moment of the occurrence of crime"—our microsocial level of explanation—and those that are "developmental" (or "historical"). The developmental levels encompass both the individual and macrosocial levels of explanation, as we are defining them, inasmuch as they are concerned with "processes operating in the earlier history of the criminal."[17] Don C. Gibbons notes that some crime "may be a response to nothing more temporal than the provocations and attractions bound up in the immediate circumstances" (our microsocial level).[18] Much violent behavior among intimates (between friends, lovers, husbands and wives, or parents and children) appears to "grow out of" the interaction of the moment. It is the task of the micro-level to explain why this is the case.

Other classification systems focus more narrowly on particular types of behavior, for example, Stanley Cohen's approach to the study of youth subcultures. Cohen distinguishes among *structure* ("aspects of society…beyond individual control," related to "the distribution of power, wealth, and differential location in the labor market"), *culture* (patterned response to structurally imposed conditions, e.g., traditions and ideologies), *subculture* (the forms of group and symbolic life by means of which structurally subordinate groups adapt to their condition), and *biography* (the "personal circumstances through which the culture and structure are experienced").[19] In terms of the tripartite classification employed in this volume, structure and culture are subsumed under the macro-level, whereas biography refers to the individual level of explanation.

Levels of explanation inform different aspects of behavior. They refer to *what is to be explained* as well as to *how it is to be explained*, and they imply different methods of inquiry and data analysis. No one level, no one analytic scheme or research method can fully comprehend the richness and complexity of human behavior, delinquent or nondelinquent. Data from one level are relevant to questions asked by the other levels; for example, data from the macro- and micro-levels help to explain the behavior of individuals located in particular social systems, structures, and cultures, who are caught up in particular ongoing events. But the focus of the questions is different for each level, and theories and methods of entire disciplines have developed around these types of questions. Disciplinary specialization has resulted in vast amounts of information and interpretation—so much so that the theorists seem often to "talk past one another" in a welter of conflicting voices and claims.

A part of this confusion stems from the level of explanation problem. Disciplinary specialists address different questions. As a result, their theories concerning delinquency causation necessarily differ. In this book, therefore, we will focus on the levels of explanation for which data and theories are appropriate, and only then attempt to explain the causes of delinquency.

Levels of explanation will be further developed and extended, and the possibilities for their integration will be explored in Chapters 7 through 10. Answers to questions posed at one level of explanation clearly have *implications* for questions posed at other levels. While disciplines often "talk past one another," answers provided by one level of explanation should not be incompatible with answers provided by another level of explanation. Indeed, explanations at one level should—and do—contribute to greater understanding at other levels, often filling in gaps, clarifying or modifying assumptions and inferences made at other levels.

RESEARCH METHODS AND THE GENERATION OF KNOWLEDGE

The complexity of human behavior is dealt with in many ways by those who have attempted to understand particular aspects of it. While the focus of a particular study may be on a specific manifestation of some phenomenon, the search always is for findings of more general significance—descriptive of the phenomenon, to be sure—but more important for the *generalization* of determining influences. Investigators necessarily choose for study "samples" of the phenomena they wish to understand. Some researchers attempt to secure a sample representative of a population. A good example is the National Youth Survey, which is based on a sample of young people in the United States. Others choose an entire population, for example, a birth cohort, to study. Some study single cases and still others choose *extreme* cases for intensive examination. Study of highly aggressive youngsters, for example, may help to understand aggression that is less extreme, and the study of gangs may inform co-offending in general, as well as other types of behavior among youth collectivities. Extrapolations of these types of behavior must be made cautiously, however, lest the results be overgeneralized and misleading.

Each method has both advantages and disadvantages. The National Youth Survey, for example, has the great advantage of being statistically representative of the entire U.S. population within the age categories selected at the time of the study. Its sample size (1,725 young people) is impressive for studies such as this. Even more important, this sample has been repeatedly interviewed since the beginning of the survey in 1974, so behavioral changes over time can be measured. When we examine this series of surveys in some detail (in Chapter 6), however, we shall see that the extent to which findings concerning some population segments can be generalized (minorities, for example) is quite limited. In addition, since the several "waves" of the survey were conducted during particular years, influences of social change during other periods cannot be determined.

Survey methods have other inherent limitations—the amount and quality of information that can be elicited in a brief encounter between an interviewer and a respondent, for example, is limited in contrast to the richness of ethnographic accounts. The latter, however, are limited in other ways, for example, the representativeness of their samples may be limited, resulting in a generalizability that is more limited than are properly conducted surveys.

All methods have limitations. The official records studied in the best known of the birth cohort studies, for example, were limited to the information about the boys and their behavior that police chose to enter into the record, supplemented by school records and data concerning population and community characteristics. Studies of extreme cases yield much valuable information but it is of unknown representativeness of larger populations or broader phenomena. Another contribution of theories is that they are useful in overcoming the weaknesses of all research methods in the search for general knowledge.

Other methods of discovery and the inferences that can be made concerning behavior causation will be discussed in the context of specific studies and theoretical perspectives. First, however, theoretical assumptions and how they have influenced the history of social thought concerning crime and juvenile delinquency are noted.

THEORETICAL ASSUMPTIONS OF CLASSICAL AND POSITIVIST CRIMINOLOGY

All theories necessarily make *assumptions* as to the nature of the phenomena they wish to explain. Most assumptions are simplifying, in order to reduce complexity and facilitate systematic study and theory. Some are necessary for purposes of generalization, so that the conditions obtaining in an experiment or observation also apply beyond the experimental or observational situation. In the history of social thought the assumptions theorists make about human behavior have been critical to their interpretations and conclusions. At the individual level, certain assumptions were critical to the emergence of perhaps the first systematic body of thought to be applied to the control of crime, namely, the *classical school* of criminology.

A product of Enlightenment philosophy, the classical school stressed the perfectibility of humankind through the exercise of reason. Led by Cesare Beccaria, whose *On Crimes and Punishments* was published in 1764, the classical school assumed that human beings were self-seeking, rational, and possessed of free will to choose among behavior alternatives. Beccaria regarded crime prevention as a primary purpose of the criminal law. After Beccaria, Jeremy Bentham (1748–1832), an English philosopher, devoted his career largely to reform of the English common law.

The classical school is sometimes referred to as "hedonistic" because it regarded human choice as being governed by considerations of pleasure and pain. A person was assumed to choose from among behavioral alternatives that course of action which would yield the most pleasure and cost the least pain. This balancing of pleasure and pain was assumed to be the basic motivation of behavior.

The classical school theorists did not ask why individuals violate the law. That question did not require inquiry because it was assumed. Their primary concern was to reduce the arbitrary nature of criminal justice of the day and the severity of punishments under that system. The classical school theorists did not critically examine their assumptions about human nature. Challenges to the assumptions and conclusions of the classical school arose during the nineteenth century, however, as scientific thinking advanced rapidly and was extended to human behavior. Growing realization of the complexity of human nature and the social order, and demands for proof through systematic observation, led to rejection of the classical school assumptions by many.

The concept of human nature adopted in this book differs considerably from the assumptions and tenets of the classical school. However, both scientific and popular thinking about crime and its control continue to be influenced by these concepts.[20]

Positivism in criminology developed, in part, on the basis of research-based challenges to classical school assertions regarding the freedom of individuals to choose between criminal and noncriminal behavior. Paradoxically positivism, too, was very much a product of Enlightenment thinking. The focus of positivism was quite different from that of the classical school theory, however, as was its most fundamental assumption. That assumption was *determinism*. Perfectibility of humankind was to be achieved through advances in knowledge about the determinants of behavior and by the application of scientific methods to the study of social control.

Positivists wanted to explain the forces that control human behavior. For some, explanation was to be found in characteristics of individuals that determined their behavior, or in their family or economic circumstances. Others sought an explanation of the social distribution of crime and other social phenomena. For them explanations lay in macro-level *conditions*, for example, in variations among nations, communities, or economic systems. Positivism flourished as new disciplines became interested in crime, and as new and more systematic and rigorous methods of inquiry were applied to its study.

Most early challenges to classical school assumptions were addressed to individual-level questions. Theories at this level tended either to ignore macro-level influences on behavior or to assume that those influences were important only as they were mediated through individual characteristics. Conversely, macro-level theories either paid little attention to individual characteristics and differences, or they assumed that, for purposes of a given situation, the individual simply reflected the operation of macro-level phenomena.

LEVELS OF EXPLANATION AND THE ORGANIZATION OF KNOWLEDGE

Organization of knowledge about juvenile delinquency, crime, and their control poses many problems. A vast array of laws and institutions, facts and beliefs, theories and assumptions confronts the student. Entries under "Crime Causation" in the *Encyclopedia of Crime and Justice*, for example, include sections on "Biological Theories," "Economic Theories," "Political Theories," "Psychological Theories," and "Sociological Theories." Daniel Glaser's introductory discussion concludes "that it is futile to argue about the superiority of one or another of [these types of] theories."[21]

The superiority of any level of explanation is not at issue here. The five sections designated in the *Encyclopedia of Crime and Justice* are products of the academic organization found in the departments of colleges and research organizations. They mirror the disciplinary affiliations of researchers, rather than the nature of the knowledge base concerning the explanation of crime. Biological theories, for example, overlap with psychological theories in focusing on processes of learning that are related to crime and delinquent behavior. Anne Dryden Witte's discussion of economic theories focuses on individual-level decision making, while Harold Pepinsky's treatment of political theories is focused primarily on (macro-level) theories of the effects of state activity on crime. Yet, theories of economic organization (macro-level) have also been brought to bear in explaining various types of crime, and political alienation (an individual-level phenomenon) has been theorized to account for such crimes as terrorism. Sociological theories also ask questions at more than one level of explanation.

There is much confusion concerning the organization of knowledge about crime and delinquency causation. Texts classify theories in very different ways. Some authors equate conflict theories and Marxist approaches, while others recognize distinctions between them. Some ignore all such theories. By classifying theories according to the types of questions they ask regarding individuals, social and cultural systems, and situations, we hope to clarify areas of agreement and of disagreement, and their implications for understanding delinquency and delinquents.

We are now ready to turn to the historical background out of which juvenile delinquency developed. That history begins with the "discovery" of childhood.

NOTES

1. The social constructionist perspective is developed in Malcolm Spector and John Kitsuse, *Constructing Social Problems*. Menlo Park, CA: Addison-Wesley, 1976. See also, Armand Mauss, *Social Problems as Social Movements*. Philadelphia: Lippincott, 1975; and Joseph

Schneider, "The social construction of social problems," pp. 209–229, in Ralph W. Turner and James F. Short (eds.), *Annual Review of Sociology*, Vol. 11 (1985), Palo Alto, CA: Annual Reviews, Inc.

2. Gordon uses the term "prevalence" rather than "participation." See Robert A. Gordon, "Prevalence: the rare datum in delinquency measurement and its implications for the theory of delinquency," pp. 201–284, in Malcolm W. Klein (ed.), *The Juvenile Justice System*. Beverly Hills, CA: Sage. The quote is from p. 270. Much confusion surrounds this term, and "incidence" or "frequency." In order to standardize the meaning of these terms, we will use "participation," rather than "prevalence," and "frequency" rather than "incidence." *Participation* refers to "the distinction between those who engage in crime and those who do not." *Frequency* refers to how often crimes are committed. The best measures of frequency refer to "the rate of criminal (or delinquent) activity *of those who are active*." See Alfred Blumstein, Jacqueline Cohen, Jeffrey A. Roth, and Christy A. Visher (eds.), *Criminal Careers and "Career Criminals,"* Vol. I, Panel on Research on Criminal Careers, Committee on Research on Law Enforcement and the Administration of Justice, Commission on Behavioral and Social Sciences and Education, National Research Council. Washington, DC: National Academy Press, 1986, p. 1. Many studies confuse these terms by including all members of a sample in the computation of measures of frequency as well as of participation.

3. Adapted from James F. Short, Jr., "Gangs and universities: observations from research and other experiences," *Washington State Review*, Spring, 1967, p. 17. See also, James F. Short, Jr., and Fred Strodtbeck, *Group Process and Gang Delinquency*. Chicago: University of Chicago Press, 1965: Chap. 1.

4. See Malcolm W. Klein and Cheryl L. Maxson, "Street gang violence," in Marvin Wolfgang and Neil Weiner, *Violent Crime, Violent Criminals*. Beverly Hills, CA: Sage, forthcoming.

5. John C. Quicker, *Seven Decades of Gangs: What Has Been Learned, What Has Been Done, and What Should Be Done*. Prepared for the California Commission on Crime Control and Violence Prevention. State of California, 1983. Quoted in *Ibid*.

6. Early self-report studies were crudely designed questionnaires or interviews, administered primarily to samples of youngsters in college classes, in high schools, in delinquency prevention programs, or among incarcerated delinquents. This experimental phase of such research has been followed by research conducted on more rigorously selected samples, using more carefully designed questionnaires and interviews. Greater attention has been paid to including behaviors that are reported in official records. The history and the scientific development of self-reported delinquency methodology is covered, and the methodology advanced, in the excellent monograph by Michael J. Hindelang, Travis Hirschi, and Joseph G. Weis, *Measuring Delinquency*. Beverly Hills, CA: Sage, 1981. There is some evidence that youngsters who are most extensively and seriously involved in criminal behavior tend most to underreport that involvement.

7. Adapted from Marcia Garrett and James F. Short, Jr., "Social class v. personal demeanor in police stereotypes of juveniles," *Social Problems*, 22 (February, 1975):368–383.

8. The major exception to this observation is that practitioners of one science, or a specialty within a science, often dispute the relevance of disciplines or specialties other than that of the person making the criticism. Such criticism also occurs within specialties, of course. This is as true of the physical and biological sciences as it is for the social and behavioral sciences. See, for example, H. F. Judson, *The Eighth Day of Creation: Makers of the Revolution in Biology*. New York: Simon & Schuster, 1979.

9. With apologies to the many others who have used this phraseology. For an early sociological treatment of the topic see Elsworth Faris, *The Nature of Human Nature*. Chicago: University of Chicago Press, 1937.

10. Albert Bandura, "Model of causality in social learning theory," pp. 81–99, in Michael J. Mahoney and Arthur Freeman (eds.), *Cognition and Psychotherapy*. New York: Plenum, 1985. The quotations are from pp. 86–96. A more extensive exposition of the theory is found in Albert Bandura, *Social Foundations of Thought and Action: A Social Cognitive Theory*. Englewood Cliffs, NJ: Prentice-Hall, 1986.

11. *Ibid.*, p. 96.

12. *Ibid.*, p. 85.

13. Levels of explanation are not, of course, restricted to delinquent behavior and delinquency. For a more extended discussion of these and other levels of explanation, see James F. Short, Jr., "The level of explanation problem in criminology," pp. 51–72, in Robert F. Meier (ed.), *Theoretical Methods in Criminology.* Beverly Hills, CA: Sage, 1985.

14. The distinction between delinquent behavior and juvenile delinquency is similar to that made by Gottfredson and Hirschi between crimes and criminality. "Crimes are short-term, circumscribed events that presuppose a peculiar set of necessary conditions (e.g., activity, opportunity, adversaries, victims, goods). Criminality, in contrast, refers to stable differences across individuals in the propensity to commit criminal or theoretically equivalent acts." Michael Gottfredson and Travis Hirschi, "A propensity-event theory of crime," in *Advances in Criminological Theory,* Vol. 1; quoted in Travis Hirschi, "Exploring alternatives to integrated theory," in *Theoretical Integration in the Study of Deviance and Crime: Problems and Prospects.* Paper prepared for a conference at the State University of New York, Albany, NY: 1987.

15. Bandura, 1985, *op. cit.,* p. 83.

16. *Ibid.*

17. In Edwin H. Sutherland and Donald R. Cressey, *Criminology* (10th ed.). Philadelphia: Lippincott, 1978, p. 79.

18. Don C. Gibbons, "Observations on the study of crime causation," *American Journal of Sociology,* 77:262–278.

19. Stanley Cohen, *Folk Devils and Moral Panics: The Creation of the Mods and Rockers.* New York: St. Martins Press, 1980, p. v.

20. See, for example, David Matza's discussion of "soft determinism" in *Delinquency and Drift.* New York: Wiley, 1964. For a discussion of economic theories of choice, see Ann Dryden Witte, "Crime causation: economic theories," pp. 316–322, in Sanford Kadish (ed.), *Encyclopedia of Crime and Justice.* New York: Macmillan and Free Press, 1983.

21. See Daniel Glaser, "Crime causation: the field," p. 308, in S. H. Kadish (ed.), *Encyclopedia of Crime and Justice.* New York: Macmillan and Free Press, 1983. The remaining topics in this section, and their authors, are "Biological Theories," by Vicki Pollock, Sarnoff A. Mednick, and William F. Gabrielli, Jr.; "Economic Theories," by Anne Dryden Witte; "Political Theories," by Harold E. Pepinsky; "Psychological Theories," by Herbert C. Quay; and "Sociological Theories," by Albert K. Cohen. See also, Robert F. Meier, *Theoretical Methods in Criminology.* Beverly Hills, CA: Sage, 1985.

CHAPTER 2
CHILD SAVING: HISTORICAL, LEGAL, AND SOCIAL CONTEXTS

SOCIAL PROBLEMS, THE PUBLIC, AND THE LAW

Social problems are by their very nature public issues, the subject of concern and controversy. What is considered problematic is always a matter of definition, and it makes a great deal of difference who is doing the defining and what they wish, and are able, to do about the problem. Modern problems of childhood, for example—including those we now call juvenile delinquency—did not exist in medieval Europe, in part, because the medieval *concept* of childhood differed from the modern conception. Historian Philippe Aries concludes that "as soon as he became weaned, or soon after, the child became the natural companion of the adult."[1] Childhood and adolescence as we know them today emerged in response to many social changes. The idea of the *family* as the special repository of moral training, with its central concern being the upbringing of children, is also a relatively recent idea in human history.[2] So, also, is the concept that adolescence is a period of special stress.

What has been considered *problematic*, and specifically delinquent, with respect to families, children, and adolescents has varied a great deal in different times and places. There can be no doubt that there was, in earlier times, much behavior by young people that today would be considered serious crime. Prior to the "invention" of juvenile delinquency, however, such behavior was not considered problematic by virtue of the youth of offenders; rather, it was simply part of the crime problem, most often attributed to the "dangerous classes."

Until recently, also, crime was regarded as a *personal characteristic* of those who manifested such behavior. The simple dichotomies of delinquent versus nondelinquent and criminal versus noncriminal were crude paradigms in terms of which sociologists, psychologists, physiologists, and endocrinologists, as well as parents, ministers, teachers, and others sought explanations of crime and delinquency. They asked what traits and experiences led some, but not other, individuals to become delinquent, criminal, or in some other way deviant. This approach also served as a guide for many of these same people—acting as "child savers," physicians, social workers, clinical psychologists, probation officers, police, prosecutors, or defense attorneys—to protect, reform, correct, rehabilitate, or punish persons defined as deviant.

This paradigm began to break down under several challenges. Vast differences were noted in the *social distribution* of crime and delinquency. There were, for example, different crime distributions among *categories* of persons in a society or between societies. Studies of the impact of law enforcement activity on young people and communities suggested that "getting caught" might be as important in determining who was and who was not delinquent as was the actual behavior of children. Self-reports of officially "nondelinquent" populations (high-school and college students and samples of the general population) found a good deal of involvement in delinquent activities by these young men and women. Finally, vague and changing definitions of delinquent behavior have rendered the simple distinction between delinquent and nondelinquent children all but useless. The simple dichotomies of the earlier paradigm thus have given way to research and to theorizing concerning the *conditions* under which a variety of delinquent behaviors occur, the *processes* leading to these behaviors, and the *persistence* of serious criminal behaviors.

Before turning to these newer paradigms, it is necessary to inquire as to how and why behaviors and persons come to be *defined* as criminal, delinquent, or sinful—or as law abiding, or in some other way praiseworthy. It is also necessary, as well, to examine the nature of the behaviors and persons so defined. This is the purpose of the present chapter.

Social problems do not spring, full blown, into social consciousness as a result of some evil or objectively seen condition. Rather, they develop as a result of the concerns and activities of individuals and groups in response to conditions that they perceive as objectionable and which they wish to change. These concerns and activities often coalesce in the form of voluntary associations, social movements, and special interest groups, which devote their efforts toward the achievement of goals which they perceive as desirable. Such groups typically make claims as to the nature of conditions that they find objectionable. Often there are counter claims by other groups. In this process, legislation may be passed and agencies of law enforcement established.

This is one way that special interest groups protect or promote their economic, political, and moral interests. Many examples of how this process works are documented in the research literature.[3] The special interests of these groups identified in these studies vary greatly, and may include economic and political gain, moral values, and the protection of social status. The power of special interest groups and favored social classes, including the power of ruling elites to influence the content of the law and its enforcement is clearly considerable. But there are limits to such power, and today's power may weaken or disintegrate in the face of opposition from other powerful groups, or from lack of support from the general public. Changing laws and practices regarding such substances as alcohol and marijuana, regarding the regulation of abortion, and regarding a variety of civil rights issues provide recent examples of both the power of special interest groups and the limitations of such power. For a variety of reasons, media of mass communication are especially important in the construction and the continuing evolution of social problems, including juvenile delinquency.[4]

The subject matter of this chapter antedates modern means and systems of mass communication, however. Here we briefly review the history of concern with childhood and youthful misbehavior, with special attention to the social forces and interest groups that were involved in the social construction of juvenile delinquency. The recent historical record, as well as that of previous centuries, is important if we are to understand continuing changes in the nature of juvenile delinquency as a social problem. A compendium of juvenile codes in the United States compiled some years ago noted that in a brief span of three years (1969–1971), 33 of the 50 states either had enacted entirely new codes or had substantially modified existing codes.[5] Most of the other states had made major code revisions within the previous decade. Revisions continue to this day.

The legal status of juvenile delinquency affects not only the activities of law enforcement agencies but also the relationships among young people, other citizens, and the juvenile and criminal justice systems. Legal status changes, in turn, are responsive in complex ways to a variety of forces in the larger society—to special interests groups such as those alluded to previously, to messages carried by the mass communications media, to changing behavior patterns, to social movements, to social customs, and to mores deeply ingrained in the social fabric. The historical context informs both the evolution of juvenile delinquency and the nature of forces and processes in its continuing evolution.

THE CHANGING STATUS OF CHILDHOOD

The behavior referred to as delinquent has a certain timeless and universal quality. It is at once as old as humankind and as new as the latest fad. As a concept, however, it is a legal invention of the late nineteenth century. As such, juvenile delinquency is but a part of the historical process in which *childhood*, and later *adolescence*, have become increasingly differentiated as distinct social categories.

The evolution of childhood and adolescence as *statuses* occurred over hundreds of years, by legal and other means.[6] More recently, differentiation has increasingly occurred *within* these broad categories, for example, between infants, preschoolers, preadolescents, adolescents, and young adults, or between kindergarten, elementary, junior high school, middle school, high school, and college students. These age-graded distinctions bring with them distinctive and changing relationships between young people, their families, and others, including educational, religious, economic, and political institutions.

As other traditional family functions have decreased in importance, attention to the family's role in child rearing—as distinct from formal educational, vocational and religious training—has increased. Early primary roles in child socialization included some that now seem anachronistic, such as wet nurses and, increasingly, apprentice relationships with adults. Following the "invention" of childhood, emphasis was placed on the family and the school as agents and as settings for proper socialization of children. When these appeared to fail, reformatories and other elements of the juvenile justice system were created.

At the same time that the *responsibility* for the proper upbringing of children was placed in the family, the *authority* of parents *vis-à-vis* their children was being eroded by the same broad social changes responsible for the new importance of the family. Scholarly debate concerning the forces at work in these changes and the specific nature of these changes continues. One such change, however, was of special importance in altering familial relationships and child rearing practices, and in changing the nature of relationships between government and citizens, namely, *the emergence of the nation-state*, with its demand for the loyalty and active political participation of citizens. The ideology of the modern nation state is based on social control of many aspects of social life. The loyalty of citizens—so necessary to the legitimacy of the state—places demands on individuals that often conflict with traditional loyalties to the more primordial groups of family, tribe, or clan.[7]

An important consequence of this development has been increasing reliance on the law—the prime instrumentality of nation states—to govern relationships among citizens. The education and control of children, once the sole province of families, became matters of concern for the law and for government. Parents were increasingly held responsible for the "proper" upbringing of their children, and what was considered proper became a matter of contention, with government as the arbiter.

PARENS PATRIAE

Legal regulation of relationships among citizens implies legal redress of grievance and legal "solutions" to problems. One of the earliest—and most important—governmental initiatives regarding children had nothing to do with juvenile misbehavior. It concerned, rather, the property rights of children.

Under feudal law, the English chancery courts (courts of equity, as distinguished from common law courts) had broad authority over the welfare of children by virtue of the doctrine of *parens patriae*, which assigned to the King (as the symbolic father of all his subjects) special rights and responsibilities. Jurisdiction was exercised almost exclusively on behalf of minors with property, because the court lacked resources to care for the poor, the neglected, and the abused. When *parens patriae* was brought to the United States, the concept was broadened considerably to include personal injury, and the *protective* powers of the court became its primary justification.[8]

Juvenile law goes back to other historical roots, as well, for example, the English common law and certain special practices with respect to juveniles that developed under the criminal law in England, Australia, and the

United States. The ancient common law of England, for example, held children under the age of seven to be "irrefutably presumed" to be incapable of criminal intent, and therefore of crime. Up to the age of 14 evidence of immaturity could be introduced to free children from the reach of the law.[9]

SOCIAL CONTROL OF CHILDREN IN THE NORTH AMERICAN COLONIES

When they were imported to the colonies in America such provisions were often altered. The common law rule under which children under seven were exempted from punishment by the courts was apparently never adopted by the Massachusetts Bay Colony, for example. In 1668, a General Court order prescribed that "in all criminal cases every person, younger as well as elders, shall be liable to answer to their own persons, for such misdemeanors as they shall be accused of." In civil cases, however, persons under 21 years of age were required to be represented by "parents, masters or guardians." The General Court preferred to set the age of responsibility for most criminal laws on a crime-by-crime basis. Penalties attached to juvenile misbehavior were often severe, as illustrated by the following examples of capital crimes:[10]

> ...for sodomy, a capital crime, children under fourteen were to be "severely punished" but not executed; for cursing and smiting parents, a capital crime, only those "above sixteen years old, and of sufficient understanding" could be put to death; for being stubborn or rebellious sons, a capital crime likewise, only those "of sufficient years and understanding (*viz.*) sixteen years of age" were liable; for arson, a capital crime, the law also applied only to those "of the age of sixteen years and upward"; for "denying the Scriptures to be the infallible word of God," again the minimum age was sixteen for those who were liable to the death penalty.

For most juvenile violations of this strict Puritan code, parents were held responsible for the conduct of their children. They might be directed to administer "due correction...in the presence of an officer," or specifically to whip a child in the privacy of the home, to pay damages (for some offenses, triple damages), or they might themselves suffer admonishment by authorities, fines, or worse. The colony was not at this point ready to assume as direct control over wayward youth as was later to be the case. While *crime* and *sin* were considered synonymous (and the natural condition of man) *poverty* and wrongdoing were not. Strongly held religious beliefs felt that poverty was a community responsibility. Belief that "the poor are always with us" must have been reinforced by the fact that there was a great deal of poverty in colonial times. Earlier, in England and in Europe, the religious doctrines that spurred charitable impulses were balanced by concerns for social control in cities where the poor were increasingly concentrated. Fear of the "disreputable poor" comprising the "dangerous classes" became a major factor in social control initiatives.[11]

It was in the new nation of the United States of America, however, that the most radical social and legal responses to poverty and crime were occurring. By the early nineteenth century much had changed in this part of the world. There was considerable wealth and great opportunities for its creation. The same forces that gave rise to profound developments in the evolution of juvenile justice changed conceptions of the relation between crime and sin, and between poverty and crime. Following upon the Renaissance and the advent of scientific thinking, Enlightenment social thought was influential.

Embracing a liberal, rationalist, and humanitarian approach to the conduct of human affairs, the Enlightenment became a cornerstone of a new optimism regarding the perfectibility of humankind. No longer considered to be inevitable or the natural condition of man, poverty and crime were the result of faults traceable to worldly conditions, for example, early family upbringing and corrupt community influences. In fact, what had happened was that the communities of colonial America, which had been founded on common religious beliefs, and which were relatively homogeneous in other respects, had become much less closely knit as *communities*. They were now composed of diverse individuals and groups. Society and community were no longer the same, as had been the case, for example, in the Massachusetts Bay Colony.

Politically, the Enlightenment enjoyed its greatest flowering as nation-states came to dominate Western societies. Among the many impacts of these developments, erosion of the authority of the family was one of the most consequential. One of the earliest manifestations of this change involved the state directly in child rearing through the creation of reformatories for juvenile offenders.

THE DISCOVERY OF THE ASYLUM[12]

Authorities in several countries sought ways nearly four centuries ago of separating juveniles convicted of crimes from convicted adults.[13] It was in the United States, however, that the reformatory movement had its fullest development. The first juvenile reformatory in this country was the New York House of Refuge, established in 1824. The Society for the Reformation of Juvenile Delinquents, founders of that institution, noted the distinction between the New York House of Refuge and earlier institutions:[14]

> It is true that before our society was thought of, Houses of Refuge existed in England, and probably elsewhere. But these were either pure charities to receive and comfort destitute children, so long as they should be in want or mere penitentiaries for the punishment of such as were convicted of crime. There was no authority to detain a child who was not criminal, and all the power and control over one who was so, was prescribed by his sentence, and ceased when that expired, and he quitted the walls of the prison. No provision could be made for his protection during his non-age.

The distinguishing feature of the child saving movement in the United States—and its hallmark in law—is revealed in the next passage:

> The legislature has very much enlarged the objects of our institution, and entrusted to its managers powers that have not heretofore been delegated.

These are essential to its beneficent action, and mark the great difference between it and other institutions that previously existed, however similar they may be in name. If a child be found destitute—if abandoned by its parents—or suffered to lead a vicious or vagrant life; or if convicted of any crime, it may be sent to the House of Refuge. There is in no case any other sentence than that it shall "there be dealt with according to law." That is, it may if not released by some legal process, be there detained, if the managers should think it unfit to be sooner discharged, until it arrives at age. Parents or guardians, from the time it is legally sentenced to the Refuge, lose all control of its person. When it is believed that a child is reformed, the managers have power, with its consent, to bind it as an apprentice, till the age of eighteen years, if a female, and if a boy till the age of twenty-one.

Reformatories for juveniles were part of a more general movement in the decades after 1820, during which "penitentiaries for the criminal, asylums for the insane, almshouses for the poor, orphan asylums for homeless children" were constructed.[15]

Asylums for juveniles, like the admonitions and punishments of the colonists who preceded them and the juvenile court movement which followed, were based on the prescriptions and proscriptions of the social and moral order in the new nation. Each of these phases of child saving, in turn, was a response to massive ideological, demographic, economic, and other social changes.

The early colonies were relatively small, isolated, and politically and economically self-sufficient. Thus, banishment could be effective, and public stocks and flogging served as relatively immediate punishment. By the mid-1820s, however, self-sufficiency had been severely eroded. Increased population size, social and physical mobility in settled areas and on the frontier, higher density and heterogeneity of population, and economic interdependency posed serious threats to the cohesiveness of the separate colonies, and to the control which could be exercised over individual citizens. Institutions which previously could be depended upon to induce conformity now seemed inadequate, or they were inhibited by the law of the land which prescribed separation of church and state. Sectarian forces played a major role in both reformatory and juvenile court movements, however. Rothman describes the perceptions of those who placed their faith in the reformatory:

> Movement to cities, in and out of territories, and down the social ladder, made it difficult...to believe that a sense of hierarchy or localism could now stabilize society. When men no longer knew their place or station, self-policing communities seemed a thing of the past. (p. 58)
>
> The child offender, no less than the adult one, was a casualty of his upbringing. The importance of family discipline in a community pervaded with vice characterized practically every statement of philanthropists and reformers on delinquency. Both mature and immature offenders were victims of similar conditions. Not that Americans, insensitive to an idea of childhood, unthinkingly made children into adults. Quite the reverse. They stripped the years away from adults, and turned everyone into a child. (p. 76)

At the heart of the reformatory movement was an abiding faith that the rehabilitative powers of a carefully designed environment could rehabilitate those in need for whatever reason. The philosophy behind this faith was intensely individualistic, reflecting the religious, economic, and political currents of the day. Paradoxically, this individualistic faith was aimed toward achieving conformity to established authority. The early reformers were guided by the notion that the Kingdom of God could be achieved on earth by the social reconstruction of individuals. Hence the "penitentiary" for adults, separation of children from adults, and the creation of special courts and programs to reform delinquents, to protect neglected children, and to *prevent* delinquency by intervention prior to youngsters' involvement in crime. Seen in this way, the concept of juvenile delinquency was as much a reaction to crime (and to sin) as it was to that part of the crime problem attributable to juveniles. Thus, the Philadelphia House of Refuge based its appeal for funds on visitors finding "the orphan, deserted or misguided child, shielded from the temptations of a sinful world."[16] Rigid daily routine and disciplinary practices with a strong military cast sought to instill absolute respect for authority and discipline in the habits of industry. If "cheerful submission" could not be obtained, obedience was to be secured by punishment. In a complete reversal of contemporary correctional philosophy, protection from corruption and temptation was directed particularly to those in the sinful world who had been closest to the wayward youngster:[17]

> The Philadelphia refuge...provided separately for various types of visitors. Reversing the natural order of things, they established regulations whereby the closer a person was to an inmate, the less he was permitted to come. Foreign tourists had no trouble gaining admission; they could inspect the premises any time with a ticket from the managers, the major, the ladies' committee, or a local judge. Interested citizens were slightly more restricted, entitled to admission on the first and third Wednesday of the month. But parents, guardians, and friends of the inmates, could visit only once in every three months...no one was permitted to converse with the children without special permission. Having rescued their charges from a foul environment, officials had no intention of bringing corruption to them.

The purpose of the reformatories, in the words of the New York Society for the Reformation of Juvenile Delinquents, was to save those "forsaken children, many of them orphans, and many who derived no protection from parents, who received no instruction from them but in wickedness and profanity, and no example but in the practice of vice and immorality."[18] Though they recognized that deviant juveniles were more victims than offenders, the reformers were interested primarily in those who could still be saved, those who in their judgment (and in the judgment of the courts) were "proper objects" for their ministrations. The primary effort was on the predelinquent, and those "who could not be rescued were to be prevented from contaminating the saving process," by consigning them to the adult criminal system.[19]

The asylums were heralded in many parts of the world as humanitarian experiments in environmental control. Commissions of inquiry and distinguished visitors came from other nations, including Charles Dickens and that most famous of all tourists to America, Alexis de Tocqueville.[20] Debates concerning prison design and the proper means of achieving penitence (between the Auburn, or congregate system, and the Pennsylvania or isolation system) concentrated on institutions for adults, but the intellectual excitement generated by the idea of the asylums was more general. The hope, and fleetingly the promise, was that they constituted a breakthrough in the efforts of a social order threatened by rapid change and loss of social control to achieve stability and cohesion.

There was in fact much social disorder in America's burgeoning cities, as well as on the frontier, but reliance on traditional methods of punishment—banishment, the stocks, whipping, fines, or hanging—and the quick justice meted out on the frontier—were no longer appropriate for increasingly crowded and interdependent cities. Historian Roger Lane notes that an early mayor of Boston, Josiah Quincy, took personal charge of a posse of citizens to put down one of that city's numerous "riots, routs, and tumultuous assemblies which had spluttered on for a full week during the long hot summer of 1825." Such "common offenses as simple drunkenness and assault," on the other hand, were paid "relatively little attention...The night watch, largely concerned with the danger of fire or arson, was afraid to enter some of the more notorious neighborhoods. No one patrolled anywhere in the daytime."[21]

But times were changing, and higher standards of public order soon came to be demanded by the good citizens of Boston and other cities. Lane continues:

> Massachusetts in 1835 had a population of some 660,940, 81 percent rural, overwhelmingly preindustrial and native born. Its citizens were used to considerable personal freedom. Whether teamsters, farmers, or artisans; they were all accustomed to setting their own schedules, and the nature of their work made them physically independent of each other. None of the more common occupations provided any built-in checks against various kinds of personal excess. Neither fits of violence nor bouts of drunkenness disrupted any vital patterns. Individual problems, sins or even crimes, were not generally cause for wider social concern.
>
> Under these circumstances, while scarcely a frontier, the Commonwealth could afford a fairly high degree of lawlessness. No city in the state boasted a professional police, and the machinery of justice was not equipped to handle many cases. Many of the more common forms of violence or crime were simply not reported to the agents of law, as those affected either shrugged off their injuries or struck back directly.
>
> But the impact of the twin movements to the city and to the factory, both just gathering force in 1835, had a progressive effect on personal behavior throughout the 19th century and into the 20th. The factory demanded regularity of behavior, a life governed by obedience to the rhythms of clock and calendar, the demands of foreman and supervisor. In the city or town, the needs of living in closely packed neighborhoods inhibited many actions previously unobjectionable. Both blue- and white-collar employees in larger establishments were mutually dependent on their fellows; as one man's work fit into another's, so one man's business was no longer his own. (pp. 364–5.)

Similar developments were occurring in other parts of the country as well, giving impetus to the reformatory movement. By 1857, a national convention of refuge superintendents was held. Another interest group—

consisting of aspiring professionals in the cause of child saving—had been added to the moral entrepreneurs who had been in the forefront of the reformatory movement.[22] Their efforts were to combine with those of energetic and gifted amateurs in the movement that resulted in the creation of juvenile courts. Before this happened, however, another important event was to occur.

THE POLICE: GATEKEEPERS TO THE JUVENILE JUSTICE SYSTEM

In 1829, Sir Robert Peel gained approval of English Parliament for a bill establishing the Metropolitan Police of London, the first of its kind.[23] With this development, the armamentarium of modern criminal justice was virtually complete. The idea was implemented rapidly in the United States; to Boston—apropos the previous discussion—in 1837.

While the crucial impetus for establishing city police may have been an increase in mob violence in major cities, the primary task of the police, then as now, was to be responsive to citizen complaints. Paradoxically, creation of a police force broadened the scope of public responsibility for wrongdoing, while at the same time setting in motion processes which rendered public responsibility problematic. Prior to the establishment of municipal police, citizens had little recourse for criminal victimization. Of equal importance, without professional assistance, behavior that was merely immoral or distasteful received little official attention. As Lane observes, "It takes real cops...to make drunk arrests" (p. 362). Lane's remark is quite appropriate, for the consumption of hard liquor was, at this time, under attack by many in the middle class, and the campaign for total prohibition was gaining strength.

More importantly, real cops—as distinguished from citizens who are bothered but not criminally victimized—can be called upon to respond to the minor crimes and peccadillos, the public nuisances and rowdiness, which bulk so large in the content of juvenile delinquency. They do so because they are expected to—this is part of the job description. The expectation that they would do so grew as citizens became conditioned to seek official help. The paradox arises because the existence of the police made it possible for citizens to escape responsibility for crime by leaving it to the police. Police roles in juvenile delinquency are treated more extensively in Chapter 3.

Creation of a full-time professional police had other consequences, adding to crime control yet another interest group. The police also made crime control somewhat more democratic, because they were recruited from many of the same groups which were the chief components of the "criminal class."

The stage was now set for the remaining elements of the "invention" of juvenile delinquency. For although the term *juvenile delinquent* had developed in the course of the reformatory movement, it was not until juvenile courts were established that it became firmly established as a legal and social category.

THE INVENTION OF DELINQUENCY

Enthusiasm for asylums began to fade relatively early in the movement. New arguments were mounted against them, practice and outcome belied the early faith in their rehabilitative influences, and the numbers of children in need continued to grow. The movement became institutionalized. Those who followed the early reformers came into established buildings and programs, with different problems than those confronting new institutions—problems of maintaining order, of day-to-day existence, which earlier had not been of primary concern. There was new focus on conditional release (probation) and on after-care (parole), both of which had been slighted in the enthusiasm for reformatory treatment of erring juveniles.[24] While a variety of probation forms were practiced elsewhere as early as the thirteenth century, it was not until late in the nineteenth century that laws relating specifically to this form of disposition for convicted criminals, juvenile or adult, were passed. Juvenile probation became firmly and widely established only after juvenile courts were legislated, as part of the juvenile court movement. Parole also was now widely established, but extremely varied in practice, and less centralized at the state level for juveniles than for adults.

Special practices for handling juveniles under the criminal law developed during the nineteenth century in Europe, the United States, New Zealand, and Australia. Simple larceny by juveniles was handled summarily by English magistrates after 1847, rather than at trial, and the Education Act, designed to assure proper education of children, was "often utilized by humane magistrates as a merciful substitute for the more severe provisions of the criminal law."[25] Groups were organized in several countries, and in some states and cities, to assist criminal courts in cases involving juveniles. These organizations performed a variety of tasks, for example, inquiring into the individual and social circumstances of offenders and counseling with the judge as to the proper disposition of cases. Morrison notes that the Probation of First Offenders Act (1887) and the Summary Jurisdiction Act (1889) in England were concerned that the character and backgrounds of young offenders be studied. But, as seems often to be the case with modern legislation as well, these acts provided neither machinery nor funds for studying these matters. The model for such inquiries developed in the midwestern United States. County agents of the Michigan State Board of Corrections and Charities were required to be notified when a criminal complaint was entered against any boy under sixteen years, or any girl under seventeen years, for any offense not punishable by imprisonment for life...[26] These agents were to represent the interest of children and perform a watchdog function over homes to which dependent and delinquent children were sent following release from incarceration.

The movement to provide special handling of juveniles appearing before criminal courts was many faceted, including separate institutions (the reformatories), provision for separate hearings and disposition under different laws, presentence investigation and sentence counseling, and various forms of probation and parole. Individually, these features developed both independently and by diffusion, as interest in child saving spread to many parts of the world.

Establishment of the first juvenile court, in Cook County (Chicago), Illinois, in 1899, culminated a century of experimentation in child saving and provided new impetus to the juvenile court movement. The law under which the juvenile court was established was more than simply a combination of previously existing elements, though it was certainly that. More important, the new law *institutionalized* a new vocabulary and new procedures for handling troublesome youth. The reach of the law over the lives of children was thereby extended, and the number of those involved in official child saving roles was expanded. Some have argued that the number of children whose lives were brought under court control was also expanded, but that is less certain. This apparently did not occur in Canada—but adequate data for the United States to test this contention are lacking.[27]

Robert M. Mennel notes that the juvenile court became both "a laboratory for the professional study of delinquency" and a Progressive political weapon by virtue of "its generally urban location" and because it was empowered to gather case histories:[28]

> The social and psychological facts about the children appearing before the court offered the most compelling evidence for the adoption of child labor laws, mothers' pensions, municipal playgrounds, compulsory school attendance, public health care for children, and rigorous regulation of tenement-building.

ASSESSING THE JUVENILE COURT MOVEMENT

The number and variety of persons with interests in, and social roles related to, child saving had, in fact, become substantial by the time the first juvenile court came into being. Social historians have documented *established interests* in the juvenile court movement, including those motivated by strong feelings of *noblesse oblige* and conscientious duty to the "less fortunate" in American society and those motivated by self-interest.[29]

Religious Interests. Reference was made, earlier, to the strongly religious, and specifically Christian, character of the early child savers. Puritan, Quaker, and Protestant groups dominated the early movement. It was not until 1863, some 39 years after the opening of the New York House of Refuge, that the Society for the Protection of Destitute Roman Catholic Children in the City of New York received its charter. In Illinois, more than a decade before passage of the Juvenile Court Act, "the four industrial schools...were evenly divided between Catholic and Protestant managements; each religious group had a school for girls and one for boys."[30] The "foreign Catholic population" was of special concern since, in the words of a Massachusetts woman speaking before the Sixth Annual Conference of Charities in 1879, it "is very large and furnishes a real proportion of our dependent and criminal class."[31] Little concern apparently was expressed for children of other religious and cultural backgrounds, beyond the wish to save them also.

Social Class Interests.   The role of economic and class interests has been pervasive in the history of social reform, including penology and child saving. Anthony Platt contends that "The reformatory plan required the teaching of lower-class skills and middle-class values."[32] The juvenile court was fundamentally authoritarian, linking family propriety with social class, and blurring the distinction between delinquent and dependent children, thus buttressing a conception of adolescent dependence and justifying and broadening court powers of intervention.

Feminism.   The juvenile court movement was spurred by the gathering momentum of women's emancipation. Indeed, since child saving was regarded as a female domain by anti-feminists as well, the movement profited from both sides of the controversy.

Anthony Platt suggests that at the turn of the century many middle-class women found themselves somewhat at loose ends. Better educated than their predecessors, and with more leisure time at their disposal, available career choices were limited. Child saving provided an eminently respectable outlet for their considerable talents and energies. "Career women and society philanthropists, women's clubs and settlement houses, and political and apolitical groups worked together on the problems of child care."[33]

Professional Interests.   The emerging class of professional child savers associated with the reformatory and juvenile court movements had a strong interest in further institutionalizing both movements. Creation of juvenile courts gave them a new legitimacy, and new claims to professional status. Child saving became a "growth industry," with new demands for judges, probation officers, other court personnel, institutional officials, and parole officials.

John Hagan and Jeffrey Leon note that, in Canada, political controversy over creation of juvenile courts centered around conflict between police and probation officers.[34] Controversy concerning the proper roles of juvenile justice functionaries, and evaluation of their performance, has been a source of continued debate. For example, the "social worker" versus "crime fighter" image of the police has often been noted.[35]

The professional identity of the child saving movement was greatly enhanced by the *medical model* of crime, delinquency, and dependency, which conceptualized these phenomena as "pathological." *Claims* concerning delinquency as a social problem were greatly facilitated by medical imagery. If delinquency was a disease, it could be treated professionally, much as was physical illness.[36]

The analogy that delinquency was like a physical illness and susceptible to treatment, enhanced the professional identity of child savers by promoting both the self-image and the public images of the reformers as something more than mere custodians. Many physicians were, in fact, involved in penal reform and other types of child saving. Their presence contributed greatly to the rehabilitative ideal that dominated the juvenile court movement. The medical model was attractive, not only because it enhanced the identities and encouraged the philanthropic and moralistic fervor of the child savers, but also because it countered powerful scientific and theological doctrines of the day. Both Darwin's science and theological beliefs in predestination held pessimistic views concerning the possibility of changing the human condition. In contrast, the child savers did not doubt that something could and should be done about delinquent and dependent children. The medical model, together with the "progressive education" of John Dewey and his followers, assured the child savers that something could be done and provided a prestigious intellectual rationale for the movement. Some have argued that the *individualistic* emphasis of both the medical model and the new progressive education were also compatible with the class interests of the child savers. Ironically, progressive education has been criticized for its "leftist" political views favoring collectivism.[37]

Private versus Public Interests. The Illinois Juvenile Court Act of 1899 was a temporary triumph of private and sectarian over public and nonsectarian child saving interests. Private institutions had been limited to receiving children who were not yet delinquent, but dependent. There was substantial opposition to the use of public funds for the private handling of these cases, and to the "practice of committing destitute children to private corporations that ran no schools themselves but forwarded the children to what purported to be industrial schools..."[38]

In 1888, the Illinois Supreme Court ruled this practice illegal. The first juvenile court bill was introduced three years later by private charity interests. These interests sought, in the words of the Visitation and Aid Society's Timothy B. Hurley, "Legislation giving them power to do what they realized it was necessary to do in order to save the child."[39] This bill failed, but the practice of committing "predelinquent" children to private charitable organizations continued, and efforts to legitimize the practice continued. The 1899 Act changed this, by authorizing the court to commit law violators, as well as dependent children, to the private charities.

The victory of private interests was short lived, however. While private agencies continued to play a major role in the handling of dependent and neglected children, public institutions soon gained ascendancy in the treatment of court-committed delinquents. Debate concerning the role of private agencies in the treatment and confinement of children has continued, however, as the effectiveness of public institutions has come increasingly under attack. Ironically, in the late twentieth century debate centers less on the role of charitable institutions and more on the appropriateness and effectiveness of profit-making institutions, some with the backing of large corporate enterprises.

Nativism, Nostalgia, and the Rural Tradition. Added to the concern with poverty, crime, and dependency—and to fear of the "dangerous classes" which were "responsible"—was a measure of fear and resentment directed toward the large number of immigrant peoples, and "foreign" influences, which flooded into the increasingly crowded cities of the land. City life, as such, was viewed by many as corrupting. Historian Richard Hofstadter argues that "The whole cast of American thinking in this period [toward the end of the nineteenth and the beginning of the twentieth centuries] was deeply affected by the experience of the rural mind confronted with the phenomena of urban life, its crowding, poverty, crime, corruption, impersonality, and ethnic chaos."[40]

Continuity from the nineteenth century roots of child saving to the twentieth century is clear. Then, as now, a society undergoing rapid change sought control over problems that could not be fully comprehended. The tendency then, as now, was to sweeten images of the rural past. Harsh and repressive features of that past were neglected or forgotten by many, while others emphasized that these same features had a positive influence by "building character."

Since the first settlers came to this country, it has been possible to find newcomers or other "outsiders" upon whom to fix blame for the perceived problems of the day. Throughout the nineteenth century many supporters of child saving reacted negatively—with varying combinations of hatred, resentment, pity, and condescension—to the latest wave of immigrants to this country. A large measure of responsibility was fixed on these groups for poverty, crime and delinquency, and immorality. It is instructive, in view of more recent concerns with other minorities, to note that most of the newcomers throughout the nineteenth and early twentieth centuries were white ethnics, for example, the Irish and, by the end of the century, Italians and Poles. Those who resisted entry of these groups into the mainstream of American society had themselves been newcomers only a few generations earlier.

Conditions of life for most immigrants were difficult, indeed:[41]

> All through the period, and especially during and after the "hungry forties," heavy Irish immigration exacerbated all of the problems of city living. By 1855, some 68,100 of the 168,031 residents of Boston (40 percent) were natives of Ireland. Uprooted from a rural setting, wholly without skills, the newcomers experienced the kind of culture shock, prejudice, and alienation which would plague other waves of migrants later. Crowded into stinking hovels, some of them underground, their miserable conditions of living strained all of the city's institutions of charity and police.

The Irish, and later the Italians and other groups, were viewed by many as "scum" and blamed for many of the ills besetting American communities. We shall have more to say about ethnicity and race as factors in juvenile delinquency in subsequent chapters.

THE REACH OF THE JUVENILE COURT: CRIME AND MORE

The legislation which created the first juvenile court was titled "An Act to regulate the treatment and control of dependent, neglected and delinquent children," thus clearly indicating the encompassing concerns of the early reformers. Whereas the first juvenile court act defined a "delinquent" simply as "any child under the age of 16 who violates any law of this State [Illinois] or any City or Village ordinance," the definition was soon broadened. In practice, courts made little distinction between the juvenile offender and the youngster who for other reasons was deemed in need of state intervention.[42]

The major thrust of the child saving movement, and of supporting legislative and judicial activity throughout most of the nineteenth century, was on protecting children from neglecting and abusing parents, and on saving the predelinquent from falling into a life of crime. Illinois laws of 1855 and 1861, for example, focused on children "who are destitute of parental care, wandering about the streets, or committing mischief or growing up in mendicancy, ignorance, idleness and vice."[43] The juvenile court was to be a "super-parent."

Though modified in recent years, the focus of contemporary juvenile courts remains similar. As previously noted, behavior defined as criminal, when committed by juveniles, is universally defined as delinquent; whereas, noncriminal behavior subject to juvenile court jurisdiction falls into two major categories. The first category is juvenile status offenses, that is, behavior which, if committed by an adult, would not be considered criminal. Such "omnibus provisions" typically are phrased in vague and general language. The 1965 California Code, for example, specified as delinquent any child who "persistently or habitually refuses to obey the reasonable and proper orders or directions of his parents, guardian, custodian or school authorities, or who is beyond the control of such person, or any person who is a habitual truant from school within the meaning of any law of this State, or who from any cause is in danger of leading an idle, dissolute, lewd, or immoral life, is within the jurisdiction of the juvenile court which may adjudge such person to be a ward of the court."[44] Or the statute in Ohio that provides that the court may have jurisdiction over any child

> who does not subject himself to the reasonable control of his parents, teachers, guardian, or custodian, by reason of being wayward or habitually disobedient; who is habitually truant from home or school; who so deports himself as to injure or endanger the health or morals of himself or others; who is found in a disreputable place, visits or patronizes a place prohibited by law or associates with vagrant, vicious, criminal, notorious, or immoral persons.

Mark Levin and Rosemary Sarri conclude that this statute "is representative, rather than unusual, in its scope, vagueness, imprecision, and opportunity for abuse."[45]

The second category of noncriminal behavior subject to juvenile court jurisdiction are cases of child neglect, including dependency, neglect, and abuse. Dependency entails no personal fault of parents or guardians, only inability to care for a child. Neglect and abuse generally imply fault, the former for inadequate care, the latter for more willful injury to a child.

While our chief concern is with delinquency, many of the same historical and contemporary interests and issues occur with respect to child neglect. Here we note simply that the lumping together of crime, status offenses, and neglect under the label delinquency has consequences that have become part of juvenile delinquency as a social problem.

Until recently, most states did not differentiate juvenile status violators from those who have committed adult offenses. Some states create a variety of categories to distinguish status violators. These labels have given rise to a set of acronyms that have become familiar in the delinquency literature: PINS (Persons In Need of Supervision), JINS (Juveniles), CHINS (Children) and, of course, MINS (Minors). Not all such labels are so easily abbreviated (unruly children, incorrigible children, and so forth), but all labels are characterized by language sufficiently ambiguous so that it allows many children to be classified. The legal provisions for the care of such children, and restrictions related thereto, are as varied as the many labels.

The recentness of legal requirements regarding the manner in which status offenders and those who have committed adult offenses are to be handled is apparent, for no such distinctions were found in codes predating 1959. The trend in recent code revisions, spurred by activities of the federal government, is to add such distinctions.

Juvenile delinquency thus lacks "objective character." The behaviors are real enough, but definitions of behaviors which constitute juvenile delinquency vary from time to time, and from place to place. The concept of juvenile delinquency continues to evolve through juvenile court legislation and practice, and as a result of many other influences. Indeed, after more than a century of experimentation, the states still have not reached consensus on such elementary matters as age specifications for defining delinquents, offenses, and other matters.

Minimum age limitations, for example, often are not mentioned in juvenile court jurisdictional statutes, but the common law practice of limiting criminal responsibility to those who have reached age seven is generally followed. The maximum age for original juvenile court jurisdiction (that is, cases for which the juvenile court is legally responsible) has declined to age 17 in most states, down from age 21 in several states. In a few states it is still lower. Most states grant *continuing* juvenile court jurisdiction until offenders reach age 21, but this, too, varies.

Tensions between juvenile and criminal courts are reflected in *limitations* placed on juvenile court jurisdiction in many states. Any juvenile, regardless of age, may be tried in criminal court if charged with certain offenses, again with a variety of age specifications. When the charge is rape or homicide, for example, juvenile court jurisdiction often is restricted to persons under the age of 14. Nearly all states permit the juvenile court to make a determination that a particular case should be tried in criminal court. In some states that decision is placed with the office of the prosecutor. The manner in which that determination is made became an important part of procedural reform, the "third round" of juvenile justice reform (following the reformatory and juvenile court movements) to be discussed in the following chapter. Here again, however, age, offense, and prior criminal history enter in the determination of such matters, with much variation from state to state. The effect of such provisions is to take determination of jurisdiction out of the hands of the juvenile court in many cases, and to place it, instead, with the prosecutor. The lack of consensus in these matters reflects the continuing struggle of state legislatures to balance special interests to provide for the protection of both the juvenile and the community.[46]

SOCIAL STRUCTURE, OBJECTIVE CONDITIONS, AND JUVENILE COURTS

This chapter has focused on what sociologists call the "structural correlates" of child saving and the juvenile court movement. Recent legal, historical, and sociological research modifies somewhat the picture of child saving as entirely conservative in nature. While the thrust was clearly moralistic and authoritarian, these values were widely shared among reformatories and court officials, many of whom "shared the disadvantaged origins of their clients."[47] Liberal and humanitarian values, and compassion for the "less fortunate," were also widely shared by the more privileged young men and women who took part in the several social movements associated with child saving. In addition, some reformers clearly possessed "broad interests, reflective attitudes toward their own policies, and distrust of panaceas, such as eugenics, that minimized human capacity to change."[48]

Scholarly attention to the special—often admittedly parochial—interests that contributed to the social construction of juvenile delinquency and child neglect as social problems has sometimes tended to be conspiratorial in tone, as though the reformers were a frightened lot engaged in a sinister plot. A more balanced view is that the child savers were greatly influenced by their (largely middle class and upper-middle class) social position. Choices among alternative values, beliefs, attitudes, and activities inevitably reflect their social position. The child savers' values and activities had important institutional consequences.

While the child savers focused on conditions and behavior which they found reprehensible, the conditions to which they drew attention—severe child neglect and abuse, extreme poverty, and the association of children with adult criminals—were, and continue to be, real. Motivations to preserve the status quo and promote the values of middle-class society were associated with a widespread humanizing trend in social relationships in general, and in child rearing in particular. Some have even charged that the "history of childhood is a nightmare from which mankind has only recently begun to awaken. The further back in history one digs, the more archaic the mode of parenting, and the more likely children are to be routinely abandoned, killed, beaten, emotionally and physically starved, and sexually molested."[49]

Much evidence attests to the accuracy of these observations. In this respect there is little controversy between admirers and critics of the course of history. Strong disagreement arises concerning the balance achieved between such values as the rights of individuals and the freedom to be different versus the protection of individuals, their persons and their property, and their collective needs for social order. And there is strong disagreement about the balance between the need for the protection of children versus the need for parental and children's rights. As we shall see in succeeding chapters, these issues continue to be debated.

LOCAL VARIATIONS VERSUS THE STRUGGLE FOR UNIFORMITY IN STANDARDS AND PRACTICES

Reform movements were broadly based and multifaceted. Failures, distortions, and excesses of earlier reforms often spurred those who came later. In

California, for example, Edwin Lemert noted the influence of the same Puritan and Calvinist values that were cited by others in legislative directives to juvenile reform schools in that state. Later reformers moved to reform the reform schools, in part against economic and sectarian exploitation:[50]

> By the end of the nineteenth century, disillusionment with reform schools that didn't reform was widespread. Furthermore, the routine and wholesale removal of children from their homes and local environments and their placement in distant areas began to be questioned. Often children were sought mainly to obtain cheap labor, without regard for their education and welfare; and those apprenticed in trades had scant protection from exploitation. Sectarian and other values frequently took precedence over the welfare of the child. It was for these and related reasons that many individuals and associations working for child welfare in the latter part of the nineteenth century began to believe that child labor and compulsory education laws had to be achieved above all. The ultimate establishment of the juvenile court was partly the result of group action seeking an effective means or agency for enforcing laws that, while expressing welfare and humanitarian goals, lacked specific applicability.

The child saving movement represented a variety of sectarian, professional, economic, social class, and humanitarian interests that coincided sufficiently and converged through political action, so as to bring about the passage of new laws concerning juveniles, and the implementation of new social machinery enforcing these laws. Prior to passage of juvenile court legislation these laws were piecemeal solutions lacking adequate means to achieve their goals. Even after juvenile court legislation, implementation was rarely uniform. The situation in California, as in many states, was aggravated by sparse settlement over large areas. Edwin Lemert emphasizes the strongly local character of the evolution of practices and programs associated with juvenile courts in California. A 1921 State Board of Charities and Corrections report noted, with what must have been resignation, that "Every county in California is a law unto itself in social matters and there is a wide diversity in understanding and administering county programs affecting dependents and delinquents."[51]

Variation depended in large part on informal understandings and procedures developed among police, sheriffs and their deputies, prosecuting attorneys, probation officers, judges, and citizens in roles outside either criminal or juvenile justice. In rural areas and smaller cities operation of juvenile justice inevitably involved ongoing relationships among offenders and their friends, parents and their friends, victims, and other community institutions. Community tolerance for behavior that might in other communities be considered delinquent was matched by more severe attention to behavior which threatened the local social fabric or economic values. "In northern or mountain counties, residents tend to overlook drinking, fighting, and sexual experimentation by boys. On the other hand, if they damage expensive ranch equipment or shoot or steal cattle, the reaction is apt to be a strong one."[52]

Lemert's observations parallel my own experience as a youth in a downstate Illinois rural community. Sexual experimentation, which sometimes resulted in the birth of children out of wedlock, was regarded as a family rather than a court matter; vandalism might be a matter between youngsters, their parents, and the school (particularly if school property was involved), but it was not brought to the attention of the single town sheriff or to the juvenile court in the county seat, some 18 miles distant. Minor thefts were dealt with directly between victims, offenders and their parents. But serious theft—as in a break-in of a local restaurant, during which a small amount of cash and a large amount of candy and liquor were stolen—was regarded quite differently. I vividly recall such a break-in, which involved two of my close friends as the culprits. In this case the sheriff and the juvenile court became involved. Of equal importance for the principals, and more so for the rest of us, the event was the subject of serious discussion among friends of the offenders. I did not realize it at the time, but we were all involved in "boundary-setting" behavior. The offenders in this case clearly had overstepped the bounds of tolerated behavior, as defined by the community and their peers. Those bounds were, after all, not all that different between the community and my peer group, despite the sense of daring which often motivated our minor confrontations with local merchants, officials, and property owners.

While wide variation in juvenile justice statutes and practices has existed from the beginning, forces pressing for greater uniformity have gathered momentum. States tend to follow one another in the specific form taken by their statutes. The bar, through local associations and organizations such as the American Law Institute, as well as associations of professionals and lay persons concerned with juvenile justice, has studied and promulgated "model statutes" and manuals of procedures, and standards for programs and facilities. Some, such as the National Probation and Parole Association (now the National Council on Crime and Delinquency) also offer evaluation services.

The movement toward professionalism among all official parties involved in juvenile justice (police, probation and parole officers, correctional institution personnel, and judges) gained strength as juvenile courts diffused throughout the country. Professional associations by no means speak with one voice; indeed, there is often conflict among them, and between them and related professions, such as social work. The trend toward professionalism inevitably focuses attention on common problems and on means and standards for coping with them.

In several states, pressure toward uniformity has focused especially on efforts to bring local practice into conformity with the law. Overseeing agencies of the state, such as the California Youth Authority (CYA), have broad powers related to sentencing, institutional construction, staffing, program design, and research. At the local level, indirect and informal influences typically outweigh direct legal influences because of the strength of local values and customs. Establishment of the CYA in 1941 provided the organizational mechanism for achieving a greater degree of uniformity. Achievements of the CYA and other overarching state agencies have accumulated over the years. Surveys requested by local courts provide opportunities for both local officials and state agencies to compare local practices with state standards, while at the same time strengthening local efforts to obtain more resources. The activities of professional associations, such as the California

Probation, Parole, and Correctional Officers Association, many of whose members have strong local ties, are closely associated with state agencies. These agencies are also looked to by the state legislature for information, expertise, and as communications links with juvenile courts.

The greatest impetus to uniformity in court standards and practices has come from activities of the federal government. Federal initiatives regarding juvenile delinquency were slow to develop. The earliest federal legislation directly affecting the juvenile justice system was the Federal Juvenile Delinquency Act of 1938. The next major legislation was the Federal Youth Correction Act of 1951. By the 1980s, following passage of the Juvenile Justice and Delinquency Prevention Act in 1974, federal activity had accelerated. A dozen more major federal acts had been passed and billions of dollars were being expended, chiefly in the form of funds channeled through state and local governments. The 1974 Act was the first to "put teeth" in the drive for uniformity, making federal funding of state and local juvenile offender programs contingent on specific actions on the state level, for example, the deinstitutionalization of juvenile status offenders.

By 1976, some 160 youth service programs were being operated within 32 federal agencies, most under the aegis of the Department of Health, Education, and Welfare.[53] The states have adopted a variety of strategies to enjoy the benefits of federal programs and to meet federal requirements, but not without costs, as we shall see in the following chapter. Most states recognize the distinction between status offenders and violators of the criminal law, but they are far from uniform in the precise distinctions which are made and in the restrictions placed on detention and institutional incarceration. Elsewhere in the country, as in California, however, the ongoing functioning of local courts and their communities probably has more to do with what happens to juveniles than do either federal or state requirements.

CONCLUSION

Juvenile delinquency continues to evolve in response to changing conditions. The growing pains of a new nation, undergoing rapid industrialization and urbanization, and the intermingling of cultures, brought about by the influx of large numbers of immigrants, threatened cherished values and institutions. Increasing interdependence of individuals and institutions, a heightened sense of propriety, and growing national self-consciousness contributed to the widespread acceptance of reform and to the cumulative process by which the system of juvenile law, courts, and corrections developed, and continues to develop in a variety of not always consistent ways. The values and special interests underlying these developments, and the existence of local variation in philosophies and practices, emphasize the multiple functions of the court. As Lee Teitelbaum notes, "The fact that the families of children brought to court tend to be poor and often to have a single parent in the home suggests that resort to official treatment is sometimes (or often) sought to relieve crushing financial burdens, to secure services that cannot be purchased, and to minimize the disruptive influence of an adolescent on both adult and younger members of the family."[54]

NOTES

1. Philippe Aries, *Centuries of Childhood: A Social History of Family Life*. Translated from the French by Robert Baldick. New York: Random House, 1962, p. 411, *et passim*. Aries' views are controversial. For a critique, and rebuttal, cf. Linda A. Pollock, *Forgotten Children: Parent-Child Relations from 1500 to 1900*. Cambridge: Cambridge University Press, 1983; and S. Ryan Johansson, "Centuries of childhood, centuries of parenting: Philippe Aries and the modernization of privileged infancy," *Journal of Family History*, Vol. 12, No. 4, pp. 343–365.

2. See Aries, *Ibid.*, pp. 25, 100, 284–285, *et passim*. For a summary of scholarly research and interpretation of this very early history, see LaMar T. Empey and Mark C. Stafford, *American Delinquency: Its Meaning and Construction*. Homewood, IL.: Dorsey, forthcoming. See research on more recent changes in parents' goals with respect to their children in Duane F. Alwin, "Historical changes in parental orientations to children," forthcoming in *Sociological Studies in Child Development*, Vol. 3, Greenwich, CT: JAI Press, 1988.

3. See, for example, William Chambliss, "The state, the law, and the definition of behavior as criminal or delinquent," in Daniel Glaser (ed.), *Handbook of Criminology*. Chicago: Rand Mcnally, 1974; Joseph R. Gusfield, *Symbolic Crusade: Status Politics and the American Temperance Movement*. Urbana, IL: University of Illinois Press, 1963; Troy Duster, *The Legislation of Morality: Law, Drugs and Moral Judgment*. New York: Free Press, 1970; Howard Becker, *Outsiders: Studies in the Sociology of Deviance*. New York: Free Press of Glencoe, 1963; S. J. Pfohl, "The 'discovery' of child abuse," *Social Problems*, 24 (1977):310–23; J. K. Tierney, "The battered women movement and the creation of wife beating," *Social Problems*, 29 (1982):207–21.

4. See Sandra Ball-Rokeach, "Media linkages of the social fabric," pp. 305–318 in James F. Short, Jr. (ed.), *The Social Fabric: Dimensions and Issues*. Beverly Hills, CA: Sage, 1986; also, Sandra Ball-Rokeach and Lois B. DeFleur, "Mass media and crime," pp. 1021–1027, in Sanford H. Kadish (ed.), *Encyclopedia of Crime and Justice*. New York: Free Press, 1983.

5. Mark M. Levin and Rosemary C. Sarri, *Juvenile Delinquency: A Comparative Analysis of Legal Codes in the United States*. Ann Arbor, MI: National Assessment of Juvenile Corrections, 1974, p. 8.

6. This topic is covered in a recent, but growing literature. See John W. Meyer and Joane P. Nagel, "The changing status of children." Paper presented at the annual meetings of the Society for the Study of Social Problems, 1975 (mimeographed). The early history of English society in this regard is summarized in John Hagan, *Modern Criminology*. New York: McGraw-Hill, 1985, pp. 8 ff.

7. See Rinehard Bendix, *Nation-Building and Citizenship*. New York: Wiley, 1964; and Guy E. Swanson, *The Birth of the Gods*. Ann Arbor, MI: University of Michigan Press, 1965; also by Swanson, "An organizational analysis of collectivities," *American Sociological Review*, 36 (August, 1971). The primacy of contemporary states with regard to children is illustrated by the fact that constitutions of "new nations" formed since World War II typically contain specific language concerning rights of children, for example, protection of education and general welfare. The U.S. Constitution contains no such provisions. See John Boli-Bennett and John W. Meyer, "The ideology of childhood and the state: rules distinguishing children in national constitutions, 1870–1970," *American Sociological Review*, 43 (1978):797–812.

8. The President's Commission on Law Enforcement and Administration of Justice, *Juvenile Delinquency and Youth Crime*. Washington, DC: U.S. Government Printing Office, 1967, p. 2. Exclusion of the impoverished and neglected is ironic, in view of the heavy representation of young people so characterized among both delinquent and dependent youth today. Sanford Fox notes that the doctrine of *parens partriae* provided the theoretical justification for subjecting predelinquent children to coercive court commitment. See Sanford Fox, "Juvenile justice reform: an historical perspective," *Stanford Law Review*, Vol. 22, No. 6 (June, 1970), p. 1190, *et passim*.

9. Other countries had similar provisions for exempting very young children from punishment under the criminal law. Morrison notes that "According to Canon law and the later Roman law a child was not punishable till he had completed his seventh year. In the Italian penal code a child cannot be punished till he has completed his ninth year, and ten is the age of penal responsibility in Norway, Denmark, Austria, and Holland. In the German Empire the juvenile must have completed his twelfth year before he is criminally

responsible. In France and Belgium no age is mentioned in the penal code at which a child is necessarily irresponsible. The question of responsibility or irresponsibility is left to the discretion of the judge. Ministerial circulars were, however, issued to the French judiciary in 1855 and 1876 to the effect that children between seven and eight years of age should not be prosecuted." William Douglas Morrison, *Juvenile Offenders*. Montclair, NJ: Patterson Smith, 1975, pp. 239–240. (Original publication date, 1896, by T. Fisher Unwin, London.)

10. Edwin Powers, "Crime and punishment in early Massachusetts, 1620–1692," reprinted in Paul Lerman (ed.), *Delinquency and Social Policy*. New York: Praeger, 1970, p. 8.

11. See Empey, *op. cit.*; and Maureece Keen, "Neediest cases," review of *The Poor in the Middle Ages*, by Michel Mollat, translated by Arthur Goldhammer, New Haven, CT: Yale University Press, 1986, in *New York Review of Books* (January 15, 1987), pp. 42–43.

12. David Rothman, *The Discovery of the Asylum*. Boston: Little, Brown, 1971. I am indebted to John Meyer for his counsel regarding this section.

13. The first Dutch House of Correction, according to Knudten and Schafer, was established in 1596. Richard D. Knudten and Stephen Schafer (eds.), *Juvenile Delinquency: A Reader*. New York: Random House, 1970, p. 331. See also, Morrison, *op. cit.*, p. 228 for discussion of developments in England and Germany.

14. The following passages are from *Documents Relative to the House of Refuge*, Instituted by the Society for the Reformation of Juvenile Delinquents in the City of New York in 1824. New York: Mahlon Day, 1832. (Reprinted in Lerman, *op. cit.*, p. 14.)

15. Rothman, *op. cit.*, p. xii.

16. *Ibid.*, p. 206.

17. *Ibid.*, p. 224.

18. *Documents*, in Lerman, *op. cit.*, p. 13.

19. See Fox, *op. cit.*

20. Dickens had more than a casual interest in the manner in which legal institutions functioned. *Bleak House*, his biting indictment of lawyers and the English Chancery courts, first appeared serially from March, 1852, through September, 1853, and then as a novel in 1853. See Charles Dickens, *Bleak House*. New York: New American Library, 1964.

21. Roger Lane, "Urbanization and criminal violence in the 19th century: Massachusetts as a test case," in Hugh Davis Graham and Ted Robert Gurr (eds.), *Violence in America: Historical and Comparative Perspectives*. Washington, DC: U.S. Government Printing Office, 1969, p. 363.

22. The phrase, "moral entrepreneurs," is Howard S. Becker's. See his *Outsiders: Studies in the Sociology of Deviance*. New York: Macmillan, 1963 (2d ed., 1973).

23. The history of policing has a rich and varied history. For a brief overview see David Bayley, "Police: History," pp. 1120–1125, in S. H. Kadish (ed.), *Encyclopedia of Crime and Justice*. New York: Free Press, 1983.

24. Practices in different countries varied greatly from the beginning. Morrison discusses conditional release and conditional liberation, the former referring to release after conviction, with or without supervision. Morrison compares the English system of releasing a prisoner "on condition he binds himself to come up for judgement when called upon" with the system in the United States in which probation officers watch over both children and parents, noting that this system is "more economical as well as more natural than the system which exists in England." Conditional liberation was a type of parole in which "juveniles committed to industrial or reformatory schools may be liberated conditionally…long before the full term of detention has expired…committed to the care of some trustworthy person, either in this country or the colonies, who is willing to take charge of them." *Op. cit.*, p. 312. O'Leary notes that the type of conditional release of prisoners referred to in Britain, the United States, and Canada as parole still is known as conditional liberation on the European continent. Vincent O'Leary, "Parole administration," in Glaser, *op. cit.*, p. 910.

25. Morrison, *Ibid.*, p. 14.

26. *Ibid.*, p. 183. The specific description is of "a society…in Paris for the legal defence of children brought before the criminal courts," but the purpose was similar elsewhere as well.

27. See John Hagan and Jeffrey Leon, "Rediscovering delinquency: social history, political ideology and the sociology of law." *American Sociological Review*, 42 (August, 1977):587–598; see also, Steven Schlossman, *Love and the American Delinquent*. Chicago: University of Chicago Press, 1977.

28. See Robert M. Mennel, "Attitudes and policies toward juvenile delinquency in the United States: a historiographical review," pp. 191–224, in Norval Morris and Michael Tonry (eds.), *Crime and Justice*, Vol. 4. Chicago: University of Chicago Press, 1983.

29. Historical, legal, and sociological reviews of these developments are found in several studies. I have relied principally on accounts provided by Mennel, *Ibid.*, Empey, *op. cit.*, Rothman, *op. cit.*, Fox, *op. cit.*, and Anthony M. Platt, *The Child Savers: The Invention of Delinquency*. Chicago: University of Chicago Press, 1969.

30. Fox, *op. cit.*, p. 1228.

31. *Ibid.*, p. 1211. Fox refers to the "coerced heresy" of the Protestant homes, *Ibid.*, p. 1195.

32. Platt, *op. cit.*, p. 69. Hagan notes that "there is little concrete information about the motives for this 'philanthropy' " or about the benefits to those who gave it. It is clear that families of the urban poor had real needs and readily availed themselves of the court's services. See Hagan, *op. cit.*, pp. 77–82. See also, Mennel, *op. cit.*, Chambliss, "The state, the law, and the definition of behavior as criminal or delinquent," *op. cit.*; and Hans W. Mattick, "Reflections of a former prison warden," in James F. Short, Jr. (ed.), *Crime, Delinquency, and Society*. Chicago: University of Chicago Press, 1974.

33. Platt, *Ibid.*, p. 77. See also, Edwin M. Lemert, *Social Action and Legal Change: Revolution within the Juvenile Court*. Chicago: Aldine, 1970.

34. Hagan and Leon, *op. cit.*

35. See, for example, Empey, *op. cit.* Empey notes that the police prefer to be viewed as crime fighters, but their jobs more often require social work skills.

36. See, for example, Arthur E. Fink, *Causes of Crime: Biological Theories in the United States, 1800–1915*. New York: Barnes, 1962. Much the same imagery was applied to the poor and otherwise dependent. It will be recalled that the immediate precursor of the Society for the Reformation of Delinquents was the Society for the Prevention of Pauperism. An 1898 report of the Illinois Board of State Commissioners of Public Charities affirmed the unitary conception of predelinquent: "If the child is the material out of which men and women are made, the neglected child is the material out of which paupers and criminals are made" (Fox, *op. cit.*, p. 1193.).

37. Hofstadter has pointed out that the "new education" had little to say concerning the class structure of American society, or of the possibility that educational opportunity might increase social mobility and break down class barriers. It was based on theory that assumed the essential similarity of interests within society. Richard Hofstadter, *Anti-intellectualism in American Life*. New York: Knopf. 1963.

38. Fox, *op. cit.*, p. 1255.

39. *Ibid.*, quoting Timothy D. Hurley, *The Juvenile Courts and What they Have Accomplished* (2d ed.), 1904, p. 18.

40. Richard Hofstadter, *The Age of Reform*. New York: Vintage Books, 1955, p. 24.

41. Lane, *op. cit.*, p. 566. See also, W. I. Thomas, Robert E. Park, and H. A. Miller, *Old World Traits Transplanted*. New York: Harper, 1921.

42. See W. Vaughan Stapleton and Lee E. Teitelbaum, *In Defense of Youth: A Study of the Role of Counsel in American Juvenile Courts*. New York: Russell Sage, 1972, p. 41.

43. Fox, *op. cit.*, pp. 1214, 1208.

44. State of California, *Welfare and Institutions Code, 1965*. Sacramento, CA: Department of General Services, 1965, p. 35.

45. Levin and Sarri, *op. cit.*, p. 12.

46. *Ibid.*, p. 18. This is not the only balance sought, however. I am told by a former reporter for the Joint Legislative Commission to revise the Penal Code of the State of California that prosecutors frequently argued for additional penalties and categories of offenses in the interest of "plea bargaining," that is, to increase their options in prosecuting cases. See John Kaplan, *Criminal Justice*. Mineola, NY: Foundation Press, 1973: p. 398, *et passim*.

47. Mennel, *op. cit.*, p. 210.

48. *Ibid.*, p. 214. See also, Steven L. Schlossman, *Love and the American Delinquent: The Theory and Practice of "Progressive" Juvenile Justice, 1825–1920*. Chicago: University of Chicago Press, 1977.

49. Lloyd DeMause, "The history of childhood: the basis for psychohistory," *History of Childhood Quarterly*, Vol. 1, No. 1 (Summer, 1973), p. 1. Cf. Pollock, *op. cit.*; Cf. Aries, *op. cit.*

50. See Lemert, *op. cit.*, p. 42.

51. *Ibid.*, p. 46.

52. *Ibid.*, p. 61.

53. See *Catalogue of Federal Youth Programs*. Washington, DC: U.S. Government Printing Office, 1976.

54. Lee L. Teitelbaum, "Juvenile status offenders," p. 990, in Sanford H. Kadish (ed.), *Encyclopedia of Crime and Justice*, Vol 3. New York: Free Press, 1983.

CHAPTER 3
PROCEDURAL
REFORM

INTRODUCTION

Federal initiatives concerning juvenile delinquency that followed the Juvenile Justice and Delinquency Prevention Act of 1974 were preceded by U.S. Supreme Court rulings which had broad repercussions throughout juvenile justice systems in this country. With few exceptions, earlier appellate court rulings at the state level had upheld the broad powers of juvenile courts. The nature of the issues and the quality of the legal debates concerning them, are the subject of the next section.

THE LEGACY OF PARENS PATRIAE

The legal status of juvenile misbehavior, child dependency, neglect, and abuse was intensely debated long before the first juvenile court legislation was passed. These debates continue as the centennial of that first legislation approaches. Early on, legal challenges to the new court, its procedures and dispositions, were frequent, but largely unsuccessful. Appellate courts upheld the lack of procedural safeguards in juvenile courts and the broad reach of state intervention into the lives of children and their parents that the juvenile courts permitted.[1] The spirit of the appeals and the decisions is exemplified in an 1876 Wisconsin case that affirmed the centrality of the doctrine of the state as *parens patriae*. Wisconsin juvenile law permitted the court to sentence a child to a state training school until the age of majority even though no crime had been committed. The court spoke eloquently to the issue:[2]

> The gravest objection…made to the statute is that the commitment of a child to one of these schools until majority except for crime, operates as an imprisonment of the child…without due process of law, and that the statute

authorizing it is therefore a positive violation of the constitution....we cannot understand that the detention of the child at one of these schools should be considered as imprisonment, any more than its detention in the poor house; any more than the detention of any child at any boarding school, standing, for the time, in loco parentis to the child. Parental authority implies restraint, not imprisonment...every school must necessarily exercise some measure of the parental power of restraint over children committed to it...when the state, as parens patriae, is compelled by the misfortune of a child to assume for its parental duty, and to charge itself with its nurture, it is compelled also to assume parental authority...

The proper *scope* of state intervention rarely has been challenged, in part because juvenile courts have occupied a position of low visibility compared to criminal courts. Until recently, the appearance of attorneys in court was rare, and often actively discouraged by judges. Judges were not required to justify accepting jurisdiction of cases, and transcripts of juvenile proceedings (essential for appeals) were not prepared. When the challenge came, therefore, it "turned...upon the *manner* of the court's intervention" primarily, and only indirectly on the power to intervene.[3]

The power to intervene may be the more fundamental issue, however. Even ardent defenders of juvenile courts recognize that juvenile court legislation often results in "normal problems of everyday life" being defined as problematic and therefore subject to state intervention.[4] Critics are more severe. Even before juvenile courts were established, an 1870 Illinois Supreme Court ruling, releasing a boy from the Chicago Reform School, sharply questioned then prevalent views and practices concerning grounds for state intervention:[5]

> What is proper parental care? The best and kindest parents would differ...there is not a child in the land who could not be proved, by two or more witnesses, to be in this sad condition....Though it is sometimes said, that "idleness is the parent of vice," yet the former may exist without the latter. It is strictly an abstinence from labor or employment. If the child performs all its duties to parents and to society, the State has no right to compel it to labor. Vice is a very comprehensive term. Acts, wholly innocent in the estimation of many good men, would, according to the code of ethics of others, show fearful depravity. What is the standard to be? What extent of enlightenment, what amount of industry, what degree of virtue, will save from the threatened imprisonment? In our solicitude to form youth for the duties of civil life, we should not forget the rights which inhere both in parents and children. The principle of the absorption of the child in, and its complete subjection to the despotism of, the State, is wholly inadmissible in the modern civilized world.

The elegant language of these rulings captures the spirit of debate which, more than a century later, continues. Arguments in the Wisconsin case carried the day for many years. The Illinois court's ruling ran counter to the gathering force of the child saving movement and had little lasting impact. Despite frequent charges and legal challenges that children's rights were being violated, appellate courts generally supported the broadened powers of intervention urged by the reformers.

The rhetoric of the juvenile court movement often seemed explicitly "anti-legal," as exemplified by Judge Ben Lindsey's comment that "a child's case is not a legal case."[6] It was especially antiprocedural, or at least *aprocedural*. Judge Lindsey was adamant concerning the lack of attention to rules of evidence:[7]

> ...[W]e pay very little attention to the rules of evidence...The whole proceeding is in the interest of the child and not to degrade him or even to punish him. We do not protect the child by discharging him because there is no legal evidence to convict, as would be done in a criminal case when we know that he has committed the offense. This is to do him a great injury, for he is simply encouraged in the prevalent opinion among city children...that it is all right to lie all they can, to cheat all they can, to steal all they can, so long as they "do not get caught" or that you have "no proof."

Appellate decisions upholding the court's broad powers and lack of due process rested also on the civil, as distinguished from the criminal, nature of the proceedings:[8]

> ...[T]he proceedings under this law are in no sense criminal proceedings, nor is the result in any case a conviction or punishment for crime. They are simply statutory proceedings by which the state, in the legitimate exercise of its police power, or, in other words, its right to preserve its own integrity and future existence, reaches out its arm in a kindly way and provides for the protection of its children from parental neglect or from vicious influences and surroundings, either by keeping watch over the child while in its natural home, or where that seems impracticable, by placing it in an institution designed for that purpose.

The irony of the distinction between the civil and criminal is that violation of the criminal law was virtually the only specific element shared by the statutes defining delinquency and delinquents. Earlier, the parental imagery of the juvenile court served also to justify the informality and consequent lack of procedural safeguards in the juvenile court:[9]

> The natural parent needs no process to temporarily deprive his child of its liberty by confining it in its own home, to save it and to shield it from the consequences of persistence in a career of waywardness, nor is the state, when compelled, as *parens patriae*, to take the place of the father for the same purpose, required to adopt any process as a means of placing its hands upon the child to lead it into one of its courts.

The impetus of the juvenile court movement thus strayed deliberately from traditional legal concerns with jurisdiction, procedure, rules of evidence and proof, or even from legally prohibited conduct. The federal presence in this process was exemplified by a 1920 publication of the United States Children's Bureau, which declared that "the fundamental purpose of juvenile court procedure is not to determine whether or not a child has committed a specific offense, but to discover whether he is in a condition requiring the special care of the state."[10]

CASE WORK THEORY VERSUS JUVENILE
COURT PRACTICE

The juvenile court movement soon came under the domination of a case work perspective that encouraged this view. "The court became, in the thought of many, the agency to which all unadjusted children or children needing care should be taken and the agency which should be directly responsible for the care and treatment of these children."[11] While this conception of the court was objected to by many, and slowed by occasional rulings and pronouncements from the bench, it prevailed for many years.[12]

Just prior to World War II, this position came under increasing attack from within the social work profession. Those who took a hard look at practice, as distinguished from philosophy, noted enormous variation from one jurisdiction to another, and failure everywhere to live up to the humanitarian rhetoric of the movement and the logic of appellate court decisions upholding the broad powers of intervention that were lodged in the juvenile court. Few courts in fact did much case work, leading some to urge that courts be strictly limited to judicial actions and that, when required, case work be performed by agencies upon court referral.

Many social workers, lawyers, and behavioral scientists agreed that what juvenile courts were doing was, in fact, punitive, and that the promise of rehabilitation was largely illusory. The first point was eloquently spoken to by Frances E. Allen:[13]

> Measures which subject individuals to the substantial and involuntary deprivation of their liberty are essentially punitive in character, and this reality is not altered by the fact that the motivations that prompt incarceration are to provide therapy or otherwise contribute to the person's well-being or reform. As such, these measures must be closely scrutinized to insure that power is being applied consistently with those values of the community that justify interferences with liberty for only the most clear and compelling reasons.

Even a casual look at the bases for possible court referral found many that were neither clear nor compelling. Behavior standards which once seemed firm and clear to the child savers continued to change—more rapidly as the technology of communication brought people once isolated into contact with one another, and as social change in many areas of life accelerated. The changes can be traced in legislative enactments, as state legislatures found specific restrictions on juveniles increasingly anachronistic. At the same time, new "problems" continually emerged. Both of these tendencies were reflected, for example, in the actions of the Washington State legislature, which, in 1961, removed from the definition of "delinquent child" reference to the "use of tobacco in any form," and added reference to use of heroin and marijuana. Also removed at that time was reference to the child "who habitually uses vile, obscene, vulgar, profane or indecent language, or is guilty of immoral conduct; or who is found in or about railroad yards or tracks; or who jumps on or off trains or cars; or who enters a car or engine, without lawful authority." In general, revisions of state statutes have tended to remove archaic language and to delete broad status categories from the definition of "delinquent child."

FAILURE OF DIAGNOSTIC PREDICTION

The juvenile court was predicated on the theory that state intervention could be justified by *diagnostic prediction* of delinquent behavior. Characteristics of children were to serve as the basis for court referral because they were predictive of future delinquent behavior. Failure of this theory seriously undermined the court.

Characteristics regarded as predictive were, in fact, so inclusive as to make virtually all children subject to court intervention. From a Children's Bureau sponsored project with the goal of identifying and treating potential delinquents, Michael Hakeem compiled the following list of "personality traits and types of behavior regarded as symptoms" calling for the referral of children for expert diagnosis and treatment:[14]

Bashfulness	Negativism
Boastfulness	Obscenity
Boisterousness	Overactivity
Bossiness	Over-masculine behavior (in girls)
Bullying	Profanity
Cheating	Quarreling
Cruelty	Roughness
Crying	Selfishness
Daydreaming	Sex perversion
Deceit	Sex play
Defiance	Sexual activity
Dependence	Shifting activities
Destructiveness	Show-off behavior
Disobedience	Silliness
Drinking	Sleep disturbances
Eating disturbances	Smoking
Effeminate behavior (in boys)	Speech disturbances
Enuresis	Stealing
Fabrication	Stubbornness
Failure to perform assigned tasks	Sullenness
Fighting	Tardiness
Finicalness	Tattling
Gambling	Teasing
Gate crashing	Temper displays
Hitching rides	Tics
Ill-mannered behavior	Timidity
Impudence	Thumbsucking
Inattentiveness	Truancy from home
Indolence	Truancy from school
Lack of orderliness	Uncleanliness
Masturbation	Uncouth personalities
Nailbiting	Underactivity

Undesirable companions	Untidiness
Undesirable recreation	Violation of street-trades regulations
Unsportsmanship	Violation of traffic regulations

The importance of this list lies neither in its obvious confusion and numerous contradictions, nor in the consequences for the vast majority of children exhibiting these behaviors. The goal of the court was not so easily encompassed. Hakeem's list is but a crude extension of the early child savers' assumption that conditions which they found objectionable were predictive of later criminality, and that intervention by the state would reduce this likelihood.

FAILURE OF THE BASIC MISSION OF THE COURT

Finally, the powers of the court were undermined by failures in what had been conceived as its *basic mission*. From the beginning, juvenile courts were in a poor position to treat delinquents, and in no position at all to prevent delinquency by the means at their disposal. The initial juvenile court legislation was an abject failure from the point of view of those who sought new programs and facilities. None were, in fact, provided. With few exceptions, the effectiveness of those that have been created since remains in doubt.[15]

The theoretical "mutual compact" between the child and the state implied in the *parens patriae* doctrine has been found wanting.[16] Anomalous practices belied the philosophy of the juvenile court from the beginning. Judges, who were supposed to be kindly and deeply concerned fathers, in many courts spent only minutes to hear a case. Detention, which was justified in the interests of clinical study, often resulted in little actual study. Treatment programs with avowed therapeutic goals often lacked adequate personnel and facilities, or demonstrable effectiveness.

Challenges to juvenile court legislation and practice were spurred by these and other factors. The underlying philosophy of the juvenile courts remained largely intact, however. Successful legal challenge, when it came, hinged not on failures of performance or on the scope of the court's authority to intervene, but on due process considerations; that is, on the *manner* in which the court intervened in the lives of children.

THE UNITED STATES SUPREME COURT RULES

The importance of United States Supreme Court rulings for the juvenile court can hardly be overestimated. The Court interprets the law of the land under the Constitution, placing legal constraints on the thousands of juvenile justice systems throughout the country.

As previously noted, frequent attempts have been made to promote uniformity in juvenile court legislation and practice, at both state and national levels. Their success has been limited. Resources available to courts vary greatly, some jurisdictions having many public and private services, programs, and institutions to which referrals can be made, others having virtually none save informal probation or incarceration in a single state reformatory. Some judges are committed to juvenile court work, devoting themselves full time to it, while others serve only parttime and often reluctantly.

The training and background of judges and of probation officers vary enormously, as do the legal requirements for these positions. Desired qualities often are phrased in extremely vague terms: A prospective juvenile court judge should be "learned, able, and discreet," for example, or (despite growing feminist awareness) a "man upright in character." A few states require that legal training be supplemented by other qualities: knowledge of family and child problems, for example, or experience and understanding regarding the problems of children and family welfare. Alaska noted only that if a lawyer were not available, "a person otherwise qualified" might be selected.[17]

Qualifications for intake and probation officers are even more varied. Some states specify that probation officers must meet civil service requirements. Others require no objective qualifications, though judges may be admonished to choose for these positions persons "of good moral character," or those who are "discreet" and who have "experience with youth."

KENT V. UNITED STATES

Given such wide variation in standards and practices among juvenile courts, and their legal independence, only a law or appellate court ruling at the federal level can exert general and compelling influence.[18] That did not happen until 1966, when the U.S. Supreme Court received from the District of Columbia the case of *Kent v. United States*.[19] That ruling was limited to the procedure by which a juvenile court might relinquish jurisdiction to the criminal court, but the majority opinion prepared by Justice Fortas spoke to larger issues:[20]

> While there can be no doubt of the original laudable purpose of juvenile courts, studies and critiques in recent years raise serious questions as to whether actual performance measures well enough against theoretical purpose to make tolerable the immunity of the process from the reach of constitutional guaranties applicable to adults. There is much evidence that some juvenile courts, including that of the District of Columbia, lack the personnel, facilities and techniques to perform adequately as representatives of the state in a *parens patriae* capacity, at least with respect to children charged with law violation. There is evidence, in fact, that there may be grounds for concern that the child receives the worst of both worlds: that he gets neither the protections accorded to adults nor the solicitous care and regenerative treatment postulated for children.

IN RE GAULT

Kent was but the opening salvo to a much more comprehensive ruling by the Court shortly thereafter. In June of 1964, 15-year old Gerald Gault had been found delinquent by the juvenile court of Gila County, Arizona, for making a lewd telephone call to a neighbor in violation of Arizona law. Young Gault was committed to the State Industrial School "for the period of his minority (in Arizona, until 21), unless sooner discharged by due process of law."[21] His offense, when committed by an adult, carried a penalty of a fine of $5 to $50, or imprisonment for not more than two months. Because no appeal was permitted in juvenile cases under Arizona law, a writ of habeas corpus was filed by an attorney representing the Gaults. The writ was dismissed by the superior court to which it had been assigned, and appeal was denied by the Arizona Supreme Court. Appeal was then made to the U.S. Supreme Court on the grounds that Gerald Gault had been denied the following basic rights under the due process (equal protection under the law) clause of the Fourteenth Amendment to the United States Constitution:

1. Right to have notice of the charges brought against him
2. Right to legal counsel
3. Right to confrontation and cross-examination of witnesses against him
4. Privilege against self-incrimination
5. Right to a transcript of the proceedings
6. Right to appellate review

The process by which Gerald Gault had been determined to be delinquent was extremely informal. Neither he nor his parents had been given notice of the charges to be brought against him. He was placed in detention without his parents being notified. The neighbor to whom the alleged lewd telephone call was made did not appear in court. Gault was unrepresented by counsel, and not informed of his right to obtain counsel. He was examined by the judge without being told of the privilege against self-incrimination. No transcript of the hearing was made, and under Arizona law no appeal was permitted. Federal appeal was the only recourse.

On May 15, 1967, the U.S. Supreme Court ruled in favor of Gault on the first four of these counts. The majority decision emphasized the anomaly that children, who require even more protection against the power of the state than adults, by virtue of their immaturity, lack of understanding, and sophistication, were in fact given less protection than adults under juvenile court law and practice. Portions of the decision follow:[22]

1. Notice, to comply with due process requirements, must be given sufficiently in advance of scheduled court proceedings so that reasonable opportunity to prepare will be afforded, and it must "set forth the alleged misconduct with particularity."
2. A proceeding where the issue is whether the child will be found to be "delinquent" and subjected to the loss of his liberty for years is comparable in seriousness to a felony prosecution. The juvenile needs the assistance of counsel to cope with problems of law, to make skilled inquiry into the facts, to insist upon regularity of the proceedings, and to ascertain whether he has a defense and to prepare and submit it. The child "requires the guiding hand of counsel at every step in the proceedings against him."
3. ...absent a valid confession, a determination of delinquency and an order of commitment to a state institution cannot be sustained in the absence of sworn

testimony subject to the opportunity for cross-examination in accordance with our law and constitutional requirements.

4. We conclude that the constitutional privilege against self-incrimination is applicable in the case of juveniles as it is with respect to adults. We appreciate that special problems may arise with respect to waiver of the privilege by or on behalf of children, and that there may well be some differences in technique—but not in principle—depending upon the age of the child and the presence and competence of parents. The participation of counsel will, of course, assist the police, juvenile courts and appellate tribunals in administering the privilege. If counsel is not present for some permissible reason when an admission is obtained, the greatest care must be taken to assure that the admission was voluntary, in the sense not only that it has not been coerced or suggested, but also that it is not the product of ignorance of rights or of adolescent fantasy, fright or despair.

Citing its own previous ruling (in *Griffin* v. *Illinois*, 1956) to the effect that the federal Constitution does not require states to provide for appellate review, the Court did not rule on this question in Gault, nor on the provision of transcripts. It warned, however, that such failures might place a considerable burden on lower courts if they were required to reconstruct a challenged record.

The Court's decision in *Gault* was not unanimous, and there were misgivings among the justices. The majority decision referred to the early reformers as possessed of "the highest motives and most enlightened impulses."[23] Justice Black's concurring opinion noted that juvenile court laws "are the result of plans promoted by humane and forward-looking people to provide a system of courts, procedures, and sanctions deemed to be less harmful and more lenient to children than to adults."[24] The Court's attack centered on the failure of juvenile courts to live up to their goals, and on their violation of constitutional guarantees:[25]

> Juvenile court history has again demonstrated that unbridled discretion, however benevolently motivated, is frequently a poor substitute for principle and procedure....Departures from established principles of due process have frequently resulted not in enlightened procedure, but in arbitrariness.

The dilemma of the Court, and of all who are concerned with individual rights, the welfare of children, and the protection of persons and property, is highlighted by portions of Justice Stewart's dissenting opinion in *Gault*. "In the last 70 years," Stewart wrote, "many dedicated men and women have devoted their professional lives to the enlightened task of bringing us out of the dark world of Charles Dickens in meeting our responsibilities to the child in our society." Recognizing the shortcomings of juvenile courts, he warned that the majority decision invited "a long step backwards into the Nineteenth Century":[26]

> In that era there were no juvenile proceedings, and a child was tried in a conventional criminal court with all the restrictions of a conventional criminal trial. So it was that a 12-year-old boy named James Guild was tried in New Jersey for killing Catherine Beakes. A jury found him guilty of murder, and he

was sentenced to death by hanging. The sentence was executed. It was all very constitutional.

OTHER SUPREME COURT RULINGS

In 1970 the Supreme Court ruled (in re *Winship*) that "proof beyond a reasonable doubt" was required in juvenile hearings, thus denying the view that such hearings were civil rather than criminal in nature, therefore requiring only a "preponderance of evidence." This ruling was further strengthened when, in 1975, the Court ruled (in *Breed* v. *Jones*) that the double jeopardy clause of the Fifth Amendment applies, through the Fourteenth Amendment, to juveniles. Earlier rulings had held that the double jeopardy prohibition did not prevent subsequent conviction in criminal courts of persons already adjudicated in juvenile courts for the same conduct, on the grounds that juvenile proceedings were civil and protective rather than criminal and punitive.

The Court also ruled, in 1971 (*McKeiver* v. *Pennsylvania*), that the federal Constitution did not compel states to provide the right to a jury trial to accused juveniles. This power was, therefore, reserved to the states, several of which have passed legislation granting that right. The so-called Miranda rights accorded adults (the right to remain silent and to be provided with counsel) also have been ruled by the Court to be not fully applicable to juveniles.

THE DIFFERENCE IT MAKES

Despite their importance, these Supreme Court decisions have left key questions unanswered. Is the delinquent essentially a child or an offender? Procedurally, as Ann Rankin Mahoney notes, the question becomes one of reconciling the determination of guilt or innocence with the "search to identify a condition requiring treatment or rehabilitation."[27]

The evolving balance struck in these rulings becomes translated into human activity in a variety of ways. The old saw that "there is more law in the end of a policeman's nightstick than in a ruling of the Supreme Court" is paralleled more abstractly (and accurately) by Justice Holmes' observation that "The life of the law...has been experience."[28] Most of that experience takes place in local courts and in the streets and institutions of local communities. And, as was the case in the establishment of the first juvenile courts, local practice is responsive to local attitudes and values, and to local relationships among authorities and other citizens.

Little systematic attention has been given to the impact of procedural reform, but findings from several studies suggest much variation. While some courts moved with dispatch to implement the due process requirements of the *Gault* decision, others were more resistive.[29] The laws in some states, for example, California, New York, and Illinois, met all or most of the requirements in *Gault* prior to the decision. In Alameda County, California, for example, advice of the right to counsel had existed for more than 30 years, whereas in other counties (notably the smaller and more rural counties) practices reflected local conditions and differing philosophies. A judge in a far northern county spoke as follows:[30]

> We're very unorthodox here. We try to keep informal. We try to get under the skin of the kids. We differ from big city courts....If a felony charge is involved I advise minors and parents of their right to counsel. However, I don't do this for the "Mickey Mouse" offenses, and I don't worry about rules of evidence in uncontested cases. Furthermore, in hearings I ask leading questions; I try to get the boy to give out a little. I try to determine if the boy needs help and guidance. Often I tell them I am not going to make specific findings. Then there are times when I make minors wards even though there is very little to go on.
>
> Appeals don't worry me in the least. If the Supreme Court wants to differ, that's OK. The opinion of the Judicial Council likewise is of no concern, except on how I administer the court. The youngster's opinion of me is important in performing my role. What parents think of me also makes a difference, and I spend a lot of time building rapport. Otherwise, I have to satisfy my own conscience.

Local variation notwithstanding, the frequency of appearance of counsel in juvenile courts increased substantially in the years following *Gault*. Lemert reports that the percentage of cases in which counsel appeared in court rose from an estimated 3 percent to 10 percent between 1961 and 1965. The *range* of estimates tells as much as does the increase. Before 1961, the range of estimates was from zero to 30 percent, whereas in 1965 it was from 0 to 99 percent. More serious cases were more likely to be represented by counsel, and the availability of public defenders greatly enhanced the likelihood of representation. Lemert also notes, however, that public defenders were more likely than privately retained counsel to be "co-opted into the organization of the court."[31]

The most ambitious studies of the impact of the *Gault* decision were conducted by Stapleton, Teitelbaum, and Lefstein, in three large cities in the midwest and eastern United States.[32] Over an eight month period immediately following *Gault*, the provisions of the decision were simulated by studying only cases involving a charge of delinquency subject to commitment to an institution, and not represented by counsel. The study examined compliance with the right to counsel, the right to confrontation and cross-examination of witnesses against the defendant, and the privilege against self-incrimination.

Great variation was found among the three courts. Advice regarding the right to counsel (without prejudice and including advice that counsel would be provided without charge, if necessary) was rarely given. The exception was in "Zenith," where the juvenile court statute had been changed to include this requirement shortly before the *Gault* decision. *No advice* in this regard was given in 85 percent of the cases in one of the other cities, and in 32 percent in the third city. Compliance was greatest with respect to the opportunity for confrontation. Only 22 percent of all cases had no witnesses present in court, and about half the cases had one or more essential witnesses present. Least compliance was found regarding the privilege against self-incrimination. Advice to this effect was never given in one of the cities, and in only a minority of cases in the other two.

Much of the variation in the handling of juvenile cases in these three courts was attributed to the changed statutes in Zenith, and to the fact that the Zenith judges were recent appointees to the juvenile bench. Their exposure to juvenile court practices was therefore relatively new. All of the judges in the other two cities had served in juvenile courts for more than four years and had been associated with juvenile courts much longer. In Zenith, unlike the other cities, a precise plea was entered to a delinquency petition, thus structuring the proceedings and making clearer the rights of all parties.

Stapleton and Teitelbaum followed this inquiry with an experimental study in one of the traditional juvenile court cities and in Zenith. The purpose of the experiment was to determine the impact of representation by counsel on both the proceedings and the outcomes of cases. Toward this end, legal services were offered to randomly selected cases meeting project criteria.[33] Project lawyers were instructed to adopt a frankly adversarial posture toward their cases.

Not surprisingly, the effect of the experimental program differed in the two cities. In the more traditional juvenile court nearly twice as many experimental cases (those provided with counsel by the project) as control cases (those not provided counsel by the project) were committed to institutions (10.7 percent versus 5.9 percent).[34] This difference was not observed in the more legalistic Zenith court, where 8.7 percent of the experimental cases were committed to institutions as compared to 12.3 percent of the controls. The largest difference between the two cities occurred with respect to dismissals and continuances under court supervision. Experimentally assigned lawyers gained dismissals in half their cases in Zenith (compared to 40 percent of the control cases), whereas dismissals were much less frequent among both experimental and control cases in the traditional court (18.5 percent and 19.2 percent, respectively).[35] Continued court supervision of cases was infrequent in Zenith (but more frequent among experimentals—10 percent as compared to 4 percent of controls), but more frequent in the traditional court (about one-third of both experimental and control cases).

Experimental differences were found to be little influenced by such factors as offense, age, race, home situation, or number of previous court appearances of the alleged offenders. Nor was variation influenced by individual judges. Between the two cities, however, differences were considerable. In the traditional court, lawyers relied more on the child's story than on legal defense tactics. In Zenith, more motions were filed, established principles of both juvenile and criminal law were appealed to in defense, and plea bargaining was more frequent (19 percent of Zenith cases, compared to 3 percent in Gotham). Lawyers appearing before the traditional court reported significantly more instances of judicial pressure against their use of classic legal steps designed to protect rights of their clients. They faced the dilemma that legalistic defense strategies might prove injurious to their clients. Such pressures also occurred in Zenith, but they were less frequent and less inhibiting.

Thus, the extent to which the courts were traditional or legalistic in their handling of juveniles influenced what happened to juveniles to a greater extent than did representation by counsel, per se. As representation by counsel becomes more common, however, and as courts become more bureaucratized and formal in procedure (as has happened increasingly in large urban courts especially), resistance to adversarial behavior by counsel has weakened. This, in turn, has created an additional problem: the defense counsel being co-opted by the court, as reported by Lemert, Emerson, and others.[36] None of these tendencies, however, has eliminated the great variation in juvenile court policy and practice that continues to exist.

Other effects of representation by counsel are even more difficult to ascertain. How do representation by counsel, and protection of procedural rights influence the juveniles who come before the court? How does "getting off" on the basis of legal tactics affect them? Stapleton and Teitelbaum present no data bearing on these questions, but they suggest that there is little evidence that the boys whose cases they studied developed a "beat-the-rap" attitude as a result of their experiences with legal counsel—despite the fact that some boys who admitted guilt did "beat-the-rap" when their lawyers entered "not guilty" pleas.

The problem thus posed bears importantly on the role of law in social control. Little systematic evidence is available, but it is generally agreed that the effectiveness of legal systems is closely related to the extent to which they are accorded legitimacy. The legitimacy of the juvenile justice system, from the perspective of juveniles caught in its web, is spoken to by a study conducted in Boston. The researchers found that the legitimacy of courts and court decisions was not questioned by boys who had been sent to a Boston Reception Center. These boys, "despite their haziness about the court proceedings, despite the fact that they have been told, oftentimes, various and conflicting things about what is happening to them, despite their shock and unhappiness at commitment...still largely accord legitimacy to the decision [to commit them to the Center]."[37]

The broader issue of law and social control is further informed by research on the moral status of the law and on political efficacy. Psychologist Lawrence Kohlberg's pioneering work suggests that a child's interpretation of the moral force of law is determined in important ways by social-class background. When 16-year-olds were asked to respond to the question, "Should someone obey a law if he doesn't think it is a good law?" typical responses from lower-class, lower middle-class, and upper middle-class boys varied considerably:[38]

> From a lower class boy: "Yes, a law is a law and you can't do nothing about it. You have to obey it, you should. That's what it's for." (For him the law is simply a constraining thing that is there. "You can't do nothing about," means that it should be obeyed.)
> A lower middle class boy replied, "Laws are made for people to obey and if everyone would start breaking them...Well, if you owned a store and there were no laws, everyone would just come in and not have to pay." (Here laws are seen not as arbitrary commands but as a unitary system, as the basis of social order. The role or perspective taken is that of a storekeeper, of someone with a stake in the order.)
> From an upper middle class boy: "The law is the law but I think people themselves can tell what's right or wrong. I suppose the laws are made by many different groups of people with different ideas. But if you don't believe the law, you should try to get it changed, you shouldn't disobey it." (Here laws are seen

as products of various legitimate ideological and interest groups varying in their beliefs as to the best decision in policy matters. The role of law obeyer is seen from the perspective of the democratic policy maker.)

Kohlberg hypothesized that the social-class differences reflected in these responses stem from variations in the extent to which children feel a "sense of potential participation in the social order." Research has repeatedly demonstrated that most children appearing before juvenile courts come from the lower or working classes. Many of these same children later appear in criminal courts, where similar class distributions are found. Thus, the paradox: Children of the social class who most uncritically accept the moral authority of the law most often come into conflict with it—and continue to do so in adulthood.

Later in life, lower-class persons tend to be less politically active and lower in political efficacy (the belief that one can affect political outcomes) than are persons higher in the social and economic order. Kohlberg's "sense of potential participation in the social order" is related to one's "stake in conformity," which has been advanced to account for conformity to laws and to other types of norms. The potential for participation in a social system is associated with the stake one has in conforming to the norms of that system.

For the present it is sufficient to note that procedural reform, like the invention of juvenile delinquency and of the institutions which preceded it, affects neither all persons nor all communities alike. Despite continued change, much of the early philosophy of the juvenile court remains in place—in statutes and in practice. In the following chapter we explore various aspects of the *practice* side of this equation.

NOTES

1. Mennel suggests that activities associated with the juvenile court "rescued" the doctrine of *parens patriae* "from the reform schools, where its credibility was being seriously undermined." Robert M. Mennel, "Attitudes and policies toward juvenile delinquency in the United States: a historiographical review," in Norval Morris and Michael Tonry (eds.), *Crime and Justice*, Vol. 4. Chicago: University of Chicago Press, p. 208. Appeals were made, with rulings sustaining juvenile courts in 40 state supreme courts. See Monrad Paulsen, "Children's court: Gateway or last resort," *Case and Comment*, 72 (November–December, 1967), pp. 3–9.

2. Paul W. Tappan, *Juvenile Delinquency*. New York: McGraw Hill, 1949, pp. 203–204.

3. W. Vaughan Stapleton and Lee E. Teitelbaum, *In Defense of Youth: A Study of the Role of Counsel in American Juvenile Courts*. New York: Russell Sage, 1972, p. 15.

4. Mark M. Levin and Rosemary C. Sarri, *Juvenile Delinquency: A Comparative Analysis of Legal Codes in the United States*. Ann Arbor, MI: University of Michigan, 1974, p. 3. As noted in Chapter 1, the first juvenile court legislation restricted the definition of delinquent child to those under the age of 16 who had violated any law of the State of Illinois, or city or village ordinances. Two years later (in 1901), however, the *Laws of Illinois* extended this definition to include any child "who is incorrigible, or who knowingly associates with thieves, vicious, or immoral persons, or who is growing up in idleness or crime, or who knowingly frequents a house of ill fame, or who knowingly patronizes any policy shop or place where any gaming device is or shall be operated." Still not content, the definition was again substantially extended in 1907 "to reach the child who ran away from home, or frequented saloons, pool rooms or bucket shops, or wandered the streets at night without being on any lawful business, or...railroad yards, or tracks, or used profanity, or was guilty

of 'indecent and lascivious conduct' " (Stapleton and Teitelbaum, *Ibid.*, p. 41). Similar provisions were found in other states in early statutes. Recent legislation has tended away from such broad "status offense" definitions, as noted in Chapter 1.

5. Quoted in Sanford J. Fox, "Juvenile justice reform: an historical perspective," in *Stanford Law Review*, Vol. 22, No. 6 (June, 1970), p. 1218. This same opinion went on to declare, "If, without crime, without the conviction of any offense, the children of the State are to be thus confined for the 'good of society,' then society had better be reduced to its original elements, and free government acknowledged a failure (p. 1219)."

6. Anthony M. Platt, *The Child Savers: The Invention of Delinquency*. Chicago: University of Chicago Press, 1969, p. 144.

7. Quoted in Stapleton and Teitelbaum, *op. cit.*, p. 20. Other judges expressed themselves in a similar vein. See, for example, *Ibid.*, p. 142.

8. Stapleton and Teitelbaum, *op. cit.*, p. 17, quoting from a 1918 Wisconsin case.

9. Quoting from a 1905 Pennsylvania Supreme Court case, *Ibid.*, p. 18. Stapleton and Teitelbaum observe that the *parens patriae* doctrine was important because it "gave the color of legal regularity to an approach that took as its model of authority the family rather than the traditional criminal justice system" (p. 13).

10. Evelina Belden, *Courts in the United States Hearing Children's Cases*. Washington, DC: United States Children's Bureau Publication No. 65, 1920, p. 11.

11. Tappan, *op. cit.*, p. 199.

12. See, for example, Judge E. F. Waite's stinging criticism, "How far can court procedure be socialized without impairing individual right?" *Journal of Criminal Law*, Vol. XII (November, 1921), pp. 339–347.

13. Francis E. Allen, "Criminal justice, legal values and the rehabilitative ideal," *Journal of Criminal Law, Criminology and Police Science*, Vol. 50 (1959), p. 226.

14. Michael Hakeem, "A critique of the psychiatric approach to the prevention of juvenile delinquency," *Social Problems*, Vol. 5, No. 3 (Winter, 1957–1958), pp. 194–205.

15. See, for example, Douglas Lipton, Robert Martinson, and Judith Wilks, *The Effectiveness of Correctional Treatment: A Survey of Evaluation Treatment Studies*. New York: Praeger, 1975.

16. Under the "mutual compact" theory the state "promises" to care for the child as a substitute parent, with fairness, lack of stigma, and treatment as by a parent, in return for the child's loss of freedom. See Judge Omar Ketcham's biting critique of the failure of the juvenile court in this regard, in "The unfulfilled promise of the American juvenile court," in M. Rosenheim (ed.), *Justice for the Child*. Glencoe, IL: Free Press, 1962.

17. See, for example, Levin and Sarri, *op. cit.*, pp. 43–44.

18. California's thoroughgoing revision of the juvenile code occurred in 1961, little influenced, apparently, by appellate decisions, but in response to the cumulative effect of "anomalies" such as discussed previously, and concerns of a variety of gathering forces. Lemert summarizes, as follows: "...social action for change emerged primarily within the context of the legal-rights issues...long-standing issues of the juvenile court were aggravated with passing time, others were redefined, and an entirely new one was created by the massive congestions in traffic court...there was no large, powerful group or alignment of groups actively pushing for change. There was instead only a small number of individuals...who agitated for the legal protection of juveniles. This 'little band of men' in no sense rode a crest of public opinion demanding change but, on the contrary, were confronted with the formidable task of welding together under the banner of legal rights a variety of interests and values, some favorable to change, some not." Edwin Lemert, *Social Action and Legal Change*. Chicago: Aldine, 1970, pp. 106–107. See also, pp. 78 ff.

19. Stapleton and Teitelbaum note that the line of decisions which led eventually to U.S. Supreme Court rulings overturning much of "traditional" juvenile court procedure began in 1932 when the court began a series of rulings that a "defendant in a state prosecution was entitled under the due process clause of the Fourteenth Amendment the protection of certain provisions of the Bill of Rights, upon the theory that each to be carried over was 'of the very essence of a scheme or ordered liberty' " (p. 19).

20. Quoted in Stapleton and Teitelbaum, *op. cit.*, p. 28. The specific ruling involved the waiver of young Kent's case to the criminal court by the District of Columbia Juvenile Court,

without a hearing to determine the appropriateness of the action, as had been requested by Kent's counsel. The court held that "under the District of Columbia Juvenile Court Act the child enjoyed a *right* to be tried in that court unless it was shown that he would not be benefited by the legal protections of the juvenile court, and further that deprivation of such a right could not be justified 'without ceremony—without hearing, without effective assistance of counsel, without a statement of reasons. It is inconceivable that a court of justice dealing with adults...would for children...permit this procedure. We hold that it does not' " (Stapleton and Teitelbaum, p. 27).

21. "In re *Gault*, Supreme Court of the United States (May 15, 1967)," reprinted in *Juvenile Delinquency and Youth Crime, op. cit.*, pp. 58–70. The court reviewed other arguments which have been made in justification of denial of the privilege against self-incrimination by juveniles, citing cases and rulings of other courts, as well as the U.S. Supreme Court. In addition to the issue of reliability of confessions obtained by coercive means, the Court rejected the theory that "Confession is good for the child as the commencement of the assumed therapy of the juvenile court process, and he should be encouraged to assume an attitude of trust and confidence toward the officials of the juvenile process" (p. 68). Citing Stanton Wheeler and Leonard S. Cottrell, Jr., and Anne Romasco, *Juvenile Delinquency: Its Prevention and Control.* New York: Russell Sage, 1966, the court stated: "it seems probable that where children are induced to confess by 'paternal' urgings on the part of officials and the confession is then followed by disciplinary action, the child's reaction is likely to be hostile and adverse—the child may well feel that he has been led or tricked into confession and that despite his confession, he is being punished." At a more philosophical level, the court noted that the roots of the privilege against self-incrimination lie deep in "the basic stream of religious and political principal" concerning the relationship of the individual and the State. "One of its purposes is to prevent the State, whether by force or by psychological domination, from overcoming the mind and will of the person under investigation and depriving him of the freedom to decide whether to assist the State in securing his conviction" (p. 67).

22. *Juvenile Delinquency and Youth Crime, Ibid.*, pp. 64–70.

23. *Ibid.*, p. 60.

24. *Ibid.*, p. 70.

25. *Ibid.*, p. 60.

26. *Ibid.*, p. 75.

27. Ann Rankin Mahoney, *Juvenile Justice in Context.* Boston: Northeastern University Press, 1987, p. 26.

28. Oliver Wendell Holmes, Jr., *The Common Law* Boston: Little, Brown, 1881, p. 1.

29. Cf. Charles E. Reasons, "*Gault*: procedural change and substantive effect," *Crime and Delinquency*, XVI (April, 1970), 163–171; and William H. Ralston, Jr., "Intake: Informal Disposition or Adversary Proceeding?" *Crime and Delinquency*, XVII (April, 1971), 160–167; Jerry Franklin and Don C. Gibbons, "New Directions for Juvenile Courts—Probation Officers' Views," *Crime and Delinquency*, XIX (October, 1973), 508–518; Lemert, *op. cit.*

30. Lemert, *Ibid.*, p. 166. That right apparently was not often exercised, for probation officers in that county estimated that, in 1961, only 5 percent of all juvenile court cases were represented by counsel. That figure rose to 17 percent by 1965 (p. 172). The following quote is from p. 170.

31. *Ibid.*, p. 178. See also, Robert Emerson, *Judging Delinquents: Context and Process in Juvenile Court.* Chicago: Aldine, 1969.

32. Norman Lefstein, Vaughan Stapleton, and Lee Teitelbaum, "In search of juvenile justice: *Gault* and its implementation," *Law and Society Review*, III (May, 1969): 491–562.

33. Stapleton and Teitelbaum, *op. cit.* Sample cases excluded homicide (since all such cases were virtually certain to be represented by counsel), neglect and dependency, and cases in which a parent was the complainant. The sample was further restricted to "those youths whose families could not afford to retain counsel." Experimental and control cases totaled more than 600 in Zenith and about 500 in Gotham.

34. *Ibid.*, p. 66. Similar findings have been reported by others. See Barry C. Feld, "Right to counsel in juvenile court: an empirical study of when lawyers appear and the difference

they make, " *Journal of Criminal Law and Criminology*, Vol. 79, No. 4, (1989): 1185-1346; also David Duffee and Larry Siegel, "The organization man: legal counsel in the juvenile court," *Criminal Law Bulletin*, VII (July–August, 1971), 655–58.

35. The finding of higher rates of dismissal of cases represented by counsel is consistent with other, nonexperimental studies. Cf. Edwin M. Lemert, "Legislating Change in the Juvenile Court," *1967 Wisconsin Law Review*, and Anthony M. Platt, H. Schechter, and P. Tiffany, "In defense of youth: a case study of the public defender in juvenile court," *Indiana Law Journal*, 43 (1968).

36. Cf. Lemert. *op. cit.*; Emerson, *op. cit.*; Aaron Cicourel, *The Social Organization of Juvenile Justice*. New York: Wiley, 1968.

37. Martha Baum and Stanton Wheeler, p. 171 in Stanton Wheeler (ed.), *Controlling Delinquents*, New York: Wiley, 1968.

38. Lawrence Kohlberg, in *Review of Child Development Research*, Vol. I. New York: Russell Sage, 1964. See also more recent work in this area by June Louin Tapp, V. Lee Hamilton, and others.

CHAPTER 4
BEHAVIORAL CONTEXTS OF JUVENILE DELINQUENCY: POLICE AND JUVENILE COURTS

INTRODUCTION

The law is a normative system, backed by governmental authority. The criminal and juvenile justice systems are instrumentalities of that system. In statutes and in tables of organization, they are at once abstract and specific—abstract in the formulations of the values and the interests of groups which have promoted them, and more or less specific in the precise language which is used. The language tends to be reasonably specific with respect to crime; not so with juvenile delinquency. The adversarial system of criminal justice, together with the specificity of the criminal law, encourages the use of legal loopholes and technical ways of avoiding liability under the law. The phrasing of most laws concerning juvenile delinquency permits fewer loopholes.

THE REALITY OF THE LAW

The reality of the law—for juveniles, and for those who are responsible for carrying out its mandates or who call upon it for assistance—assumes concrete form in the actions of relevant parties with respect to acts or conditions. *It is in the interaction of parties that the effects of laws become realized.*

Regardless of the language of the law, and of the institutions and roles set up to control behavior, what actually happens to juveniles as a result of lawmaking and enforcement is dependent on considerations and contingencies about which it is difficult to generalize. This chapter shows that juvenile delinquency refers not only to the behavior of juveniles, but also to the behavior of others as well—parents, neighbors, teachers, peers, police, judges, probation officers, others professionally involved in the juvenile justice system, shopkeepers and their patrons, park and recreation program personnel, and so forth. All the elements in the "social construction" of juvenile delinquency are present, including the beliefs about childhood and children, the laws, the theories, and the institutions. But most important, people are acting and interacting in ways which make juvenile delinquency a reality. The chapter describes some of the types of behavior that bring juveniles to the attention of authorities, but it is chiefly concerned with the types of actions taken by police and others who screen that behavior and the youngsters involved in it in a variety of ways.

THE POLICE—GATEKEEPERS OF THE SYSTEM

In the mid-1960s the President's Commission on Law Enforcement and Administration of Justice noted that there were more than 40,000 public law enforcement organizations in the United States.[1] There are many more now. The bulk of these—some 33,000 according to the Crime Commission—are found in boroughs, towns, or villages. They were, and are, small, *the modal size then being fewer than five police officers.* At the other extreme are the agencies of the federal government, the approximately 200 agencies with state jurisdiction, and the large city and county agencies.

Add to these agencies the thousands of private security agencies and their employees, and the sizeable industry involved in law enforcement and security is apparent. In his study of "The Police and the Public," Albert J. Reiss noted that persons employed in public or private law enforcement or security work composed approximately 1 percent of the civilian labor force of the United States.[2] Law enforcement has been a growth industry in this country and elsewhere.[3]

These numbers, and the variations they mask, have important consequences. They point up the importance—potential and real—of the police as an interest group, and they suggest the difficulty of generalization concerning relationships between the police and juveniles before the law. Because most public information concerning crime and delinquency comes from law enforcement agencies, variation in standards and performance among these agencies makes it impossible ever to know the true amount of lawbreaking in the society.

It will never be possible to know all of the behavior that could be officially labeled and classified as criminal or delinquent. This is especially the case with respect to the minor delinquencies, which are virtually universal among young people. The consequences of these observations are profound for understanding the extent and nature of crime and delinquency, for control of these phenomena, and for assessment of the justice of the juvenile and criminal justice systems.

THE SCREENING FUNCTION OF THE POLICE

This chapter is concerned with the two most important official social settings in which juvenile behavior becomes classified as juvenile delinquency: the police departments and the juvenile courts. These are the primary agencies that screen youngsters into categories of delinquent, criminal, or one of the subcategories known by the acronyms (e.g., PINS) noted in Chapter 2. We begin with an overview of such screening, as revealed in a study conducted

TABLE 4.1   Distribution of Juvenile Dispositions, 1958–1962

POLICE DEPARTMENT	N	%
NUMBER OF CASES	9,023	100.0
Released	8,014	88.8
Referred to Social or Welfare Agency	180	2.0
Referred to County Probation Department	775	8.6
Referred to State Dept. of Public Welfare	54	0.6
PROBATION DEPARTMENT	**N**	**%**
NUMBER OF CASES FROM POLICE	775	100.0
Released	229	29.5
Informal Supervision	243	31.4
Referred to Juvenile Court	246	31.7
Waiver to Criminal Court	57	7.4
JUVENILE COURT	**N**	**%**
NUMBER OF CASES FROM PROBATION DEPARTMENT	246	100.0
Formal Supervision	94	38.2
Institutionalized	152	61.8

Source: Robert M. Terry, "Discrimination in the handling of juvenile offenders by social-control agencies," *Journal of Research in Crime and Delinquency,* 4 (July, 1967):218–230. Reprinted by permission of Sage Publications, Inc.

some years ago in Racine, Wisconsin, by Robert M. Terry. Table 4.1 presents the essential details.

In Table 4.1, note that fewer than 3 percent of all cases processed by the police department reached the juvenile court (divide the 226 cases referred by the probation department by the total number of cases, 9,023). Fewer than 2 percent of cases were sent to institutions.

The most consequential screening of children who became officially labeled as delinquent clearly occurred at the level of the police. Of the 11 percent who were not released by the police, most (9 percent) were referred to the county probation department. Of these, a few were waived to criminal court, while the remainder were released, placed under informal supervision, or sent to the juvenile court, in approximately equal proportions. Terry reported that only serious offenses and, usually, repeat offenders ever got to the court.

This conclusion is supported by several studies, which also yield other conclusions:

1. Police departments vary enormously in their policies and practices with respect to release or referral of persons with whom they have contact.[4]
2. Most persons apprehended are reported by citizen complaints, rather than on police initiative.
3. Police handling of *serious* offenses is based chiefly on *legalistic* criteria, rather than upon class or racial distinctions.

4. With respect to less serious offenses, decisions to arrest are based principally upon *complainant preference,* but what is defined as offensive behavior is influenced by other, extralegal factors.

Police referral of juveniles, when it does occur, most often involves passing children to the other major gatekeeper in the juvenile justice system, the juvenile court. Table 4.2 presents relevant nationwide data for juveniles taken into police custody since 1961, by size of jurisdiction reporting.

TABLE 4.2 Police Disposition of Juveniles Taken into Custody, 1961–1985, by Size of Place*

DISPOSITION	YEAR	ALL CITIES REPORTING	LARGE CITIES 250,000+	CITIES 100,000 TO 249,999
HANDLED WITHIN	1961	45.3%	36.2%	44.4%
DEPARTMENT	1965	47.1%	38.5%	48.9%
AND RELEASED	1970	45.7%	37.7%	43.6%
	1975	42.8%	29.5%	44.3%
	1980	34.5%	26.0%	35.8%
	1985	31.4%	25.7%	30.8%
REFERRED TO	1961	48.9%	59.8%	52.7%
JUVENILE COURT	1965	45.8%	53.6%	44.8%
	1970	49.8%	58.9%	52.7%
	1975	51.7%	67.0%	51.4%
	1980	57.2%	69.2%	57.7%
	1985	60.9%	71.0%	64.2%
REFERRED TO	1961	2.0%	1.8%	1.3%
WELFARE AGENCY	1965	3.1%	6.1%	1.4%
	1970	1.6%	2.2%	1.6%
	1975	1.4%	1.6%	1.5%
	1980	1.5%	1.1%	2.6%
	1985	1.9%	1.6%	2.9%
REFERRED TO OTHER	1961	2.9%	2.0%	1.2%
POLICE AGENCY	1965	2.7%	1.5%	3.0%
	1970	2.1%	1.0%	1.7%
	1975	1.8%	1.1%	1.3%
	1980	1.7%	2.4%	2.0%
	1985	1.1%	1.2%	.7%
REFERRED TO	1961	.9%	.1%	.4%
CRIMINAL OR ADULT	1965	1.4%	.4%	1.9%
COURT	1970	.8%	.2%	.5%
	1975	2.3%	.9%	1.5%
	1980	5.1%	1.3%	1.8%
	1985	4.6%	.5%	1.3%

*Source: Federal Bureau of Investigation, Uniform Crime Reports for 1961, 1965, 1970, 1975, 1980, 1985, U.S. GPO

Table 4.2 reveals a somewhat different pattern than that suggested by the Racine study. Early in the series, slightly less than one-half of all juveniles taken into police custody were released, or referred, to juvenile court, but the percentage released has decreased significantly, whereas referrals to juvenile courts have increased. These trends have occurred in all sized jurisdictions.

Whereas there is not much variation to be accounted for in the remaining dispositions, referrals to criminal or adult courts have increased substantially in all jurisdictions over the reporting period, particularly in more recent

TABLE 4.2   Police Disposition of Juveniles Taken into Custody, 1961–1985, by Size of Place* (cont.)

CITIES 50,000 TO 99,999	CITIES 25,000 TO 49,999	CITIES 10,000 TO 24,999	UNDER 10,000	SUBURBAN[a]	RURAL
50.1%	53.9%	54.4%	51.5%	(no report)	43.4%[b]
54.6%	51.5%	52.5%	50.4%	56.3%	29.6%
50.2%	48.6%	51.0%	48.7%	52.6%	33.4%
49.1%	46.2%	47.8%	43.7%	49.6%	29.8%
35.9%	37.8%	38.0%	34.8%	38.8%	27.4%
35.1%	34.1%	34.8%	30.5%	29.3%	20.8%
40.7%	39.0%	38.9%	38.8%	(no report)	47.3%
39.2%	42.0%	40.6%	42.3%	37.6%	56.4%
45.4%	45.4%	44.2%	45.9%	42.0%	58.1%
45.1%	47.8%	46.2%	48.2%	45.1%	61.7%
55.4%	54.4%	52.8%	51.9%	52.6%	61.8%
56.1%	56.9%	56.0%	56.4%	65.6%	67.8%
2.8%	2.6%	1.7%	1.7%	(no report)	1.6%[b]
2.1%	1.2%	1.2%	1.3%	1.0%	2.0%
1.4%	1.8%	.8%	.9%	1.2%	2.2%
1.5%	1.2%	1.2%	1.3%	1.1%	2.0%
2.3%	1.4%	1.2%	1.1%	1.2%	2.3%
2.1%	2.4%	1.4%	1.4%	1.7%	2.2%
5.6%	3.0%	3.6%	4.2%	(no report)	3.9%[b]
3.3%	3.5%	3.4%	3.2%	3.6%	3.7%
2.4%	3.0%	2.7%	2.7%	3.2%	4.3%
2.5%	1.9%	1.9%	2.3%	2.0%	2.8%
1.6%	1.8%	1.3%	1.4%	1.4%	2.6%
1.4%	1.1%	1.1%	1.3%	.9%	2.5%
.7%	1.5%	1.3%	3.8%	(no report)	3.8%[b]
.7%	1.7%	2.3%	3.7%	1.5%	8.3%
.6%	1.3%	1.3%	1.7%	1.0%	2.0%
1.8%	3.0%	2.9%	4.5%	2.2%	3.6%
4.8%	4.6%	6.7%	10.8%	6.1%	5.9%
5.3%	5.4%	6.7%	10.3%	2.5%	6.7%

[a]Suburban includes areas in other city groups.

[b]"County agencies" reported in 1961; rural agencies thereafter.

years. In smaller cities and rural areas, higher percentages of juvenile cases are referred to criminal or to adult courts than is the case in larger cities.

These data reflect changes in juvenile law and procedure, as well as in other elements of juvenile delinquency.

HOW DO THE POLICE "DISCOVER" DELINQUENCY?

Most persons apprehended by the police are reported by citizen complaints rather than by police initiative. Observational studies are revealing. Albert J. Reiss and his colleagues studied three locations, all high crime rate, low-income areas: Boston (with a traditional police department based on an ethnic occupational culture—in Boston, the "Irish Cop"); Chicago (to represent the model of the modern bureaucratically organized department based on systems analysis and centralized command and control); and Washington, D.C. (a department in process of professionalizing staff and modernizing command and control systems).[5]

Observers accompanying police reported every encounter with citizens. More than 5,000 mobilizations of the police were reported. Eight out of ten of these mobilizations originated with citizens telephoning police for service, followed by police dispatch of a one- or two-man "beat car" to handle the incident. Fourteen percent originated on the initiative of police while on patrol; 5 percent when a citizen mobilized police in a field setting. The police, therefore, are largely *reactive* rather than proactive with respect to common crime.

Contrary to the violent crime-fighting world of police conveyed by television and other media, less than 1 percent of the time that officers were on routine preventive patrol was spent in actually handling criminal incidents (Reiss, 1971, p. 95). Most incidents that occurred "on view" were noncriminal, as were incidents to which police were dispatched.

Police youth divisions in the departments studied produced few juvenile offenders (only 7 percent of all arrested juveniles in Washington, D.C. in 1965, as compared to 83 percent of all arrested juveniles by the patrol division). Juvenile division personnel typically were involved in preventive activity and in handling juveniles only after they had been arrested.

Reiss notes that these data reflect our liberal system of restricting police access to places where crimes occur. Homes and businesses are considered private places, and are protected from encroachment by police initiative. "Citizens thus have discretionary control over *knowledge of crimes* committed in private places."[6]

INFLUENCES ON POLICE DISPOSITION OF CASES

Police *disposition* of cases is most heavily influenced by the *seriousness of crime* and by *complainant preference*. Reiss and Donald Black found that "the police did not file an official report in a single instance where the complainant expressed a preference for unofficial handling of a felony or misdemeanor."[7] Police compliance with a complainant's preference for official action occurred most often when suspects were strangers to the victim and when felony charges were made. Complainant behavior toward the police also influences police action. When complainants were *deferential* to the police, their preferences were more likely to be followed.

POLICING AND THE POLICE SUBCULTURE

Police relationships with the public, including their handling of juveniles, are embedded in the history of municipal police, the nature of policing, and everyday police experience. Out of these factors a widely shared police subculture was formed, with important consequences for both the police and the public. Egon Bittner has described the police subculture as secretive, defensive, and distrustful of the society being policed, and of other levels of the criminal justice system.[8] While there is much local variation on these themes, it is useful to examine their historical and contemporary roots.

First, historically, as today, policing is fundamentally concerned with *order*. The influx of poor and dispossessed people to cities, which resulted from the commercial and industrial revolutions of the eighteenth and nineteenth centuries (soon to be identified as the "dangerous classes"), led to the invention of the police. From the beginning, the police have been associated with the dangerous classes and the very activities they were charged with policing. Instances of police corruption and complicity in these activities reinforce this association.

Second, police work often "requires peremptory solutions for complex human problems" (Bittner, p. 12), problems involving "subtle human conflicts and profound legal and moral questions." Most police officers are ill-equipped to deal with these questions. In any case, demands of the moment preclude their adequate consideration, for reflection on the merits of a decision typically is possible only *after* a suspect is arrested, or after some untoward course of events has been stopped.

Third, central to the police role in such problems is that force may have to be used. This is understood by those who call the police, those against whom police proceed, and by the police themselves.

> ...the role of the police is to address all sorts of human problems when and insofar as their solutions do or may possibly require the use of force at the point of their occurrence. This lends homogeneity to such diverse procedures as catching a criminal, driving the mayor to the airport, evicting a drunken person from a bar, directing traffic, crowd control, taking care of lost children, administering medical first aid, and separating fighting relatives. (Bittner, p. 44)

The importance of force to the police role has been challenged on grounds that other social roles also involve use of force or its threat, and that police use force infrequently and only as a last resort.[9] Nevertheless, the ambivalence felt by many citizens toward police—demanding aid and protection, but resentful and fearful of police presence and interference—reflects this importance of force in policing perhaps more than any other thing, and this ambivalence contributes to the strained quality of police-citizen relationships. Official policing involves taking charge in a multitude of situations. While force is not often used or necessary, its threat is ever present, for both the police and the policed.

Fourth, the public expects the police to be crime fighters, and the police share this expectation. Mass media portrayals of police work (public and private) reinforce these expectations, although in distorted fashion, stressing violence, frequent use of firearms, and often illegal means of crime control. Yet, most police work consists of routine surveillance and regulation of human activities, such as patrol, security, traffic control, crowd control, and settlement of family and neighborhood disputes. The latter, in particular, is very like social work, for which most police are ill-prepared. It is not surprising, therefore, that both the public and the police are often confused and resentful of each other. Role conflict among police is built in to these different expectations and tasks.[10]

Fifth, the public puts pressure on the police to stop crime, focusing on this or that type of crime, often as a result of media exposés of crimes for which there is widespread public involvement (e.g., gambling, prostitution, illicit drug trade). While other segments of the juvenile and criminal justice systems may share the blame, the police—as the front line of defense against crime—are the most vulnerable to public condemnation.

Sixth, the ecology of police work has a socially divisive effect. Guided by computer analyses which target locations and situations where the action is, surveillance and intervention are selectively distributed, focused primarily on lower socioeconomic areas and people. Despite the fact that citizen complaints about the inadequacy of police protection are highest in lower socioeconomic areas occupied by minority populations, the selective distribution of police surveillance and intervention "inevitably entails the consequence that some persons will receive the dubious benefit of extensive police scrutiny merely on account of their membership in those social groupings which invidious social comparisons locate at the bottom of the heap" (Bittner, p. 10).

Seventh, juvenile and criminal justice systems contribute to police distrust by failing to affirm arrest decisions. When persons arrested are returned to the community, they become once again a police responsibility, and the police feel rebuffed. More than half of the officers in the Reiss study were dissatisfied with both juvenile and municipal court judges because they were too lenient. In the view of many police, the juvenile court fails in its role as a "backup institution" for other youth serving agencies. All aspects of the justice systems, therefore, are caught up in conflicting demands, frustrated interdependence, and failures, which often are celebrated in the media.

Eighth, the criminal justice system is characterized by status and prestige inequalities, with the police typically occupying the lower rungs of the status system. Lawyers, prosecutors, and judges are often condescending toward police officers and fail to treat them as professionals. Officers are particularly incensed when judges fail to regard the lack of deference to police authority as serious, while demanding total deference to judicial authority.[11]

Finally, constant exposure to the "seedy" side of life leads many police to a cynical and often simplistic view of the nature of the citizens they encounter, and their communities and their problems.

Structural characteristics of policing thus combine to impart unique qualities to police work and to the police subculture. While all types of cultural solidarity are at peak strength in confrontation with outsiders, Bittner suggests that the police subculture "is *only* outward oriented"; that is, it coheres and promotes solidarity only in relation to the world being policed. As a consequence, the police subculture interferes with effective cooperation throughout police systems.[12]

This combination of solidarity against the outside world and independence within the police subculture places a heavy burden on the individual officer and his or her closest partners. And when, as is the case in many communities and among many groups, attitudes of distrust and hostility are reciprocated, the potential for conflict is very high.

These and other characteristics of police work (the low rate of on-view police mobilization and stringent legal protections against the invasion of personal privacy) are associated with the "method of suspicion," an important operating principal of policing based in the police subculture.[13] Police tend to divide the public into "respectables," who are generally assumed to be innocent of wrongdoing, and "suspects." Based on common police beliefs, attitudes, and experiences, this method of suspicion exacerbates tensions and potential conflicts between the police and the policed. The consequences are especially great for lower-class minority populations, because it is they who are most subject to police scrutiny.

THE POLICE VIEW

This aspect of police work has been nicely captured by Carl Werthman and Irving Piliavin's description of "Gang Members and the Police":[14]

> From the front seat of a moving patrol car, street life in a typical black ghetto is perceived as an uninterrupted sequence of suspicious scenes. Every well-dressed man or woman standing aimlessly on the street during hours when most people are at work is carefully scrutinized for signs of an illegal source of income; every boy wearing boots, black pants, long hair, and a club jacket is viewed as potentially responsible for some item on the list of muggings, broken windows, and petty thefts that still remain to be cleared; and every hostile glance directed at the passing patrolman is read as a sign of possible guilt.
>
> The residents of these neighborhoods regard this kind of surveillance as the deepest of insults. As soon as a patrolman begins to interrogate, the suspect can easily see that his moral identity is being challenged because of his dress, his hair style, his skin color, and his presence in the ghetto itself.
>
> Black gang members are constantly singled out for interrogation by the police and the boys develop their own techniques of retaliation. They taunt the police with jibes and threaten their authority with gestures of insolence, as if daring the police to become bigots and bullies in order to defend their honor…[and] these techniques of retaliation often…succeed in provoking this response. When suspect after suspect becomes hostile and surly, the police begin to see themselves as representing the law among a people that lack proper respect for it. They too begin to feel maligned, and they soon become defensively cynical and aggressively moralistic. From the point of view of a patrolman,

night sticks are only used upon sufficient provocation, and arrests are only made with just cause.

THE MEANING AND USES OF STREETS
FROM THE PERSPECTIVE OF GANG MEMBERS

Gang members perceive the situation of conflict between the police and themselves quite differently. City blocks and street corners become invested with new meanings when they are transformed into a gang "hangout," its "territory," or its "turf." Werthman and Piliavin describe the gang hangout as a sort of "home" or "private place," noting Sheri Cavan's observation that "a house is a place where activities which would be unlawful in public places, such as poker games and nudity, and activities which would be a source of embarrassment in public places such as family arguments and lovemaking, can be fully enjoyed."[15] Gangs use the street, its corners, alleys, parks, pool rooms, and candy stores, for behavior that most adolescents confine to their homes or cars. Gang boys are more at home in their turf than elsewhere. Indeed, they are often ill at ease when outside "the area." An aim of many delinquency prevention programs has been to expose youngsters to the social worlds outside their limited experience.

Harassment of others is also a gang tactic, especially of rival gang members or adolescent nonmembers of the gang who come into the gang turf. "Regular" adults usually are ignored, but any and all perceived intrusions of their private club are resented by the gang. Strangers are often forced to walk around a group of youngsters blocking the street, and embarrassed in other ways. Young people may be taunted or assaulted if they do not quickly move away from the group.

Werthman and Piliavin note that the police are resented by gangs in part because they threaten the "private space" conception of gang hangouts. Indeed, the police impose their own set of normative claims on the proper uses of the streets. Places that are defended like homes by gang members are, after all, not legally defined as private places. For the police, they are places of work, and the homelike uses to which gang members put them are often perceived as threats to the patrolman's task of maintaining the conventional rules that ordinarily govern behavior. "The relationship between gang members and policemen thus has its roots in an ecological conflict over claims to final authority in the same setting."[16] Police in one major city have a phrase that expresses this relationship. When they are annoyed with gang behavior on a street corner hangout, they will demand, "Gi'me that corner!"

Relations between gang members and police are further strained by the police role in conflicts between gang members and other segments of the community, for example, local store owners, and school and park officials who look to the police for backup authority.

Werthman and Piliavin's research illustrates some of the consequences of the method of suspicion for residents of local communities, juvenile and adult alike. Police often adopt a strategy of harassing gangs, in part as a response to public pressure to do something about gangs, but also because gangs represent a constant threat to police authority, and a major source of crime in the areas for which the police have responsibility. Pressure on the police fluctuates, spurred on by periodic media exposés (which may exacerbate the problem by providing status to the youngsters' delinquent behavior). In many cities pressure is more immediate at the neighborhood level, where adults and nongang members are fearful of gangs (often with justification) and disapproving of their activities. Adult residents are also often fearful and resentful of the police—for it is from the ghetto that the loudest complaints of police brutality and ineffectiveness most often come.

POLICE DECISIONS AND PREDICTIONS: AN EVALUATION

Out of the richness of their experience police develop attitudes and understandings that influence the way they go about their jobs. In Chapter 3, it was noted that the "predictive theory" of the traditional juvenile court was not validated by juvenile court practice. What of predictions based on police experience? An experiment conducted in Seattle yields some intriguing answers.[17]

Marcia Garrett asked Seattle police to estimate what proportion of boys in each of five types of families (described in social class terms) would be likely to commit a variety of offenses. Boys from lower-class families were, as expected, estimated to be much more likely to engage in nearly all offenses than boys from middle-class families. The officers were also asked to what extent boys from these classes and family backgrounds were "cooperative or uncooperative toward police," and "respectful or disrespectful." The officers were also asked if these boys were "sorry for committing an offense or proud of it," what types of companions the boys were expected to have, and how the boys would dress (their general appearance). A strong association was found between social class and family background and the stereotype of delinquents as uncooperative, disrespectful, proud of their offenses, friendly with delinquent companions, and disreputable in appearance. Statistically, appearance and demeanor predicted delinquent behavior more strongly than did social class and family background.

Demeanor and appearance serve as sensitizing criteria, and as cues in situations requiring (or seeming to require) action. Assumptions as to class and family background may be made on the basis of other criteria, as well, for example, the community or neighborhood in which interaction takes place.

Between July and December, 1964, Seattle police were asked to predict whether or not boys they encountered for the first time would commit further delinquent acts. Six years later, Garrett examined police records to determine which boys had, in fact, repeated as delinquents (in the sense of having a police contact recorded after December, 1970). The results are reported in Tables 4.3 and 4.4.

TABLE 4.3   Police Predictions for First Offenders (in 1964) Compared to Actual Outcomes (in 1970)*

	POLICE PREDICTIONS, 1964	ACTUAL OUTCOMES, 1970
	(July–December, 1964; N=429)	(as of December 31, 1970)
Repeat offenders	248 (58%)	149 (35%)
Nonrepeaters	181 (42%)	280 (65%)
	429 (100%)	429 (100%)

*73 "undecideds" (14.5% of the total number of boys first contacted in 1964) are eliminated from Tables 4.3 and 4.4.

TABLE 4.4   1970 Outcomes of 1964 First Offenders, by Police Predictions

	POLICE PREDICTIONS, 1964		
OUTCOMES, 1970	REPEAT OFFENDERS	NONREPEATERS	TOTAL
Repeat offenders	111 (45%)	38 (21%)	149 (35%)
Nonrepeaters	137 (55%)	143 (79%)	280 (65%)
Total	248 (100%)	181 (100%)	429

Table 4.3 indicates that the police overpredicted future delinquency involvement by a considerable margin. Predictions of further delinquency were made for 248 (58 percent) of the boys, whereas only 149 (35 percent) had been arrested again by July, 1970.

Table 4.4 reports the *efficiency* of both types of predictions, judged by actual outcome of the 1970 follow-up. Of those who in 1964 were predicted to repeat, about 45 percent did so (111 out of 248), while more than half (55 percent) were "false positives" in the sense that Seattle police records contained no further entries for these boys. Predictions of nonrepeating were more efficient— 143 correct predictions—or 79 percent. The remaining 21 percent were "false negatives" in that they did, in fact, repeat. Errors were made in both directions.

The efficiency of the police predictions in these cases can be compared with that which would have resulted had all the boys been predicted as nonrepeaters, in which case predictive efficiency would have been 65 percent. Note in Table 4.4 that 254 "correct" predictions were made (111 plus 143). This is 59 percent of the total numbers of repeat and nonrepeat predictions made. Thus, higher predictive efficiency would have been achieved had the officers simply predicted that none of the boys would repeat.

The lack of efficiency in police prediction of future involvement in delinquency is hardly surprising, but it cautions us against easy assumptions as to the efficacy of predictions made on the basis of practical police experience. Neither "knowing the territory" (as in the case of the police) nor "good intentions" (as was the case with the early reformers, and is the case, for the most part, with police and others concerned with juvenile justice) is sufficient to insure predictability. The problem of false positives plagues all predictive research, even that conducted by more scientific means.[18]

DILEMMAS, PARADOXES, AND POSSIBLE SOLUTIONS

Police-citizen relationships are often paradoxical, the result of dilemmas deeply ingrained in the experiences, beliefs, and customs of police and policed. On the one hand police interference is resented; on the other, police protection of persons and property is demanded. Greater police efficiency is demanded, yet police are restricted from access to places where crimes most often occur. For their part, the police require the cooperation of citizens for knowledge of crimes, yet are suspicious of those who possess such knowledge. Police resent playing the role of social worker, yet that is mostly what they do. They reflect the prejudices of their own backgrounds, yet on many occasions find themselves involved in civil rights conflict, charged with the responsibility to protect those rights, as well as the property and persons of affected citizens.

There is much debate and disagreement concerning what to do about these problems. General agreement exists on the necessity for greater racial and ethnic equity in the composition of police departments, so that "armies of occupation" are not structured along racial lines. While progress has been made, much remains to be done.[19] Another suggestion is that police should become more professional.

POLICE PROFESSIONALIZATION

Professionalizing the police is associated with higher educational standards and technical improvements in command, communications, and crime detection. It has also been advanced as a counter to the influence of the police subculture, and there is evidence to support this view.[20] Serious limitations to professionalism as a solution to police problems remain, however. Professionalism is based on (1) the existence of a systematic body of theory, knowledge, and practice—as in medicine and the law—and (2) fiduciary responsibility; that is, devotion to the ideal that a client's interests, rather than personal or commercial profit, are the primary purposes of practice.

The police have a hard time on both counts. There remains much disagreement concerning the proper body of theory, knowledge, and practice for the police; and, as we have seen, the interests of police and their clients are often in dispute. Police educational standards have followed an unsteady course over recent decades, and such standards have progressed more rapidly in some places than in others.

A variety of procedures have been undertaken to achieve the professional integrity of the police, for example, bureaucratization, elaborate rules concerning procedure, mandatory training in police academies—all intended to limit discretion of the line officer. While these changes all seek better control of the abuse of police discretion and the arbitrary exercise of power, they conflict with the exercise of decision making that is critical for line officers. The police subculture also counters efforts of professionals in the command hierarchy to control the actions of line officers. Under the tutelage of experienced policemen in the streets, rookie cops quickly learn to disregard many of the lessons learned in the police academy.

There is, of course, much variation in such matters. James Q. Wilson's early study of police handling of delinquents in two cities chosen to represent variation in professionalization of police is illustrative.[21] The "Western City" department was highly professionalized, operating according to universalistic standards in recruiting and in law enforcement, without regard to political connections or to citizens' race, ethnicity, or local residence. The "Eastern City" department, in contrast, was characterized as "fraternal." Most members were recruited locally, many with the proper political credentials. Law enforcement in Eastern City was less rigorous, more informal, and given to favoritism. Black and white juveniles in Western City received quite similar treatment for comparable offenses, whereas in Eastern City black youth were taken to court (rather than released with a warning or reprimand) nearly three times as often, proportionately, as were whites. One out of four black youngsters apprehended for assault were taken to court, compared to 11.5 percent of the whites, but for burglaries these figures were 100 percent and 11.8 percent, respectively.

Wilson interviewed police officers in the two departments and found great differences in their attitudes toward delinquency and juveniles (p. 14):

> ...Western City's officers have more complex attitudes toward delinquency and juveniles than their colleagues of Eastern City...[The former]...tend to be less moralistic, less certain as to causal factors, more therapeutic, and more frequently couched in generalizations than in anecdotes. Eastern City's officers, by contrast, are more likely to interpret a problem as one of personal or familial morality rather than of social pathology, to urge restrictive and punitive rather than therapeutic measures, to rely on single explanations expressed with great conviction and certainty, and to confine discussions of juveniles almost exclusively to anecdotes and references to recent episodes than to generalizations, trends, or patterns.

The more professional Western City police were more likely than the Eastern City police to take official actions and thereby to restrict the freedom of juveniles with whom they came in contact. Wilson's study suggests that professional norms make the police less discriminatory but more severe, a consequence, perhaps, of weakened identification with the community. A variety of programs have sought to combine the advantages of professional training with those of community support, chiefly by bringing citizens and police together in the interest of crime prevention and better citizen-police relationships. While some progress has been made, the manner in which relationships between citizens and police are socially structured ensures that problems will always remain. In addition, as a recent assessment of professionalism in criminal justice concludes, "It seems fair to say...that some communities prefer an 'old boy' police force."[22]

Professionalization is but one aspect of police reform in the interest of preventing crime, removing corruption and undue political influence, and making the police more responsive to the citizenry. A variety of initiatives have been proposed and tried in efforts to achieve these and other goals (see, for example, the discussion in Chapter 10.[23]

THE JUVENILE COURT: SUPER-PARENT VERSUS BACK UP INSTITUTION

The juvenile court movement was a startling success. A short two decades after passage of the Illinois statute in 1899, all but three states had enacted juvenile court laws, as had many other countries. The court quickly came to function as a backup to other institutions: police, families, schools, local businesses, and social agencies.

If police are the gatekeepers of the juvenile justice system, juvenile courts have been the chief adjudicators and arbiters of its justice. For many years, however, information on how the courts function was limited to a few case studies. It is possible to construct a reasonably comprehensive picture of the composition and functioning of juvenile courts during the mid-1970s on the basis of survey data.

THE NATIONAL ASSESSMENT OF JUVENILE CORRECTIONS

The nature of the court's relationship with other institutions is suggested by data from a nationwide comparative study of juvenile courts in the United States, the first study of its kind.[24] A mailed survey was begun early in 1974, with supplementary field observations continuing for more than a year. The National Assessment study provides a useful overview of U.S. juvenile courts at a time when juvenile justice policies and practices were being critically examined, following congressional passage of the Juvenile Justice and Delinquency Prevention Act in 1974.

REFERRALS TO JUVENILE COURTS AND CASE DISPOSITIONS

The National Assessment survey collected data on sources of referral to juvenile courts—the "other side of the coin," as it were, from Table 4.2. The police accounted for the bulk of court referrals (about 75 percent), while parents (about 10 percent), schools (about 8 percent), and social service agencies (4.4 percent) were also substantial sources of referral. Court jurisdiction size made little difference in source of referral, though schools accounted for a smaller proportion of referrals in the largest jurisdictions, while parents referred more of the children seen in courts in smaller jurisdictions.

Young people come to the attention of juvenile courts for many reasons. Petition rates for court referral reflect the historical focus of the juvenile court on family problems (dependency and neglect, and CHINS—Children in Need of Supervision) and delinquency, as well as traffic offenses. The total referral rate of courts reporting to the National Assessment survey was 42.0 per thousand of the youth population. Referral for delinquency composed the bulk of this figure (averaging 24.4 per thousand, or slightly less than 2.5 percent of the youth population, during a given year). Referral for traffic offenses was the next highest (averaging 12.5 per thousand), but this was much higher in very large jurisdictions than in less populated areas. CHINS (8.5 per thousand) and dependency and neglect (4.0 per thousand) followed.

Courts vary in the extent to which they handle cases formally (by petition, with a formal hearing and decision) or informally (comparable to police handling within the department, usually followed by release). Proportionately more cases are handled formally in urban jurisdictions, whereas more are dealt with informally in semi-urban and rural jurisdictions.[25] Since 1957, when reasonably accurate data on the matter were first collected, the trend has been toward handling more cases informally. By the end of the 1970s, more than half of all cases coming before juvenile courts in the United States were handled by informal means. The National Assessment study suggests that most of these were either dismissed outright, or the offenders were counseled, warned, and released. When informal supervision (which typically entails little in the way of obligation by the child) is taken into account, it appears that *juvenile courts exercised little or no continuing authority over about two-thirds of the children who appeared before them.* The majority of the remainder were handled by formal probation, with smaller proportions either referred to other agencies, committed to correctional institutions, or waived to criminal court (the latter only in about 1 percent of the cases).

The juvenile court movement had a clear preference for diagnosis and probation rather than incarceration, particularly of status offenders. Yet the National Assessment study found that a third of the juveniles in correctional facilities were status offenders. Incarceration clearly has not been reserved for the most serious offenders.

By offering strong incentives to states and local jurisdictions to eliminate institutionalization of status offenders, the Juvenile Justice and Delinquency Prevention Act of 1974 gave impetus to a nationwide movement aimed at this goal. A few states moved vigorously in this direction, some diverting status offenders from juvenile courts altogether and placing responsibility for such children with other agencies. A major problem with this policy, as Solomon Kobrin and Malcolm Klein note, however, is that few offenders are involved solely in either status or delinquent offenses. They argue that "[if] the aim is humaneness and equity, [such] programs are perhaps best centered in the courts, where the critical disposition decisions can be made to avoid secure confinement as a response to a noncriminal offense."[26]

This argument presumes a type of court oversight that may not exist in many courts, however. Michael Sosin found that *intake workers* (who may be social workers, probation officers, representatives of the prosecutor's office, or simply clerks) played the most critical role in case disposition in courts surveyed by the National Assessment study.[27] Ironically, Sosin reports that due process protection of children's rights were especially weak at the intake level, leading to the paradox that juveniles charged with serious criminal offenses were more likely to have their rights protected than were status offenders or those charged with less serious crimes.

Sosin's analysis suggests that local crime rates and community attitudes toward juvenile crime had little impact on intake decisions. Of far greater importance was the *local court context*. Small civil courts and the juvenile courts attached to them handled most cases informally; many cases also were processed without trial in misdemeanor courts and in their adjacent juvenile courts. Juvenile court judges tended to commit to institutions a percentage of cases very close to the national average (13.5 percent). Variation in rates of incarceration, therefore, was mainly a function of intake workers' prior screening rather than of judges' decisions.

JUVENILE COURT GOALS AND PRIORITIES

The National Assessment survey asked judges and probation officers about their *goals*, both in an ideal sense and in actual practice. Both placed *protecting the rights of offenders* at the top of their actual ratings, and only slightly lower as an ideal. Protection of the rights of offenders was not regarded as inconsistent with a *service orientation* to youth.

Judges and probation officers accorded some goals lower priority, both in an ideal sense and in actual practice. These lower priority goals included restricting court intervention to behaviors that are crimes for adults (note the inconsistency with the federal Juvenile Justice and Delinquency Prevention Act of 1974), punishment of offenders, upholding moral standards, increasing fiscal support for the court, and processing cases quickly.

The area of greatest *disagreement* between judges and probation officers was *changing juveniles' attitudes and values*, which was ranked first by judges as an ideal, and second in actual practice. Probation officers, who have far more contact with juveniles than do judges, rated this goal very low as an ideal, while acknowledging that it was more important in actual practice.

There was agreement that considerable discrepancy existed between the ideal and the actual practice with respect to the goal of *protecting the community from dangerous youth*. Both assigned low rank to this goal as an ideal, but noted that it was very important in actual practice. Discrepancies also were noted regarding the *provision of services to the community*, both judges and probation officers ranking this goal higher as an ideal than in actual practice. *Developing ties with social agencies* also was ranked higher as an ideal by probation officers than by judges, but both ranked this goal relatively low in actual practice.

Findings such as these take on added significance in view of the complex nature of the "network of organizations and groups concerned with juvenile matters" that composes the "task environment of the court."[28]

THE TASK ENVIRONMENT OF THE COURT

The complexity of the task environment of the court is suggested by Figure 4.1, reproduced from the National Assessment study. The organizations and groups represented in the diagram have complex relationships with one

THE JUVENILE COURT AND ITS TASK ENVIRONMENT

It is impossible to comprehend the complexity of the activities of the juvenile court or appreciate the various issues confronting it without recognizing the consequences of the court's intertwinement in a network of organizations and groups concerned with juvenile matters. It is from this network, termed the "task environment," that the court receives its major inputs of resources and to which it "delivers" its outputs. Analytically, the task environment can be conceptualized as (a) agencies that refer youth to the court, (b) organizations that provide financial resources, (c) agencies and groups that monitor and legitimate the activities of the court, (d) organizations that provide complementary services, and (e) agencies that receive court referrals. Empirically, of course, any given organization in the environment may serve several of these functions for the court.

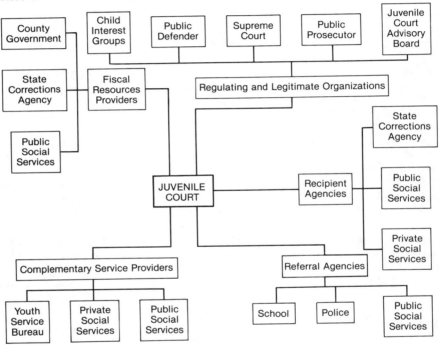

FIGURE 4.1 The Task Environment of the Juvenile Court SOURCE: Rosemary Sarri and Yeheskel Hasenfeld (eds.), *Brought to Justice? Juveniles, Courts, and the Law.* National Assessment of Juvenile Corrections. Ann Arbor: University of Michigan Press, 1976.

another, which influence their relationships with the court and with children and their parents.

Judges, court administrators, and probation officers were asked how *influential* they felt the organizations diagrammed in Figure 4.1 were to the court. There was general agreement that police and the schools exerted the most influence, with public social service agencies, state supreme courts or court administrators, public prosecutors, and state juvenile corrections agencies also ranking relatively high in influence. None of these, however, was rated as having a great deal of influence on the court.

Each of the groups and organizations in the court's task environment has goals and task environments of its own. Awareness of the backup role of the court was indicated by the perception that police, schools, and public prosecutors demanded isolation of more offenders from the community. "More legalistic case processing methods" were perceived as important to police, prosecutors, public defenders, and state supreme courts. Public and private social service agencies, correctional agencies, civic and child interest groups, youth service bureaus, and the schools press for more court services. These same groups, with the exception of schools, also were perceived as advocating diversion of cases from formal court handling, and as seeking provisions for the individual treatment of cases.

With few exceptions, these perceptions are consistent on the part of judges, court administrators, and probation officers. Thus, there is widespread agreement by court personnel that some part of the court's task environment demands that the court take a "legalistic" orientation and isolate the offenders, whereas others demand a service/treatment orientation.

Yeheskel Hasenfeld, one of the coauthors of the National Assessment report, concludes that, overall, juvenile court personnel see their community mandates as requiring social control and deterrence, despite the fact that most juvenile court cases are for status offenses or less serious criminal offenses. In addition, however, the courts must assume responsibility for troubled youth who are victims of social and economic instability and of the failure of other community institutions.[29]

The central finding which emerges from Hasenfeld's analysis is that, despite close involvement with key external organizations, *courts are little influenced by them and seldom in conflict with them.* Contrary to the underlying assumptions of the court, little use is made of resources in the environment. Instead, juvenile courts tend to be reactive to their external environment and to youth in trouble. The consequences are discouraging, for *"once children enter the court's orbit, they are less likely to benefit from the services of other youth-serving agencies"* than are other children. They are likely instead "to be thrust into a very narrow and limited pool of court services and [to] be excluded from a wide variety of community youth services just at the time they need access to as many services as possible" [emphasis added].[30]

This conclusion is reinforced and elaborated by a field study of a juvenile court in a large northern U.S. city. Robert Emerson spent many months observing proceedings in this court and interviewing the participants. Emerson emphasizes that the court's *coercive* power to commit children to the state youth authority is critical to its role as a "dumping ground" for cases judged hopeless or uncontrollable by the local child welfare department.[31] Many youth serving agencies, faced with high case loads, look to the court to rid themselves of their least desirable and most troublesome clients in order to protect themselves from failures with these most difficult cases. The result is that the court, lacking substantial resources of its own, becomes co-opted into a system that seeks to rid itself of "hard-core" cases that other agencies do not want.

The National Assessment survey concludes that such vast variation exists among courts that it is doubtful that even the basic elements of the juvenile court can be adequately defined, let alone definitively described. This confused picture is the result both of local variation and the inherent incompatibility of the two primary objectives of the court—social control and rehabilitation. The consequences are often deleterious for both objectives.

ADAPTING TO CHANGE

Juvenile courts are faced with the necessity to adapt to continuous change in the larger society as well as in the immediate task environment. New laws often mandate change in the court, and new agencies and new programs become a part of that task environment. The result, concludes Anne Rankin Mahoney, is that courts have become victims of "change overload."[32] Change requires investment of time and energy, often involving new personnel and procedures, and new relationships with other agencies. Declining resources and overcrowded court dockets further complicate the court's task.

One result of this combination of circumstances is *delay in the administration of juvenile justice.* Delay affects a variety of court functions and the people involved in them. Mahoney and Carole Fenster distinguish between "court time," "case time," "child time," and "intervention time."[33] Court time ("the time available to the court, each day, to deal with the cases on that session's calendar") may be eroded by many types of change, for example, the opening of a shopping mall that attracts teenagers or the rapid growth of population that drives up case loads. Case time—time spent in processing cases, from apprehension to final disposition—has been the subject of much professional as well as community concern. Delays in case time undermine both the court's rehabilitative and its control objectives, in part by impacting child time ("the *quality* of time that is given to the court appearances of an accused person") and intervention time, the latter drawing attention to the importance of timing in the court's intervention into children's lives.[34]

There is disagreement concerning the causes and effects of time thus conceived. Time standards set by professional groups, such as the American Bar Association and the Conference of State Court Administrators, tend to be shorter for juvenile than for adult offenders. However, Mahoney notes that defense attorneys have sometimes argued that delay in bringing cases to final disposition permits the child to demonstrate improvement in the condition or behavior that has brought him or her to the court.

"Mass processing" of cases is a common practice in many jurisdictions, especially those jurisdictions in which large numbers of juveniles must be handled with limited resources. Under such circumstances little diagnostic time is spent on cases and decisions become routinized, based on stereotypical criteria rather than on individualized treatment or justice criteria. Even in "good courts" there is great variation in the time taken for various stages of case processing, and relatively few meet the standards suggested by professional groups.[35] Delays are the result of many factors, including the procedural reforms discussed in the previous chapter. Although rarely studied systematically, the presence of attorneys in court seems likely to increase delays at several stages of court processing.[36]

COMMUNITY SETTINGS, AGENCIES, AND DELINQUENCY

We turn next to the community setting in which all the agencies of juvenile justice (and their task environments) function, with special attention to the school as a behavioral context of juvenile delinquency.

NOTES

1. President's Commission on Law Enforcement and Administration of Justice, *The Challenge of Crime in a Free Society*. Washington, DC: U.S. Government Printing Office, 1967.

2. Albert J. Reiss, Jr., *The Police and the Public*. New Haven, CT: Yale University Press, 1971.

3. The literature on police and policing is extremely large and diverse. Recent summaries on a variety of police-related topics may be found in S. H. Kadish (ed.), *Encyclopedia of Crime and Justice*. New York: Free Press, 1983. See also, Clifford D. Shearing and Philip C. Stenning, "Modern private security: its growth and implications," pp. 193–245, in Michael Tonry and Norval Morris (eds.), *Crime and Justice: An Annual Review of Research*, Vol. 3. Chicago: University of Chicago Press, 1981; and Shearing and Stenning (eds.), *Private Policing*, Sage Criminal Justice System Annuals. Beverly Hills, CA: Sage, 1987.

4. Several studies demonstrate the first conclusion. Goldman, studying a mill town in Allegany Co., Pennsylvania, reported 64 percent of juveniles apprehended were handled without court referral. Great variation was noted by offense, however: 91 percent of auto thieves, but only 11 percent of mischief cases were sent to court, for example. See Nathan Goldman, *The Differential Selection of Juvenile Offenders for Court Appearance*. New York: National Council on Crime and Delinquency, 1963. Bordua found that Detroit police reported 106,000 "encounters" with juveniles. Interviews were held with 23,645 suspected offenders (and more than 10,000 other youths) in gathering evidence. "Official contacts" numbered 9,445 (9 percent of total encounters) involving 5,282 juveniles. Nationally, Bordua examined data for over 2,000 police agencies from FBI reports. See David Bordua, "Recent trends: deviant behavior and social controls," *Annals of the American Academy of Political and Social Science* 359 (January):149–163. Some 385 (19 percent) of the agencies reported that they released less than 5 percent of the juveniles they contacted, while 60 agencies (3 percent) released more than 95 percent. At least 50 agencies were found in every 5 percent interval between these extremes.

5. Reiss, *op. cit.*

6. *Ibid.* See also, by Reiss, "The legitimacy of intrusion into private space," pp. 19–44 in Shearing and Stenning (eds.), *op. cit.*

7. Donald J. Black and Albert J. Reiss, Jr., "Police control of juveniles," *American Sociological Review* 35 (February):63–77. This conclusion is confirmed by Philadelphia research. When victims told police they were against prosecution of a sample of juveniles taken into custody, regardless of the seriousness of the crime alleged or the previous record of the juvenile, no further prosecutional action was taken. See William H. Hohenstein, "Factors influencing the police disposition of juvenile offenders," pp. 138–149, in Thorsten Sellin and Marvin E. Wolfgang (eds.), *Delinquency: Selected Studies*. New York: Wiley, 1969.

8. Egon Bittner, *The Functions of the Police in Modern Society*. Washington, DC: National Institute of Mental Health, 1970; also, Peter K. Manning, *Police Work*. Cambridge, MA: MIT Press, 1979.

9. Richard E. Sykes; "A regulatory theory of policing: a preliminary statement," pp. 237–256, in David H. Bayley (ed.), *Police and Society*. Beverly Hills, CA: Sage, 1977.

10. See LaMar T. Empey, *American Delinquency: Its Meaning and Construction* (rev. ed.). Homewood, IL: Dorsey, 1982, pp. 310–317.

11. Reiss, *op. cit.* See also, Dale Bowlin, "Police and the courts," pp. 12–13, in Geoffrey P. Alpert and Roger G. Dunham, *Policing Urban America.* Prospect Heights, IL: Waveland Press, 1988.

12. Bittner, *op. cit.*, p. 65.

13. See David Matza, *Becoming Deviant.* New York: Wiley, 1970. Arthur Stinchcombe notes that justice systems in the United States provide extraordinary protection to private space, as well as to private property, and that this limits police access to many places where crimes occur. See Arthur L. Stinchcombe, "Institutions of privacy in the determination of police administrative practice," *American Journal of Sociology,* 69 (September, 1963):150–160. See also, Reiss, 1971 and 1987, *op. cit.*

14. Carl Werthman and Irving Piliavin, "Gang members and the police," pp. 56–98, in David Bordua, *The Police: Six Sociological Essays.* New York: Wiley, 1967.

15. Sherri Cavan, "Interaction in home territories," *Berkeley Journal of Sociology,* VIII, p. 18, quoted in *Ibid.*

16. Werthman and Piliavin, *op. cit.*

17. This section is based largely on Marcia Garrett and James F. Short, Jr., "Social class v. personal demeanor in police stereotypes of juveniles," *Social Problems,* 22 (February, 1975):368–383.

18. For extended discussion of this issue see Alfred Blumstein, Jacqueline Cohen, Jeffrey A. Roth, and Christy A. Visher (eds.), *Criminal Careers and "Career Criminals",* Vol. I. Panel on Research on Criminal Careers, Committee on Research on Law Enforcement and the Administration of Justice, Commission on Behavioral and Social Sciences and Education, National Research Council. Washington, DC: National Academy Press, 1986.

19. See the discussion in Sandra Ball-Rokeach and James F. Short, Jr., "Collective violence: the redress of grievance," pp. 155–180, in Lynn A. Curtis, *American Violence and Public Policy: An Update of the National Commission on the Causes and Prevention of Violence.* New Haven, CT: Yale University Press, 1985. See also, Jerome Skolnick, *The Politics of Protest: A Report to the National Commission on the Causes and Prevention of Violence.* Washington, DC: U.S. Government Printing Office, 1969.

20. See, for example, Robert Regoli, *Police in America.* Washington, DC: University Press of America, 1977.

21. See James Q. Wilson, "The police and the delinquent in two cities," pp. 9–30, in Stanton Wheeler, *Controlling Delinquents.* New York: Wiley, 1968. Wilson notes that, when the study was done in 1962 official crime rates of the two cities were quite similar.

22. Geoffrey C. Hazard, Jr., "Criminal justice system: overview," pp. 450–470, in S. H. Kadish (ed.), *Encyclopedia of Crime and Justice,* Vol. 2. New York: Free Press, 1983. The quote is from p. 456.

23. See, for example, Robert M. Fogelson, *Big City Police.* Cambridge, MA: Harvard University Press, 1977; Chap. 11; also, Mark H. Moore and Robert J. Trojanowicz, *Corporate Strategies for Policing.* National Institute of Justice. Washington, D.C.: U.S.G.P.O., 1988.

24. Rosemary Sarri and Yeheskel Hasenfeld (eds.), *Brought to Justice? Juveniles, the Courts, and the Law.* National Assessment of Juvenile Corrections. Ann Arbor, MI: University of Michigan Press, 1976.

25. See Ellen H. Nimick, Howard N. Snyder, Dennis P. Sullivan, and Nancy J. Tierney, *Juvenile Court Statistics, 1983.* Pittsburgh, PA: National Center for Juvenile Justice, 1985.

26. Solomon Kobrin and Malcolm Klein, *Community Treatment of Juvenile Offenders: The DSO Experiments.* Beverly Hills, CA: Sage, 1983, p. 318.

27. Sosin's research is summarized in Institute for Research on Poverty, *Focus,* Vol. 4, No. 3 (Spring, 1981), pp. 5–6, 17–18.

28. Sarri and Hasenfeld, *op. cit..*, p. 83.

29. Hasenfeld, in *Ibid.*

30. *Ibid.*, p. 42; See also, M. A. Bortner, *Inside a Juvenile Court: The Tarnished Ideal of Individualized Justice.* New York: New York University Press, 1982.

31. Robert M. Emerson, *Judging Delinquents: Context and Process in Juvenile Court.* Chicago: Aldine, 1969, p. 63.

32. Anne Rankin Mahoney, *Juvenile Justice in Context*. Boston: Northeastern University Press, 1987.

33. Carole Fenster and Anne Rankin Mahoney, "Time and process in juvenile court," *The Justice System Journal*, Vol. 10, No. 1 (1985):37–55.

34. *Ibid.*, pp. 40–43 (emphasis in original).

35. See Margaret K. Rosenheim, "Juvenile justice: organization and process," pp. 969–977 in S. H. Kadish, *op. cit.*; see also, Bortner, *op. cit.*

36. Fenster and Mahoney, *op. cit.*, p. 50, found that among youths appearing before a suburban court on a single petition alleging burglary or theft, "those with attorneys took, on the average, three times as long to move from filing to adjudication as youths without attorneys (74 days compared to 24 days)." Neither other factors in these cases nor case outcomes could account for these differences. See also, Barry C. Feld, "The right to counsel in juvenile court: an empirical study of when lawyers appear and the difference they make," *Journal of Criminal Law and Criminology*, Vol. 79, No. 4 (1989): 1185-1346.

CHAPTER 5
SCHOOLS AND COMMUNITIES AS BEHAVIOR SETTINGS FOR JUVENILE DELINQUENCY

HISTORICAL NOTE

Most northern states in the United States had free education laws by the mid-nineteenth century, but the nation's first *compulsory* schooling law was not passed until 1852, in Massachusetts. It was twelve years before another state did so, but by the end of the century most states had such laws, and by 1918, all did. The movement for universal, compulsory education was similar in motivation and participation to the juvenile court movement and the movement against child labor. Even more than the other two, the public schools movement became a fundamental building block of the American nation—a primary means by which American citizenship came to be defined. The success of the movement was primarily attributable, John Meyer and his colleagues argue, to the "common consciousness of the laws of God and the demands of rational human order."[1] Politically, the movement was shaped by intense activity at the local and state levels before it became a matter of abiding federal interest.

There was much disorder in the burgeoning cities of the United States and on its frontiers throughout most of the nineteenth century. Public education during this century evidenced a good deal of obstreperous behavior on the part of students, and classroom discipline was enforced by physically coercive and sometimes brutal methods.[2] Despite the infusion of new philosophies of education stressing personal and intellectual development, and new methods of instruction designed to enhance learning possibilities, discipline and control remain as basic goals of most public and private schools. The success of universal compulsory education—unlike the success of the movement which gave it birth—continues to be hotly debated.[3]

Like the juvenile court movement, the drive for universal education was at once political, economic, religious, and nativistic. Once achieved it, too, quickly became institutionalized. At the turn of the century, when the first juvenile courts were being established, education was already highly professionalized and becoming increasingly so. It was also becoming increasingly centralized in formal government structures and increasingly bureaucratic in organization.

The legal requirements of school attendance placed constraints on families and other institutions, as well as on children. In the early days of compulsory schooling, vaguely drawn laws lacking in provisions for enforcement combined with the limited capacity of schools to minimalize such constraints. Increased capacity of schools, increased professionalism of teachers, administrators, and enforcement personnel (the fabled "truant officer"), and increased standardization brought on by a centralized and bureaucratic organization greatly strengthened these constraints. Schools soon joined the police as the primary institutions for maintaining community order and law enforcement.

LOOKING TO THE COURT FOR BACKUP AUTHORITY

These developments virtually insured that "problem children" would emerge, and of course they did. In most school districts problem children could be dealt with by school authorities using locally determined disciplinary procedures and with little involvement of police or courts.[4] In larger cities, however, highly mobile and heterogeneous populations created special problems for neighborhood institutions. Backup authority was sought in the juvenile justice systems. For many years, schools—some created specifically for problem children processed by the court—served both as sources of referral of children to the court and recipients of children from the court.

Two brief excerpts from Robert Emerson's field study nicely capture the nature of these relationships. A truant officer, replying to Emerson's question as to when he referred youngsters to the court, replies: "Only when it's impossible. You try everything and get nowhere....The only time's where nothing works. Then you have to do something." And the principal of a "small special public school for boys in the middle grades [about sixth to eighth grade] who have been expelled from the regular school system for various kinds of misbehavior" brings two boys and their parents for an informal hearing before the chief probation officer of the juvenile court. Emerson then describes a typical lecture as follows: "Would you like me to bring you into court? Have the judge send you away to training school?...You're going to go to school, and when you're in school you're going to sit in your seat, and you're not going to move."[5]

Emerson notes that the police, school authorities, and representatives of other institutions look to the juvenile court as a backup institution. The court is expected to affirm their actions and to confirm their authority.

In the latter half of the twentieth century schools once again have become social settings in which delinquent behavior takes place, and performance in school has become a critical element in delinquent and criminal careers.

WHAT IS TO BE EXPLAINED?

How much delinquency occurs in school settings? A great deal, if the only comprehensive study of the matter is to be believed.[6] Known by its title, the "Violent Schools—Safe Schools" study was conducted in the mid-1970s. Principals in more than 4,000 schools completed questionnaires distributed under the auspices of the National Institute of Education. More than 31,000 students and nearly 24,000 teachers from a large sample of junior and senior high schools completed questionnaires concerning their experiences with school crime. More than 6,000 of these students were randomly selected and personally interviewed, and intensive field studies were conducted in ten schools that reported progress in coping with serious crime problems.

This massive study suggests that students and teachers in many schools are victims of acts that could be defined as delinquent, including a good deal of crime. Jackson Toby notes, for example, that "a majority of American junior high-school teachers were sworn at by their students or were the target of obscene gestures within the month preceding the survey."[7] Criminal victimization, though much less frequent, was not uncommon, as Tables 5.1 and 5.2 demonstrate. Thefts were especially pervasive. Teacher victimization tended

TABLE 5.1 Percent of Teachers Victimized in Public Schools over a Two-Month Period in 1976

SIZE OF COMMUNITY	BY LARCENIES IN JUNIOR HIGH SCHOOLS	BY LARCENIES IN SENIOR HIGH SCHOOLS	BY ASSAULTS IN JUNIOR HIGH SCHOOLS	BY ASSAULTS IN SENIOR HIGH SCHOOLS	BY ROBBERIES IN JUNIOR HIGH SCHOOLS	BY ROBBERIES IN SENIOR HIGH SCHOOLS
500,000 or more	31.4% (56)	21.6% (59)	2.1% (56)	1.4% (59)	1.4% (59)	1.1% (59)
100,000–499,999	24.5 (45)	22.8 (36)	1.1 (45)	1.0 (36)	0.7 (45)	0.9 (36)
50,000–99,999	21.0 (23)	19.3 (31)	0.2 (23)	0.3 (31)	0.3 (23)	0.4 (31)
10,000–49,999	20.8 (94)	16.5 (75)	0.6 (94)	0.3 (75)	0.5 (94)	0.4 (75)
2,500–9,999	16.9 (41)	19.1 (47)	0.3 (41)	0.2 (47)	0.4 (41)	0.4 (47)
Under 2,500	15.9 (42)	18.5 (53)	0.2 (42)	0.2 (53)	0.0 (42)	0.4 (53)
All communities	22.1 (301)	19.3 (301)	0.8 (301)	0.5 (301)	0.6 (301)	0.6 (301)

N.B.: Numbers in parentheses refer to the number of schools on the basis of which the average percentage of personal victimization was calculated for each cell.

Source: Special tabulation of data from U.S. Department of Health, Education and Welfare, 1978. Published in Jackson Toby, "Crime in the Schools," p. 71, in James Q. Wilson (ed.), *Crime and Public Policy*. San Francisco: Institute for Contemporary Studies, 1983.

TABLE 5.2   Percent of Students Victimized in Public Schools over a One-Month Period in 1976

SIZE OF COMMUNITY	BY LARCENIES OF MORE THAN $1		BY ASSAULTS		BY ROBBERIES OF MORE THAN $1	
	IN JUNIOR HIGH SCHOOLS	IN SENIOR HIGH SCHOOLS	IN JUNIOR HIGH SCHOOLS	IN SENIOR HIGH SCHOOLS	IN JUNIOR HIGH SCHOOLS	IN SENIOR HIGH SCHOOLS
500,000 or more	14.8% (56)	14.9% (59)	8.5% (56)	3.7% (59)	5.7% (56)	2.8% (59)
100,000–499,999	18.0 (45)	16.8 (36)	7.8 (45)	2.7 (36)	3.6 (45)	1.9 (36)
50,000–99,999	18.0 (23)	15.3 (31)	7.7 (23)	2.9 (31)	3.8 (23)	1.3 (31)
10,000–49,999	15.5 (94)	15.8 (74)	6.8 (94)	2.7 (74)	3.3 (94)	1.4 (74)
2,500–9,999	16.1 (41)	14.6 (47)	7.4 (41)	3.1 (47)	3.5 (41)	1.4 (47)
Under 2,500	15.8 (42)	14.2 (53)	6.2 (42)	3.5 (53)	3.8 (42)	2.0 (53)
All communities	16.0 (301)	15.2 (300)	7.3 (301)	3.1 (300)	3.9 (301)	1.8 (300)

N.B.: Numbers in parentheses refer to the number of schools on the basis of which the average percentage of personal victimization was calculated for each cell.

Source: Special tabulation of data from U.S. Department of Health, Education and Welfare, 1978. Published in Jackson Toby, "Crime in the Schools," p. 72, in James Q. Wilson (ed.), *Crime and Public Policy.* San Francisco, Institute for Contemporary Studies, 1983.

to be higher in larger than in smaller communities, and except for robbery, slightly higher in junior than in senior high schools. Student victimization likewise was higher in junior than in senior high schools, but was less closely related to the size of the community.

The most likely students to be victimized were those who were young, male, and members of racial and ethnic minorities (very like the profile of the perpetrators of crime, as we shall see in the next chapter). Male teachers also reported higher percentages of victimization, as did the youngest and least experienced teachers. Because they lack seniority, these teachers are also found most frequently in troubled inner-city schools where attendance and disciplinary problems are the greatest.

WHO ARE THE OFFENDERS IN SCHOOL-RELATED CRIME?

The survey could provide little information concerning the perpetrators of school crime, since self-reports of this sort were not gathered. Based on extensive observations and intensive interviews of school counselors, security personnel, parents, and representatives of community organizations, the field study reached the conclusion that[8]

...a small percentage of students—the figure 10 percent was frequently cited—form a hard core of disruptive students who are responsible for most of the vandalism and violence in schools. While this troublesome group did not seem to be identifiable in terms of any specific racial, ethnic, or socioeconomic status background, school staff commonly described them as students who were also having difficulty academically, were frequently in trouble in the community, and tended to come from troubled homes. These students were easily identifiable and generally seemed to be known both to staff and other students because of the frequency with which they were in trouble....this group of troublesome students could find allies among the other students when specific issues, situations, or problems arose. Violence and disruptive behavior is thus...interactive with a small group of students frequently causing problems and at times setting off a chain reaction among other student groups.

The report also concluded that most school crime was committed by current students, rather than by intruders, as has often been supposed. Even the majority of cases of breaking and entering were attributed to current students. Of special interest was the reported link between offending and academic ability and achievement. Teachers who said that a majority of their students had low academic ability were far more likely to report that they had been attacked or robbed than were teachers who perceived less than a third of their students to be of low ability. This factor far outweighed the relationship of racial balance to school crime, although schools in which racial and ethnic minorities predominated reported higher rates of victimization of both students and teachers.

The research literature confirms the relationship between delinquent behavior and academic ability and performance.[9] It is less consistent concerning the effects of dropping out of school.[10] Many studies find higher rates of delinquent behavior among students who eventually drop out of school, but dropping out of school has sometimes been reported to decrease involvement in delinquency.[11]

SERIOUS CRIME AND FEAR IN SCHOOLS

The "Violent Schools—Safe Schools" study found victimization figures for *serious* crimes to be low. Also some among these violent crimes were probably of minor consequence, since few of the assaults were reported to require medical attention. The fact that they occurred over such short periods of time magnifies their significance, however.

The survey also found that *fear* of victimization was an important factor in school nonattendance. Eight percent of the largest city junior-high students (5 percent among suburban and smaller cities, and 4 percent among rural school students) reported that they stayed at home at least once during the previous month, "because someone might hurt or bother you at school." As Toby notes, "Since the students who had an opportunity to reply to this question were those attending school on the day the questionnaire was administered (or on a subsequent make-up session), students in the sample who failed to fill out their questionnaires may have contained a higher proportion of victims of school crime and a higher percentage of those frightened into truancy."[12]

SCHOOL CRIME, SOCIAL CONTROL, AND SOCIAL CHANGE

School crime occurs primarily, but not exclusively, at times and in places when supervision is lacking or diminished, for example, in places such as hallways, stairs, cafeterias, toilets, and locker rooms. The survey did not ask students about harrassment and attacks that occur *during the journey to and from school*. Given the data on fear, however, before- and after-school times and places clearly are important to school-related crime, as well.

Respondents were asked their opinions as to what might be done to make schools safer places. The most frequent recommendation among principals, teachers, and students concerned better discipline and supervision. A variety of disciplinary actions and security precautions were also mentioned. Some schools require students to carry hall passes when out of class, and visitors must check in at the office. Security measures in some inner-city schools have since become even more restrictive. More security officers have been employed, and some schools require all who enter the school to do so by one entrance or a very few entrances (a few require passage through surveillance devices similar to those used in airport security). Audio and visual monitoring of hallways, classrooms, and other areas where trouble might break out also have become more common.[13]

The reported consensus among principals, teachers, and students concerning better discipline and supervision may be more apparent than real, as ethnographic studies suggest. Parents must also be considered in this equation, and much local variation exists in this respect (see the following discussion). Historical and contemporary forces combine to render the effectiveness of discipline and supervision extremely difficult. While the discoveries of childhood and adolescence resulted in greater attention to child rearing and child saving, the provision of educational institutions for the young led inevitably to increased separation of children from the adult world, thus making control over children both problematic and more difficult.

THE COMMUNITY CONTEXT OF SOCIAL CHANGE

Professionalism and the bureaucratic organization of schools have resulted, also, in increased separation of schools from their communities. In this process schools have gained greater autonomy to determine what should be taught and how it should be taught, and a measure of protection from parochial interests in local communities. The resulting loss of contact with parents, however, has diminished the ability of both the schools and the parents to control students. These separations of schools, children, and parents have also enhanced the formation of youth subcultures and their influence on young people, further challenging traditional social controls.

The extension of civil rights movements to "children's rights" has contributed to schools' social control problems, eroding their authority and curtailing disciplinary prerogatives. Procedural reform has made many juvenile courts reluctant to involve themselves in school disciplinary problems, thus further weakening the school as a social control institution.

The impact of these trends has been magnified by demographic changes. Many inner-city schools now must cope with highly mobile student populations. It is sometimes difficult even to know which children are, or should be, included in the student population. A high proportion of enrolled students may be absent on an average school day in some schools. In others, school authorities are uncertain as to which children should be expected to be in attendance, so great is community instability.

Stanford sociologists have studied how schools have adapted to these conditions and to the turbulence of crime and disorder. Their investigations, conducted half a dozen years before the National Institute of Education studies, anticipated many of the problems later identified by those studies. In addition, the Stanford researchers wanted to know how phenomena such as urban riots, civil rights activities, and anti–Vietnam War protests had influenced schools. Their studies provide important insights into the changing nature of schools and their relationships with constituencies.

School administrators studied by the Stanford researchers did not view discipline and order as their primary problems. Their major concern was rather with what they regarded as their most important *constituency*—students:[14]

> The crucial idea which is necessary to understand what has taken place is the concept of *externalization*. The schools have come to terms with the idea that contemporary secondary school students have interests, roles, qualities, or commitments, entirely outside of both their families and the schools themselves. This development is greatly aided by changes in our wider society. Most Americans—partly because of all the public discussion about the problems of young people, and the problems of controlling them—have come to see a series of youth problems as quite general in our society, and in no way the particular responsibility of a given set of schools or school administrators.

The problem of student drug use is illustrative. Observing that most students who use drugs regulate their drug consumption sufficiently so that they are able to conform to school rules, administrators chose to handle exceptional problems on a case-by-case basis. A massive drug problem may exist, but it is neither peculiar to, nor the responsibility of, the schools. The problem has been externalized.

Similarly, racial conflicts and the political and ethnic commitments of students are defined by school authorities, and by many others, as legitimate interests related to societal problems. They are, therefore, *external* to the schools. School administrators consequently regarded adaptation to demands based on these interests as legitimate. Suggestions from the Violent Schools—Safe Schools study that most school crime is committed by current students notwithstanding, much school crime also can be externalized as a manifestation of more general youth problems in society. Schools are able to absolve themselves of responsibility for solving social problems, in part, because others agree that these are social, not simply school, problems:[15]

...young people are widely seen as independent *persons*, or *citizens*...a major social change is occurring in the position of young people in society. They are increasingly asserting, and tacitly being allowed and encouraged to assert, their independence from familial and school controls. The schools have by and large been forced to acknowledge much of this independence, and have developed more limited controls and demands on student behavior.

Many schools, like juvenile courts, have retreated from their traditional *in loco parentis* role. While no Supreme Court ruling of the critical nature of *Gault* compelled such changes, the social forces responsible for them have produced equally profound and far-reaching consequences for schools, courts, and other institutions. Schools often have been viewed as primary vehicles for changing social conditions, or for adapting to them. Examples abound—racial prejudice, discrimination, and segregation; poverty; adaptation to scientific and technological change; declining physical fitness; and drug abuse—are some of these areas of change. Although schools continue to be the focus of social policy initiatives, that role now seems increasingly problematic thereby increasing pressures on an already beleaguered institution.

The Stanford researchers concluded that, while the schools had "managed to get out of the line of fire" during a time of increasing youth turbulence, "appeal to the educational interests of young people" remained problematic.[16] Defining students as "citizens first" has additional consequences for families, labor markets, and other institutions. All of these problems appear to have been exacerbated since those words were written. Juvenile delinquency is, by definition, a problem of youth, but it is also a problem of relationships between young people and the larger society. Schools thus remain important behavior settings for many problems.

COMMUNITY SETTINGS AND JUVENILE DELINQUENCY

The bleak picture of crime in and around schools portrayed by the National Assessment survey should not be allowed to obscure the extent of local variation. To introduce the broader context of regulatory forces at work in communities we turn to human ecology.

The Ecological Context. Arrests of juveniles and other measures of official handling occur most frequently in economically marginal, or "slum," neighborhoods and communities. Many of these localities are also occupied primarily or exclusively by racial or ethnic minorities. The "ecological conflict" between police and youth in such communities, briefly touched upon in the previous chapter, is part of this broader ecological context.

Early in the nineteeth century European scholars called attention to the geographic patterning of crime, and its joint distribution with social characteristics of populations, for example, poverty, ethnicity, and a variety of social ills. Modern ecological studies of crime and delinquency emerged only later, however, as part of the Chicago School of Urban Sociology.

The Chicago sociologists were interested in urban structure, in characteristic patterns of city growth and development, and in related social and economic processes, and their consequences.[17] Clifford Shaw and Henry McKay studied the distribution of addresses of official cases of delinquency, first in Chicago and later in other cities.[18] By relating these distributions to a variety of land use characteristics, other social ills, and social and economic characteristics of areas within the city, a consistent pattern emerged.

Within physical limitations (e.g., Chicago's location along Lake Michigan) delinquency rates for both boys and girls, and for adult criminals, were highest in the area immediately surrounding the central business district. Rates declined progressively in concentric areas the further away from this zone one moved. The area nearest the central business district had been designated by Ernest W. Burgess as the "zone in transition," indicative of the changing character of land use, from predominantly residential use to industrial and commercial use.[19]

Similar results were obtained when delinquency rates were computed for traditional and officially designated local community areas.[20] Similar *gradients* were found for measures of poverty and economic dependency, for the physical deterioration of neighborhoods, for high population density and turnover, for truancy, and for other social problems.

Shaw and his colleagues observed that many areas with high delinquency rates had been so characterized for many years, while the racial and ethnic character of residents had changed a great deal. Further, delinquency rates of racial and ethnic groups exhibited similar patterns, that is, higher rates for residents of a given race or ethnicity in areas near the central business district, lower rates for members of these groups who lived in areas further removed from that district. Neither race nor ethnicity per se, therefore, could explain delinquency rates.

Variations in the ecology of delinquency, and their interpretation, have been the subject of a great deal of speculation, research, and theory, and the object of much social policy debate and practice, matters to which we will return in later chapters.

Other Institutional Settings. Of all institutional contexts of delinquent behavior the greatest amount of attention has focused on the *family*. At the same time that the discovery of childhood increased family responsibilities for child socialization, the rise of the nation state challenged—some would say usurped—family authority, as families became the target for early reform efforts.

A good deal of early scholarly research on juvenile delinquency also focused on family influences. In the early 1930s, however, this focus changed as study of broader forces influencing delinquency, crime, family dissolution, and other social problems accumulated. Other studies emphasized the importance of peer influences on delinquents. While each of these influences continues to be found in more recent studies, interest in the family setting has revived as more sophisticated research methods and theories have emerged.[21]

The association of broken homes (households severed by the divorce or the separation of parents) with official cases of delinquency has long been observed. The significance of the statistical relationship was questioned, however, when more sophisticated research revealed that the association was weak. Later research provided important clues as to the nature of the relationship, for example, that the statistical association of broken homes and delinquency is closer for girls than for boys, and that the association varies by type of delinquent behavior. The statistical association is also closer for status offenses and other minor delinquencies than for more serious offenses. Poor family relationships, however, also feature prominently in the careers of those who are most persistently and seriously involved in crime. Several studies also report that the *quality* of marital and parent-child relationships, and of family economic circumstances, is more closely associated with delinquent behavior than is family dissolution.[22]

Other aspects of family structure and culture that have been studied for their association with delinquency include family size, birth order, and criminality among other family members. While statistical relationships tend to be weak, delinquents are reported to come disproportionately from large families and to be intermediate in birth order, rather than the first or last born child. Assessment of the significance of these and other findings in particular studies has been hampered by the lack of more complete information (concerning, for example, the family structure, the economic circumstances, the quality of marital and parent-child relationships, the disciplinary practices, criminality among parents and siblings, and still other factors). Lack of a compelling theory has been an even more important impediment to the advance of knowledge concerning these and many other relationships, though this, too, is changing as we shall see in Chapter 8.

Evidence concerning the influence of *religion*—affiliation, belief, and extent of participation—is inconclusive.[23] Empirical support can be found suggesting that religious variables are both negatively and positively related, and even unrelated to delinquent behavior.

Descriptive relationships such as those between delinquency and institutions such as the family and religion do not explain. They require explanation. That task is facilitated by taking a more holistic perspective on youth-adult relationships as a context for delinquent behavior.

Youth-Adult Relationships as a Context for Delinquent Behavior. Communities vary a great deal in the nature of institutional influences on delinquency. In this section we deal with this complexity by focusing on ethnographic and sociological studies of community relationships that subsume family, school, religious, economic, and political institutions.

We turn first to Gary Schwartz's ethnographically based interpretations of *authority relationships* between young people and adults in several communities. Schwartz argues that broader cultural influences (such as the empirical regularities discussed previously) must be understood in the context of the local events and institutions that give them meaning.

BEYOND CONFORMITY OR REBELLION: YOUTH AND AUTHORITY IN AMERICA[24]

The autonomy of local communities (as distinct from larger political and economic forces) is much debated in the scholarly literature. Schwartz reminds us, however, "that young people rarely choose where they will grow up. The local community is the place where most of them go to school, form friendships, find things to do in their spare time, and, more generally, explore ways of defining themselves in relation to the world outside of their families" (p. 15).

Schwartz and his colleagues studied six midwestern communities, pairing them on the basis of a variety of characteristics, but primarily for the purpose of comparing how local "cultures reflect different resolutions of similar issues" concerning youth (p. 10).

"Ribley" and "Patusa" (the community names are pseudonyms) are small towns, the former in an economically depressed coal mining area, the latter a more affluent community with an agricultural economic base. Schwartz observes that "[t]here is a democratic flavor to the inward-looking quality of small-town life." While awareness of social class is pervasive, class interests do not dominate institutional life. Much of Ribley's and Patusa's "civic life revolves around the symbol of small-town unity, high school basketball" (p. 33).

The issue that concerns Schwartz in these small towns is their handling of troublesome youth. The manner in which this issue is resolved reflects fundamental differences in values and in the ethics that govern personal relationships in the two communities. The nature of these differences, and the consequences for youth culture, are suggested in Figure 5.1.

The policies of local institutions reflect the normative contrasts depicted in Figure 5.1. The "moral boundaries" of Patusa define permissible public behavior, whereas Ribley seeks to create a protective shield around young people.[25] Acceptance by the community does not follow automatically from simply growing up in Patusa, or even from knowing other people on a personal basis for "living harmoniously together entails constant vigilance against threatening outside influences and internal disturbances" (p. 33). In contrast, tolerance of others flows naturally from living together in Ribley.

In both of these communities the police role in social control is secondary to that of the schools. There the similarity ends, however. "In Patusa, any form of expressive behavior that goes beyond very narrow bounds is seen as a potential slap in the face of authority" and the impulse is nearly always to "clamp down" before the problem gets out of control (p. 33). Relatively minor issues often become major violations of the rules. Discipline is often harsh and personally demeaning to the offender.

FIGURE 5.1

Ribley	Patusa
Troublesome youth are protected by the community	Troublesome youth are extruded from the community
Values: Freedom and personal expressiveness	Values: Order and security
Ethics: Personal understanding, tolerance of differences	Ethics: Vigilance against outside influences and internal disturbance
Basis for authority: Reasonableness	Basis for authority: Commitment to order and stability
Consequence: Continuity between segments of youth culture and with the adult world	Consequence: Fragmentation of peer groupings, oppressive penetration of adult authority into the way young people organize their lives

In Ribley tolerance of youthful deviance is imbedded in caring and in concern based on intimate familiarity with personal and family history. "Extrusion into the formal legal system is seen as the absolute last resort: something that breaks the moral bonds between the generations and disrupts the solidarity of the community as a whole" (p. 34). The solidarity of intergenerational relationships is characterized by "a certain amount of formality and distance," however, "because these qualities allow both parties to see the differences in experience and judgment" that are the basis for authority. In Ribley, "tolerance has its rules, and the primary one is not backing others into a corner" (p. 52).

Contrasting community cultures are reflected in differences between youth cultures in these two towns. Youth styles and identities in Ribley are richer than in Patusa, though not sharply opposed to one another. There is considerable continuity within the youth world of Ribley, whereas peer groups are highly fragmented in Patusa. The contrast is greatest in allowable public behavior. In Ribley, "[Y]oung people are permitted to engage in a good deal of expressive behavior in public without adult resistance," whereas in Patusa, the lines of such behavior are sharply drawn and enforced (p. 34).

Control in Ribley is based on reasonableness. "What matters...is the sense of the dignity of each person. It is only when a person intentionally and repeatedly does not respect the norm of mutual tolerance that the community reacts punitively" (p. 34).

Patusa's rational mold of authority enforces rules "in a manner that is consistent with the goals of local institutions...however, authority is less concerned with the instrumental efficacy of the rules than with its power to contain and suppress any form of youthful expressiveness that would disrupt the equanimity of adults...The basic thrust of authority is to let young people know that the first item of business is knowing how to stay out of trouble" (pp. 34–35).

Schwartz next compares two working-class communities: "Parsons Park" and "Cambridge," the former located in a large city, the latter a suburban community. As depicted in Figure 5.2, in both, "loyalty to local traditions" versus "social mobility" are at issue.

Cambridge is a nearly all-white suburb of a large city, while Parsons Park is located directly in the path of the invading black population out of the inner city. Residents of Parsons Park are proud of their common heritage,

FIGURE 5.2   The Issue: Loyalty to Local Traditions Versus Social Mobility

Parsons Park	Cambridge
Values: Mutual support of working-class, ethnic, and Catholic values by families and other community institutions	Values: Conflict between traditional working-class family values and middle-class mobility values represented by school
Authority: Perceived as rational, based on commonly accepted values, but often rigid and unyielding, at home and school	Authority: Perceived as patently irrational (because it has no instrumental value) and unreasonable (because it is humiliating)
Consequence: Continuity of youth culture with white ethnic working-class adult culture and social world	Consequence: Fragmentation of youth culture; rebellion of youth against adult authority

but there is a good deal of anxiety about the viability of established patterns of social life. Adults worry more about this than do young people, many of whom find the local community parochial and stifling. Racially motivated incidents between the youth of Parsons Park and black youth occasionally occur (at football games and other places of interracial contact), but these are peripheral to youth culture. Of greater concern is the fact that adults regard deviance as equivalent to moral corruption. Nevertheless, "few youth base their social identity upon the rejection of adult values. There is a spirit of fraternal solidarity in the youth world which stresses experiences that bring different youth groups together" (p. 108).

In Cambridge, that solidarity and common bond are lacking. The community is torn between conflicting values embodied in the home and the school. Parents expect their children to "get ahead in life," and they view the school as a vehicle to social mobility. Yet the gulf between the working-class parents and the middle-class professionals who run the school is obvious to both and deeply resented by the parents. Parents demand harsh policies toward drug use and violence, and expect their children to accept the rational authority of the school, but they resent the school's attempts to enforce discipline when their own children are involved. There is little involvement of parents in school affairs. "For the youth of Cambridge, the school stands for ambitions that run against their sense of themselves as autonomous persons. Adult authority is experienced as infantilization that fails to recognize their strong need for independence from adult controls....[Here] the reaction of youth to adult authority...[has] a much more aggressive character...[and] the youth world is also split into groups that despise one another. In Cambridge, drug use and fights often have serious repercussions. Youth who are seen as compliant to adult authority are targets of real hostility, and a code of personal honor that is hypersensitive to insult sets youth groups against one another" (p. 108).

Schwartz next compares an all-white affluent suburb and a Mexican-American inner-city community. Seemingly a strange comparison, the comparison is nevertheless instructive. In both of these communities "the American dream of success" contends with "investment in the expressive satisfactions of peer group sociability" for the time and commitment of young people (p. 10).

"Glenbar's" affluence protects its residents from the disorder of inner-city life. In contrast, "while "32nd Street" is not the poorest or the most disorganized inner-city community, conflict is very much part of everyday life. Armed youth shoot and occasionally kill one another" (p. 193).[26]

> The comparison between youth who take privilege for granted and youth who must struggle to get a decent education or job reveals a good deal about how class and ethnicity shape the lives of young people in urban America. Yet this comparison also discloses continuities...In both communities, young people accept conventional images of success...[they] believe that an affluent way of living is highly desirable and that education is the primary route to getting the kinds of jobs that support such a mode of living...the means to this end—education—[is accorded] only instrumental significance...education is useful to the extent that it helps one get ahead in the world. Where they differ is the way in which they work out the expressive component of their peer cultures. (p. 193)

Glenbar is homogenously white and upper middle class, whereas 32nd Street is distinctively Mexican. The school systems in the two communities are at opposite ends of the spectrum of educational resources, academic standards, and social order, yet in neither are youth committed to education other than in a strictly instrumental fashion. Youth in 32d Street share in their rich ethnic heritage, yet they are oriented chiefly to the street world and to standards of personal honor that often involve them in conflict with other youth and which are counterproductive to success in school.

Except for their common cultural identity, the people of 32nd Street lack the intergenerational alliances among nonfamilial authority figures and youth that exist in Parsons Park. Few, if any, coaches, priests, teachers, politicians, or policemen command enough respect among 32nd Street young people to protect them from peer pressures.

Glenbar has neither the sense of community nor the cultural traditions that are found in 32nd Street. Nor is there a dominating value (such as "honor," found in 32nd Street) that leads inevitably to deviant behavior. Alcohol and marijuana use are the chief forms of deviance in Glenbar. The deep friendship relations of youth constitute a mild form of rebellion against adult values, which youth experience as abstract, impersonal, and overly instrumental.

Youth in both communities are very much involved in the expressive rather than the instrumental side of youth culture. Both accept the rationality of conventional adult values, but for different reasons. Glenbar youth "conform because the payoff is so tangible that it would be foolish to do otherwise. In 32nd Street, youth do not conform to conventional norms with much consistency because the payoff is so remote and problematic" (p. 194).

FIGURE 5.3   The Issue: Success Values Versus Expressive Satisfactions of Peer Group Sociability

32nd Street	Glenbar
The rationality of conventional adult values is accepted by youth in both communities.	
Honor and reputation are individual and group values; reciprocity	Intimacy, friendship, individuality; coolness (avoidance of public airing of private problems)
Family and peer group values separated from values of school, and other public institutions	Parents stress doing well in school, rely on school for expertise; but adult values experienced as impersonal
Adult authority weak due to lack of status and power in larger society	Bond between generations weak; youth compliance instrumental
Authority perceived as unreasonable (because payoff is remote and problematic)	Authority perceived as unreasonable (because overly instrumental, future-oriented)
Public high school is disorganized and dangerous; students pushed through regardless of academic performance	School viewed as strictly instrumental; a chasm exists between school and friendship
Peer culture is often violent; trust is rare, so great is value placed on honor	Dominated by personal identity, deep friendships; deviance minor (marijuana, alcohol; "rebellion" in form of sharing only with friends)

These diagrams, excerpts, and brief summaries do not do justice to the richness of data and interpretation provided in Gary Schwartz's fine monograph. Heuristically, the comparisons serve well to demonstrate the complexity and variability of issues, cultures, and social relationships that influence the behavior of both youth and adults. They illuminate the subtle ways in which relationships within and between generations are shaped by the presence or absence of hopes and fears, traditions and respect (or their lack).

Still other issues divide youth and adults in other communities, of course, and the manner in which they are resolved quite likely ranges across continua, rather than the stark contrasts portrayed by Schwartz. We gain further insight into the nature of these issues and their resolutions from a second set of exemplars of the consequences of youth-adult interaction, this one a study of lower-class black and white gangs and communities in Chicago, conducted approximately a decade prior to the Schwartz study.

A COMPARISON OF BLACK AND WHITE GANG COMMUNITIES[27]

The black gang boys in this study were more firmly embedded in the lower regions of the lower class than were the white gang boys. Median income levels in the black communities were much lower than those in the white communities. Unemployment levels among the black communities studied averaged more than twice those in the white communities. The contrasts in income levels and in overcrowded living conditions were even more striking. No white community studied was as disadvantaged as the least disadvantaged black community in these respects. The black communities were also more disadvantaged with respect to family stability and other institutional measures. In sum, members of the black gangs lived in communities described by S. M. Miller as the "unstable poor," while the white gangs came principally from working-class communities and the "stable poor."[28]

Field observers noted that delinquent behaviors were not clearly differentiated from nondelinquent behaviors among the black gang members. Systematic behavior inventories confirmed these observations. Assuming responsibility for domestic chores and participation in adult-organized sports activities were positively correlated with delinquent activities among members of black gangs, for example, whereas these activities were more clearly differentiated among members of the white gangs studied. An extensive and rich literature on lower-class black community life supports this conclusion, among adults as well as children.[29] Delinquent behavior in lower-class black communities, compared with lower-class white communities, was more a part of a total life pattern in which delinquency was not as likely to create disjunctures with other types of behavior.

Differences in lifestyles between white and black communities were economic as well as ethnic, historical as well as current. Community life in the white and black communities differed for both youth and adults. In most of the white areas, neighborhood taverns—often with a distinct ethnic clientele—were the exclusive domain of adults. At times these became the focus of tensions between adolescents and adults.

Life in the white areas revolved around conventional institutions such as the Catholic church and local political and "improvement" associations (a euphemism, in some instances, for an agreement to keep blacks from moving into their neighborhoods). Ethnic organizations and extended kinship groups, unions and other job relationships, and formally organized recreational patterns (e.g., bowling leagues) were important sources of community stability for both adults and young people. Similarities between these communities and Parsons Park (discussed previously) are striking.

Life in the lower-class black communities was characterized by informal neighborhood gathering from the vantage of front door steps or stair landings, neighborhood taverns and pool halls, and other quasi-public settings and institutions. The following description of incidents occurring in one of these institutions—a "quarter party"—is illustrative. The incident involved the Rattlers, a gang of tough black youngsters with a well-deserved reputation for gang fighting and strong-arming persons who came into the commercial area adjacent to their territory for legitimate or illegitimate purposes (seeking prostitutes, or patronizing the numbers racket).

"Quarter parties" did not follow any single format, but there were common objectives in all such gatherings. An adult would host the party in his or her (usually her) home for other adults, or teens, or both. The objective of the host was to make money. (Some such gatherings were called "rent parties.") There might be an entrance charge of a quarter, and refreshments were sold—most commonly at a quarter per drink. The objective of guests at such a party was, of course, to have fun, but the type of fun varied for different classes of party goers. The following gang worker's report is illustrative (adapted from Short and Strodtbeck, pp. 110–111):

> This woman who is called "Ma" was giving the party. She gives these parties. Charges 25 cents. There was a lot of drinking—inside, outside, in the cars, in the alleys, everywhere. There were Rattlers and a bunch of boys from the [housing] projects. They had two rooms, neither of them very large. There was some friction going on when I got there—boys bumping each other, and stuff like this.
>
> There were a lot of girls there. Must have been about 50 to 75 people in these two rooms, plus another 20 or 25 outside. There were some older fellows there, too—mainly to try and grab one of these younger girls.
>
> The girls were doing a lot of drinking—young girls, 12- and 13-year olds. This one girl, shortly after I got there, had passed out. I took her home. Nobody there, but two of the other girls stayed with her.
>
> The age group in this party amazed me—must have been from about 11 to the 30's. There were girls there as young as 11, but no boys younger than about 15. The girls are there as a sex attraction, and with the older boys and men around, you know the younger boys aren't going to do any good.
>
> We had one real fight. One of David's sisters was talking to one of these boys from the projects—a good-sized boy, bigger than me. I guess she promised to go out to the car with him—this is my understanding. Anyhow they went outside. To get outside you had to go out this door and down this hall, and then out on the porch and down the stairs. She went as far as the porch.

As she got out there, I guess she changed her mind. By this time the guy wasn't standing for any "changing the mind" business, and he started to pull on her—to try and get her in the car. She yelled for David, and he came running out. All he could see was his sister and a guy he didn't know was pulling on her. David plowed right into the guy. I guess he hit him about 15 times and knocked him down and across the street, and by the time I got there the guy was lying in the gutter. David was just about to level a foot at him. I yelled at David to stop and he did. I took him off to the side and told Gary to get the guy out of there.

(The worker walked down the street with David, trying to cool him down. What happened next very nearly precipitated a gang fight.) Duke, Red, and Mac were standing eight or ten feet away, sort of watching these project boys. This one boy goes up the street on the other side and comes up *behind* David and me. We don't see him. All of a sudden Duke runs right past me. I was wondering what's going on and he plows into this guy—crashed the side of his mouth and the guy fell flat. Duke was about to really work the guy over when I stopped him.

Duke said, "Well look, man, the guy was sneaking up behind you and I wasn't gonna have him hit you from behind! I did it to protect you."

I got the guy up and he said, "I wasn't going to hit you—I just wanted to see what was going on," and this bit.

By now Duke says, "Well, the heck with it. Let's run all these project guys out."

They banded together and were ready to move, but I said, "Look, don't you think you've done enough? The police aren't here yet, but if you start anything else they'll be here. Somebody is bound to call them. The party is still going on so why don't we all just go back inside. No sense in breaking up a good thing—you paid your quarter."

White gang boys often found themselves openly at odds with proprietors of local hangouts and other adults and adult institutions, particularly concerning drinking (which was virtually universal in this group), drug use (which was rare among these boys), sexual delinquency, and general rowdyism. Stealing was tacitly condoned by adult "fences" and other purchasers of stolen goods, so long as local residents were not victimized. In communities undergoing racial transition (during the period of study this included nearly all lower-class white communities in Chicago), the rowdyism was at times turned to advantage by adults and encouraged. An apposite case is an incident that occurred shortly after midnight on a late summer night. The scene was typical of gatherings of boys and girls at "their" park in a neighborhood that was unsuccessfully resisting invasion by black families. Again, a gang worker's report provides the data (adapted from pp. 112–114):

At approximately 12:30 at night, I was hanging with a group of teenage kids at the corner of the park, which is immediately across the street from the Catholic church. The group was a mixed one of boys and girls ranging in age from 16 to 20. There were approximately 15–20 teenagers, and, for the most part, they were sitting or reclining in the park, talking, drinking beer, or wrestling with the girls. I had parked my car adjacent to where the group was gathered and was leaning on the fender, talking to two boys about the remainder of the softball season. The group consisted of members of the Amboys, Bengals, Sharks, and a few Mafia. They were not unusually loud or boisterous this particular hot and humid evening because a policeman on a three-wheeler had been by a half hour earlier and had warned them of the lateness of the hour.

While I was talking to two of the Amboys, I noticed a solitary teenage figure ambling along on the sidewalk heading toward the Avenue. I paid no particular heed, thinking it was just another teenager walking over to join the park group. However, as the figure neared the group, he made no effort to swerve over and join the group but continued by with no sign of recognition. This was an oddity, so I watched the youth as he passed the gathered teenagers and neared the curb where I was sitting. At this point, I suddenly realized that the boy was black, and in danger if detected. I did not dare do or say anything for fear of alerting the kids in the park, and for a few minutes I thought the black youth could pass by without detection. However, Butch, a Bengal who had been drinking beer, spotted the youth and immediately asked some of the other teenagers, "Am I drunk or is that a Nigger on the corner?" The attention of the entire group was then focused on the black youth, who by this time had stepped off the curb and was walking in the center of the street toward the opposite curb. The youth was oblivious to everything and was just strolling along as if without a care in the world.

Behind him, however, consternation and anger arose spontaneously like a mushroom cloud after an atomic explosion. I heard muttered threats of "Let's kill the bastard," "Get the mother-fucker," "Come on, let's get going." Even the girls in the crowd readily and verbally agreed.

Within seconds, about a dozen of the kids began running in the direction of the black youth. Realizing that I was unable to stem the tide, I yelled out to the black youth something to the effect of "Hey man, look alive." The boy heard me as he paused in mid-stride, but did not turn around. Again I found it necessary to shout a warning as the white teenagers were rapidly overtaking him. At my second outcry, the black youth turned around and saw the white kids closing in on him. Without hesitation, he took off at full speed with the white mob at his heels yelling shouts of "Kill the bastard—don't let him get away."

I remained standing by my car and was joined by three Amboys who did not participate in the chase. The president of the Amboys sadly shook his head, stating that his guys reacted like a bunch of kids whenever they saw a colored guy, and openly expressed his wish that the boy would get away. Another Amboy in an alibi tone of voice, excused his nonparticipation in the chase by explaining that he couldn't run fast enough to catch anybody. Harry merely stated that the black kid didn't bother him, so why should he be tossed in jail for the assault of a stranger.

As we stood by the car, we could hear the actual progress of the chase from the next block. There were shouts and outcries as the pursued ran down the street and his whereabouts were echoed by the bedlam created by his pursuers. Finally, there was silence and we waited for approximately fifteen minutes before the guys began to straggle back from the chase. As they returned to my car and to the girls sitting nearby, each recited his share of the chase. Barney laughingly related that Guy had hurdled a parked car in an effort to tackle the kid, who had swerved out into the street. He said that he himself had entered a coal yard, looking around in an effort to find where the boy had hidden, when an adult from a second floor back porch warned that he had better get out of there as the coal yard was protected by a large and vicious Great Dane.

The black youth apparently had decided that he couldn't outrun his tormentors and had begun to go in and out of back yards until he was able to find a hiding place, at which point he disappeared. His pursuers then began to make a systematic search of the alleys, garages, back yards, corridors, etc. *The boys were spurred on to greater efforts by the adults of the area who offered advice and encouragement.* One youth laughingly related that a woman, from her bedroom window, kept pointing out probable hiding places in her back yard so that he would not overlook any sanctuary. This advice included looking behind tall shrubbery by the fence, on top of a tool crib by the alley, and underneath the back porch. Other youths related similar experiences as the adults along the Avenue entered gleefully in the "hide-and-seek." Glen related that as the youths turned onto X street, he began to shout to the people ahead in the block that "a Nigger was coming" so that someone ahead might catch or at least head off the boy. The other pursuers also took up the hue and cry, which accounted for all the loud noises I had heard.

CONCLUSION

This chapter presents "social facts" regarding delinquency in institutional relationships and more holistic and naturalistic analyses of delinquency in a variety of community contexts. Both are necessary for understanding, the former for their objectivity and generalizability, the latter for the insights they provide into the subjective meaning and interpretation of apparently similar conditions and life circumstances. Individuals, groups, institutions, and communities experience life in different ways, as both objective and subjective data demonstrate.

We shall have more to say about the social settings for delinquent behavior as we pursue the elusive goal of explanation. Family and peer relationships in particular will be emphasized for their influence on individual and group behaviors. Situational influences will be examined for their relevance in making choices among behavior alternatives. Larger social forces, such as those that produce the ecological variations noted in this chapter, will be analyzed for their special relevance. Before doing so, however, we must discuss more specifically what it is that we wish to explain. Given the long history of delinquency, that is no simple task.

NOTES

1. John W. Meyer, David Tyack, Joane Nagel, and Audri Gordon, "Education as nation-building in America: enrollments and bureaucratization in the American states, 1870–1930," *American Journal of Sociology,* 85 (November, 1979): 591–613; see also, David B. Tyack, *The One Best System: A History of American Urban Education.* Cambridge, MA: Harvard University Press, 1974; and Morris Janowitz, *The Rediscovery of Patriotism: Education for Civic Consciousness.* Chicago: University of Chicago Press, 1983.

2. See, for example, Joan Newman and Graeme Newman, "Crime and punishment in the schooling process: a historical analysis," in Keith Baker and Robert J. Rubel (eds.), *Violence and Crime in the Schools.* Lexington, MA:D.C. Heath, 1980.

3. Cf. Charles Silberman, *Crisis in the Classroom.* NY:Random House, 1970; Craig Haney and Philip G. Zimbardo, "The blackboard penitentiary—it's tough to tell a high school from a prison," *Psychology Today,* 9 (June 1975):16–20; Jackson Toby, "Schools and crime: policy

issues," in James Q. Wilson (ed.), *Crime and Public Policy*. San Francisco: Institute for Contemporary Studies, 1983.

4. See Robert M. Emerson, *Judging Delinquents: Context and Process in Juvenile Court*. Chicago: Aldine, 1969, p. 39. In many *rural* school districts schools were, in fact, the primary institutions for maintaining community order. In the small town in Illinois in which I "grew up" (population about 600) there was no police force. A single, part-time sheriff was the symbol of official authority, but he rarely had anything to do. So unimpressive was he that he often was the butt of youthful pranks and jokes, among adults as well as young people. The town jail had a single cell which served chiefly as a way station for occasional transients who had no place to sleep at night. My father served for many years as high-school principal, and later superintendent of schools in the "township" school district. School security and disciplinary problems almost never extended beyond school authorities, which usually meant my father. He "ran a tight ship" with respect to discipline, with no truant officers, counselors, or disciplinary committees, and without resort to corporal punishment.

5. Emerson, *Ibid.*, p. 53.

6. U.S. Department of Health, Education, and Welfare, *Violent Schools—Safe Schools: The State School Study Report to the Congress*. Washington, DC: National Institute of Education, 1978. The following report of this study is based largely on Jackson Toby, "Crime in American public schools," *Public Interest*, 58 (Winter 1980):18–42; and Jackson Toby, "Schools and crime: policy issues", *op. cit.*

7. Toby, "Crime in American public schools," *Ibid.*, p. 20.

8. Francis A. J. Iani, director of the field studies, quoted by Toby, "Crime in American public schools," *op. cit.*, pp. 23–24.

9. Data from the most rigorous of these studies are summarized in Alfred Blumstein, Jacqueline Cohen, Jeffrey A. Roth, and Christy A. Visher (eds.), *Criminal Careers and "Career Criminals,"* Vol. 1. Panel on Research on Criminal Careers, Committee on Research on Law Enforcement and the Administration of Justice, Commission on Behavioral and Social Sciences and Education, National Research Council. Washington, DC: National Academy Press, 1986, pp. 282–286.

10. For a more detailed summary of studies on this topic see Terrence P. Thornberry, Melanie Moore, and R. L. Christenson, "The effect of dropping out of high school on subsequent criminal behavior," *Criminology*, 23 (February, 1985):3–18.

11. See Delbert S. Elliott and Harwin Voss, *Delinquency and Dropout*. Lexington, MA: Lexington, 1974. No such dampening effect on *arrests* was found in a Philadelphia cohort study which reports that dropping out of school was related to higher rates of arrest through the early years of adulthood, regardless of race, socioeonomic status, employment, or marital status. See Thornberry, et al., *op. cit.* The relationship between dropping out of school, employment, and delinquency is extraordinarily complex. Farrington, et al. note that the peak age of offending in England and Wales occurs consistently during the last year at school for most young people. This has been true since World War II even though the minimum school leaving age has changed, first from 14 to 15, and later to 16. The Cambridge Study in Delinquent Development, a longitudinal survey of more than 400 "overwhelmingly white, urban, working-class" males living in London when the study began, finds unemployment consistently related to higher rates of offending. However, "leaving school and obtaining a full-time job had a negligible effect on crime rates." See David P. Farrington, Bernard Gallagher, Lynda Morley, Raymond J. St. Ledger, and Donald F. West, p. 351, in "Unemployment, school leaving, and crime," *British Journal of Criminology*, 26 (October, 1986):335–356.

12. Toby, *op. cit.*, p. 21. Many *teachers* in large inner cities also reported being afraid of their students. *School buildings* are also extensively victimized. Based on principals' reports, the national survey estimated that the annual cost of replacing broken windows and other damaged or stolen school property was approximately $200 million.

13. At the 1984 meetings of the American Society of Criminology, a session on school crime and its control featured speakers who detailed such procedures. The speakers conveyed the distinct impression that many inner-city schools were by necessity becoming fortresses.

14. John Meyer, Chris Chase-Dunn, and James Inverarity, *The Expansion of the Autonomy of Youth: Responses of the Secondary Schools to Problems of Order in the 1960s.* Technical Report No. 41, Laboratory for Social Research, Department of Sociology, Stanford University, Stanford, CA, August, 1971. The quotation is from p. 7.

15. *Ibid.*, p. 8.

16. *Ibid.*, p. 10.

17. See James F. Short, Jr., *The Social Fabric of the Metropolis.* Chicago: University of Chicago Press, 1971. Human ecology is also interested in more general relationships between social systems and the environment. See Amos H. Hawley, "Human ecology: persistence and change," pp. 119–140, in James F. Short, Jr. (ed.), *The State of Sociology: Problems and Prospects.* Beverly Hills, CA: Sage, 1981.

18. Clifford R. Shaw, Frederick M. Zorbaugh, Henry D. McKay, and Leonard S. Cottrell, *Delinquency Areas.* Chicago: University of Chicago Press, 1929. See also, Clifford R. Shaw and Henry D. McKay, *Juvenile Delinquency and Urban Areas.* Chicago: University of Chicago Press, 1942 (rev. ed., 1969). Frederic M. Thrasher had earlier documented the concentration of juvenile gangs in these same areas. See Frederic M. Thrasher, *The Gang.* Chicago: University of Chicago Press, 1927. More recent ecological studies are discussed in Albert J. Reiss, Jr. and Michael Tonry (eds.), *Communities and Crime,* Vol. 8 of *Crime and Justice.* Chicago: University of Chicago Press, 1986.

19. Ernest W. Burgess, "The growth of the city: an introduction to a research project," pp. 47–62, in Robert E. Park, et al. (eds.), *The City.* Chicago: University of Chicago Press, 1925.

20. See Albert Hunter, *Symbolic Communities.* Chicago: University of Chicago Press, 1975.

21. See Karen Wilkinson, "The broken family and juvenile delinquency: scientific explanation or ideology," *Social Problems,* 21 (June, 1974):726–739.

22. Many of these studies are summarized and interpreted in Joan McCord, "Family relationships and crime," pp. 759–764, in S. H. Kadish (ed.), *Encyclopedia of Crime and Justice.* New York: Free Press, 1983. See also, Jackson Toby, "The differential impact of family disorganization," *American Sociological Review,* 22 (1957):505–512; Thomas P. Monahan, "Family status and the delinquent child: a reappraisal and some new findings," *Social Forces,* 35 (1957):250–258; F. Ivan Nye, *Family Relationships and Delinquent Behavior.* New York: Wiley, 1958; William McCord, Joan McCord, and Irving Zola, *Origins of Crime.* New York: Columbia University Press, 1959; Martin Gold, *Delinquent Behavior in an American City.* Monterey, CA:Brooks/Cole, 1970; Roland J. Chilton and Gerald E. Markle, "Family disruption, delinquent conduct and the effect of subclassification," *American Sociological Review,* 37 (February, 1972):93–99.

23. See Joseph P. Fitzpatrick, "The role of religion in programs for the prevention and correction of crime and delinquency," pp. 317–330, in *Task Force on Juvenile Delinquency,* President's Commission on Law Enforcement and Administration of Justice, Juvenile Delinquency and Youth Crime. Washington, DC: U.S. Government Printing Office, 1967. See also, Travis Hirschi and Rodney Stark, "Hellfire and delinquency," *Social Problems,* 17 (Fall, 1969):202–213; Steven R. Burkett and Mervin White, "Hellfire and delinquency: another look," *Journal for the Scientific Study of Religion,* 13 (December, 1974):455–462; Gary F. Jensen and Maynard L. Erickson, "The religion factor and delinquency: another look at the hellfire hypothesis," in Robert Wuthnow (ed.), *The Religious Dimension: New Directions in Quantitative Research.* New York: Academic Press, 1979.

24. This section is based on Gary Schwartz, *Beyond Rebellion or Conformity: Youth and Authority in America.* Chicago: University of Chicago Press, 1987.

25. Kai Erikson discusses the "moral boundaries" of communities in *Wayward Puritans.* New York: Wiley, 1966.

26. A more detailed discussion of youth on 32d Street is found in Ruth Horowitz, *Honor and the American Dream.* New Brunswick, NJ: Rutgers University Press, 1983.

27. This section is based on James F. Short, Jr. and Fred L. Strodtbeck, *Group Process and Gang Delinquency.* Chicago: University of Chicago Press, 1965.

28. See S. M. Miller, "The American lower class: a typological approach," *Social Research* (Spring, 1964). Reprinted in the Syracuse University Youth Development Reprint Series, pp. 1–22. Our use of the term *unstable poor* to describe the families and communities of the

black gang boys we studied refers to the instability of circumstances in their lives. It is not evaluative. For discussion of the relationship between unemployment, family disruption, and violence among urban blacks, see Robert J. Sampson, "Urban black violence: the effect of male joblessness and family disruption," *American Journal of Sociology* Vol. 93, No. 2, pp. 348–82 (1987); See, also, Valentine, *op. cit.*

29. See, for example, St. Clair Drake and Horace R. Cayton, *Black Metropolis: A Study of Negro Life in a Northern City.* New York: Harper and Row, 1962; Ulf Hannerz, *Soulside: Inquiries into Ghetto Culture and Community.* New York: Columbia University Press, 1969; Bettylou Valentine, *Hustling and Other Hard Work: Life Styles in the Ghetto.* New York: Free Press, 1978; Elijah Anderson, *A Place on the Corner.* Chicago: University of Chicago Press, 1978. cf., Jay MacLeod, *Ain't No Makin' It: Leveled Aspirations in a Low-income Neighborhood.* Boulder, CO: Westview Press, 1987.

CHAPTER 6
THE SOCIAL DISTRIBUTION OF DELINQUENT BEHAVIOR: PROBLEMS OF MEASUREMENT AND INTERPRETATION

INTRODUCTION

This chapter has a dual focus: first, on the types of behavior that bring juveniles to the attention of police and courts; second, on the manner in which such behavior is distributed among social categories. We are interested in the "categoric risks" of becoming delinquent; that is, the risk or probability that persons in different social categories (based on age, gender, race, ethnicity, and certain other social characteristics) will become delinquents.

The first concern is behavioral. Unlike previous chapters, the primary focus is on the behavior of young people, although we will be looking also at how officials classify that behavior. The second concern is with the distribution of behaviors among various categories of young people, depending upon their age, gender, race or ethnicity, and social class. The emphasis will be on measuring rates of occurrence of behaviors among these categories. Categoric risks refer to *rates of involvement* in delinquent behaviors by *categories* of persons (and *rates of responses* by social control institutions).

Both concerns are primarily *descriptive*, rather than explanatory, and they are inevitably linked to each other and to the settings and patterns of interaction discussed in previous chapters. Information concerning the extent of juvenile involvement in delinquency and the responses of control agents and agencies is relevant to causal processes, but neither type of information *explains* the linkage. Categoric risks result not only from the behavior of juveniles, but from countless decisions by others, as well, including the police, judges, school officials, ordinary citizens, and parents. They represent "facts theories must fit" in order to explain how and why juvenile behavior becomes juvenile delinquency and juveniles become delinquents. They are relevant, as well, to the efficacy of control strategies and the future of juvenile delinquency as a social problem.

Identification of delinquent acts and youngsters is clearly not simply a matter of locating names and descriptors of behavior and characteristics of perpetrators in police and court files, or on institutional rosters, or elsewhere in the community. Strengths and limitations of official sources of information were discussed briefly in Chapter 1. Here we review, equally briefly, the two primary nonofficial methods that have been used both to identify delinquents and to measure delinquency: self-reports and victim reports.

Self-Reported Delinquency Studies. Some *self-reported* delinquency (SRD) studies have focused on the proportion of respondents who have engaged in delinquent acts, inquiring, for example, "Have you ever stolen something?" or "Have you stolen something since you were ten years old?" These data provide information on the extent of *participation* among members of a social category or an entire population. Other studies ask about the *frequency* of respondents' involvement in delinquent acts over a specified period, for example, *within the past year* or some other time-bounded period. Studies that have no time bounds, or very long ones, are less useful for research purposes because of problems of recall.

The most comprehensive and representative study of participation in SRD behavior in the United States is the National Youth Survey (NYS), conducted by Delbert Elliott and his colleagues. The NYS is a longitudinal *panel* study of a carefully drawn sample (N = 1,725) of the 11 to 17 year old population (as of 1976). Respondents were first interviewed between January and March, 1977, concerning their behavior during the previous calendar year, and they were interviewed again during this three month period in five successive years. A seventh round of interviews was conducted in 1987.

This chapter focuses on the first five years of the study, during which the panel age ranged from 11 to 17, in 1976, to 15 to 21, in 1980. The NYS researchers paid particular attention to problems of SRD reliability ("the extent to which a measure contains…errors which vary from person to person on a single survey, or from survey to survey for a given person assuming that no real change has occurred between surveys") and validity ("the degree to which a measure actually describes what it is intended to describe").[1]

Victimization Studies. Large scale *victimization* studies began in the mid-1960s under sponsorship of the President's Commission on Law Enforcement and Administration of Justice. These studies were later continued in the form of the National Crime Survey (NCS), with the cooperation of the United States Bureau of the Census, during the 1970s.[2] No SRD studies on such a large scale have been conducted. SRD studies also have tended to be less consistent and rigorous in approach than have victimization studies.

The first NCS was conducted in 1973. Respondents were chosen by means of a carefully drawn sample of households and businesses—about 65,000 households (representing 130,000 individuals) and 15,000 businesses. The method of study was face-to-face interview. In contrast, SRDs typically have been conducted within school settings, and have rarely included more than a few hundred respondents. A few nationwide studies are now available, and one statewide study. The largest of these—conducted in Illinois— included more than 3,100 respondents.

LIMITATIONS AND ADVANTAGES OF ALTERNATIVE METHODS

The major strength of SRD and victimization studies is that the information gathered has not been filtered through the processes discussed in previous chapters. It is not always clear, however, that the behaviors reported by individuals when they are surveyed—their own behavior or their victimization—are criminal or delinquent, *by legal standards*. The NYS and Hindelang (et al.) projects attempt to overcome this problem by rigorous matching of legal and behavioral categories, and by studying large numbers of behaviors of interest to investigators.

Both self-reports and reports of victimization are subject to problems of recall, or "memory decay." The NYS attempts to overcome this problem by limiting inquiries to behavior engaged in over a one-year period and by detailed questioning of some respondents to ascertain the validity of reports of their most recent delinquent behaviors. A tendency to "telescope" events into the time periods studied has also been noted. When asked to recall events (such as victimizations) that occurred within the past year or six months, there is a tendency to reach back in memory beyond the six months or year specified, and to report events which happened somewhat earlier. This may account for inconsistencies between reports of behavior over shorter and longer periods, for example, over the past month as compared to the past year.

While improvements in SRD methodology encourage confidence in their reliability and validity, detailed probing of answers to questions related to behavior often reveals inconsistencies in response. Some of these reflect efforts to conceal the truth, whereas others hinge on differing interpretations of questions.[3] Because investigators go to great lengths to solve these and other problems, data from all three sources (official reports, self-reports, and victimization surveys) may be compared with some confidence. At the very least it is clear that people in all walks of life, of all ages, races, and genders, are willing and able—within acceptable or known limits (which therefore can be taken into account)—to report both their involvement in illegal behavior and their victimization, *to the extent they are knowledgeable*.[4]

The conclusion to be derived from consideration of the limitations of data sources is not that one source is more reliable or valid than another; rather that each has advantages and limitations, often for particular purposes. The trick is to capitalize on the advantages in order to overcome the limitations. One way to do this is by using *different methods* to examine the *same relationships*. Convergence of findings builds confidence that they are true. When findings diverge, artifacts of source and method may be helpful in explaining why, and the knowledge gained thereby may be helpful in establishing "facts theories must fit."

BEHAVIOR FOR WHICH JUVENILES ARE REFERRED TO JUVENILE COURTS

The National Assessment of Juvenile Corrections found that slightly less than 2.5 percent of the youth population in the United States were referred annually to juvenile courts for delinquency. National Center for Juvenile Justice (NCJJ) reports indicate that the delinquency *case rate* has averaged nearly twice that figure (4.35 percent, or 43.5 per 1,000 children aged 10–17) between 1976 and 1983. This rate has more than doubled since 1957, when it was 19.8 per 1,000.[5] The *number* of delinquency cases disposed of in 1983 was about 1,275,600, *the lowest such number since 1974,* but exceeding the number of cases in 1957 by more than 800,000 cases.

Petitions alleging property offenses constitute the largest single category for referral, composing between 40 percent and 45 percent of all referrals. Status offenses, dominated by curfew, runaway, truancy, and incorrigibility, compose between 20 percent and 25 percent, while referrals for violent crimes and drug or alcohol offenses each account for about 10 percent. Courts in the largest cities tend to report higher percentages of criminal offenses, and lower percentages of status offenses, than do courts in smaller jurisdictions.

Juvenile courts also receive cases of child dependency, abuse, and neglect. The number of case dispositions in these categories handled by courts of juvenile jurisdiction in 1983 was 196,200 (3.07 per 1,000 children under 18 years of age). This figure was the highest recorded for dependency, abuse, and, neglect over the 1957 to 1983 time period.

AGE AS A CATEGORIC RISK

As juvenile law has continued to evolve, new behaviors have come under court jurisdiction and some have been removed. All the while, except for restrictions concerning the age of criminal responsibility, juveniles also have been subject to the prohibitions of *criminal* law, though sanctions for such behavior often differ for juveniles and adults.

Self-reports of many populations and over a period of more than three decades indicate that participation in some form of delinquent behavior is virtually universal. The NYS found a participation rate of 81 percent in one or more of the 35 delinquency items on a general delinquency measure during the first year of the survey.[6] The delinquency items in this measure ranged in seriousness from "lied about age" and "hitchhiked" to "aggravated assault" and "stole something worth more than $50." The annual rate of participation *in some type of delinquent behavior* was relatively constant between 1976 and 1980.

The probabilities of involvement in delinquent behavior vary considerably by age, as well as by offense. Between 1976 and 1980, as the NYS panel aged, the participation rate for more serious criminal behaviors (UCR *index offenses*) declined from 21 percent to 12 percent.[7] Index offenses in this NYS study included those which best matched the UCR index category, except for homicide. Participation in crimes against persons (which included the UCR index crimes against persons, plus "hit teacher," "hit parent," and "hit student") declined even more strikingly. Participation in acts of general theft (based on the UCR property crimes of motor vehicle theft, stole something worth more than $50, and broke into a building or vehicle, plus "bought stolen goods," "stole something worth $5 to $50," "stole something worth less than $5," and "joyriding") declined only slightly.

In contrast, rates of participation in status offenses (including runaway, "skipped classes," "lied about age," and sexual intercourse) increased substantially with the aging of the panel, from less than 50 percent to more than 60 percent. Smaller increases occurred for public disorder offenses ("hitchhiked," disorderly conduct, public drunkenness, "panhandled," and obscene calls) and illegal services (prostitution, "sold marijuana," and "sold hard drugs"). The greatest increases occurred for sexual intercourse (from 13 percent to 44 percent), public drunkenness (14 percent to 37 percent), and selling marijuana (4 percent to 10 percent), offenses associated with or symbolic of adulthood.

In contrast to participation, *frequency* of offending among the NYS panel increased substantially over the reporting period. The increase in the general delinquency scale was from 36 to 53 offenses per respondent between 1976 and 1980, that is, a 47 percent increase. When the more minor delinquencies were eliminated from this measure, the increase was even more dramatic, from 19 to 32 offenses per respondent, an increase of 68 percent. As was the case with participation, however, frequency of involvement in the more serious (index) offenses *declined* as the panel aged, from a low of 1 per respondent in 1976 to an even lower 0.6 per respondent in 1980. The overall increase in the self-reported frequency of offending was accounted for by the same types of offenses for which participation increased between 1976 and 1980, that is, status, public disorder, and illegal services offenses.

In summary, increases in both participation and frequency of offending occurred for only a few offenses as the panel aged—most dramatically for those associated with adulthood, that is, sexual intercourse and drunkenness. The general pattern observed is one of *countertrends associated with age.* On the one hand, "adult" type delinquent behaviors tend to increase as adulthood is approached. On the other, involvement in serious criminal behavior tends to decrease as adulthood becomes imminent.[8] Serious criminal behavior thus is not tied in any simple or inevitable way to the life cycle. It is not simply the culmination of involvement in previous, less serious, types of delinquent behavior. There is a good deal of overlap in reports of status offenses and criminal behavior.

ARREST RATES

It is difficult to get an accurate picture of arrest rates over the entire country because the necessary data are not available. A reasonable approximation can be obtained by using United States Census Bureau figures as a population base, and by calculating arrest rates on the basis of Uniform Crime Reports, which for many years have received reports from jurisdictions covering more than 90 percent of the total U.S. population.

After eliminating persons below age ten and over 65 (the very low rate age groups at both ends of the age spectrum),[9] the overall *ratio* of arrest rates for persons aged 10–19, compared to those aged 20–64, was 1.60 in 1980. That is, compared to their proportion of the total population, persons aged 10–19 were arrested 1.6 times as often as were persons aged 20–64. For index violent crimes this ratio was 1.48, but for serious property crimes it was 3.77. For non-index offenses, which tend either to be less serious or less likely to be discovered or reported (e.g., statutory rape, other sex offenses, embezzlement, liquor laws, and vagrancy), the ratio of juvenile (aged 10–19) to adult (age 20–64) arrest rates in 1980 stood at .80, *after excluding curfew and runaways which are exclusively juvenile offenses.*

Juveniles thus are overrepresented in arrests for the *more serious* crimes, especially so for more serious property crimes. They are underrepresented (relative to their numbers in the population) in arrests for more-difficult-to-measure offenses, which—with certain exceptions—tend to be less serious. Thus, while *most* juvenile delinquency consists of behavior that is not very serious, juveniles are responsible for a disproportionate amount of serious crime, as measured by arrests. Stated another way, while *greater numbers* of juveniles are arrested for the less serious offenses (even excluding the status offenses on which UCR data are collected), *relative to their proportion of the total population* juveniles are underrepresented for these offenses; conversely, while fewer juveniles are arrested for serious crimes, they are overrepresented in arrests for these crimes.

Most juveniles arrested for violating the liquor laws, for disorderly conduct, for offenses against family, for vagrancy, and for suspicion, have been detained in part because of their youth. While seriousness of offense is a major factor leading to official intervention, discretionary behavior often results in *less serious* charges against suspected offenders than might be warranted under the law. We should, therefore, expect to find that "official delinquents" commit a good deal more delinquent behavior than those who are not officially delinquent. Self-reports clearly indicate that this is the case.

COMPARING OFFICIAL DELINQUENTS WITH OFFICIALLY NONDELINQUENT YOUTH

An early study conducted in three small city public high schools and in state training schools found that higher proportions of the training school boys and girls admitted committing *all of the offenses* studied, and to committing them more frequently.[10] Differences between the incarcerated training school youngsters and public school youngsters were especially great for the more serious status offenses (running away and school probation or expulsion) and criminal (stealing expensive items and narcotics use) offenses.

These findings have been confirmed many times by other investigators, on different populations, at different times, and using somewhat different methods. Maynard Erickson and LaMar Empey, for example, found dramatic differences in the self-reported delinquency of four samples of boys designed to represent gradations of delinquency as determined by official actions.[11] Similar findings have been reported in other studies conducted in the United States and in Sweden, Norway, and England. *The relationship between the frequency and seriousness of delinquent behavior and being officially defined as delinquent thus is positive, strong, and broadly generalizable.*[12] The "risk" that a child will become "officially" delinquent clearly is higher for those youngsters who, by their own admission, more frequently engage in behaviors defined as delinquent. This conclusion is all the more impressive in view of evidence that youngsters who have police records are less likely than those without such records to participate in self-report surveys.[13]

AGE OF MAXIMUM CRIMINAL INVOLVEMENT

SRD studies are virtually useless for comparing youth versus adult involvement in crime in the general population, since representative samples of adults have not been studied using these methods. UCR arrest data and a detailed study of an entire cohort of males in Philadelphia are in agreement, however, that *arrests for both status offenses and most criminal offenses tends to peak in the later adolescent years, and to decline thereafter.*[14]

The pattern is dramatically illustrated for robbery, burglary, and aggravated assault in Figure 6.1.[15] Arrest rates for all three of these offenses rise very rapidly during the early adolescent years, followed by rapid decreases. The decline is less rapid for the two violence-related offenses (robbery, which involves at least the threat of violence, and aggravated assault). By age 21 the arrest rate for burglary has declined to 50 percent of its peak. Not until age 24 does the rate of arrests for robbery reach this level, and for aggravated assault the 50 percent level is reached only at age 36.

GENDER AS A CATEGORIC RISK

While virtually all children engage in behavior that might bring them to the attention of legal authorities, all sources of data agree that there is much variation in the distribution of such behavior by social categories. Among the categoric risks of *participation in crime,* gender is the most consistently differentiating. Higher proportions of males than females commit most delinquent behaviors, and gender differences are greater for serious crimes than they are for less serious behaviors. There is, however, much variation in gender ratios of crime and delinquency.[16]

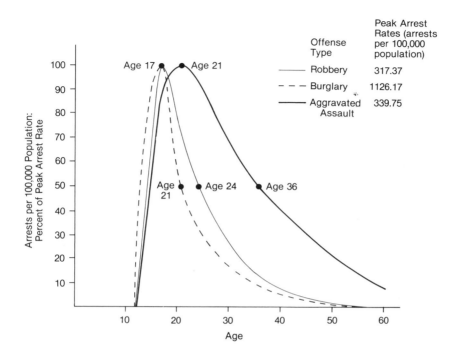

FIGURE 6.1   1983 U.S. age-specific arrest rates (arrests per 100,000 population of each age). The curve for each offense type is displayed as a percentage of the peak arrest rate. The curves show the age at which the peak occurs (at 100 percent) and the age at which the rate falls to 50 percent of the peak rate.   SOURCE: Alfred Blumstein, Jacqueline Cohen, Jeffrey A. Roth, and Christy A. Visher (eds.), " Criminal Careers and Career Criminals," 1986. Reprinted with permission from National Academy Press, Washington, DC.

In traditional societies, such as pre–World War II Algeria, Tunis, Ceylon, and Japan, gender ratios for court referrals were typically very high—3,000 to 4,000 males for each female referred to the courts. They are much lower in "modern" societies, where gender *roles* are less differentiated and where females, like males, are more involved in a wider range of activities, both as children and as adults. The basic principle can be generalized: As gender roles become less differentiated, gender ratios in crime and delinquency decline.

JUVENILE COURT DATA

Gender ratios of youngsters appearing in U.S. juvenile courts earlier in history, when gender roles were more sharply differentiated in this country, also were high relative to more recent ratios. According to the National

Assessment study the mean rate of referral of young male offenders to the courts surveyed was 41.9 per 1,000, compared to a rate of 7.5 females per 1,000 females, a ratio of 5.59.[17] There was, however, much variation in these rates, especially among courts in smaller cities. Gender ratios were higher in smaller jurisdictions.

NCJJ data indicate that 81 percent of the delinquency cases handled by juvenile courts were male during the early years of the 1957–1983 series, but that percentage declined slightly after 1965, reaching a low of 74 percent. The *number* of female delinquency cases increased more rapidly (by 260 percent) than did the number of male cases (174 percent) between 1957 and 1983. Slightly more female than male cases of dependency and neglect were handled by juvenile courts.

SELF-REPORT GENDER RATIOS

Gender ratios tend to be higher the further one moves into the justice system; that is, from first contact with the system (usually the police), through the juvenile court, to incarceration. Conversely, gender ratios are lower for measures that are closer to the behavior being measured. SRDs (the closest to actual behavior of all data sources) consistently find lower gender ratios than do official data, suggesting that boys and girls are not so different in behavior as the official data indicate.

Hindelang and his associates' analysis of SRD studies confirms higher gender ratios (that is, proportionately more males than females) for more serious than for less serious offenses. For example, as the value of goods stolen increases, so does the gender ratio for stealing, and ratios tend to be higher for violent offenses than for stealing, except for the most serious of stealing offenses. Gender ratios also are consistently low for status offenses.[18] The NYS reports that for several status offenses, and a few crimes, participation of males and females was very similar. This was the case for such offenses as lying about age, cheating on school tests, skipping classes, hitting a parent, making obscene calls, panhandling, using a credit card fraudulently, and writing bad checks.

The relationship between gender and delinquency thus is complex. In general, when measured by self-reports, gender ratios for frequency tend to be higher than are participation ratios. About three males to every two females reported *some* involvement in the behaviors measured by the NYS each year. This figure for frequency ranged from three to two to about three to one. As the NYS panel matured, gender differences for serious and violent offenses tended to peak when the age range of the panel was 12–18 or 13–19, after which gender differences declined. For less serious offenses gender differences were either constant or increasing monotonically each year. Male and female frequency rates for most theft offenses appeared to be converging over time, while differences in participation were becoming more pronounced.[19] As the panel aged, more males than females were participating in theft, but *among* those participating the frequency of theft by males and females was growing closer.

GENDER RATIOS OF ARRESTS

Arrest data confirm substantial gender differences in serious involvement in delinquent behavior. Data from the 1985 Uniform Crime Reports are presented in Table 6.1.

Note that, with the exception of larceny-theft—a large component of which consists of shoplifting—the *male percentage* is higher for the more serious Class I offenses than it is for the less serious offenses. Except for such "traditional" female offenses as prostitution and running away from home, males also predominate in arrests for the less serious offenses. Note also, that gender ratios are higher for serious violent crimes than they are for serious property crimes (8.1 as compared to 3.9 in Table 6.1). Both these ratios have declined in recent decades. In 1960, the average gender ratio for serious violent crimes was 14.2, in 1970 it was 9.8, and in 1980 it was 8.7. For serious property crimes these averages were in 1960 10.0, in 1970 4.8, and in 1980 4.4.

Other research demonstrates that the decline in gender ratios for most crimes has been especially pronounced *for persons under the age of 18.* That is, arrests of young females—compared to young males—have experienced greater increases than is the case for gender comparisons of older persons, and they have been greater for serious property crimes than for violent crimes.[20]

Detailed analyses of gender-specific rates of arrests for persons under age 18 suggest that adolescent females continue to be arrested primarily for traditional female offenses (running away and larceny-theft, mostly in the form of shoplifting).[21] *Young* females have accounted for a higher proportion of all arrests of females than young boys have of all arrests of males in recent years (about one-third compared to a quarter or less).[22] For more serious offenses, however, boys and girls are remarkably alike, each accounting for about 40 percent of all arrests for their respective genders–about two and one-half times their proportion in the population.

PATTERNING OF DELINQUENT BEHAVIOR AMONG MALES AND FEMALES

Gary Hill and Anthony Harris demonstrate that there is greater similarity in the *patterning* of arrests for UCR offenses among younger males and females (aged 17 and under) than among those who are older.[23] While this suggests greater gender similarity in criminal behavior among adolescents than among adults, arrest rates are limited in what they can tell us about such matters. As routinely collected, they provide no information on how different behaviors relate to one another.

Patricia Miller's analysis of SRD participation data is important in this respect. By factor-analyzing Illinois data separately for males and females, Miller found a remarkable degree of similarity in the manner in which self-reported participation in delinquent behaviors *clustered.*[24] Drug use offenses clustered together for both boys and girls, as did status offenses, personal violence offenses, minor and more serious criminal property offenses, and car-related offenses. The picture that emerged from her analysis

TABLE 6.1 Total Arrests, 1985, by Age and Gender

OFFENSE CHARGED	TOTAL NUMBER OF PERSONS ARRESTED—1985	MALES UNDER 18		FEMALES UNDER 18		SEX RATIO
		1985	PERCENT	1985	PERCENT	
TOTAL	10,289,609	1,368,035	13.3	394,504	3.8	3.5
Murder and nonnegligent manslaughter	15,777	1,189	7.6	122	7.8	9.8
Forcible rape	31,934	4,733	14.9	97	3.0	48.8
Robbery	120,501	28,108	23.3	2,046	1.7	13.8
Aggravated assault	263,120	30,635	11.7	5,622	2.1	5.4
Burglary	381,875	134,742	35.2	10,512	2.8	12.9
Larceny—theft	1,179,066	281,204	23.9	105,013	9.0	2.7
Motor vehicle theft	115,621	39,014	33.8	4,932	4.2	8.0
Arson	16,777	6,248	37.2	658	4.0	9.4
Violent crime[1]	431,332	64,665	15.0	7,887	1.9	8.1
Property crime[2]	1,693,339	461,208	27.2	121,115	7.1	3.9
Crime Index total[3]	2,124,671	525,873	24.8	129,002	6.0	4.0
Other assaults	550,104	64,157	11.7	19,254	3.6	3.3
Forgery and counterfeiting	75,281	5,363	7.1	2,458	3.2	2.1
Fraud	286,941	13,732	4.8	4,048	1.4	3.3
Embezzlement	9,799	480	4.9	216	2.2	2.2
Stolen property; buying, receiving, possessing	110,415	25,072	22.8	2,619	2.3	9.6
Vandalism	224,046	91,833	41.0	8,520	3.9	10.8
Weapons; carrying, possessing, etc.	157,304	24,107	15.3	1,756	1.1	13.8
Prostitution and commercialized vice	101,167	732	7.2	1,715	1.7	2.3
Sex offenses (except forcible rape and prostitution)	86,861	13,630	15.7	1,206	1.3	11.3

TABLE 6.1 Total Arrests, 1985, by Age and Gender (cont.)

OFFENSE CHARGED	TOTAL NUMBER OF PERSONS ARRESTED—1985	MALES UNDER 18		FEMALES UNDER 18		SEX RATIO
		1985	PERCENT	1985	PERCENT	
Drug abuse violations	702,882	68,493	9.8	11,898	1.7	5.8
Gambling	28,034	717	2.6	37	1.3	19.3
Offenses against family and children	48,699	1,545	3.1	855	1.8	1.8
Driving under the influence	1,503,319	17,737	1.1	2,697	1.8	6.6
Liquor laws	467,149	86,170	18.4	31,142	6.7	2.8
Drunkenness	834,652	20,014	2.3	3,874	4.7	5.1
Disorderly conduct	583,532	67,148	11.6	16,055	2.8	4.1
Vagrancy	29,825	2,232	7.8	497	1.7	4.7
All other offenses (except traffic)	2,142,121	223,337	10.4	58,140	2.8	3.9
Suspicion (not included in totals)	11,229	2,017	18.0	583	5.1	3.4
Curfew and loitering law violations	71,608	53,948	7.6	17,660	2.4	3.0
Runaways	139,970	59,698	4.2	80,272	5.8	.7

[1]Violent crimes are offenses of murder, forcible rape, robbery, and aggravated assault.

[2]Property crimes are offenses of burglary, larceny-theft, motor vehicle theft, and arson.

[3]Includes arson, a newly established Index offense in 1979.

*Source: U.S. Department of Justice, Federal Bureau of Investigation, Crime in the United States, 1985. Washington, DC: U.S. Government Printing Office, 1986, p. 174–178.

is one of continued—though perhaps declining—*higher participation* in most delinquent behaviors among boys, but *similarity in patterning* of behaviors among boys and girls. That is, boys were more frequently and extensively delinquent than were girls, but boys and girls who participated in delinquent behavior did so in quite similar behavior configurations.

Illinois boys and girls who reported engaging in one of the clusters tended also to participate in one or more of the others. Delinquent behavior tends not to be highly specialized. Those who participate tend to be involved in more than one type of behavior—in status and drug use offenses, for example, and in car-related and property offenses. Delinquent behavior clearly is not random, however, and relationships among offenses inform the nature of the behavior.

The Illinois study found that use of marijuana was closely related to status offenses (driving without a license, use of alcohol, truancy, and sexual intercourse). Participation in status offenses, however, was not closely related to the use or sale of other drugs (psychedelics, heroin, barbiturates, and amphetamines). Conversely, sale of drugs and use of drugs other than marijuana was rare and not closely related to any of the other clusters of offenses. Use of marijuana among most of these youngsters thus appeared to be casual, unrelated to more serious delinquent behaviors. Hard drug use was not significantly related to the amount of criminality committed by these young people. However, "drug use, measured either currently or over time," has been found to distinguish the highest-rate offenders in self-report studies of convicted adult felons.[25]

Miller also found that "strong-arming" offenses clustered with violent offenses as well as with other criminal offenses, and the use of weapons was related to criminal as well as violent offenses, indicating some affinity between these clusters. A less serious cluster of property offenses was related, also, to fist fighting for boys, driving recklessly for girls, and anonymous phone calls for both sexes. These relationships, plus the close relationship of vandalism to less serious property offenses, suggest that for many youngsters these offenses constituted expressive "hell raising" rather than instrumental behavior. For girls, purchasing alcohol was related to both status and car-related offenses, while for boys purchasing alcohol was related only to status offenses. Purchasing alcohol, among boys, thus appeared to be routine adolescent behavior, whereas for girls it was perhaps an indication of participation with boys in car-related offenses as well.[26]

By the late 1970s, 56 percent of U.S. high-school seniors surveyed by the University of Michigan Survey Research Center had used marijuana (compared to about 20 percent of the Illinois boys and girls aged 14–18 that had been studied earlier in that decade).[27] Daily or near daily use of marijuana rose to 11 percent of the high-school seniors studied in 1978. There was speculation that marijuana might become a permanent "recreational drug" among young people. Yet, a decade later, daily use of marijuana had declined to 3.3 percent, and occasional use had dropped as well. Knowledge of the effects of marijuana use grew rapidly during this period and was widely disseminated. In contrast, use of cocaine—the "glamour drug" of earlier years—continued to rise among young people until the late 1980s. The Michigan researchers reported a decrease in "current" cocaine use (use within the past 30 days) between 1986 and 1987; 4.3 percent in 1987 compared to 6.2 percent in 1986. A ten-year follow-up of the class of 1976 found that nearly 40 percent had tried cocaine by that time.

These data suggest the complex and dynamic character of gender relationships and delinquent behavior in general, and of drug offenses in particular. More than most delinquent acts, patterns of drug use are "trendy," reflecting changing historical influences[28] and subject to changes in fashion. Drug use is also influenced by public (and especially youth) awareness of the effects of drugs, law enforcement policies, and other broad social forces.

Alcohol remains the drug of choice among most adolescents, with little change in consumption patterns evident from the survey data. Two-thirds of the high-school seniors surveyed in the Michigan studies reported being current users, about 5 percent were daily drinkers, and more than a third indicated they had consumed five or more drinks in a row over the past two weeks. Similarly, tobacco use, while not as high as alcohol use, did not decline in the late 1980s. Nearly one in five high school seniors indicated they were daily smokers.

These data—enlightening as they are—mask a great deal of variation in drug use among adolescents. National surveys of high-school seniors, for example, do not provide information on those who have dropped out of school. Estimated nationally to constitute 15 to 20 percent of students entering high school, these youngsters who drop out appear to be the most vulnerable to serious drug abuse, especially to "crack," the cheap, powerful, and highly addictive form of cocaine.

Research reports over a period of many years document much variation both in the extent and the patterning of drug use in local communities, for example, among different ethnic groups and the youth groups associated with them.[29] Observational studies such as those discussed in the previous chapter (and later, in Chapters 7 and 9) note that different types of drugs are used by different groups of young people, for example, "hard" as opposed to "soft" drugs. Also patterns of drug use are related to participation in different "social worlds" and to a variety of causal processes.

CHRONIC OFFENDERS

Several studies report that relatively few adolescents account for a high proportion of all serious criminal behavior committed by young people. Marvin Wolfgang and his colleagues traced the police records of an entire cohort of Philadelphia males who had been born in that city in 1945. After excluding traffic offenses, 35 percent of the nearly 10,000 boys in the cohort had at least one recorded police contact by the time they had reached age 18. Slightly more than one-half of these "official delinquents" had more than one police contact. A smaller group of 627 boys (18 percent of all offenders, but only 6.3 percent of the cohort) had five or more police contacts. These boys accounted for well over half of all offenses (61.7 percent) for which police contacts were recorded for the cohort. These "chronic" offenders had been arrested at younger ages than had the other arrestees, and they were more involved in serious offenses than were other offenders.[30] Similar findings have been reported elsewhere.

Chronic offenders in the Philadelphia study were more often nonwhite and of low socioeconomic status (SES) than were either nonarrestees or boys with only one police contact. They had experienced more family moves and school discipline problems, had completed fewer grades in school, and had measured lower on intelligence tests than other boys.

Study of a second cohort of Philadelphia youth born in 1958 has yielded similar findings, with an important difference. The proportion of males who had at least one recorded police contact by age 18 was slightly lower than for the 1945 cohort (32.6 percent compared to 35 percent), but the 1958 cohort arrestees were more recidivist and more violent. Chronic offenders (those with five or more arrests) composed 7.5 percent of the 1958 cohort. These boys were responsible for 68.5 percent of all index offenses committed by the cohort, 60.7 percent of the criminal homicides, 76.2 percent of the aggravated assaults, and 66.4 percent of all offenses involving injury.[31]

Other longitudinal studies confirm that males commit more delinquencies and commit them more frequently than do females. Lyle Shannon's study of Racine, Wisconsin cohorts did not find the progression from less serious to more serious behaviors reported by Wolfgang and his associates, nor did researchers who studied young people who had been arrested for violent offenses in Columbus, Ohio.[32] In general, juveniles evidence little tendency to specialize in offense patterns, but females are more likely than males to cease offending or move to status offenses, such as running away.

RACE AND ETHNICITY AS CATEGORIC RISKS

While self-report and official data concerning gender—and, to a lesser extent, age—are reasonably consistent with one another, they diverge considerably for race. R. D. Peterson and John Hagan note that the focus of research on crime among different races and ethnic groups reflects larger social concerns.[33] Early in the history of the United States, much concern focused on the plight of the Irish. In the early twentieth century crime and other social problems associated with other newly arrived immigrants (e.g., those from Italy and Poland) were of primary concern. Still later, with the increased migration northward of blacks from the South, major controversy centered on crime among blacks. In the last quarter of the twentieth century increased attention was focused on Hispanics and recently arrived Asian immigrants.

Most statistical research has concerned delinquency and crime among blacks. Official data, whether at the level of police contact, arrest, court appearance, conviction, or institutionalization, consistently find that blacks are more delinquent than whites. In contrast, SRD studies find relatively few and smaller differences between black and white youth.

Race-specific arrest rate ratios (black to white) for UCR offenses vary for different types of offenses. For all UCR offenses, except traffic offenses, the ratio of black to white arrest rates in 1980 was 2.4.[34] That is, proportionate to their representation in the population, 2.4 times as many blacks as whites were arrested. For *all index crimes,* this figure was 3.7; for *index property crimes,* 3.2; and for *index violent crimes,* 4.6. The higher ratio for crimes involving violence was especially great for robbery (10.3). All of these figures have declined by about one-third since 1970. Declines are equally large when ratios are calculated for the youthful population only.

The black-white participation ratio for all nontraffic offenses was the same for the 1945 and 1958 Philadelphia cohorts of males (1.8 to 1 for each cohort). For UCR index crimes and offenses with injury, however, black-white arrest rates appeared to be converging.

Victim Reports. Higher rates of violent crimes among blacks is confirmed by victimization studies and death statistics. In 1985, a federal government task force, convened to study and make recommendations regarding minority group health problems, reported that prevention of homicide should be considered a public health problem. The task force noted that the death rate was 51 percent higher for blacks than for whites and that homicide was second only to heart disease in accounting for this disparity. Further, in 1983, when the data were gathered, homicide was the leading cause of death among black males, aged 14–44.[35]

Self Reports. For the most part, self-reports fail to confirm higher rates of either participation or frequency of involvement in delinquent behavior (including serious crimes) among black young people. During the early years of the NYS, higher proportions of blacks than whites reported some involvement in violent offenses. The black-white ratio of participation in robbery during the initial year of the survey, when respondents ranged in age from 11–17, was 2.25 to 1 (9 percent for blacks, 4 percent for whites). By 1980, when the respondents ranged in age from 15–21, both participation and the black-white ratio for robbery had declined, the latter to 1.5 to 1 (3 percent for blacks, 2 percent for whites). Differences in both participation and frequency for individual offenses found whites more involved in some offenses (e.g., public disorder, drug use, and school-related offenses), whereas blacks reported consistently more involvement in sex-related offenses.[36]

As was the case with male-female comparisons, black-white differences are greater as one moves further into the justice system. Rates of incarceration are even higher for blacks, relative to whites, than are arrests. There is much debate as to why this should be the case, for example, to what extent does this reflect discriminatory treatment within the criminal justice system? Or is it because of other factors? Research in this area has focused largely on adults, rather than juveniles, and is by no means conclusive.[37]

Exhaustive research into the reliability and validity of self-reports provides a possible basis for reconciling inconsistent findings regarding race as a categoric risk. Black males more often fail to self-report involvement in serious crimes for which they have been arrested.[38] While the reasons for this are not entirely clear, several possibilities have been suggested, including discrimination by police, or prejudice and lying (by the victims), faulty memory, a lack of understanding of complex questions, and "social desirability" (i.e., giving the most socially desirable answer rather than the true answer to questions). Hindelang and associates found that social desirability could not account for lower validity scores of black males in their Seattle sample. Black males performed poorly on a "knowledge scale," however, suggesting that these boys may have had more difficulty than others in interpreting questions and instructions. In any case, caution must be observed when comparing black male involvement in serious crime with that of other categoric risks.

Given the overwhelming dependence of arrest on complainant reports and preferences, and on the seriousness of a reported offense, discriminatory treatment certainly is not the only cause of racial and ethnic disparities in official measures of delinquent and criminal behavior. Higher rates of juvenile court appearance of racial and ethnic minority children who are otherwise *in need* is consistent with traditional juvenile court philosophy and practice, yet there is evidence of discriminatory practice here, as well.

SOCIAL CLASS

No categoric risk for delinquent behavior has received more empirical and theoretical attention than social class. Yet, as was the case for race, self-report and official measures often disagree, and victim reports do not provide even a partial solution to the puzzle. Issues raised by this controversy are exceedingly complex, involving emotionally charged political philosophies, disagreement over the meaning and measurement of social class, and methodological problems.

The ecological research reviewed briefly in the previous chapter found a strong negative relationship between a variety of measures of socioeconomic status (SES) and delinquency rates of *communities*.[39] These studies did not relate SES and delinquent behavior of individuals, however. So strong was the ecological relationship between lower SES and rates of delinquency that for many years investigators failed to measure the relationship at the individual level. When this was done the relationship between individual SES and participation in delinquent behavior was found to be weak, and in several studies nonexistent. Several studies have concluded that both official and self-report data suggest only a slight tendency for greater involvement in delinquent behavior among lower-class, compared to middle-class, youth.

The NYS found class differences in the commission of delinquent acts to be somewhat stronger and more persistent for males than for females. Most observed differences involved lower participation and frequency rates among middle-class, compared to working-class or lower-class youth. The few offenses for which middle-class youth reported higher participation rates tend to be minor, for example, lying about age, cheating on school tests, skipping classes, stealing from family members, buying liquor for minors, being drunk in public, being disorderly, and evading payment. For no offense, however, did middle-class youth report higher *frequency* of involvement when compared to working-class or lower-class youth. Class differences thus appear to be stronger for frequency than for participation. Table 6.2 reports participation and frequency rates for the 1979 survey (when respondents ranged in age from 14–20) for several groups of offenses, by gender, after adjusting the self-reports for "appropriate and trivial events."[40]

The significance of the NYS findings is enhanced by the fact that the age range of the sample in 1979 spans the ages of maximum criminal involvement for most serious crimes. Nevertheless, the relationship between social class and delinquent behavior remains a matter of considerable controversy.

OTHER CATEGORIC RISKS

The institutional settings and relationships examined in previous chapters result in differential risks of delinquency involvement.[41] The NYS researchers note "small but significant differences" in participation between urban, suburban, and rural youth, with lower percentages of the latter reporting involvement in most delinquent behaviors, thus confirming at the individual level observed ecological urban-rural differences. Differences in frequency were less pronounced. Marijuana and cocaine participation were substantially lower among rural than among suburban and urban youth, and sale of hard drugs was even more distinctively urban.

NYS youth living with both biological parents reported less participation and less frequent involvement than did youth living either with a single parent or with one parent and a stepparent. More respondents who reported family crises (e.g., divorce or separation, death of a family member, or prolonged unemployment) also reported more participation in delinquency, and their reported frequency was about twice that of those who did not report such crises. The marital status of respondents also was related to involvement in delinquency, the married generally reporting less participation and frequency. Being in school also affected delinquency involvement by the NYS panel. Youth in school reported higher percentages of participation in minor assaults, vandalism, and measures of school and home delinquency. Out-of-school youth were more likely to report participation in felony-level assault and theft, hard drug use, illegal services, public disorder, and in involvement in a general delinquency scale. Frequency differences were similar but limited to hard drug use, school delinquency, and general delinquency. Relationships between employment and delinquency in the NYS panel were similar to the school-related statistics, with the employed generally reporting more involvement in the more serious offenses. Both of these relationships are confounded with age, but age alone cannot account for the higher rates of involvement in felony theft and assault, both of which *decline* with age.[42]

TABLE 6.2 Adjusted Delinquency Rates by Class and Gender: 1979 (age range = 14–20)

MALES

SCALE (N)	PREVALENCE (PERCENTAGE)				INCIDENCE (RATE PER 100 YOUTH)			
	MIDDLE (176)	WORKING (233)	LOWER (348)	Sig*	MIDDLE (176)	WORKING (233)	LOWER (348)	Sig**
Felony Assault	6.3	12.0	11.8		16	61	67	
Minor Assault	13.7	22.3	19.3	a	21	88	52	b
Robbery	1.1	4.7	4.6	b	3	23	15	
Felony Theft	7.4	15.9	15.8	ab	15	93	153	ab
Minor Theft	19.3	21.0	18.7		91	190	139	
Damage Prop.	23.3	21.9	25.0		56	118	72	
Illegal Serv.	10.3	19.3	14.7	a	86	477	769	ab
Crimes/Persons	16.5	28.3	25.9	ab	40	171	134	ab
General Theft	22.7	25.8	25.3		106	283	292	a
Index Offenses	10.2	18.0	19.0	b	28	131	145	
General Del.-B	62.3	70.3	71.4		1545	3322	3584	ab

TABLE 6.2 Adjusted Delinquency Rates by Class and Gender: 1979 (age range = 14–20) (cont.)

| | FEMALES | | | | | | |
| | PREVALENCE (PERCENTAGE) | | | | INCIDENCE (RATE PER 100 YOUTH) | | |
SCALE (N)	MIDDLE (184)	WORKING (222)	LOWER (298)	Sig*	MIDDLE (184)	WORKING (222)	LOWER (298)	Sig**
Felony Assault	3.3	4.1	5.4		49	5	17	
Minor Assault	3.3	3.6	7.7		124	6	55	
Robbery	0.5	0.5	0.7		1	5	1	
Felony Theft	2.2	2.7	3.7		11	6	49	
Minor Theft	7.1	7.2	9.4		203	27	78	
Damage Prop.	6.5	6.3	7.4		34	24	47	
Illegal Serv.	4.4	4.1	5.4		22	29	95	
Crimes/Persons	4.4	5.9	10.1	b	174	16	73	
General Theft	8.2	9.9	10.4		214	33	126	
Index Offenses	3.8	4.5	5.4		53	11	55	
General Del.-B	52.5	50.7	50.3		1758	1877	2688	

* a = middle versus working p ≤ .05; t = 2.32
b = middle versus lower p ≤ .05
c = working versus lower p ≤ .05

** a = middle versus working p ≤ .05; t = 2.14
b = middle versus lower p ≤ .05
c = working versus lower p ≤ .05

NYS respondents who reported regular attendance at religious services reported less involvement in virtually all delinquent behaviors.

THE COLLECTIVE NATURE OF JUVENILE DELINQUENCY

More than half a century ago, Clifford R. Shaw, Henry D. McKay, and their colleagues documented that delinquent boys most often committed their delinquencies in the company of others. Court records of boys appearing in court on delinquency petitions indicated that fewer than one in five were lone offenders. Of boys brought to court for stealing, only one in nine committed his offense alone. A series of case studies further documented the relationship of companionship with offending. Frederic Thrasher's classic study, *The Gang*, added to this picture.[43]

Since much nondelinquent behavior also involves age peers, that fact alone cannot account for delinquent behavior. The *nature* of the group context in which delinquent behavior occurs, however, may be different from that which does not produce such behavior. It may also be different for different categories of persons; that is, the categoric risks of delinquency may be different for various types of collectivities and for lone offenders.

Early studies of the group nature of delinquency proved to be so convincing that their conclusions came to be taken for granted. The advent of SRD studies continued to document delinquent behavior as a group phenomenon. However, most of these focused on the nature of delinquent subcultures, rather than on the nature of groups.

None of the empirical studies suggested that companionship involved more than a few boys in most delinquent episodes. Based on official records, the early research suggested that delinquents acted typically in groups of two or three. This finding has been confirmed by SRD and observational studies. More recent research adds an important distinction between *offenders* and *offenses*. A study of "juveniles taken into custody for residential burglary" in Peoria, Illinois, between 1971 and 1978 (467 youths in all), found that about one-half of all *burglary incidents* were committed by offenders acting alone.[44] Two-thirds of all burglary *offenders* committed their offenses with at least one other person, however.

National Crime Survey (NCS) robbery data for the United States present an even more dramatic example of the contrast in group involvement between incidents and offenders. While slightly more than one-half of all *robberies* were reported to involve a single offender, only half that proportion of *robbery offenders* acted alone. Nearly one-half of the offenders committed their robberies with one or two companions, while another 26 percent had three or more companions. Approximately three-quarters of all robbery offenders thus committed their robberies with at least one accomplice.

These seeming anomalies occur because many burglars commit more than one burglary and most do not exclusively act alone or with others. Reiss notes that "good estimates are not available of the variation among criminal histories in the mix of lone and group offenses, of variation in the number of accomplices, and of the consistency and variation of co-offending in an individual's history."[45] Self-reports indicate higher rates of lone offending" among boys than do official records for the same offenders. Group offenders also engage in illegal behavior more frequently than do lone offenders.[46] It also appears that lone offenders commit less serious crimes than do group offenders.

Until recently, little research has focused specifically on the nature of group-delinquency relationships. Jerzy Sarnecki's study of delinquent networks in a medium-sized Swedish city is, therefore, of special interest.[47] Police records of boys and girls *suspected of involvement in specific delinquent episodes* over the period 1975 through 1980 were studied. Corroborative information was obtained by interviewing some offenders as well as "social workers, police and other persons who came into contact with the investigated juveniles in the course of their daily work" (p. 34). Participants overwhelmingly committed offenses with others, though 41 percent of all *offenses* involved a single offender. Nearly eight out of ten *participants* in all offenses committed their offenses with others. Delinquent groupings were small, 56 percent of all "offense participations" involving two or three offenders and only 8 percent five or more. Delinquency groupings were of short duration, only 13 percent persisting more than six months. Most delinquent "careers" also were of short duration, and those who persisted in delinquent behavior tended to change their associates in offending.

CATEGORIC RISKS AND GROUP OFFENDING

Swedish studies confirm findings in other countries that most delinquents are males (79 percent of the delinquents in the network study were males) and that more males than females persist in delinquency. Seventy percent of the girls, compared to 43 percent of the boys identified in police files, were suspected of only one offense. Female participation in the largest and most seriously delinquent networks was even smaller than that in the general population of suspected offenders, ranging from 10 percent to 12 percent. Further, "girls were always situated on the periphery of the gangs" and they "most frequently became involved with a gang when they were together with one of the boys belonging to the gang" (p. 72).[48] Sarnecki also concludes that girls were accepted in the gangs on the basis of their association with one of the boys, but that they lacked high status in the gangs. Involvement in delinquency was higher among gang-affiliated girls than among non–gang-affiliated girls, and was highest among the largest and most delinquent gangs.

No age-graded pattern of gangs such as has been reported in several U.S. studies was found in the Swedish study. However, recruitment of new members into the gangs was associated with intensive involvement in delinquent behavior. The definition of a gang in the Swedish study (see footnote 48) may simply mean that more members of gangs took part in co-offending at times of heightened delinquent activity. This would be consistent with findings from a Chicago study in which *both* delinquent and nondelinquent group activities occurred as members of the gang being observed sought to develop greater group cohesion.[49] While it is not possible to determine how alike the U.S. and Swedish gangs and networks are, the descriptive characteristics noted by Sarnecki suggest many similarities.

Finally, to repeat a point made in the previous chapter, highly delinquent gangs are most common in the lower socioeconomic areas of large cities where official measures of delinquency also are high.[50] Discussion of the significance of this finding and of the nature of the group-delinquency relationship is deferred to the following chapters.

CAREER DELINQUENTS AND DELINQUENT CAREERS

As a final note to this chapter, we explore briefly the relationship between categoric risks and persistent offending, and the notion of delinquent and criminal careers. The Natural Research Council Panel on Research on Criminal Careers has summarized all known research in these areas. Citing longitudinal studies conducted on Philadelphia, Racine, Wisconsin, and London cohorts, the Panel reports that "between one-half and two-thirds of first offenders are rearrested (Philadelphia and Racine) or reconvicted (London). After each subsequent (criminal) event, the persistence probability increases, reaching a plateau range of 0.7 to 0.9 by the fourth event.[51] That is, the probability of another offense increases with each offense, leading ultimately to the "chronic offenders" discussed previously.

The chief concern in this context is whether persons who are the most seriously and frequently involved in criminal behavior are distinguished by particular patterns of behavior or by particular social characteristics. We know that the differences in categoric risks discussed in this chapter are *not* as pronounced among those who, by their own admission, are most frequently and seriously involved in criminal behavior. As previously noted, they are, however, distinguished by *high frequency of prior offending, early onset of delinquency*, and *drug use* (current or over time). A fourth factor, "unstable employment in the recent past," also characterizes these high-rate offenders. The first three of these characteristics of criminal careers involve delinquent behavior, but no specific pattern of types of offenses has been shown to be related to later high-rate offending. Indeed, authors of *The Violent Few* were impressed with the seemingly *incidental* character of violence in the lives of the young men studied.[52]

Those who become involved in serious delinquent and criminal behavior also report that they have committed less serious delinquencies. But involvement in status offenses is not predictive of later involvement in more serious behaviors. Those who *persist* in delinquency, however, typically escalate the seriousness of their offenses. Adult offenders tend to specialize in either property or violent offenses; juveniles typically switch between these offenses.

ON TO EXPLANATION

Previous chapters and this brief review of the social distribution of delinquent behavior prepare us for the task of explanation. We begin this complex topic with the macrosocial level of explanation.

NOTES

1. See Delbert S. Elliott, Suzanne S. Ageton, David Huizinga, Brian A. Knowles, and Rachelle J. Canter, *The Prevalence and Incidence of Delinquent Behavior, 1976–1980: National Estimates of Delinquent Behavior by Sex, Race, Social Class, and Other Selected Variables*. National Youth Survey Report No. 26. Boulder, CO: Behavioral Research Institute, 1983. The quotes are from pp. 29 and 30 of this report. See also, Michael J. Hindelang, Travis Hirschi, and Joseph G. Weis, *Measuring Delinquency*. Beverly Hills, CA: Sage, 1981; and Joseph G. Weis, "Issues in the measurement of criminal careers," pp. 1–51, in Alfred Blumstein, Jacqueline Cohen, Jeffrey A. Roth, and Christy A. Visher (eds.), *Criminal Careers and "Career Criminals"*. Washington, DC: National Academy Press, 1986. These reports examine the methodology of SRD and summarize evidence as to SRD reliability and validity.

2. See National Criminal Justice Information Statistics Service, *Criminal Victimization in the United States: Summary of Findings 1977–78, Changes in Crime and Trends in 1973*. Washington, DC: U.S. Government Printing Office, 1979; see also Ellen H. Nimick, Howard N. Snyder, Dennis P. Sullivan, and Nancy J. Tierney, *Juvenile Court Statistics, 1983*. Pittsburgh, PA: National Center for Juvenile Justice, 1985.

3. See, for example, Barry Glassner and Julia Loughlin, *Drugs in Adolescent Worlds: Burnouts to Straights*. London: Macmillan, 1987.

4. These matters are dealt with more extensively in Hindelang, et al., *op. cit.* (for self-reports) and in Michael R. Gottfredson and Michael J. Hindelang, "Sociological aspects of criminal victimization" (for victimization surveys), pp. 107–128, in Alex Inkeles and Ralph H. Turner (eds.) *Annual Review of Sociology*, Vol. 7. Palo Alto, CA: Annual Reviews, 1981. Because they inquire only as to *criminal* victimization, the latter cannot inform the extent or the nature of the vast amount of behavior falling under the rubric of status offenses. Nor do they report other behaviors covered under juvenile court statutes, such as child neglect, dependency, or abuse. Much criminal behavior also is not included in the NCS, though more extensive coverage is provided in a few studies. The NCS does not collect information on homicide or on so-called victimless offenses (such as gambling, drug use, prostitution, and drunkenness), or on crimes committed by organizations. Data concerning *offender* characteristics based on victimization studies are especially limited—to offenses in which victims confront, or are at least able to *see*, the offenders. Even then, victims' perceptions of the age, race, and even the gender of offenders are subject to error. Estimates of "categoric risks," based on reports of victims are, therefore, of limited value.

5. See Nimick, et al., *op. cit.*, p. 10. The year 1957 is the first year for which reasonably reliable data are available.

6. This section is based on Elliott, et al., *op. cit.*

7. UCR index offenses include four crimes of violence (homicide, forcible rape, robbery, and aggravated assault) and four property crimes (burglary, larceny-theft, motor vehicle theft, and arson). The history of the UCR system, offense definitions, and data are reported annually by the Federal Bureau of Investigation, U.S. Department of Justice. See, for example, U.S. Department of Justice, *Crime in the United States, 1986*. Washington DC: U.S. Government Printing Office, 1987.

8. The NYS researchers also note that the trend in serious offenses appears to occur as a result of changes in *termination* rather than *initiation* of participation in these offenses, since the initiation rates were fairly constant over the period of study.

9. In 1980, children under the age of 10, who composed 14.6 percent of the total U.S. population, accounted for only 0.6 percent (that is, 0.006) of all arrests reported to the FBI, while persons over 65, who compose 11.3 percent of the population, accounted for 1 percent (.01) of all arrests. Sources: Uniform Crime Reports and U.S. Bureau of the Census. The following comparisons are necessarily approximate. The Census Bureau categorizes age by 5-year segments (e.g., 10–14 and 15–19, as here combined), rather than the UCR age designation of "under the age of 18."

10. See James F. Short, Jr. and F. Ivan Nye, "Extent of unrecorded juvenile delinquency: tentative conclusions," *Journal of Criminal Law, Criminology and Police Science*, 49 (December, 1958):296–302.

11. Maynard L. Erickson and LaMar T. Empey, "Court records, undetected delinquency, and decision-making," *Journal of Criminal Law, Criminology and Police Science,* 54 (December, 1963):456–469.

12. See S. A. Cernkovich, Peggy C. Giordano, and M. D. Pugh, "Chronic offenders: the missing cases in self-report delinquency research." Paper presented at annual meetings of the American Society of Criminology, Denver, CO. Bowling Green, OH: Bowling Green State University, Department of Sociology, 1983; Leroy C. Gould, "Who defines delinquency: a comparison of self-reported and officially reported indices of delinquency for three racial groups," *Social Problems,* 16 (1963):325–336; Travis Hirschi, *Causes of Delinquency.* Berkeley, CA.: University of California Press, 1969; Delbert S. Elliott and Harwin Voss, *Delinquency and Dropout.* Lexington, MA: D. C. Heath, 1974; K. Elmhorn, "Study in self-reported delinquency among school children in Stockholm," pp. 117–146, and Nils Christie, J. Adanaes, and S. Skirbekk, "A study of self-reported crime," pp. 86–116, in K. O. Christiansen (ed.), *Scandinavian Studies in Criminology,* Vol. 1. London: Tavistock, 1965; David Farrington, "Self-reports of deviant behavior: predictive and stable?" *Journal of Criminal Law and Criminology,* 64 (1973):99–110.

13. Hindelang, Hirschi, and Weis, *op. cit.,* p. 249.

14. See Marvin E. Wolfgang, Robert M. Figlio, and Thorsten Sellin, *Delinquency in a Birth Cohort.* Chicago: University of Chicago Press, 1972.

15. Blumstein, et al., *op. cit.*

16. Gender ratios customarily report the number of males per 100 females (arrested, for example). A ratio over 100 thus indicates that males exceed females. Conversely, a ratio under 100 indicates that females exceed males. A ratio may also be expressed as the number of males per female, in which case unity (1.0) indicates equal numbers of males and females, 2.0 indicates two times the number of males as females, and so forth.

17. Rosemary Sarri and Yeheskel Hasenfeld (eds.), *Brought to Justice? Juveniles, the Courts and the Law.* National Assessment of Juvenile Corrections. Ann Arbor, MI: University of Michigan Press, 1976, p. 19.

18. Hindelang, et al., *op. cit.*

19. Elliott, et al., *op. cit.,* p. 70.

20. See Rita James Simon, "Women and Crime," pp. 1664–1669, in S. H. Kadish (ed.), *Encyclopedia of Crime and Justice,* Vol. 4. New York: Free Press, 1983; see also, Freda Adler, *Sisters in Crime: The Rise of the New Female Criminal.* New York: McGraw-Hill, 1975.

21. See, for example, Darrell J. Steffensmeier and R. H. Steffensmeier, "Trends in female delinquency: an examination of arrest, juvenile court, self-report and field data," *Criminology,* Vol. 18, No. 1, pp 62–85 (1980); see also, Lois B. DeFleur, "Biasing influences on drug arrest records: implications for deviance research," *American Sociological Review,* 40 (February, 1975):88–104.

22. See LaMar T. Empey, *American Delinquency: Its Meaning and Construction.* Homewood, IL: Dorsey, 1982, pp. 82–83.

23. Gary D. Hill and Anthony R. Harris, "Changes in the gender patterning of crime, 1953–77: opportunity v. identity," *Social Science Quarterly,* 62 (December, 1981):658–671.

24. See Patricia Miller, unpublished paper, Institute for Juvenile Research, Chicago, 1977. The five offenses for which female rates did not increase were curfew, sex offenses, suspicion, vagrancy, and gambling—all offenses of broad and vague definition, subject to extreme variation in enforcement practice. Male arrest rates for these offenses also declined between 1965 and 1976. Male rates for auto theft also declined.

25. See Blumstein, et al., *op cit.,* p. 94. Other factors found to distinguish "the most active 10 percent of offenders who commit crimes at rates that may exceed 100 per year" include "high frequency of prior offending; early onset of delinquency as a juvenile; and unstable employment in the recent past." The relationship between drug use and delinquency appears to be quite different than that between drug use and adult crime. Cf. Glassner and Loughlin, *op. cit.*

26. Miller, *op., cit.,* p. 14. Lee Bowker reports that boyfriends exercise greater influence on girl's use of alcohol and marijuana than do girlfriends. He relates use of these drugs to the double standard of sex behavior. That is, boys seek sexual favors from girls and employ drugs for

this purpose. Being under the influence of drugs is then used by girls as a rationalization for "giving in" to their boyfriends. See Lee H. Bowker, *Women, Crime, and the Criminal Justice System*. Lexington, MA: Lexington Books, 1978, p. 90. Glassner and Loughlin find that friendship and sociability are of critical importance to both drug users' and non-drug users' social worlds.

27. Data reported are drawn from a series of reports from the University of Michigan and the Alcohol, Drug Abuse, and Mental Health Administration, U.S. Department of Health and Human Services. See Institute for Social Research, "Marijuana shows signs of becoming youths' permanent recreational drug," *ISR Newsletter*, University of Michigan, Ann Arbor, MI (Summer, 1978): 6–7. Also see subsequent issues: "Drug use down," (Winter, 1984–85):4–5; "Cocaine use rising," (Winter, 1985–86):5,8; "Patterns of drug use," (Fall/Winter, 1987–88):3,6.

28. Glassner and Loughlin, *op. cit.*, p. 276, note that "historical location of cohorts" may change empirical relationships between behavior and other phenomena of interest. College-bound high-school students studied by Maus in the 1960s reported more drug use than did their non–college-bound counterparts. Johnston, studying high-school students in the 1970s, reports just the opposite finding. Cf., Armand Maus, "Anticipatory socialization toward college as a factor in adolescent marijuana use," *Social Problems*, 16:357–64; Lloyd Johnston, *Drugs and American High School Students, 1975–1983*. Washington, DC: National Institute of Drug Abuse, 1984.

29. See, for example, Glassner and Loughlin, *op. cit.*; Bill Barich, "Los Angeles County Gangs," *The New Yorker* November 3, 1986, pp. 97–130; Stephen C. Cook, "The drugs of choice among the city's teens," *San Francisco Examiner*, June 3, 1986, p. A-1; Joan W. Moore, with Robert Garcia, Carlos Garcia, Luis Cerda, and Frank Valencia, *Homeboys: Gangs, Drugs, and Prison in the Barrios of Los Angeles*. Philadelphia: Temple University Press, 1978; Harold Finestone, "Cats, Kicks, and Color," *Social Problems*, V (July, 1957): 3–13.

30. Wolfgang, et al., *op. cit.* See also, Lyle W. Shannon, *Criminal Career Continuity: Its Social Context*. New York: Human Sciences Press, 1988.

31. Interview with Marvin E. Wolfgang, in Clemens Bartollas, *Juvenile Delinquency*. New York: Wiley, 1985, pp. 25–27. Females were also studied in the 1958 cohort, but data had not been analyzed as of the date of this writing.

32. See Lyle W. Shannon, *Assessing the Relationship of Adult Criminal Careers to Juvenile Careers: A Summary*. Office of Juvenile Justice and Delinquency Prevention. Washington, DC: U.S. Department of Justice, 1982; D. Hamparian, R. Schuster, Simon Dinitz, and John Conrad, *The Violent Few: A Study of Dangerous Juvenile Offenders*. Lexington, MA: Lexington Books, 1978.

33. R. D. Peterson and John Hagan, "Changing conceptions of race: towards an account of anomalous findings of sentencing research," *American Sociological Review*, 49 (February, 1984):56–70.

34. See Blumstein, et al., *op. cit.*, p. 25. All known studies are summarized in Appendix A of this volume, "Participation in Criminal Careers," by Christy A. Visher and Jeffrey A. Roth, pp. 211–291.

35. National news media carried this story in 1985. My source is the Spokesman Review (Spokane, WA.), October 17, 1985.

36. Elliott, et al., *op. cit.*, p. 75; see also Blumstein, et al. *op. cit.*

37. Blumstein finds that incarceration rates for blacks and whites do not differ significantly when seriousness of offense is statistically controlled. This finding has been challenged by others. Cf. Alfred Blumstein, "On the racial disproportionality of U.S. prison populations," *Journal of Criminal Law and Criminology*, 73 (Fall, 1982):1259–1281; and George S. Bridges, Robert D. Crutchfield, and Edith E. Simpson, "Crime, social structure and criminal punishment: white and nonwhite rates of imprisonment," *Social Problems*, 34 (October, 1987):345–361. See, also Stephen P. Klein, Susan Turner, and Joan Petersilia, *Racial Equity in Sentencing*. Santa Monica: RAND, 1988.

38. See David Huizinga and Delbert S. Elliott, *Self-Reported Measures of Delinquency and Crime: Methodological Issues and Comparative Findings*. Boulder, CO: Behavioral Research Institute, 1984. See also, Hindelang, et al., *op. cit.*, pp. 157 ff.

39. This research is reviewed in Hindelang, et al., *Ibid.*, pp. 181 ff.; see also, Robert A. Gordon, "Issues in the ecological study of delinquency," *American Sociological Review*, 32 (December, 1967):927–944.

40. See Delbert S. Elliott and David Huizinga, "Social class and delinquent behavior in a national youth panel: 1976–1980," *Criminology*, 21 (May, 1983):149–177. Table 6.2 is adapted from pp. 170–173.

41. The following discussion is based on Elliott, et al., *op. cit.*, pp. 105–115.

42. Examination of the effects of dropping out of high school on arrests of the 1945 Philadelphia cohort yields the "ineluctable conclusion" that "dropping out of high school is positively associated with later criminal activity" even after controlling for employment and marital history. See Terence P. Thornberry, Melanie Moore, and R. L. Christenson, "The effect of dropping out of high school on subsequent criminal behavior," *Criminology*, 23 (February, 1985):3–18.

43. Clifford R. Shaw, F. M. Zorbaugh, H. D. McKay, and L. S. Cottrell, *Delinquency Areas*. Chicago: University of Chicago Press, 1929; see also by Shaw, *The Jack-Roller* (1930); *The Natural History of a Delinquent Career* (1931); *Brothers in Crime* (1938), all published by the University of Chicago Press; and Shaw and McKay, *Social Factors in Juvenile Delinquency*. Vol. 2, No. 13. Washington, DC: U.S. Government Printing Office, 1931. See also, Frederic M. Thrasher, *The Gang: A Study of 1,313 Gangs in Chicago*. Chicago: University of Chicago Press, 1927 (abridged edition, with a new introduction, published in 1963). The general topic is discussed in James F. Short, Jr., "Collective behavior, crime and delinquency," pp. 403–449, in Daniel Glaser (ed.), *Handbook of Criminology*. Chicago: Rand McNally, 1974.

44. This study is discussed in Albert J. Reiss, Jr., "Co-offending influences on criminal careers," pp. 121–160, in Blumstein, et al., *op cit*.

45. Reiss, *Ibid.*, p. 123.

46. See Maynard L. Erickson, "The group context of delinquent behavior," *Social Problems*, 19 (Summer, 1971):114–129; Michael J. Hindelang, "The social versus solitary nature of delinquent involvements," *British Journal of Criminology*, 11:167–175; and "With a little help from their friends: group participation in reported delinquency," *British Journal of Criminology*, 16:109–125.

47. See Jerzy Sarnecki, *Delinquent Networks*. Stockholm: National Council for Crime Prevention, Report No. 1986:1.

48. The gang was defined in this study as "a group of juveniles who have been linked to each other by being suspected of joint delinquency by the...police" (p. 60). While this definition is quite unconventional, since it relies on police information rather than on study of gang members, it is useful for the study of youth networks. See Chapter 9, below, for a more extended discussion of criteria for designating youth groups as gangs.

49. See Leon R. Jansyn, "Solidarity and delinquency in a street corner group," *American Sociological Review* 31 (October, 1966):600–614; see also, Chap. 9.

50. In his Preface to Thrasher's classic study, Robert A. Park remarked that "a study of the gang...is at the same time a study of 'gangland'; that is to say, a study of the gang and its habitat, and in this case the habitat is a city slum." Robert E. Park, "Editor's Preface," p. vii, in Thrasher, *op. cit.* For a review of recent research on gangs and delinquency, see Mark C. Stafford, "Gang delinquency," pp. 167–190, in Robert F. Meier (ed.), *Major Forms of Crime*. Beverly Hills, CA: Sage, 1984.

51. See Blumstein, et al., *op. cit.*, pp. 89 ff.

52. See Donna M. Hamparian, Richard Schuster, Simon Dinitz, and John Conrad, *The Violent Few: A Study of Dangerous Juvenile Offenders*. Lexington, MA: D.C. Heath, 1978.

CHAPTER 7
MACROSOCIAL
FORCES
AND PRINCIPLES

INTRODUCTION

The primary focus of the next several chapters is on explanations of juvenile delinquency and juvenile delinquents—in contrast, that is, to dependency, neglect, or abuse, or, for the most part, status offenses or status offenders. Juvenile delinquency occurs in widely varying macrosocial contexts. This chapter focuses on how macrosocial forces have been and are related to variations in delinquency rates in different social systems, cultures, and social structures.

COMPARATIVE AND HISTORICAL STUDIES

Comparative, historical, ethnographic, and sociological research has demonstrated enormous variation in the quantity and quality of delinquent and criminal behavior between different societies and cultures, and, over time, within the same societies. We know, for example, that infanticide and behaviors now considered abusive of children have been common practice throughout most of recorded history. Many child-rearing practices once considered proper and even necessary would now be considered illegal and child abusive.[1] Variations among local communities in delinquent behavior, and the beliefs and practices regarding such behavior, have also been studied, as noted in earlier chapters. Macro-level variables are involved in the explanation of all the categories of delinquent behavior, and of the ways in which families and communities contribute to and attempt to control such behavior.

POLITICAL AND ECONOMIC THEORIES

Crime, by definition, is behavior lawfully punishable by the state. We begin our examination of theories at the macro-level, therefore, with consideration of the impact on these theories of the technologies and political and economic systems that underlie modern industrial societies.

Political and economic theorists focus on both the etiology of delinquency and its control. With the emergence of the nation-state as the dominant form of modern political organization, the primary concern with the evolving concepts of crime and juvenile delinquency was on their *control*. These developments had major consequences for the manner in which societies were organized, especially with regard to relationships among citizens and between citizens and the state. Thus, there is good reason for theories of crime *causation* as well as crime control "to rest on assumptions about the relation of people to a state."[2] Theorists have emphasized very different aspects of political and economic organization in this respect.

MARXIST THEORIES

Theories in the *Marxist* tradition focus on the importance of ownership and control of the means of economic production and distribution, and on changes in social life associated with the rise of capitalism and the industrial revolution. Initially the Marxist focus was on Europe, especially in England during the fifteenth and sixteenth centuries. Disruption of traditional economic and social relationships associated with capitalism and the industrial revolution left in their wake a large unemployed segment of the population, which came to be identified as the "dangerous classes." Cut adrift from traditional crafts and communities, thousands roamed the countryside, subsisting as best they could off the land or by victimizing travelers. Most eventually settled in cities, again to survive by whatever means were available, including various forms of crime. Criminal subcultures and organizational networks often developed under such circumstances.

Capitalism, the Marxist theory argues, was responsible not only for creating the "dangerous classes," but for a spirit of competitiveness, of acquisitiveness, of individualism, and of exploitation of others throughout society. Capitalism required the creation and maintenance of "surplus labor," which keeps wages down and ensures the economic profits enjoyed and controlled by the capitalist class. The surplus labor supply was both created and maintained with the support of emerging nation-states.[3]

The most ambitious attempt to apply Marxist theory to juvenile delinquency has been undertaken by Herman and Julia Schwendinger who argue that sixteenth century capitalism "ripped apart the ancient regime and introduced criminality among youth in all stations of life."[4] By investing control over the means of economic production in the capitalist class and by separating workers from the fruits of their labors, capitalism created the conditions for the emergence and reproduction of the adolescent subcultures that mediate relationships between social class, scholastic achievement, and delinquent behavior. Criminal subcultures and criminal organizational networks flourished as traditional economic and social relationships were disrupted on a vast scale.

Capitalism created the conditions for crime and delinquency within higher levels of the social order as well. "White-collar offenses" flourished among the gentry, and their children often formed their own status groups. Many of these were responsible for behaviors which, if not explicitly criminal, were often dissolute and characterized by disregard of others' persons and property. Conspicuous consumption and the ethics of individualism encouraged exploitation of others throughout the society. With the support of emerging and greatly strengthened nation-states, capitalism created the conditions for modern juvenile delinquency and criminality.

Elements of the Marxist theory and its application to modern day conditions are open to debate, but many of the historical conditions basic to the theory are not in dispute. While capitalism did not *create* greed and avarice, it encouraged such sentiments and influenced their social distribution. All advanced industrial and postindustrial societies "reproduce surplus labor" and capitalist and socialist nations alike apparently undergo similar changes in crime patterns in various stages of development. Profitability and competition in international markets motivate capitalist, socialist, and mixed economies; and technological developments are critical to the quantity and types of personnel required for the production and distribution of goods and services in all economies. Organizational arrangements change for a variety of reasons, often related to technology, but including international economic and political developments, as well.

Careful historical analysis of the conditions under which capitalism emerged and has changed, and of the consequences of these developments, suggests caution regarding any simple or straightforward interpretation of these events or of their consequences for contemporary societies.[5] The connection between such global developments and the occurrence of juvenile delinquency is mediated by particular historical, cultural, and local circumstances—by the historically concrete, as Charles Tilly notes (*As Sociology Meets History*. New York: Academic Press, 1981).

Thus, while many of the facts upon which Marxist and other "radical" theories are based are generally accepted, much debate centers on specific interpretations. Although the levels and types of unemployment and the levels of alienation of labor vary a great deal among nation-states, they are more or less constant features of capitalist, socialist, and mixed economies in today's economically interdependent world.

Louise Shelley finds that capitalist and socialist nations undergo similar changes in *crime patterns* in various stages of development. Shelley regards the influence of industrialization and urbanization as the primary forces propelling change. Variations in observed patterns can be accounted for, she suggests, by such factors as the degree of control exercised over internal migration and the degree to which traditional ways of life can be successfully maintained. These developments were, and continue to be, extremely complex, greatly influenced by particular historical, cultural, and social (often local) circumstances.[6]

Conflict theories of law, crime, and delinquency developed in reaction to theories that, explicitly or implicitly, emphasized *consensus* as the basis for law and law enforcement, and their functional nature. They share with Marxist theories the notion that law and law enforcement emerge out of conflicting interests. The nature of those interests extends beyond the Marxist emphasis on class conflict, however. As we have seen, many interests were involved in the invention of delinquency. Conflict theorists stress the importance of economic and political power in the determination of what is considered to be criminal or delinquent. Other sources of power also are recognized, for example, religious and professional groups, but the interests of these groups are sometimes seen to be manifest in or derivative of political and economic interests.

Recent scholarly work helps to resolve theoretical disputes between conflict theorists and others. These studies leave no doubt that "law and order" are not based solely on consensus regarding social values and objectives. The existence, if not always the precise nature, of conflicting interests in the determination of what is considered criminal or delinquent is clear. The power of the state vis-à-vis other institutions and social forces has been the focus of much controversy, however. Three examples of research concerning the nature of state power all make somewhat the same point.

John Brewer and John Styles conclude that the law—the prime instrumentality of states—was a potent force in seventeenth and eighteenth century England, constraining as well as empowering state (and other) authority. Some parts of the country, they suggest, "were virtually 'lawless zones'; the practice of local courts sometimes deviated considerably from the letter of the law as enacted or interpreted" by the central government. In addition, "most legal officials were rank amateurs who were as much concerned with the preservation of local harmony as they were with the (often divisive) business of litigation."[7]

Michael Ignatieff notes that crimes resulting in state sanctions are but "the tip of an iceberg...a small part of those disputes, conflicts, thefts, assaults too damaging, too threatening, too morally outrageous to be handled within the family, the work unit, the neighborhood, the street." Ignatieff urges attention to "how agents like the police worked out a tacit agreement with the local enforcers of norms, determining which offenses were theirs to control, and which were to be left to the family, the employer, or the neighborhood."[8]

Finally, Ira Katznelson documents differences between England and the United States in social class formation and maintenance, and in relationships between social classes and the state, which greatly influenced the consciousness of class and of class-based politics in the two countries.[9] In all three of these examples, the state is seen as a powerful, but limited force, constrained as well as constraining.

Conflict theories have been especially effective in analyzing influences on the timing and the form of legislation, and on statutory sanctions, as noted in Chapter 2. The role of elites is clearly important in the making of law and its enforcement, but so also are other interest groups, social values in the larger community, and communications media.

Attempts by conflict theorists to explain the "categoric risks" of delinquency and crime in terms of racism, sexism, and class conflict in the administration of justice have been less successful. Theoretically, the influence of racism and sexism on the juvenile and criminal justice systems should be similar, operating to the disadvantage of racial and ethnic minorities, and of females. As noted in the previous chapter, blacks do have exceptionally high official crime rates compared to whites, but females have exceptionally low crime rates, compared to males. Support for the conflict theory position that discriminatory enforcement practices account for differences in delinquency rates among racial and ethnic minorities, and among lower socioeconomic strata, is found in empirical studies conducted in some jurisdictions. Studies comparing imprisonment rates of whites and nonwhites in states and regions of the United States have been able to account for most of the variation in racial differentials in arrests, convictions, and sentencing on the basis of the *seriousness of crimes* for which official actions are taken. When such comparisons were made across counties in Washington state, however, rates of imprisonment for nonwhites, Hispanics, and Native Americans were higher, and rates of imprisonments of whites were lower, even when seriousness and violence of offense were controlled.[10] Interviews of justice officials and community leaders revealed much concern and fear that minorities represented a threat to public order, and that crime and violence were primarily minority problems. These perceptions were associated with an informal screening process in which crimes involving minorities were handled more severely than were those committed by whites.

These findings suggest that prejudice and discrimination continue to be important influences in law enforcement. More important, they direct attention to economic and political forces that are fundamental to social structure and to culture—to macro-level forces that are important to lawmaking and lawbreaking, as well as law enforcement.

At the community level, conflict theories help to explain why apparently similar behaviors are regarded differently by the law, for example, why the lower-class "Roughnecks" are regarded as delinquent, whereas the unruly middle-class "Saints" in a community are not[11]; why the upper-class "playboy" without a job is not regarded as a criminal, whereas the lower-class vagrant may be; and why some property offenses (such as many white-collar violations) are more likely to be subject to less harsh civil penalties, whereas criminal sanctions apply to others (for ordinary theft and burglary), despite the fact that the former are far more costly to the victims than are the latter. Conflict theories are helpful, too, in analyzing the social construction of other social problems, both historical context and in contemporary societies.[12]

CULTURE, SOCIAL STRUCTURE, AND DELINQUENT SUBCULTURES

Culture and social structure are interdependent. The combination of new technology and political and economic organization, associated with modernization and the industrial revolution, increasingly separated the work place from the family, changing beliefs about children, and increasing structural differentiation of communities, as well as families, based in part on age. New institutions were created to carry out the new functions brought about by these changing beliefs, and by the changing technologies and political and economic organization. Many established institutions changed the nature of their relationships with young people. The result was that children were increasingly separated from the normal round of adult activities.

As age-grading has become ever more refined and institutionalized, the consequences have been profound. The resulting changes in institutions and socialization practices, and in adult perceptions and expectations of children, also weakened traditional forms of social control. Childhood and adolescence became problematic. Adolescence, especially, became a period of social and psychological turmoil, of identity confusion and diffusion.

The connection between macrosocial forces and the situations of childhood and adolescence can be seen in the contrast between modern Western societies and their earlier counterparts, and with primitive societies. Ethnographic studies of primitive societies find continuity between childhood, adolescence, and adulthood quite unlike that experienced by most children in modern societies. Erik Erikson contrasts the *cultural coherence* of primitive tribes with the fragmented and individuated exposure to culture experienced by young people in highly stratified and specialized modern societies.[13] Hans Sebald and others have noted that the lack of meaningful *rites of passage* associated with puberty and initiation into adult status creates role confusion and identity problems for youth in modern societies.[14]

SOCIAL CHANGE

Even before G. Stanley Hall gave adolescence its name (in 1904) it was recognized that that period of life posed special problems of adjustment and of preparation for adulthood. More recently, James Coleman suggests, the term *youth* has in important respects superceded adolescence. A variety of factors combined to produce the phenomena of *youth culture* during the 1960s: the large numbers of young people, the result of the "baby boom" following World War II; the increasing affluence of these young people, which enabled them to "back up their tastes with their money" and create a youth market with enormous economic power; the extension of the period of education prior to entering the labor market; the increased number of women who joined the work force, further separating them from youth in the home and in the neighborhood; the increased extent to which adults worked "in large organizations where youth are not present"; and the expansion of the mass media, which catered increasingly to the youth market.[15]

These social changes had far-reaching consequences for the social, economic, and political life of the community—for adults as well as young people. Among these consequences was the creation of conditions conducive to the formation of delinquent subcultures.

PRINCIPLES OF SUBCULTURAL FORMATION

In common parlance, a *subculture* denotes the special interests and identities that characterize certain individuals, groups, and larger aggregations, setting them apart from the larger society. The importance of social change to the etiology of delinquent subcultures is captured in the following two fundamental principles:

1. *"social separation produces cultural differentiation,"*[16] that is, when groups or categories of people are separated socially, conditions are ripe for subcultural formation. But more is required for this to happen, however.
2. The "crucial condition for the emergence of new cultural forms," Albert Cohen theorizes, "is the existence, *in effective interaction with one another, of a number of actors with similar problems of adjustment.*" (Emphasis is original.)[17]

THE NATURE OF SUBCULTURES

We speak of youth subcultures, delinquent subcultures, ethnic subcultures, regional subcultures, subcultures associated with particular occupations, and subcultures that develop among people who share special interests, such as stamp collecting, bird watching, or drug use. Neither membership in a particular category (e.g., race, ethnicity, age, sex, occupation, or area of residence) nor behavior (bird watching or delinquency) is sufficient to define a subculture, however. The critical element, rather, is the degree to which values, norms, artifacts, activities, and identities are shared, and the extent to which those who have these elements in common differ from others within a society or some larger cultural system.

The notion of delinquent subcultures refers to the relationship of these elements to delinquent behavior, rather than simply to co-offending. It is helpful for analytical purposes to distinguish subcultures from the groups and individuals who share subcultural elements. Indeed, failure to make this distinction has led to confusion. While members of a particular group may be the sole *carriers* of a subculture, subcultures often are shared by many individuals and groups. Conversely, some subcultures are more *group-oriented* than others. "Conflict subcultures," in particular, tend to be shared by "fighting gangs" whose identity involves such values as "defense of turf." In contrast, drug use, though it typically occurs in a group context, tends to be less restricted to a particular group, since the subcultural orientation is toward drugs and experiences associated with their acquisition and use.

As the term suggests, subcultures exist in relation to larger cultures and societies. The nature of these relationships is critical to the origin, development, and status of subcultures within societies.

DELINQUENT AND CRIMINAL SUBCULTURES

Donald R. Cressey notes that "[m]any types of delinquent and criminal subcultures have long been present in industrialized societies."[18] For this reason the origins of such subcultures are difficult to trace. As noted, above, the earliest *criminal* subcultures in modern states probably emerged from the large numbers of unemployed persons set adrift by the advent of mercantile capitalism and the industrial revolution. Young people were a significant component of the "dangerous classes," and many grew up under the active tutelage of adult criminals in the "lawless zones" of larger cities. Many of their problems were those of similarly circumstanced adults.

In the more recent past, large numbers of immigrants have settled in major cities in many parts of the world, creating massive problems of adjustment for children and their parents. Many of these problems are especially acute for young people. Frederic Thrasher's classic study of juvenile gangs in Chicago noted that gangs of young boys from different nationality groups often reenacted clashes with one another that resembled those occurring in their (or their parents') former countries.[19] Other conflicts were rooted in the collision of old and new cultural traditions, and in racially or ethnically based prejudices, and in discriminatory institutional practices, especially in schools. Marshall Clinard and Daniel Abbott's study of Kampala, Uganda (a less developed, but modernizing country) indicates that the degree of tribal homogeneity was a major factor distinguishing a low-crime slum community from a high-crime slum community in that city.[20]

MODERNIZATION THEORY

These types of conflicts exist today, though the cast of racial and ethnic groups continues to change. Modern industrial and postindustrial societies place a premium on certain skills and personal characteristics. Among these are symbolic skills (especially language and arithmetic), interpersonal skills, adaptability and dependability (for example, regarding punctuality and effort), motivation for achievement, and self-control of aggressive impulses.[21] The "life chances"—including the risk of delinquency—of young people are related to their ability to acquire these skills and characteristics. Opportunities to do so are unevenly distributed among social strata in all modern societies.

The bases for the distribution of such opportunities are both cultural and structural. Many racial and ethnic minorities are disadvantaged in both respects. Groups possessing these skills and embodying these characteristics find assimilation into American society easier than do groups lacking them.[22]

Shelley places the relationship between crime and modernization in both historical and contemporary perspective, among capitalist, socialist, and mixed economic systems. The results of her review suggest that the early effects of modernization lead to increases in both property and personal offenses in urban areas, while crime rates in rural areas are lowered as people leave these areas and move to the cities. Rural areas continue to have high rates of violent crime, however.

Increased mobility and communication made possible by modern technology have speeded up contemporary modernization processes. To a major degree this has been due to rapid urban migration in contemporary developing nations. The result has been that delinquency and crime have become major social problems in all modern and modernizing societies.

Following the initial phase of modernization, societies once characterized primarily by violent crime (often taking traditional forms) become dominated by property crime. While violent crimes against persons decrease in relative frequency, however, increasingly they become "associated with the commission of property crimes as individuals are willing to resort to whatever means [are] necessary to secure desired goods."[23]

In this process, most nations experience rising overall rates of crime. A few nations have not, however. Where this is the case, the explanation appears to lie in the ability of these nations to maintain the strength of traditional social control institutions, such as religion, the family, and broader cultural identities.[24] "Police states," such as Spain under Franco, also are able to reduce, at least temporarily, the impacts of modernization through controls over internal migration, long prison terms for offenders, and at times by the virtual annihilation of offenders.

Historically, the concrete conditions of individual nations greatly influence the impact of modernization on delinquency and crime. The Caribbean nations and the United States, for example, are alike in the great gap between rich and poor citizens, and they are alike in that the *relative deprivation* experienced by the poor is exacerbated by the *public nature* of this gap. In the Caribbean the contrast between affluent tourists and the poor among the citizenry fosters feelings of relative deprivation, while in the United States mass media advertising and conspicuous consumption patterns of the rich foster these feelings. In other developing nations, for example, Nigeria and Argentina, *acute* deprivation of youth accompanying rapid urbanization is the problem. Even those developed and developing countries that have not experienced spiralling crime rates have not been able to resist other trends associated with modernization, namely, increases in juvenile offending, offending by females, and gang delinquency. Delinquent gangs apparently develop only in such societies, influenced by traditions as well as by modernization.

SOCIAL STRUCTURE AND CONTEMPORARY CULTURE

Cultural themes define what is valued in societies. Rules based on these themes prescribe acceptable ways of achievement in accord with these values. Some societies—the United States is generally cited as the prime example—place extraordinary value on achieving material success. However, opportunities and the special skills and characteristics associated with the achievement of success are unevenly distributed among social strata in all modern societies.

Robert K. Merton's seminal paper, "Social structure and anomie," sketches a theoretical paradigm concerning the relationship between certain features of culture and social structure and their impacts on behavioral adaptations. Later elaborations by others have attempted to explain delinquent subcultures. Basic to Merton's theory of social structure—its "core process," as Arthur Stinchcombe notes—is the social structuring of available alternative courses of action.[25] In this conception, choices among behavior alternatives are neither entirely free nor completely determined. Rather, possible alternatives are constrained by the social structure. The socially structured nature of alternatives, in turn, has both individual and institutional consequences.

Merton theorized that pressures "to engage in nonconforming rather than conforming conduct" (for example, crime and delinquency) differ among people located in different structural positions. The nature of these pressures can be understood by analytically separating *culturally defined goals* and *culturally acceptable means* for their achievement. Societies differ in the relative emphasis that is placed on each. "Contemporary American culture" "appears to approximate the polar type in which great emphasis upon certain success-goals occurs without equivalent emphasis upon institutional means."[26]

For persons disadvantaged with respect to institutional access, pressures to deviate from acceptable (legal) means for achieving success can be considerable. Disadvantage, like delinquency, varies among categories of persons. Yet, most adolescents who are disadvantaged by social position do not deviate, at least to the extent that they engage in extensive criminal activity. The theory is more successful in explaining serious criminal behavior among persons located in some categoric risks than others.

Answers to questions raised by these seeming anomalies involve individual- and microsocial-level processes, as well as crosscutting macro-level forces. While traditional institutional access to material success is more limited for females than for males, criteria for success also have been defined differently according to gender. Traditional gender roles protect young females from most such pressures, while exercising greater controls over their behavior and urging upon them different sets of goals and expectations, for example, cultivation of desirable "feminine characteristics" in order to make a "good marriage" and as preparation for managing a household.

Albert K. Cohen's adaptation of Merton's theory argues that pressures to achieve in American society are linked to both age and gender.[27] We tend to "measure" ourselves against "all comers" *of our own age and gender*. A certain amount of "hell-raising" and "sewing wild oats," Cohen notes, is expected of young males—even approved as a masculine virtue *because* it is distinctly unfeminine, so long as "real trouble" is avoided. Of equal importance, material success is not the only social measuring rod. Indeed, among adolescents it appears to be less important than is concern for *status* among age peers. Status and material possessions may, of course, be linked.

The delinquent subculture, Cohen concluded, was formed in reaction to status problems experienced by working-class males in middle-class institutions, especially the school. Inadequately prepared for formal education, their behavior found wanting in terms of the "middle-class measuring rod," working-class boys are confronted with difficult choices, and opportunities that are themselves socially structured.

ALTERNATIVE ADAPTATIONS TO SOCIALLY STRUCTURED DISADVANTAGE

Cohen discusses the relationship of three alternative adaptations to gender and social class. The "college-boy" adaptation is most consonant with the functional requisites of modern society and with the cultural goal of material success. But that adaptation is hardly viable for youngsters who perform poorly in school and who lack both the motivation to do better and the necessary social skills for "making it" in middle-class terms. One alternative is to give up middle-class aspirations, to perform well enough only to "get by," and to identify with working-class status. This is the corner-boy adaptation, described in William Foote Whyte's classic study, *Street Corner Society*.[28]

Cohen's depiction of the delinquent alternative emphasizes the *expressive* nature of much delinquent behavior, and its status-providing (as opposed to utilitarian) value for delinquent boys. Many youngsters steal items in order to show off for their friends. Cohen also emphasizes the malicious and negativistic character of the delinquent subculture, hypothesizing that it signifies rejection of the middle-class measuring rod, in effect, turning middle-class values upside down.

Cohen was aware that the delinquent subculture he described and sought to account for was probably only one among many delinquent subcultures. His general theory of subcultures seems more on target than is his attempt to account for qualities that appear to be associated with vandalism, rather than with other common types of delinquency. Much stealing, while primarily expressive, is not malicious or particularly negativistic. Cohen also failed to appreciate the power and attractions of lower-class culture and organization.

LOWER-CLASS CULTURE AS A GENERATING MILIEU OF GANG DELINQUENCY[29]

The research literature supports the position that some middle-class goals are highly regarded by lower-class as well as middle-class young people, by gang members as well as those who are not members of gangs, and by many drug users as well as non–drug users.[30] Lower-class boys and girls are more likely, also, to value lifestyles that hinder middle-class achievement. This is especially the case for lower-class gang members whose lifestyles include a variety of unconventional activities, many of them quasi-legal or illegal hustles. Some of these are especially damaging to the life-chances of adolescent girls, for example, attaching themselves to boys' gangs, prostitution, and bearing out-of-wedlock children.

OPPORTUNITY STRUCTURES AND DELINQUENT SUBCULTURES[31]

The degree of integration between conventional and criminal value systems in lower-class communities has a profound impact on the character of delinquency. In some communities adults who are engaged in organized criminal activities also participate in conventional (economic, political, and religious) institutions. Both conventional and criminal adult role models for young people are available, and adult criminals are often more successful than are their conventional counterparts. Adults share an interest in containing youthful excesses of violence and other criminal activities, except as they may be controlled by adults. Delinquent activities in such integrated communities tend to be relatively orderly, rational, and systematic.

In communities lacking in integration in the previous sense, adult criminals are less successful and do not participate in conventional institutions, neither successful conventional nor criminal role models are available. Adult controls, which might emanate from either sector, are therefore weak. The lack of social controls in such communities gives rise to conflict gangs.

Richard Cloward noted that Merton's paradigm did not regard the availability of illegitimate means for achievement of goals as problematic. Theft and other criminal means of achieving material success were viewed simply as innovative, albeit illegal, means to that end. Cloward's position is firmly grounded in a rich research tradition that demonstrates the importance of cultural transmission of values, techniques, and traditions supporting delinquent and criminal behavior. Becoming a successful thief is by no means a simple matter, nor are delinquent gangs equally accessible to all adolescents. Cloward and Lloyd Ohlin attempt to account for delinquent subcultures in terms of the paradigm outlined in Figure 7.1.

The basic elements of the Merton paradigm relevant to delinquent subcultures are reproduced by Cloward and Ohlin as independent

FIGURE 7.1   Opportunities, Gang Membership, and Delinquency   SOURCE: James F. Short, Jr., Ramon Rivera, and Ray A. Tennyson, "Perceived Opportunities, Gang Membership and Delinquent Behavior," *American Sociological Review*, 30 (February, 1965):56–67.

OPPORTUNITIES, GANG MEMBERSHIP, AND DELINQUENCY	TYPE OF SUBCULTURE	
STRUCTURAL FEATURES	CRIMINAL	CONFLICT
I. *Independent Variable*	(Integrated Areas)	(Unintegrated Areas)
A. Culturally prescribed success goals	Internalized	Internalized
B. Availability of legitimate means to success goals	Limited; hence intense pressures toward deviant behavior	Limited; hence intense pressures toward deviant behavior
II. *Intervening Variables*	Incomplete internalization	Incomplete internalization
A. Institutional norms	Available	Unavailable
B. Availability of illegal means to success goals	Accommodative; each participates in value system of other	Conflicted; neither group well organized; value systems implicit, and opposed to one another
1. Relations between adult carriers of conventional and criminal values	Available; offenders at different age levels integrated	Unavailable; attenuated relations between offenders at different age levels
2. Criminal learning structure	Stable sets of criminal roles graded for different ages and levels of competence; continuous income; protection from detection and prosecution	Unarticulated opportunity structure; individual rather than organized crime; sporadic income; little protection from detection and prosecution
3. Criminal opportunity structure	Strong controls originate in *both*	Diminished social control; "weak" relations between adults and adolescents
4. Social control	legitimate and illegal	
III. *Dependent Variable*	structures. Pressures toward deviance originate in limited	Pressures toward deviance
A. Expected type of collective response among delinquents	accessibility to success goals by legitimate means, but are ameliorated by opportunities for access by illegal means. Hence, delinquent behavior is rational, disciplined, and crime-oriented.	originate in blocked opportunity by *any* institutionalized system of means. Hence, delinquent behavior displays expressive conflict patterns.

variables in this figure: structural features, and institutional (conventional) norms. Up to this point integrated and unintegrated lower-class areas are the same. They diverge sharply with respect to the availability of illegal means to success goals: Intervening Variable B, elaborated in terms of (1) relations between adult carriers of conventional and criminal values, (2) criminal learning structure, (3) criminal opportunity structure, and (4) social control.

The dependent variables (those to be explained), III in Figure 7.1, refer to the types of delinquent subcultures that are expected to emerge from the structural and cultural variables listed as independent and intervening: criminal, in the case of integrated areas, conflict, in unintegrated areas. Cloward and Ohlin hypothesized that a third type of subculture (retreatist, e.g., oriented around drug use) emerges among "double failures," that is, those who fail in both conventional and illegal (criminal or conflict) means of achievement.

RESEARCH ON DELINQUENT SUBCULTURES

Research focused on "opportunity structure theory," as the Cloward and Ohlin paradigm has come to be called, both offers limited support for the theory and clarifies the nature of the reality it seeks to explain. The Chicago gang study referred to in earlier chapters found that perceptions of legitimate and criminal opportunities by black and white lower-class gang and non-gang boys, and middle-class boys of both races, generally supported the paradigm, *up to the point of the specification of the dependent variable; that is, the predicted delinquent subculture.* White boys and middle-class boys tended to perceive legitimate opportunities as available to a greater extent than did black and lower-class boys, and gang boys of both races were the least optimistic in this regard.

Conversely, responses to questions concerning relationships between adult carriers of conventional and criminal values and criminal learning and opportunity structures, indicated that lower-class boys perceived criminal opportunities as open to them to a greater extent than did middle-class boys, as did black compared to white boys, and as did gang boys of both races compared to non-gang boys.[32] Similar differences were found in the boys' perceptions of the "clout" and the "helpfulness" of adults in their residential areas (as a measure of social control emanating from adults).

Given these findings, the clearest implication of the Cloward and Ohlin paradigm is that a delinquent subculture should not be found among the white middle-class boys studied. Such, indeed, was the case. However, the most evident delinquent orientation among several of the black gangs was toward *gang conflict* rather than property crimes. Quantitative analysis of behavior ratings of the gang boys identified a conflict pattern characterized by individual and group fighting, the carrying of concealed weapons, and assault, but this cluster of offenses also was associated with robbery, and to a lesser extent with many other behaviors, delinquent and nondelinquent alike.[33]

Both quantitative measures and field investigations revealed a great deal of diversity in both delinquent and nondelinquent patterns of behavior. Additionally, while the gang boys engaged in a great deal of theft behavior, no clear pattern of such behavior could be identified and no gang could be classified as criminal on the basis of field work.

ADULT-ADOLESCENT RELATIONSHIPS

Adult controls and opportunity structures for youth are further informed by data concerning the nature of adult-adolescent relationships. When asked to identify the adults with whom they had the *most contact*, gang members named fewer adults than did the other boys. More importantly, gang boys nominated far fewer adults occupying "caretaker" roles.[34]

When adults identified by the boys were interviewed, those nominated by gang members (in contrast with adults nominated by the other boys) reported that their interaction with boys in the strata from which their nominations had come occurred primarily *around the neighborhood* in which the boys lived. Non-gang strata adults more frequently saw the boys in centers for organized adolescent activities or in their own homes or the boys' homes.

Differences in reported topics of conversation that the gang and non gang nominees had with the boys also were striking. School problems were noted by about half or more of the adults named by non-gang boys, but by few of the gang nominees. Analysis of responses to questions concerning school problems revealed especially dramatic differences between black gang boys and non-gang nominees of both races, with more of the latter indicating that they had discussed and given advice concerning school problems. Neighborhood gossip and casual greetings predominated as topics of conversation between gang boys and the adults they nominated, quite in contrast with topics reported by adults nominated by other boys.

The data present a consistent picture: Gang members were more isolated from the conventional adult world, more embedded in the lower-class milieu, and less likely to receive assistance from adults than were non-gang members from the same communities. Black gang members were especially disadvantaged, and white middle-class boys were the most favored in each respect. These data, and analysis of specific comments by their nominators concerning the boys, strongly suggest that gang members, compared to the other boys, had little reason to perceive adults as willing or able to help them in substantial ways.[35]

SUBCULTURAL THEMES AND DELINQUENCY

Subcultures are defined in terms of shared values and norms and the personal identities of those who share them. Most definitions of subcultures stress "conduct norms," and they explain delinquent behavior largely as conformity to these norms. Conversely, nondelinquent behavior is explained by rejection of delinquent norms and conformity to conventional norms. However, normative properties of groups are inadequate to explain many aspects of group behavior. Members of even the most delinquent gang are not engaged in delinquent behavior most of the time, and delinquent episodes rarely involve all members of the group who share the relevant norm (see Chapter 9).

Youth groups are among the most important macro-level influences on much delinquency, and micro-level processes often determine the outcome of behavior episodes, as we shall see in Chapter 9. While the *origins* of delinquent subcultures in modern societies are difficult to trace, it is possible to study some of the processes by which subcultural themes are adopted and adapted by particular groups.

FURTHER OBSERVATIONS OF THE CHICAGO GANG COMMUNITIES

As noted in Chapter 5, life in the white gang areas in Chicago was dominated by conventional institutions such as the Catholic church, local political organizations, and voluntary associations which were attempting to prevent blacks from moving into their neighborhoods. Ethnic organizations and extended kinship groups, unions and other job relationships, and formally organized recreational patterns (e.g., bowling leagues) were important sources of community stability for both adults and young people.

The reaction of white gang members to the presence in "their" park of a black teenager (presented in Chapter 5) is illustrative of the racially tense situation in many of Chicago's white neighborhoods at the time of the study. Here, macro-level phenomena (the ecological setting, the normative properties of the community, and the general structure of relationships between young people and adults) set the stage for an event that produced delinquent behavior.

There is, of course, much we do not and cannot know about this event and others like it—for example, the great variety of possible outcomes, why different boys responded as they did to the appearance of the black youngster, why none of the girls joined in the chase, and what might have happened had the black youngster been caught. More detailed observations at the microsocial level might have provided answers to some of these questions. Given the information available, it is clear that macrosocial phenomena set the stage for the playing out of microsocial interaction of individuals and groups. Similarly, the informal mingling of adolescents and adults characteristic of the black gang communities, illustrated by the "quarter party" in Chapter 5, is a setting for behavioral events which often have delinquent outcomes. At the time of this study quarter parties were a recurring form of social interaction in many lower-class black communities.

Because of the ecology of racial occupancy of Chicago communities, black and white gangs never engaged in conflict with one another. Some black families in the vanguard of invasion were able to move into white residential areas as a result of relative economic affluence. Others did so by overcrowding dwelling units.[36] Gang boys' families sometimes followed these early arrivals. When they did so, members of gangs often returned to the gang neighborhoods they had left in order to be with the gangs. When a critical mass of black youngsters had arrived, "branches" of the gangs to which the boys belonged sometimes were formed in these areas.

GANGS AND DELINQUENT SUBCULTURES

The fact that most delinquent behavior takes place in groups was noted in Chapter 6. While microsocial processes do not necessarily involve groups, they always involve interaction, and it is in the group context that most interaction involving delinquent behavior occurs. Adolescents belong to many types of groups, and delinquent behaviors are common among many of these. One type of group—the gang—has been notorious for its association with delinquent behavior.

The viability of the gang as a scientific concept is controversial. Research has failed to confirm the commonly held image of "that old gang of mine." Nor has it confirmed the image of delinquent gangs as made up of "vicious hoodlums" lurking in the street, who commit mayhem in neighborhoods and destroy property. Both of these images are misleading, the first overly romantic, the other simplistic, incorporating only some of the behavior to be explained.

For present purposes the *gang* is defined as *a group whose members meet together with some regularity, over time, on the basis of group-defined criteria of membership and group-defined organizational structure, and with some sense of territoriality.*[37] Gangs are to be distinguished both from adult-sponsored youth groups and more free-floating aggregations of young people who sometimes gather in particular places, but which have not coalesced into gangs.

Gangs exist as parts of other social systems, just as subcultures exist in relationship to larger cultures. Gangs are *carriers* of subcultures, but they do not *constitute* them. A drug user subculture, for example, may be shared by members of a gang, but most such subcultures are not exclusive to a single group. Particular variants of drug user subcultures may be identified with particular gangs, however. The relationship of conflict gangs to conflict subcultures is typically quite different, inasmuch as conflict gangs depend in part on rival gangs. A reputation for toughness and fighting may be acquired by acting tough and fighting with peers who are not members of gangs, but the existence of other conflict gangs, and of a conflict subculture, enhances the prospects for status in the social world of conflict gangs. Consider the following field reports. The first is an example of a drug-using subgroup within a larger gang of white youngsters; the second involves a gang fight between members of two black gangs noted for their fighting reputations.

A DRUG-ORIENTED GANG

After nearly six months in the field, the observer of the "Pill Poppers" (the gang used many drugs, but chiefly pills, which were cheap and readily available) submitted the following description of a "hanging session" of the group. Members of the group and the detached worker assigned to them exchanged anecdotes of numerous incidents in which various members of the group had been involved. A few of the incidents follow:[38]

> The time Willie was so high he walked off a roof and fell a story or two and broke his nose. The worker thought he had been on a roof, while Butch maintained he fell from a boxcar. Butch said it was over a week before he went to the doctor....Harry said he walked around the hospital in a crazy looking green coat whenever the guys went to visit him.
>
> The time Snooks, Baby, and Jerry climbed on a roof to wake Elizabeth. One of the guys reached through the window and grabbed what he thought was Elizabeth's leg and shook it to wake her up. It turned out to be her old man's leg and it woke him up.
>
> A more recent incident in which Sonny leaped over the counter to rob a Chinese laundryman, who proceeded to beat him badly. When the police came, Sonny asked that they arrest the man for having beaten him.
>
> Walter got into an argument with a woman over whose car it was they were standing by. He insisted they call the police, and waited confidently until the police showed and took him away.
>
> Sonny tried to break into a building and was ripping off a door when the police found him.
>
> Some of the guys slept out in a car and woke the next morning to find the car was being pulled away. They asked the tower to stop just long enough so they could get out.
>
> One of the guys broke into a car and just about tore the door off doing so. All the windows of the car were broken out, but he was too high to notice.
>
> One of the boys tried to start a car but just could not manage. The car had no motor.

The group assembled clearly enjoyed these stories. The observer commented that "these tales may be in the process of becoming legendary within the group. They are so characteristic...and describe it so well." Originally a segment of a larger gang, this group's preoccupation with drugs and their refusal to participate in the more bellicose activities of the larger gang, led to their increasing isolation.

The research literature provides conflicting accounts of the extent and nature of subcultures supportive of hard drug use. An earlier Chicago study of young addicts found evidence of an elaborate subculture formed around "kicks," "hustles," "cool" behavior, and esthetic tastes in clothes and music.[39] A New York study, focusing primarily on individual personality characteristics, found that addicts had weak egos, inadequate superegos, and suffered extreme problems of masculine identity.[40]

Both of these studies located addicts primarily among minority populations in lower socioeconomic areas. The New York study reported that, while most addicts had belonged to gangs, following their addiction most had become peripheral members of their gangs. Personality characteristics of the Chicago addicts were not studied. The two studies, therefore, did not so much contradict one another as address different levels of explanation.

CONFLICT GANGS

The contrast between the "Pill Poppers" and the "Knights" and "Vice Kings," two conflict gangs, could hardly be greater. The Knights and the Vice Kings regularly engaged in the guerrilla warfare typical of conflict gangs in Chicago during the late 1950s and early 1960s. A detached worker with the Knights described an incident involving the two gangs as follows:[41]

> While I was sitting there in the car talking to William, the remaining guys having gotten out of the car in pursuit of some girls around the corner, William told me that a couple of Vice Kings were approaching. I looked out the window and noticed two Vice Kings and two girls walking down the street by the car. I didn't know them as Vice Kings because I only know the chiefs like Garroway, Pappy…William then turned around and made the observation that there were about fifteen or twenty Vice Kings across the street in the alley and wandering up the streets in ones and twos.
>
> At this point, I heard three shots go off. I don't know who fired these shots, and no else seemed to know, because the Vice Kings at this point had encountered Commando, Jones, and a couple of other Knights who were coming from around the corner talking to the girls. The Vice Kings yelled across the street to Commando and his boys, and Commando yelled back. They traded insults and challenges, Commando being the leader of the Knights and a guy named Bear being the leader of the Vice Kings. At this point I got out of the car to try to cool Commando down, inasmuch as he was halfway across the street hurling insults across the street and daring them to do something about it, and they were doing the same thing to him. I grabbed Commando and began to pull him back across the street.
>
> By this time the Vice Kings had worked themselves into a rage, and three of them came across the street yelling that they were mighty Vice Kings and to attack Commando and the Knights. In trying to break this up, I was not too successful. I didn't know the Vice Kings involved, and they were really determined to swing on the Knights, so we had a little scuffle around there. I did see one Vice King who I did know. That was Jr. Smith, and I asked him to help me break it up. At this point, along the street comes Henry Brown, with a revolver, shooting at the Vice Kings. Everybody ducked and the Vice Kings ran, and Henry Brown ran around the corner. I began to throw Knights into my car because I knew that the area was "hot," and I was trying to get them out of there. Henry came back around the corner and leaped into my car also. I asked him if he had the gun, and he told me that he did not, and since I was in a hurry, I pulled off in the car and took him and the rest of the boys with me.
>
> Asked how the boys felt and acted after this incident, the worker's reply is quite revealing: In the car, Commando and the other boys were extremely elated. There were expressions like: "Baby, did you see the way I swung on that kid"; "Man, did we tell them off"; "I really let that one kid have it"; "Did you see them take off when I leveled my gun on them"; "You were great, Baby, and did you see the way I…" It was just like we used to feel when we got back from a patrol where everything went just right (the worker had been a paratrooper in the Korean conflict). The tension was relieved, we had performed well and could be proud.

In this brief excerpt the status function of the conflict subculture is seen in bold relief. Both the Knights and the Vice Kings experienced the thrill of the conflict. They had faced great danger. The Vice Kings could explain their failure to defeat the enemy by virtue of the Knights' superior weaponry. The Knights could believe they were prevented from complete triumph only by the intervention of the detached worker. Participants on both sides shared the elation and the status-conferring glow of the encounter.

Events are not always so easily and painlessly resolved, of course. Though the extent of violence and lethal weapons on the street are exaggerated in popular lore and media accounts, guns have become more accessible since this research was conducted. Casual encounters between gangs often result in serious injuries or death. Planned violence, such as drive-by shootings, also have become more common. Under such circumstances gang conflict may become a deadly zero-sum game.

The events described in these field reports involve the microsocial level of analysis and explanation. The "Pill Poppers' " tales and the reactions of the gang to their telling, and the encounter between the Knights and the Vice Kings, tell us a great deal about the nature of these groups and their behavior.

PROPERTY CRIMES, COMMUNITIES AND DELINQUENT GANGS

As noted in Chapter 6, property crimes constitute the largest number of serious crimes in statistical pictures of crime and delinquency. Members of gangs engage in a great deal of such behavior. Cliques that engaged in theft activities existed in several of the Chicago gangs. The membership of those cliques frequently shifted, and larger "criminal gangs" were not found. Irving Spergel has described patterns of delinquent behavior, including economic crimes, that are more confirming of the Cloward and Ohlin paradigm.[42] A "racket" subculture was found in a residentially stable lower-class community in which organized crime existed. Gang members from this community had a stronger criminal orientation than did those in other lower-class communities. A second community, "Slumtown," exhibited high rates of public assistance, high infant mortality, high population density and congestion, low income, and physical deterioration. Here gang delinquency took a more conflict-oriented form. A third community, "Haulburg," was described as standing midway between Racketville and Slumtown in neighborhood integration and criminal organization. This community was characterized by a delinquency pattern dominated by car theft, burglary, store holdups, and some violent behavior.

Available data do not permit resolution of theoretical issues raised by studies such as these. It seems clear that the influence of lower-class cultural values and behavior patterns has been underestimated by theorists in the delinquent subculture tradition. Yet, those who emphasize the lower-class milieu as the critical factor shaping delinquency also underestimate the strength and appeal of values associated with material success and the constraints of conventional values. Just how these factors interact varies among individuals, families, and communities; and chance factors doubtless play an important role also. But chance factors are also socially structured, as will be discussed in Chapter 9.

The *nature* of available criminal opportunities is critical to delinquent subcultures. While organized crime has been an important factor in Chicago for more than half a century, it has taken many different forms. In the black communities studied in Chicago the numbers racket was well entrenched, as were prostitution, drug dealing, and a great deal of petty crime. Pimps were quite visible role models in a few of these communities, and one of the gang leaders we studied worked as a "runner" for a numbers dealer. The most available role models for black gang members were petty thieves, small-time pimps, burglars, young men involved in robbery, low-level drug dealers, and other functionaries in the rackets. Yet, like Glassner and Loughlin's drug-dealers, few of these young men aspired to such roles, or to more affluent and powerful criminal occupations.[43]

CATEGORIC RISKS, SUBCULTURES, AND DELINQUENCY

Chapter 6 documented the failure of most SRD studies to find higher delin-quency rates among working-class or lower-class youngsters than their middle-class counterparts. This failure has been viewed as a refutation of the class-linked nature of delinquency, or at least as weakening its theoretical basis. How can this apparent contradiction be reconciled?

Self-report data demonstrate that participation and frequency of in-volvement in delinquent behaviors differs less among young people from differing social-class backgrounds than some theories suggest. Survey data also document that delinquency is overwhelmingly a group phenomenon, but tell us very little about the subcultural nature of delinquency. Nor do they reveal much about the community context of such behavior.

Macro-level factors linking patterns of social control and the distribu-tion of incentives and opportunities for the commission of delinquent acts appear to explain much of the variation in delinquency rates among cate-goric risks. Residential segregation in American cities is strongly related to social class, as well as to race and, in many cities, ethnicity. Residential segregation is reflected, also, in the social class, the racial and ethnic composition of schools, both important contexts for the generation of common "problems of adjustment," and "effective interaction," as pre-viously noted. It is in local communities, in schools and parks, on the streets, and in other specific locales that interaction related to delinquent behavior takes place.

Clues to the nature of these relationships are found in many of the studies previously cited. A study conducted by Albert J. Reiss and Lewis Rhodes also is informative.[44] Reiss and Rhodes found that official delin-quency rates and self-reported delinquency of boys from varying social-class backgrounds in Nashville, Tennessee, were related to the *social-class structure of schools*. While lower-class boys had generally higher rates of delinquency than boys from other social-class backgrounds, the chances of juvenile court referral for lower-class boys residing in predominantly high-status areas with low delinquency rates was virtually zero. This finding is especially impres-sive because lower-class boys in high-status areas most often chose other lower-class boys as friends (and had those choices reciprocated), and "delinquent organization" was more frequent among lower-class than middle-class boys as well.

Behavior choices occur as a result of individual-level and micro-level, as well as macro-level, influences. The availability of role models and opportunities, the nature of formal and informal control structures, and the nature of supports for delinquent behavior (adult and age peers alike), and the availability of reward structures for conventional as well as delinquent behavior all influence individuals. Choices are *not determined*, but they are *limited*, by position in the social order. Individual behavioral choices are based in part on *personal assessments* of macro-level factors. These assessments make it a good deal easier for middle-class children to acquire a stake in conformity to middle-class values and expectations regarding school attendance and performance—and a good deal harder to avoid such commitment—than is the case for lower-class children.

Values and practices regarding socialization and supervision vary for young people in different risk categories. A point made by Robert J. Sampson with respect to the effectiveness of cohesive family structures in controlling delinquency is equally applicable to age, gender, and other categoric risks. "Cohesive family structures," he notes, "are probably effective not because they intervene in actual criminal acts but because they are aware of and control peer-group activities that often set the context for more serious crime."[45] Closer supervision of younger children than of adolescents, and of females than of males, results in more effective control. As we shall see in the next chapter, bonds of attachment and commitment to parents generally result in more effective behavior controls for all young people.

ECOLOGICAL AND DEMOGRAPHIC TRENDS

The ecological patterns of delinquency rates have inspired a great deal of research and a variety of interpretations. Shaw and his collaborators conducted extensive case studies of delinquents, in addition to their ecological studies.[46] Their findings may be summarized as follows: (1) Delinquent behavior comes to be "traditional" in some neighborhoods, being passed on from year to year—and from generation to generation—by siblings, delinquent gangs, the persistence of criminal activities, and the presence of adult criminals in the community; and (2) community control of delinquent behavior is weakened in areas of ecological transition as a result of changing land use patterns in the city, high population density and turnover, and ineffective conventional institutions.

Research on delinquent gangs and delinquent subcultures has elaborated the first of these findings. The second finding developed out of studies of urban ecology that attributed community change to metabolic processes of growth. The theory held that *social disorganization*, which followed from these processes, resulted in weakened social control. This theory was criticized for ignoring the influence of cultural factors on these processes and for failing to recognize important forms of social organization to be found in communities that appear by conventional criteria to be socially disorganized.

Recent research helps to reconcile conflicting claims regarding community and ecological relationships with delinquency. The early ecological model assumed the *stability* of the ecological structure of city growth in explaining *how* communities change and the consequences of change. This assumption was valid until World War II. Since that time, however, *planned* activities affecting urban structure and growth expanded greatly, changing classical ecological processes of invasion and succession. Large-scale public housing, shopping centers, gentrification and suburban development occurred. Highway construction and major institutional development projects also modified the physical and, therefore, the community structure of many cities. These types of activities resulted from political and economic considerations, and cultural images of what cities ought to be like. They altered the operation of forces basic to the earlier models of ecological change.

Some neighborhoods and communities have been completely destroyed by large-scale planned activities. Dramatic changes in other communities have resulted in quite different community populations and the creation of "artificial neighborhoods."[47] The impact of these changes on ecological processes and on crime and delinquency has been profound. Studies conducted in both Los Angeles and Chicago find that the assumption of ecological stability is no longer valid. The theory that delinquency rates reflect the ability of communities to sustain social control, however, is supported.

Urban redevelopment activities, often undertaken to replace physically deteriorated areas and to relieve economic deprivation, do not insure effective social control. Shaw and McKay had argued that economic deprivation and physical deterioration tended to be associated with high rates of population turnover and heterogeneity, which in turn rendered social control difficult. More recent research suggests that change of any sort that disrupts institutional and community stability has similar effects. Planned human activities may destroy neighborhoods and entire communities. The resulting population shifts create new residential areas and alter existing neighborhoods beyond the boundaries of new construction, disrupting institutional and personal networks. When local networks lack stability, the research suggests, informal social control based on primary associations is less likely to develop or to be maintained.[48]

Research on the impact on crime of post–World War II housing policy in Great Britain also is instructive. Anthony E. Bottoms and Paul Wiles find that these impacts depend on a variety of related factors, for example, the local "reputation" of an area with respect to crime or respectability, the activities of local residents, the types of public housing constructed in an area (high-rise buildings or single family houses), as well as the decisions of local housing authorities. Areas of similar class composition can have quite different criminal careers. Among the more significant social aspects of Britain's housing policies, Bottoms and Wiles suggest, is that they have "reflected and reinforced, in bricks and mortar, class divisions in Britain."[49]

Local and national governments play a more active role in housing construction and allocation in Britain than in the largely market-driven housing industry in the United States. Social class divisions in Britain also have been more pervasive and rigid than in the United States. There is growing evidence of the emergence of a "ghetto underclass" in the inner cities of the United States, however. While public housing provides the physical location for much of this segment of the population, structural changes in the economy appear to play the most important role in this relatively new development.

William J. Wilson and Robert Aponte note that in little more than a decade poverty has become "urbanized" in the United States. While the change has affected both whites and blacks, other qualitative shifts have led to problems of longterm poverty and welfare dependency, particularly among blacks. Wilson and Aponte note that "poor inner-city minorities have been especially vulnerable to the structural transformation" of many cities "from centers of production and distribution of physical goods to centers of administration, information exchange, trade, finance, and government services." Millions of jobs have been lost in this process and many of those that have been created have not benefited the poor. Growth sectors in the economy have left the central city or require skills that the poor do not possess. The result is that:[50]

> ...female-headed families are heavily represented in the poverty population, are highly urbanized, and are disproportionately black; that black female heads are much less likely to marry if single, or to remarry if divorced or widowed, and therefore that female-headed families among whites tend to be of relatively short duration, whereas among blacks they tend to be prolonged; that teenage pregnancies are strongly associated with being reared in female-headed families, poverty, and ghetto residence; that black children are increasingly growing up in families without fathers not only because more black women are getting divorced, separated, or are becoming widows, but also because more black women are not marrying; and that the increasing joblessness of black men is one of the major reasons black women tend not to be married. This research strongly suggests that the urban core has spawned a sizable and growing black underclass of marginally productive and unattached men, and of women and children in female-headed homes.

Specific implications of these developments for juvenile delinquency have not been systematically studied, although crime and delinquency are among the accompaniments of longterm poverty and welfare dependency that are most often noted in journalistic accounts. Other consequences include deterioration of schools and widespread lack of community participation in efforts to overcome problems associated with poverty, unemployment, and teenage pregnancy.

Whatever the implications of a relatively permanent ghetto underclass in this country, it is clear that restoration of the emphasis on ecological processes, social change, and adaptation both strengthens and modifies Shaw and McKay's interpretation of the relationship between social disorganization and social control.

DEMOGRAPHIC FACTORS

"Society at large is faced perennially with an invasion of barbarians."[51] So Norman Ryder introduces his discussion of *demographic* metabolic processes that characterize all societies. Ryder's point is that the young must be socialized. Rapid social change exacerbates problems associated with that task. Ryder focuses on the post–World War II "baby boom," which grossly distorted the U.S. age distribution. Relevant data are presented in Tables 7.1 and 7.2.

TABLE 7.1   Size of population aged 14–24, 1890–1990, and percent change per decade.

YEAR	SIZE (IN MILLION)	PERCENT CHANGE
1890	14.2	
1900	16.5	+16
1910	20.0	+21
1920	20.8	+4
1930	24.8	+20
1940	26.3	+6
1950	24.2	−8
1960	26.7	+10
1970	40.5	+52
1980	44.8	+11
1990	41.1	−8

Source: James S. Coleman, et al., *Youth: Transition to Adulthood*. Report of the Panel on Youth of the President's Science Advisory Committee. Chicago: University of Chicago Press, 1974, p. 46. Based on the 1890–1960 statistics of the U.S. Bureau of the Census, *U.S. Census of Population: 1960. General Population Characteristics, United States Summary*. Final Report PC(1)-1B. Washington, DC: U.S. Government Printing Office, 1961. Table 47.

TABLE 7.2   Ratio of the population aged 14–24 to the population aged 25–64, 1890–1990, and percent change per decade.

YEAR	RATIO	PERCENT CHANGE
1890	0.566	
1900	0.519	−8
1910	0.496	−4
1920	0.430	−13
1930	0.431	0
1940	0.400	−7
1950	0.322	−20
1960	0.322	0
1970	0.449	+39
1980	0.423	−6
1990	0.332	−21

Source: James S. Coleman, et al., *Youth: Transition to Adulthood*. Report of the Panel on Youth of the President's Science Advisory Committee. Chicago: University of Chicago Press, 1974, p. 46. Based on the 1890–1960 statistics of the U.S. Bureau of the Census, *U.S. Census of Population: 1960. General Population Characteristics, United States Summary*. Final Report PC(1)-1B. Washington, DC: U.S. Government Printing Office, 1961. Table 48.

Table 7.1 demonstrates the extent to which the decade of the 1960s witnessed an unparalleled increase in the size of the most crime-prone age group, 14–24. Of equal importance, relative to the older age groups that are responsible for socializing the young, for teaching them, and for accommodating them into the work-force, during that decade the ratio of the population aged 14–24 to that aged 25–64 (see Table 7.2) experienced a large increase, the only such increase in this century.

Ryder's analysis indicates that the schools absorbed about 90 percent of the increase of persons aged 16–19 during the 1960s. Schools thus were confronted with a very rapid increase in enrollments on an unprecedented scale.

Except for the baby boom, the United States had experienced declining fertility for many years. After reaching a peak in 1957, the general fertility rate declined to the lowest rate in history during the 1980s. Resumption of the lower fertility trend is reflected in lower numbers of delinquency cases. Demographic changes cannot account for all the observed changes in numbers of delinquency cases, however, since *rates* of delinquency cases in juvenile courts have increased in recent decades. Rates increased steadily throughout the 1960s but did not reach their peak until 1970 (when babies born during the record fertility year of 1957 were thirteen years old).

ROUTINE ACTIVITIES, LIFESTYLES, AND DELINQUENT BEHAVIOR

Lawrence E. Cohen, Marcus Felson, and others have studied the impact on the crime of demographic trends, broader social changes, and human ecology.[52] The basic proposition of their perspective is that crime occurs with the convergence of motivated offenders, suitable targets, and the absence of suitable guardians. Social changes have altered "routine activities" and "lifestyles" of large numbers of people: More women work outside the home, the number of single-person households and single-parent families has increased, adolescents spend less time with their parents than they did in pre–World War II days, and more people travel away from the home. These changes weaken guardianship. Consumer products have become more widely distributed, thus increasing the supply of suitable targets for theft. The numbers of motivated offenders increased significantly following the "baby boom" noted previously. Under circumstances of economic adversity, such as occurs in downturns of the business cycle, in economic dislocation, and in the creation of an underclass, the supply of offenders motivated to commit property crimes is increased.[53]

Empirical studies have generally supported this theoretical perspective. Based on data from the 1975 National Crime Survey, Terance D. Miethe, Mark Stafford, and J. Scott Long report that routine activity and lifestyle variables strongly influence the risk of property victimization but not of violent crime victimization.[54] This is consistent with the property crime focus of the routine activities approach, with its emphasis on motivated offenders, suitable targets, and guardians. Miethe and his associates note that many questions remain unanswered, however. The relative importance of the three major components is not clear, nor are the circumstances under which their convergence results in criminal acts. Some of these questions will be addressed in Chapter 9, following discussion of how and why *individuals* become delinquent.

NOTES

1. See LaMar T. Empey, *American Delinquency: Its Meaning and Construction*. Homewood, IL: Dorsey, 1982, pp. 23–34; see also, Ruth Shonle Cavan and Jordan T. Cavan, *Delinquency and Crime: Cross-Cultural Perspectives*. Philadelphia: Lippincott, 1968; T. C. N. Gibbens and R. H. Ahrenfeldt (eds.), *Cultural Factors in Delinquency*. London: Tavistock, 1966.

2. Quoting Harold E. Pepinsky, "Crime causation: political theories," pp. 323–330, in S. H. Kadish (ed.), *Encyclopedia of Crime and Justice*. New York: Free Press, 1983. See also, Stanley Cohen, *Visions of Control: Crime, Punishment and Classification*. Cambridge: Polity Press, 1985.

3. See Albert K. Cohen, "Crime causation: sociological theories," pp. 342–353, in S. H. Kadish (ed.), *Encyclopedia of Crime and Justice*. New York: Free Press, 1983, especially pp. 349–350; see also, Herman Schwendinger and Julia Siegel Schwendinger, *Adolescent Subcultures and Delinquency*. New York: Praeger, 1985, pp. 3–17. The most prominent precursor of modern Marxist theories of crime was William Bonger.

4. Schwendinger and Schwendinger, *Ibid.*, p. 3.

5. See Daniel Chirot, "The rise of the west," *American Sociological Review*, 50 (April, 1985):181–195.

6. See Louise I. Shelley, *Crime and Modernization: The Impact of Industrialization and Urbanization on Crime*. Carbondale, IL: Southern Illinois Press, 1981. While Shelley's focus is on crime rather than juvenile delinquency, the fact that so much crime is committed by the young suggests that her analysis is equally applicable to delinquency. See also, Lois B. DeFleur, *Delinquency in Argentina: A Study of Cordoba's Youth*. Pullman, WA: Washington State University Press, 1970; E. P. Thompson, *Whigs and Hunters*. London: Allen Lane, 1975; D. Hay, P. Linebaugh, J. Rule, E. P. Thompson, and C. Winslow (eds.), *Albion's Fatal Tree*. London: Allen Lane, 1975.

7. J. Brewer and J. Styles, *An Ungovernable People: The English and their Law in the 17th and 18th Centuries*. New Brunswick, NJ: Rutgers University Press, 1980.

8. Michael Ignatieff, "State, civil society, and total institutions: a critique of recent social histories of punishment," pp. 153–192, in Michael Tonry and Norval Morris (eds.), *Crime and Justice: An Annual Review of Research*, Vol. 3. Chicago: University of Chicago Press, 1981, p. 186.

9. Ira Katznelson, "Working-class formation and the state: nineteenth-century England in American perspective," pp. 257–284, in Peter B. Evans, Dietrich Rueschemeyer, and Theda Skocpol, *Bringing the State Back In*. Cambridge: Cambridge University Press, 1985.

10. Cf., Alfred Blumstein, "On the racial disproportionality of U.S. prison populations," *Journal of Criminal Law and Criminology*, 73 (Fall, 1982):1259–1281; and George S. Bridges, Robert D. Crutchfield, and Edith E. Simpson, "Crime, social structure and criminal punishment: white and nonwhite rates of imprisonment," *Social Problems*, 34 (October, 1987):345–361.

11. See William Chambliss, "The Saints and the Roughnecks," *Society*, 11 (November–December, 1973):24–31. Sanctioning is a complex process, however. See Peggy C. Giordan, "Sanctioning the high-status deviant: an attributional analysis," *Social Psychology Quarterly*, 46, 4 (1983):329–42.

12. For a comprehensive review of conflict theory see Austin T. Turk, *Criminality and the Legal Order*. Chicago: Rand McNally, 1969. See also, Pat Lauderdale, "A power and process approach to the definition of deviance," pp. 3–14 in Pat Lauderdale, *A Political Analysis of Deviance*. Minneapolis, MN: University of Minnesota Press, 1980. Social constructionist theories of social problems are reviewed in Joseph W. Schneider, "Social problems theory:

the constructionist view," pp. 209–229, in Ralph H. Turner and James F. Short, Jr. (eds.), *Annual Review of Sociology*, 11. Palo Alto, CA: Annual Reviews, 1985.

13. Erik H. Erikson, *Childhood and Society* (2d ed.). New York: Norton, 1963.

14. Hans Sebald, *Adolescence: A Social Psychological Analysis* (2d ed.). Englewood Cliffs, NJ: Prentice-Hall, 1977, p. 90, *et passim*.

15. See James S. Coleman, Robert H. Bremner, Burton R. Clark, John B. Davis, Dorothy H. Eichorn, Zvi Griliches, Joseph F. Kett, Norman B. Ryder, Zahava Blum Doering, and John M. Mays, *Youth: Transition to Adulthood*. Report of the Panel on Youth of the President's Science Advisory Committee. Chicago: University of Chicago Press, 1974, pp. 114–119.

16. Glaser refers to this principle as a "fundamental law of sociology and anthropology." See Daniel Glaser, *Social Deviance*. Chicago: Markham, 1971, p. 35.

17. Albert K. Cohen, *Delinquent Boys: The Culture of the Gang*. Glencoe: Free Press, 1955, p. 59.

18. Donald R. Cressey, "Delinquent and criminal subcultures," pp. 584–590, in S. H. Kadish (ed.), *Encyclopedia of Crime and Justice*. New York: Free Press, 1983.

19. See Frederic M. Thrasher, *The Gang: A Study of 1,313 Gangs in Chicago*. Chicago: University of Chicago Press, 1927 (rev. ed. 1936, abridged, with a new introduction by James F. Short, Jr., 1963). See also, W. I. Thomas, Robert E. Park, and Herbert A. Miller, *Old World Traits Transplanted*. New York: Harper, 1921; see also, Thorsten Sellin, *Culture Conflict and Crime*. New York: Social Science Research Council, 1938

20. Marshall B. Clinard and Daniel J. Abbott, "Community organization and property crime: a comparative study of social control in the slums of an African city," pp. 186–206, in James F. Short, Jr. (ed.), *Delinquency, Crime, and Society*. Chicago: University of Chicago Press, 1976; see also by Clinard and Abbott, *Crime in Developing Countries: A Comparative Perspective*. New York: Wiley-Interscience, 1973. See also, Eugene Havens and Elsa Ugandizaga, *Tres Barrios de Invasion*. Bogota: Ediciones Tercer Mundo, 1966.

21. The precise meaning and significance of terms denoting modernity, industrialization, and postindustrial development is a matter of much theoretical and empirical controversy. The functional requirements of modern societies are discussed in Alex Inkeles, "Social structure and the socialization of competence," *Harvard Educational Review*, 36 (Summer, 1966):265–283. See also, John Walton, "Theory and research on industrialization," forthcoming in Ralph H. Turner and James F. Short, Jr., *Annual Review of Sociology*, Vol. 13. Palo Alto, CA: Annual Reviews, pp. 89-108, 1987.

22. Ironically, persons possessing these and other valued personal characteristics sometimes create, or exacerbate, problems in their relationships with others by competing "too successfully." When women and members of minority groups do this, existing orders and organizations may be threatened. Resentment thus created may add to the burdens of prejudice and discrimination faced by less powerful segments of society.

23. Shelley, *op. cit*, p. 139. The following discussion is based largely on Shelley's work. The association of violence with illegal markets has been extensively documented and frequently dramatized. See, for example, John Kaplan, *Marijuana: The New Prohibition*. New York: World, 1970; Kettil Bruun, Lynn Pan, and Ingemar Rexed, *The Gentlemen's Club: International Control of Drugs and Alcohol*. Chicago: University of Chicago Press, 1975.

24. See Marshall B. Clinard, *Cities with Little Crime: The Case of Switzerland*. Arnold Rose Monograph Series, American Sociological Association. Cambridge: University of Cambridge Press, 1978.

25. See Arthur L. Stinchcombe, "Merton's theory of social structure," pp. 11–33, in Lewis A. Coser (ed.), *The Idea of Social Structure: Papers in Honor of Robert K. Merton*. New York: Harcourt Brace Jovanovich, 1975.

26. See Robert K. Merton, "Social structure and anomie," *American Sociological Review*, 3:672–682; revised and expanded with the same title, pp. 131–160, in Robert K. Merton, *Social Theory and Social Structure*. Glencoe, IL: Free Press, 1957, p. 132. Though written approximately four decades ago, the article's characterization of American culture seems even more applicable today.

27. Albert K. Cohen, *Delinquent Boys: The Culture of the Gang*. Glencoe, IL: Free Press, 1955.

28. See William Foote Whyte, *Street Corner Society*. Chicago: University of Chicago Press, 1943.

29. See Walter B. Miller, "Lower class culture as a generating milieu of gang delinquency," *Journal of Social Issues*, XIV (1958):5–19.

30. See, for example, Robert A. Gordon, James F. Short, Jr., Desmond S. Cartwright, and Fred L. Strodtbeck, "Values and gang delinquency: a study of street-corner groups," *American Journal of Sociology*, LXIX (September, 1963):109–128; Laura Thomasson Fishman, *Aspirations and Delinquency: The Case of Negro Girls*. Master's thesis, Department of Sociology, University of Chicago, 1966; Gary Schwartz, *Beyond Rebellion or Conformity: Youth and Authority in America*. Chicago: University of Chicago Press, 1987; Barry Glassner and Julia Loughlin, *Drugs in Adolescent Worlds: Burnouts to Straights*. New York: St. Martin's Press, 1987. cf., John Hagedorn, Perry Macon, *People and Folks: Crime and the Underclass in a Rustbelt City*. Chicago: Lake View Press, 1988.

31. See Solomon Kobrin, "The conflict of values in delinquency areas," *American Sociological Review*, 16 (December, 1951): 653–661; Albert K. Cohen and James F. Short, Jr., "Research in delinquent subcultures," *Journal of Social Issues*, XIV (1958):20–37; Richard A. Cloward, "Illegitimate means, anomie, and deviant behavior," *American Sociological Review*, 24 (April, 1959):164–176; see also, Richard A. Cloward and Lloyd E. Ohlin, *Delinquency and Opportunity: A Theory of Delinquent Gangs*. New York: Free Press, 1960.

32. No clear pattern emerged among gang and nongang, lower-class and middle-class black respondents with respect to the opportunity to "make it big" in illegal enterprise. Among white respondents, gang members tended to perceive no greater availability of elite criminal opportunities than did respondents from the other groups.

33. See James F. Short, Jr., Ray A. Tennyson, and Kenneth I. Howard, "Behavior dimensions of gang delinquency," *American Sociological Review*, XXVIII (June, 1963):411–428.

34. See Ramon Rivera and James F. Short, Jr., "Significant adults, caretakers, and structures of opportunity: an exploratory study," *Journal of Research in Crime and Delinquency*, 4 (January, 1967):76–97. *Caretakers* were defined as any adult, who, in the course of his or her ordinary daily activities, comes into contact with adolescents *as a representative of some larger adult-dominated institution that is formally committed to guide or to change the behavior of youth,* for example, youth workers, teachers, counselors, clergy, defense lawyers.

35. Analysis of the boys' evaluations of adult roles in their communities confirms this interpretation. See James F. Short, Jr., Ramon Rivera, and Harvey Marshall, "Adult-adolescent relations and gang delinquency," *Pacific Sociological Review*, 7 (Fall, 1964):59–65. Social relationships with adults were closely associated with the occupational choices of these boys, further operating to the disadvantage of the gang boys. See Ramon Rivera and James F. Short, Jr., "Occupational goals: a comparative analysis," pp. 70–90, in Malcolm W. Klein and Barbara C. Meyerhoff (eds.), *Juvenile Gangs in Context: Theory, Research, and Action.* Englewood Cliffs, NJ: Prentice-Hall, 1967.

36. See Robert J. Bursik, Jr., "Ecological stability and the dynamics of delinquency," pp. 35–66, in Albert J. Reiss, Jr. and Michael Tonry (eds.), *Communities and Crime*, Vol. 8 of *Crime and Justice*. Chicago: University of Chicago Press, 1986.

37. Walter B. Miller has been the most persistent investigator and definer of gangs and other youth aggregations. See Walter B. Miller, "Gangs, groups, and serious youth crime," pp. 115–138, in David Shichor and Delos H. Kelly (eds.), *Critical Issues in Juvenile Delinquency.* Lexington, MA.: D.C. Heath, 1980, p. 119, *et passim.* Miller includes illegal activity as a defining criterion of gangs. We do not, since this is what we wish to explain. Miller's further comment, however, is most appropriate: "police departments in large cities apply the term (gang) quite narrowly, police in smaller cities and towns less narrowly, most media writers more broadly, and most distressed local citizens very broadly" (p. 116).

38. Adapted from Short and Strodtbeck, *op. cit.*, pp. 208–209. The pill-poppers' preoccupation with drugs was extreme. Drug use among adolescents is typically but one of many activities shared by those who use drugs. The primary motivation for drug use in most cases appears simply to be sociability with friends. See Glassner and Loughlin, *op. cit.*; also Schwartz, *op. cit.*

39. See Harold Finestone, "Cats, kicks, and color," *Social Problems*, 5 (1957):3–13.

40. Isidor Chein and Eva Rosenfeld, "Juvenile narcotics use," *Law and Contemporary Problems*, 22 (1957):52–68.

41. Adapted from Short and Strodtbeck, *Ibid.*, pp. 200–202.

42. See Irving Spergel, *Racketville, Slumtown, and Haulburg.* Chicago: University of Chicago Press, 1964.

43. The enormous profits to be made by the manufacture and distribution of illegal drugs since this study was conducted have altered these aspirations for at least some gang members. Firearms have also become more accessible, leading to the escalation of gang- and drug-related violence. See Mercer L. Sullivan, *Youth Crime and Employment Patterns in Three Brooklyn Neighborhoods.* New York: Vera Institute of Justice, 1984.

44. Albert J. Reiss, Jr., and A. L. Rhodes, "The distribution of juvenile delinquency in the social class structure," *American Sociological Review,* 26 (October, 1961):720–732

45. Robert J. Sampson, "Crime in cities: the effects of formal and informal social control," pp. 278–279, in Albert J. Reiss, Jr. and Michael Tonry (eds.), *Communities and Crime,* Vol. 8 of *Crime and Justice.* Chicago: University of Chicago Press, 1986.

46. See, for example, Clifford R. Shaw, *The Jackroller: A Delinquent Boy's Own Story* (with a new introduction by Howard S. Becker). Chicago: University of Chicago Press, 1966 (originally published in 1930); and by the same author and publisher, *The Natural History of a Delinquent Career,* 1931; *Brothers in Crime,* 1938.

47. See Gerald D. Suttles, *The Social Construction of Communities.* Chicago: University of Chicago Press, 1972.

48. See Leo Schuerman and Solomon Kobrin, "Community careers in crime," pp. 67–100, in Reiss and Tonry, *op. cit.;* see also, Robert J. Bursick, Jr., "Ecological stability and the dynamics of delinquency," pp. 35–66, in Reiss and Tonry (eds.), *op. cit.;* Bursik and Jim Webb, "Community change and patterns of delinquency," *American Journal of Sociology,* 88 (1982):24–42. Bursik notes that his research supports a model of community structure advanced in Brian J. Berry and John D. Kasarda, *Contemporary Urban Ecology.* New York: Macmillan, 1977. See also, Sheldon Ekland-Olson, "Deviance, Social Control and Social Networks," pp. 271–299, in Steven Spitzer and Rita Simon (eds.), *Research in Law, Deviance, and Social Control,* Vol. 4. Greenwich, CT: JAI Press, 1982.

49. Anthony E. Bottoms and Paul Wiles, "Housing tenure and residential community crime careers in Britain," pp. 101–162, in Reiss and Tonry (eds.), *op. cit.,* p. 111.

50. See William J. Wilson and Robert Aponte, "Urban poverty," pp. 231–258, in Ralph H. Turner and James F. Short, Jr., (eds.), *Annual Review of Sociology,* Vol. 11. Palo Alto, CA.: Annual Reviews, 1985. See also, William Julius Wilson: *The Truly Disadvantaged: The Inner City, the Underclass, and Public Policy.* Chicago: University of Chicago Press, 1987. Robert J. Sampson, "Urban black violence: The effects of male joblessness and family disruption," *American Journal of Sociology,* 93 (1987):348–82.

51. Norman Ryder, in Coleman, et al., *op. cit.,* p. 45.

52. Lawrence E. Cohen and Marcus Felson, "Social change and crime rate trends: a routine activity approach," *American Sociological Review,* 44 (June, 1979):588–608. The relationship of this perspective to juvenile crime is analyzed in Lawrence E. Cohen and Kenneth C. Land, "Age structure and crime: symmetry versus asymmetry and the projection of crime rates through the 1990s," *American Sociological Review,* 52 (April, 1987):170–183; see also, Lawrence E. Cohen, Marcus Felson, and Kenneth C. Land, "Property crime rates in the United States: a macrodynamic analysis, 1947–1974; with ex ante forecasts for the mid-1980s," *American Journal of Sociology,* 86 (January, 1980):90–118; and Marcus Felson and Michael Gottfredson, "Social indicators of adolescent activities near peers and parents," *Journal of Marriage and the Family,* 46 (August, 1984):709–714.

53. David Cantor and Kenneth C. Land, "Unemployment and crime rates in the post–World War II United States: a theoretical and empirical analysis," *American Sociological Review,* 50 (June, 1985):317–332.

54. See Terance D. Miethe, Mark C. Stafford, and J. Scott Long, "Social differentiation in criminal victimization: a test of routine activities/lifestyle theories," *American Sociological Review,* 52 (April, 1987):184–194.

CHAPTER 8
THE INDIVIDUAL IN THE EQUATION

If everyone responded to macro-level influences in the same way, the explanation of human behavior would be greatly simplified. Of course we do not. It is the task of this chapter to explain some of the reasons for individual variations in response to environmental conditions, including delinquent responses.

The search for the sources of individual differences in delinquent behavior has taken many forms, depending on the purpose of the inquiry and who is asking the questions. A clinical psychologist, for example, will want to know why an individual who has been referred for diagnosis or treatment committed the offense for which he or she has been referred. Questions of this kind will be greatly influenced by what the psychologist has been trained to observe and by his or her interpretations, guided by that training.

Because individual-level questions have been the most often asked, the body of knowledge at this level is extremely varied and complex. Its contributors have come primarily from the several branches of biology, psychology, and sociology that compose the behavior and life sciences. Today, most scientists from these disciplines stress the importance of both macro-level (environmental) and "within the individual" influences on behavior, although they vary a great deal in emphasis, and on precisely which influences are most important.

This ecumenical spirit is not universally shared. Sciences and their practitioners tend to be specialized and parochial. As a general rule, the more advanced the science, the higher the degree of specialization of subject matter, theory, and research methods. Scientists of a particular stripe (geneticists, behavioral psychologists, or sociologists) are often unacquainted even with the questions posed by others, and little concerned with their answers. Since a critical stance regarding theory and evidence is a hallmark of scientific disciplines, disputes within as well as between disciplines are endemic and frequently confusing. This chapter presents a broad overview of these theories and the state of knowledge with respect to them.

The study of the characteristics of individuals—what they are, how they develop, and the nature of their relationship to delinquent behavior—begins with biologically based theories. Biology—more particularly medicine—was the first of the sciences to direct systematic research to the problem of why individuals commit crimes.

BIOLOGICAL CONTRIBUTIONS: HISTORICAL CONTEXTS

Our interest in this book is in the *general nature* of biological phenomena and their interactions with psychological, situational, social structural, and cultural factors in the production of delinquent behavior. Most of the research and theory in this area has focused on physiological, genetic, developmental, or other biological *characteristics of persons* who have been officially identified as delinquent or criminal. Our focus will be on how such characteristics might relate to *personal development and to the individual's interaction with others* (e.g., parents, teachers, police, and other authorities), and how these characteristics might *combine* to produce delinquent behavior. Because knowledge in this area is quite limited, much of what we have to say is little more than informed speculation. It is on the basis of such limited knowledge, however, that more powerful theory, better research, and better integration of knowledge may become possible.

Biological theories have attributed crime to simple and direct connections with a physical type (or other hereditary characteristic), to complex mechanisms involving underlying biological conditions (e.g., brain damage or glandular functioning), and to complex and sophisticated mechanisms that involve the growth, development, and functioning of the human organism. While a variety of biologically based explanations of crime were advanced as early as the mid-sixteenth century, the first such theory to gain wide acceptance was not published until late in the nineteenth century. Cesare Lombroso, an Italian military physician, was attracted to positivist thinking and the work of Charles Darwin. He observed Italian prisoners and soldiers. His research led him to the conclusion that criminals were *atavistic*; that is, they had reverted to an earlier biological stage that could be identified by a variety of physical stigmata.[1] Persons possessed of five or more such characteristics, he theorized, were lacking in personal control and predisposed to crime. Other aspects of his theory today seem equally anachronistic, for example, his attribution of atavism to physical characteristics associated with "colored" races, and his explanation of the paradox that, while females were "more primitive" than males, they were nonetheless not criminal unless possessed of masculine characteristics. Lombroso reconciled the paradox by theorizing that female primitive qualities, which would predispose a person to jealousy, revenge, insensitivity to pain, and diminished moral sensibility, were "neutralized by piety, maternity, want of passion, sexual coldness, weakness, and an undeveloped intelligence."[2]

Lombroso later concluded that fewer than half of all criminals were "born criminals," and he altered his theory to include the influences of social and economic circumstances and mental illness. His identification with biological determinism has persisted, however, and it was this aspect of his theory that was subjected to the most severe criticism. The heritability of crime, albeit in another guise, was soon advanced by some of those critics.

THE ADVENT OF INTELLIGENCE TESTING

Intelligence testing became possible and popular with advances in experimental psychology toward the turn of the twentieth century. In 1913, an English prison physician, Charles Goring, published the results of extensive comparisons of criminals and noncriminals. Goring found little evidence of Lombroso's physical stigmata. He concluded instead that criminals differed from noncriminals in intelligence, also regarded as an inherited trait. About this same time, Henry Goddard, an American psychologist, began to publish research that reached much the same conclusion. Goddard estimated that at least 25 percent of all delinquents, and perhaps as much as 70 percent, could be characterized as mentally defective.

Studies using improved methods of measuring intelligence and better samples of the general population found much smaller differences between delinquents and nondelinquents, and between criminals and noncriminals. The heritability of intelligence also was questioned as evidence of environmental influences on socialization accumulated. The fact that delinquents and criminals chosen for study were nearly always *incarcerated* led many to challenge even small observed differences in intelligence between offenders and nonoffenders.

As a result of such challenges, intelligence and physiological characteristics faded as correlates and the causes of crime, only to be resurrected by anthropologist Ernest A. Hooten.[3] Hooten's comparisons of reformatory and jail prisoners with college students, firemen, policemen, and hospital patients convinced him that criminals were physically and mentally inferior, and that both conditions were caused by poor heredity.

Like his predecessors, Hooten was severely criticized, on logical and empirical grounds. Hooten's logic, his critics charged, was circular. He had first used conviction for crime to distinguish criminals. After measuring the physical characteristics of the criminals and finding them *different* from the noncriminals, he concluded that these characteristics were inferior. Physical and mental inferiority was then employed to explain criminality. To make matters worse, many of the physical differences between the two samples were arguably not inferior, for example, lower body weight, a low forehead, small ears, or a long neck. In addition, Hooten's noncriminal sample consisted of disproportionate number of firemen and policemen, two groups selected on the basis of physical fitness.

SOMATOTYPES AND DELINQUENT BEHAVIOR

The next, and by extension the most recent, theory in this tradition was advanced by William H. Sheldon.[4] Sheldon's theory was based on the hypothesized linkage between genetically determined "somatotypes" (body types) and temperament. Three basic somatotypes were distinguished, each associated with a distinct temperament: *mesomorphs* were large-boned and muscular, *endomorphs* were corpulent and soft muscled, and *ectomorphs* were lean and delicate. The corresponding temperamental types were, for mesomorphs: physical vigor, social assertiveness, and deficiency in internal control mechanisms; for endomorphs: sociability, an easy going nature, and love of comfort; and for ectomorphs: sensitivity, introversion, and nervousness.

Sheldon compared boys confined in a private institution for delinquents with an equal number of college boys. His findings suggested that higher proportions of delinquents than nondelinquents were mesomorphic. More recent studies also have found some support for the relationship between somatotype and officially defined delinquents, and among adult felons. The relationships reported generally are weak, but they appear to be strongest among those more seriously involved in crime, both delinquents and adults. Sheldon's theory has had little impact on the field, however, even among some of the major proponents of the role of biology in delinquent behavior. The relationship between physiology, temperament, and behavior remains an important issue, in need of further theoretical and empirical specification.[5]

RECENT INQUIRIES AND A CONCEPTUAL FRAMEWORK

The most general point to be made about biological correlates of crime and delinquency is that biological variables should be considered as part of a more comprehensive system of explanation. Despite decades of often fruitless "nature versus nurture" debate, consensus does exist on this point. A few additional principles are helpful as guides to further inquiry.

The first is that *any condition that influences how one interacts with others inevitably influences behavior.* These influences vary greatly. A condition that irritates one person, for example, or which is interpreted as aggressive or provocative to another, may lead to altercations between individuals. The result of such interaction is, of course, subject to many influences and may take a variety of forms, for example, an argument or physical attack on a person or property, or quite the opposite, a withdrawal or retreat from the scene. Conditions that one person may find irritating or in some way provocative may be much less so for another person. Appearance and demeanor are signals to others with whom we interact. Just as an innocent remark or gesture may be misinterpreted, leading to misunderstanding, so may appearance, demeanor, and other behaviors.

Biological factors influence how persons perceive and interact with one another. Physical appearance,[6] an epileptic seizure, or impulsive behavior related to some biological pathology (e.g., a brain tumor) serve as cues to others with whom we interact. The meaning of such cues also is influenced by cultural patterns and by the social experience of the perceiver.

Saleem A. Shah and Loren A. Roth note that most biological factors and mechanisms *interact with social experience* and are "considerably shaped and modified by social experience."[7]

ACCOUNTING FOR MALE/FEMALE DIFFERENCES
IN DELINQUENT BEHAVIOR

Perhaps the best example of a general biological characteristic that may be related to some types of crime is the male sex hormone, testosterone. Testosterone levels vary among males and they are higher among males than among females. The fact that crime rates are higher among males than among females has led to the suggestion that testosterone and crime levels are causally related. Some evidence suggests that this may be the case, and that the differences male and female crime rates cannot be accounted for solely in terms of learning. Developmental studies find that children do not begin to imitate the behavior of adults of their own sex until the age of six. Yet, Eleanor Maccoby and Carol Jacklin's review of studies of children *under* that age indicates that three-quarters of the studies found boys to be more aggressive than girls and that no study reported higher levels of aggressive behavior among girls than among boys.[8] Crosscultural studies yield similar results, as do studies of chimpanzees. Evidence that differences in reinforcement or punishment could account for the results was not found.

Pollock and associates also report that experimental work with pregnant female monkeys finds that exposure to high levels of testosterone during prenatal development is associated with aggressive behavior and masculine sexual behaviors.[9] In addition, studies of criminal or aggressive behavior among prisoners and 16-year-old males support the relationship between testosterone level and aggressive behavior.

The effects of testosterone levels also have been shown to vary in relation to *social* factors. Speaking to the age distribution of crime and delinquency, Walter Gove notes that "in combination with the adolescent role and peer pressure, [testosterone] should greatly increase one's willingness to take risks and participate in strenuous physical activity."[10] It has been noted, also, that testosterone levels are correlated with assertive (aggressive) behavior among adolescents males, but not among older men, a difference Alice S. Rossi attributes to greater *social maturation* associated with impulse control among the latter.[11]

Other biological phenomena also appear to be related to the gender distribution of crime and delinquency, though the evidence is far from clear as to precisely how they operate, and socialization certainly shapes such biological influences.

BIOLOGICAL PATHOLOGIES AS CAUSAL FACTORS

Research suggesting that certain biological pathologies may be more directly related to delinquent behavior has also been reported. Tumors and other forms of brain pathology appear to be related to some cases of serious crime and delinquency, in the sense that individuals who have exhibited no assaultive or predatory behavior prior to the appearance of the pathology do so following its occurrence. Thus, very young children who had not previously exhibited such behaviors have been observed after their survival of acute encephalitis disorders, to engage in several types of deviant behavior that might be considered delinquent.

The effects of some disorders may be spectacular, as in cases of "abnormal or explosive behavior resulting from 'misfires' in the system," for example, the model citizen who goes berserk or the quiet person who suddenly and irrationally becomes assaultive. Because they are infrequent, the relationship of such occurrences to delinquency is weak. Their occurrence may have less direct influences on behavior, however.[12]

BIOLOGICAL FACTORS AND DELINQUENT LABELING

Persons who exhibit biologically pathological symptoms, for example, those associated with epilepsy, may become *labeled* as delinquent, or otherwise deviant. Most epileptic children are likely to be recognized as epileptic and treated accordingly. Occasionally, however, such symptoms may be associated with a delinquent act—or be interpreted and reacted to as delinquent behavior.

Children with less obvious symptoms of brain pathology (for example, those with the syndrome known as minimal brain damage), but who evidence erratic behavior or moodiness attributable in some way to brain damage, are less likely to be diagnosed properly. The likelihood that they will be reacted to (by parents, peers, and others) in ways that may contribute to delinquent behavior is thereby enhanced. Labeling may, in turn, have further consequences for the person so labeled, for example, by affecting his or her self conception and interaction with others.

The point is more general. *Any biological factor that affects learning, mood, or the modulation of behavior may be linked to particular behaviors.* Because many such factors are rare, they cannot account for a large proportion of delinquent behavior, though the cumulative effects of many such conditions may be quite significant. Other conditions, such as learning disabilities, are more prevalent and, therefore, of greater importance. Learning disabilities, which may be genetically linked, affect the ability to communicate, which in turn influences interpersonal interaction. The same can be said for intelligence. Other examples that have been cited in the research literature include hyperkinesis among children, and irritations experienced during phases of the menstrual cycle among some women. Identification of such factors, and the *mechanisms by which they influence behavior* is a challenge of great significance for theory, research, and social policy.

THE LINKAGE OF COMMON BIOLOGICAL AND SOCIAL CHARACTERISTICS

For most crime and delinquency common biological factors are important to delinquent etiology, although they are not fully understood. Links between biological and social correlates of behavior are not hard to find, but the theoretical development and empirical research that would explain them are scant. Biological and social scientists continue to work largely in isolation from one another. Integration of the two disciplines remains largely at a descriptive and elementary level. Yet, clearly, there are linkages. Epidemiological studies, for example, note that certain biological and social phenomena have similar distributions. Thus, some biological disorders (notably epilepsy, endocrine-related problems, perinatal pathology, minimal brain disorder, and some chromosomal disorders) are known to result, in part, from inadequate nutrition, birth trauma, and poor prenatal and postnatal care—all with important social linkages.

The precise relationship of such disorders to social factors and to behavior is not clear. Like the ecology of crime and delinquency, however, some biological phenomena (such as prenatal, paranatal, and postnatal problems) are heavily concentrated in lower-class communities and among lower-class groups. Infants born in these circumstances, therefore, are at greater risk prenatally and continue to suffer disadvantages in nutrition, in general physical and medical care, and in the availability of other resources. Biological factors thus are heavily influenced by environmental, as well as inherited, characteristics and developmental processes.

GENETIC STUDIES AND A BIOLOGICALLY BASED THEORY OF LEARNING

The most convincing evidence of genetic linkage with criminality comes from extensive studies of the criminality of twins and of children who have been adopted.[13] The former can be distinguished, between monozygotic (MZ) and dizygotic (DZ) twins. Monozygotic twins result from the fertilization of a single egg, which subsequently divides, thereby insuring that the twins are identical in genetic makeup. Fraternal twins (dizygotic) result from separately fertilized eggs. Only about half their genes are alike, as is the case with other nontwin siblings. Studies conducted in several countries report that identical twins are more alike with respect to criminality than are fraternal twins. While this finding is impressive, critics have noted that identical twins are more likely to be treated identically, in the family and by others, than are fraternal twins even of the same sex. The case for a genetic basis for the findings, therefore, remains questionable.

This problem has been addressed by researchers in several countries who have compared the criminality of adopted children whose biological and adopted parents differ with respect to criminality. These studies suggest that the criminality of adopted children is more closely related to that of their biological than of their adoptive parents. The highest crime rate (24.5 percent) was among sons whose biological and adoptive parents were both criminal. However, if only one biological parent was criminal and the adoptive parents were not, the rate of criminal convictions among adopted sons was 20 percent. A rate of 14.7 percent was shown if the adoptive parents exhibited criminality, but the biological parents did not. If neither biological nor adoptive parents had criminal convictions, the rate of conviction of adopted sons was 13.5 percent.[14]

This study also found that chronic offenders (the 4 percent who had been convicted of crime more than twice) were responsible for 69.4 percent of the convictions of the adoptees studied (cf. the discussion of chronic offenders among the Philadelphia cohort in the previous chapter). Further, chronic offenders, who made up about 1 percent of the adoptees studied, whose biological parents were also chronic offenders accounted for nearly a third of all court convictions of adoptees. While this study has been criticized for its possible selection biases in the placement of children and on its statistical criteria, it is, nevertheless, the strongest empirical evidence for a genetic role in criminal behavior.[15]

Mednick and Jan Volavka draw upon a large body of central and autonomic nervous system studies, as well as studies of neuroendocrinology and neurochemistry, to develop a psychobiological theory of learning that might account for the role played by biological factors in criminality.[16] These studies involve genetic and environmentally influenced biological phenomena and social experience. While the technical details are of little concern in the present context, the outlines of the theory are simple and straightforward. Several types of evidence suggest that criminals (usually incarcerated older adolescents or adults) have biological deficiencies that contribute to learning difficulties. One theory is that biological deficiencies interfere with learning moral precepts by diminishing the critical *fear* response to punishment or its threat, and by weakening the *anticipatory* ability which is necessary for learning to take place.

Most biological theories stand firmly in the *control* tradition, though they differ greatly in their assumptions and specifications as to what is not controlled in order for crime to occur. Convergence on principles acceptable to scientists from a broad spectrum of the life sciences may be occurring through the integration of biological theory, behavioral psychology theory, social cognitive theory, and other theories concerning learning and motivation. Some of these consider positive motivations for crime, as well as controlling mechanisms and processes.

PSYCHOLOGICAL PERSPECTIVES: OVERVIEW

Herbert Quay has observed that "Bootleggers, burglars, and bank robbers little resemble one another in what they actually *do*. Criminals constitute a class of individuals only insofar as they all break the law; they are far from being a class in the psychological sense of being homogeneous in their behavior or motivations for crime" (emphasis in original.)[17]

Psychologists have developed several theoretical schools to account for this diversity. Three are of particular interest with respect to juvenile delinquency: psychoanalytic theory, behavior theory, and social learning or social cognitive theory.[18]

Psychoanalytic Theory.   Psychoanalytic theory, identified with Sigmund Freud, begins with the premise that human behavior is motivated by fundamental biological energy, or drives, that are innately aggressive. Failure to develop adequate internal (that is, within the individual) controls over innate aggressiveness results in its expression in a variety of forms, including crime. Freud identified this innate disposition for aggression as the libido, or *id*.

Freud's follower and noted child psychiatrist, August Aichhorn, applied psychoanalytic theory to delinquent behavior. For Aichhorn the id represented the child's primitive, instinctual demands, made without regard for others. In the course of socialization the id must be modified by the development of the *ego* (the capacity for rational thought) and the *superego* (internal controls, or, in common parlance, the conscience). Failing the development of adequate controls, and a normal course of libinal development, the id will break through for satisfaction. In the classic psychoanalytic formulation, the ego and the superego operate as controls over the innate tendency to aggress.

General Principles and Questions. In modified form the assumption that aggression is innate is retained in some learning theories and in social control theory. All theories accept the insight of these theories *that every human being has the capacity to commit the most objectionable antisocial acts.*[19] The roles of the ego and superego also have been modified in more recent formulations in recognition of the deliberate and rational character of much law violation. The ego performs motivational as well as control functions. Similarly, the superego may motivate crime, as in crimes of conscience.

Another fundamental principle of human behavior to emerge from research and theory in psychiatry and the other life sciences is that *behavior is adaptive*, or, put slightly differently, *problem solving.* Note the corollary, that the behavior of those who interact with children in behavior settings of delinquent behavior also is adaptive. Two basic questions concerning the individual-level etiology of delinquency thus become apparent: (1) Why is it that some juveniles solve their problems by engaging in delinquent behavior while others do not? Or, more aptly, under what circumstances does juvenile delinquency occur? (2) Under what circumstances do those who interact with juveniles define their behavior as delinquent? Or do those who interact with juveniles react in ways that provoke delinquent behavior?

DELINQUENCY AS LEARNED BEHAVIOR

Behavior theory, social learning theory, and *social-cognitive theory* regard delinquent behavior as *learned*. In general, application of these theories to delinquency simply extend general principles of learning.

Classical experiments established the principle that behavior could be shaped, or conditioned, by associating stimuli with one another (e.g., food and an auditory stimulus). These were followed by experiments in which responses were shown to vary according to whether the stimulus was rewarding or punishing. From these early experiments the basic principle of behavior theory evolved, namely, that *behavior is a function of its consequences*. That is, learning occurs as a result of the *reinforcement* of behavior. Reinforcement occurs by means of rewards and punishments. The effectiveness of reinforcement is enhanced by its immediacy, intensity, and repetition. Behavior theory thus views learning as a process in which behavior can be controlled by means of the administration of appropriate rewards and punishments.

Social cognitive theory builds on the principles of behavior theory by emphasizing cognitive processes and learning from observation of models that are present in the environment. Social cognitive theory holds that a great deal of learning is anticipatory; and that learning occurs chiefly by observing other people's behavior and its consequences.[20] Observing others provides both negative (aversive or punishing, by example) and positive (rewarding, by example) reinforcement for learning. A person acquires a repertoire of behaviors, which may or may not be invoked, depending on such factors as the nature of stimuli, situational factors, personal goals, rationalizations, self-evaluation, and a sense of personal efficacy. Social cognitive theorists and experimenters emphasize the *reciprocal* nature of behavior, cognitive and other processes within the individual, and the external environment.

BEHAVIOR TYPOLOGIES

One of the chief strategies used by psychologists to study delinquents has been to develop typologies of offenders. The etiological task is thereby simplified, since each type is believed to have a common etiology. While "pure" types are rare, typologies are useful in that they permit careful examination of the correlates of, and processes associated with, classes of behavior. The etiology of similar cases may be informed by comparison with cases more closely conforming to theoretical types.

Children Who Hate.   Research attention has focused most often on extremely aggressive and otherwise chronically delinquent children. One of the more dramatic studies of these was carried out by Fritz Redl, a psychiatrist, and David Wineman, a social worker. Redl and Wineman studied a small group of 10 boys, aged 8 to 11, who had been brought together in a treatment institution. Their vivid description of these boys contrasts them with others who are less extreme in their maladjustment:[21]

> ...there is still a wide gap between the hatred which a well taken care of middle class child develops as a side line to his anxiety or compulsion neurosis and that of the slum area delinquent who has to survive by aggression in a world of struggle. And there is still a great difference between the child who occasionally kicks back at frustrations or expresses the negative side of an ambivalent feeling toward brother or sister and the child who has been reeling under the impact of cruelty and neglect to such a degree that the acid of counter-aggression has eaten itself by now into the very stomach linings of his adaptational system. There is a great difference between a child whose basic personality is still in good enough shape to be approached through psychiatric treatment or through the design of a benevolent institutional program and the child in whom some of the normal behavior controls have already been destroyed by those who hated him so much when he was dependent and weak and who by now is but a helpless bundle of aggressive drives. There is also a great difference between the child who breaks out into some minor aggressive rebellion from time to time in the classroom, or who betrays deep seated death wishes against us through the medium of finger paint, and the child whose aggression seems to flow uninhibited, skipping even the in-between stage of fantasy, into direct action of reckless destruction or into flare-ups of blind and murderous rage.

These are "Children Nobody Wants," say Redl and Wineman. They document the severe parental rejection, as well as rejection by siblings, peers, and others in their communities, experienced by these boys:[22]

> If prevailing criteria for what constitutes an adequate child-adult relationship pattern are used as a basis for reaching conclusions, we can see very little in the case history profiles of our children that would satisfy even the most naive clinician or educator that they had had anything even approaching an "even break." In very few instances were we able to gather any evidence that there had been even continuity of relationship with original parent images. Broken homes through divorce and desertion, the chain-reaction style of foster home placements and institutional storage, were conspicuous events in their lives...the quality of the tie between child and adult world was marred by rejection ranging from open brutality, cruelty, and neglect to affect barrenness on the part of some parents and narcissistic absorption in their own interests which exiled the child emotionally from them....One of the things that constantly amazed us when we would observe the parents and children together was how much like strangers they were to one another....we were impressed by how little interest the parents took in what was happening to the children in treatment. Contrary to our expectations that they might become competitive with the treatment milieu on the basis of feelings of guilt for placing the child and for their own inadequacy, they never became involved on any level at all. Their main, unconcealed reaction was: "We're glad you've got them, not us. Life is so peaceful without them."

Life with siblings, and in the school and community was no more pleasant for these children, and their aggression extended into these areas. While the boys sometimes associated with other delinquent children, they often were "lone wolves." Often shifted about, they also lacked roots and identity in school and community. Where some degree of continuity was found, the boys' behavior had become legendary.

Rarely, apparently, did *anything* good happen to these boys. Redl and Wineman describe six "missing links" in the boys' backgrounds that constitute a reasonable list of generally agreed upon requirements for normal, healthy childhood:[23]

1. Factors leading to identification with adults, including feelings of being loved and wanted; encouragement to accept values and standards of the adult world.
2. Opportunities for and help in achieving a gratifying recreational pattern.
3. Opportunities for adequate peer relationships.
4. Opportunities for community ties, of establishing a feeling of being rooted somewhere where one belongs, where other people besides your parents know and like you.
5. Ongoing family structures which were not in some phase of basic disintegration.
6. Economic security sufficient for the basic necessities of life.

It is not difficult to appreciate how deficits in socialization and extreme rejection such as these might lead to extreme aggression, and how these processes might reflect macro-level influences. The learning processes previously discussed provide a menu of mechanisms involved in the etiology of behaviors of everyone who took part in the scenarios described by Redl and Wineman: parents, siblings, teachers, and peers of the boys, as well as the boys themselves. Precisely how these mechanisms operated in individual cases is less important for present purposes than is identification of these general mechanisms. It is more difficult to judge how generalizable they may be. Clues are found in studies of boys who were somewhat less aggressive than the "children who hate."

A Study of Less Extreme Rejection and Aggression. Bandura and Walters compared some two dozen "aggressives" with a similar number of nonaggressive boys of the same age. Their summary of differences between the two groups of boys recalls the "children who hate," though in less extreme form:[24]

> The fathers of the aggressive boys were typically hostile to, and rejecting of their sons, expressed little warmth for them, and had spent little time in effective interaction with them during the boy's childhood. Although the mothers' greater warmth had apparently sufficed to establish *dependency needs* during the boys' infancy, their tendency to punish and discourage *dependency behavior* reduced the boys' striving for secondary rewards in the form of *dependency gratification*, thus reducing the effectiveness of important sources of control. (Emphasis added)

The combination of fathers' rejection and mothers' inconsistent handling of dependency, Bandura and Walters argue, created a great deal of conflict and anxiety among the boys regarding dependency. To the extent that the boys were exposed to values supportive of a "macho" image of masculinity, dependency conflicts were exacerbated. Dependency conflict tended to be generalized to others, to authority figures and even to peers, thus limiting their influence on the boys. "The parents' use of punitive methods of discipline not only further alienated their sons but fostered the hostility and aggression with which the boys had responded to emotional deprivations."[25] The boys' aggressive behavior was reinforced, while self-control lacked clear direction.

If we assume that "normals" and the "children who hate" represent extremes not only in aggressive behavior, but also in etiology, and that Bandura and Walters' "aggressives" occupy a point somewhere in between these extremes, important principles of socialization emerge. Of special importance is the quality of parent-child interaction, for example, the amount and type of nurturance (versus neglect, rejection, and hostility), the handling of dependency needs and behavior, the consistency of parental demands and discipline, and the type of discipline employed by parents.

This research emphasizes the importance of avoiding extremes of neglect, rejection, and overdependency. Dependency needs must be developed sufficiently to foster *sensitivity to others* and to motivate the child to seek the interest, attention, and approval of others.[26] Conversely, dependency must not become so overwhelming that it hinders rationally independent thought and action. What is "proper" and "normal" in this respect is heavily value-

As a general goal for all children, however, self-respect and respect for others, the capacity for rational thought and independence of action can perhaps be taken as a standard.

If it is to be successful in these terms, socialization requires restrictions on conduct, just as it requires teaching (of information, skills, and knowledge) and training (of values, purposes, preferences, and moral codes).[27] Relationships within the home are critical in this process because they are the earliest and most intimate associations experienced by the child. They shape emotional and self-development, as well as sensitivity to others. The home is the child's most important learning environment throughout the early years.

A longitudinal study of English boys confirms the relationship between aggression and parent-child relationships, though the distinction between the effects of rejection and of neglect appears to be less important than is suggested by some typologies. David Farrington found that the most violent delinquents in his sample tended to come from families marked by the lack of harmony, and to have cold, harsh, and poorly supervising parents. Parents of these boys also were more likely to have been convicted of crime themselves than were parents of less violent boys.[28]

A Study of Social Aggressors, Stealers, and Normals.   The importance of specific antecedents for different types of crime has not been established theoretically or empirically. Gerald R. Patterson's typology of "deviancy progressions" is suggestive, however. Patterson notes that very young children (two- and three-year-olds) "commit frequent 'crimes against property.' "[29] Some research suggests that acts of stealing and aggression among normal children peaks between the ages of two to four and declines thereafter. For some children, however, socialization appears to be arrested in the sense that the high rates of aversive behavior characteristic of two- to four-year-olds persists among eight-year-olds.

Patterson studied children averaging a little over eight years of age who were classified as "Normals," "Social Aggressors," and "Stealers." Studied again at age 14 or older, the "Stealers" were the most likely to have later delinquent careers.[30]

Qualities of parent-child interaction found in the series of studies based on this typology appear similar to others in the research literature noted previously. Patterson observes that "[t]he overwhelming impression about the homes of these children [Stealers] is that of a distant, uninvolved pattern of familial interaction."[31] Fathers were least likely to punish aversive behavior by the Stealers. While this is suggestive of neglect, the correspondence is by no means clear. Similarly, parents of both Social Aggressors and Abused Children were more likely to be hostile and socially aggressive toward their children than were parents of Normals and Stealers, suggesting rejection. Specific dynamics of parent-child relationships and how they relate to the behavior of both parents and children remain matters for theoretical development and empirical inquiry.

"Coercion theory" (Patterson's term) bears certain similarities to behavior theory and social cognitive theory. These theories emphasize the *interactive effects* of parent-child behavior, that is, that parental behavior is modified by child behavior, just as child behavior is modified by parental behavior. These theorists challenge the conventional wisdom that takes for granted parenting *skills,* arguing instead that parents often lack the knowledge and skills necessary for proper parenting. This is especially the case with increasing numbers of young single parents, many of whom lack appropriate role models, information, and support systems.

This program of research also suggests that effectively changing ("extinguishing" in the language of behavioral psychology) antisocial behavior requires punishment and that simply developing prosocial skills is insufficient.

The children studied by Patterson were quite young. The more general principle, so far as adolescents are concerned, may have more to do with perceptions of the rationality and the reasonableness of authority as these relate to community culture, as suggested in Chapter 5.

SOCIOLOGICAL PERSPECTIVES ON MOTIVATION AND LEARNING

The data and the theories of psychologists, psychiatrists, and sociologists regarding individual development find many areas of agreement, though they often speak to different issues and aspects of socialization. Sociologists, for example, study factors associated with *what is learned* somewhat more than *how it is learned*, though an early statement by a sociologist—Edwin H. Sutherland—bearing on both of these problems and on the social distribution of crime has endured for nearly half a century.[32]

DIFFERENTIAL ASSOCIATION

Sutherland's principle of *differential association* holds that delinquent and criminal behaviors are learned in interaction with others. Sutherland emphasized the importance of communication, especially that which "occurs within intimate personal groups."[33] *Motivation* for criminal behavior "is learned from definitions of the legal codes as favorable or unfavorable," and he argued that a "person becomes delinquent because of an excess of definitions favorable to violation of law over definitions unfavorable to violation of law."[34]

The principle of differential association was a bold affirmation of the learned nature of behavior at a time when this was not the accepted view. While it has been faulted on several grounds, the principle is consistent with many of the macro-social observations discussed in the previous chapter. Sutherland's original purpose was to explain "the process by which a particular person comes to engage in criminal behavior,"[35] but at this level other learning theories are more adequate to account for the mechanisms by which differential association (as it has come to be understood) produces delinquent behavior. The "translation" of differential association into the more formal language of behavior theory has demonstrated its compatibility with these theories.[36]

ROLE THEORY, THE SELF, AND REFERENCE GROUPS

Other social psychological theories at the individual level emphasize particular aspects of socialization. Role-self theory holds that behavior is oriented
toward the creation, maintenance, and enhancement of one's concept of
self—the image one has of oneself.[37] These notions are compatible with
psychological theories of learning, but they stress different aspects of personal development. Like social cognitive theory, sociological self theory is
more explicit concerning cognitive aspects of self-regulation and processes
associated with its development.

Self-development, role taking and role-playing all involve learning.
Self-concept theory holds that self-development in very young children
occurs in the process of association and identification with "significant
others," that is those with whom the child experiences intimate and sustained
interaction. Somewhat later, these significant others and broader categories
of persons become important as reference groups for the child. Reference
groups continue to be important throughout life. They often change in
response to changed circumstances, as for example when the child becomes
a "preteen," later an adolescent, and still later passes through phases of
adulthood.

Some groups are important primarily as *status* reference groups; that
is, for answering such self-directed questions as, "Who am I? Where do I
fit in the scheme of things? What do I want to be or do?" Other groups are
especially important for normative development; that is, for shaping judge-
ments as to ethical and moral beliefs and behavior. Some groups, especially
those with whom interaction is most intimate and long-lasting, for example, parents and peer groups, function in both capacities in varying degrees.

It follows from these observations that self-development is not fixed in
infancy, although most theories emphasize the importance of very early
childhood experiences. Changes in self-concept occur for many reasons as a
result of social expectations associated with changes in life circumstances.
Sociological social psychologists distinguish between expectations (and
changes) associated with social positions (statuses) that are ascriptive (e.g.,
on the basis of one's age, sex, race or ethnicity, and social class) and those that
are achieved (i.e., by virtue of role performance).[38]

Several investigators have studied the importance for youthful behavior of both ascribed and achieved statuses, and of *social types,* that is,
configurations of roles and values that differentiate among young people.[39]
Some examples of the latter which bear on delinquent behavior are "socies"
or "socialites" and "greasers" (middle-class and working-class or lower-
class youth, respectively, who reject conventional authority and whose
lifestyles often violate conventional standards of behavior), and "freaks"
or "hippies" (whose lifestyle treats conventional authority and standards
of behavior with indifference). Behavior choices, including criminal and
noncriminal choices, are socially structured and heavily influenced by the
extent to which the individual identifies with social types, as well as by
other circumstances, such as the presence or absence of others of a given
social type.

Students of deviant adolescent social types generally agree that they characterize a minority of adolescents. Most adolescents are sufficiently attached to conventional persons and involved in conventional pursuits that they do not attach themselves to deviant social types. For those who do, however, roles associated with those types may become central to self-concepts and so of critical importance to their behavior. Behavior patterns become motivated by *values* associated with the social type, by one's *self-identity* with the social type, and by *association* with others who share this identity; in other words, by participation in a subculture that embodies the social type.

Control of deviant behavior is not the primary focus of social type theory, although relationships between young people and authorities, and symbols of authority, are major concerns. The notion is not that young people who find a social type attractive become totally committed to the subculture, though for some this may be the case. Rather, most young people who participate in delinquent behavior drift between conventional values and situations and those that are delinquent or otherwise deviant. Situational pressures are, therefore, critical to understanding much youthful behavior.

Gary Schwartz argues that the significance of social types extends beyond the minority of young people who exemplify them. His ethnographic studies convince him that "young people who are invested in youth culture styles and identities stand out from the crowd in the eyes of their peers." Even those who may be rejected or feared are usually regarded as the *kinds of persons* who can be expected to take a stand "on issues that concern most of the young people in the community."[40]

Self-regulatory functions may encourage or discourage crime or other types of behavior considered deviant. These functions involve *self-observation* (in effect, making an object of oneself in terms of moral and legal considerations; e.g., "Am I this or that type of person?"), *judgments* (based on such factors as personal standards, performance comparisons, and evaluations), and *self-evaluations* (in the light of such observations and judgments). Bandura notes that "[a]ctivation of self-evaluative processes...requires both *personal standards* and *knowledge of the level of one's performance.*" Further, "[s]elf-evaluative regulators do not operate unless activated, and many factors affect the selective activation and disengagement of internal control."[41]

Application of self-concept theory and measures to juvenile delinquency has been disappointing, perhaps because they have been oversimplified and fail, therefore, to capture subtle theoretical nuances. Simple measures of self-esteem have not proven to be very predictive of delinquent behavior. Such single measures fail to comprehend the dynamic character of the self, the many (often changing) representations of the self held by each individual. Daphna Oyserman and Hazel Markus note that, for adolescents especially, the *future* and considerations of *potential* may be particularly important aspects of the self. "Choosing among competing actions and pursuing the chosen action," they argue, "depends on the nature of one's set of possible selves."[42] For maximal motivational relevance, possible selves should balance one another. A "feared" possible self should be balanced by an "expected" possible self, for example.

Oyserman and Markus studied young people aged 13–16 in the Detroit, Michigan, area. Samples were chosen from public schools and from three types of treatment programs for youth with varying degrees of officially adjudged involvement in delinquency. While the samples were small (108 students were selected from seven inner-city schools, 40 from community placement programs, 31 from group homes for delinquents, and 59 from the state training school), the results are suggestive. When gender, age, grade in school, and race were controlled, the more seriously involved delinquents reported more negative "feared" and "expected" selves, and less balance of possible selves than did official nondelinquents and the less seriously involved delinquents.

Because personal evaluative standards and judgments reflect cultural standards and positions within social systems, concepts such as the *self* and *social types* bridge the three levels of explanation distinguished in this book. Their activation occurs within situational contexts. In both macro-level and micro-level respects the nature of processes at work is informed by the labeling perspective.

INSIGHTS OF THE LABELING PERSPECTIVE

Once in place, laws make it possible to identify young people as delinquents. An early seminal book by historian Frank Tannenbaum suggested that application of the machinery of juvenile justice to the normal mischievous play of young people had the dual effects of (1) dramatizing for the child that his behavior is evil and (2) identifying the child as delinquent within the community. "The first dramatization of 'evil' which separates the child out of his group for specialized treatment plays a greater role in making the criminal than perhaps any other experience....The process of making the criminal, therefore, is a process of tagging, identifying, segregating, describing, emphasizing, making conscious and self-conscious; it becomes a way of stimulating, suggesting, emphasizing, and evoking the very traits that are complained of."[43] In this way, Tannenbaum argued, the "normal child" becomes the "delinquent."

Building on Tannenbaum's insight, Edwin Lemert distinguished between *primary* and *secondary* deviance. Primary deviance refers to delinquent acts which go undetected and, therefore, are not labeled as such. Lemert's major interest was what happens to the child after he or she is officially identified as delinquent. Official labeling, he hypothesized, may result in assignment to and acceptance by the child of a deviant *role*: "When a person begins to employ his deviant behavior as a role...as a means of defense, attack, or adjustment to the overt and covert problems created by the consequent societal reactions to him, his deviance is secondary."[44]

The converse of labeling is that rule making, boundary setting, and boundary maintenance are a necessary part of socialization and the maintenance of social order.[45] A great deal of research and theory have been devoted to study of rule making, rule makers, and rule enforcers. The communication of rules to children is critical to their socialization. The tension between boundary setting and labeling informs the nature of social control.

SOCIAL CONTROL THEORY

As the term implies, the emphasis of social control theory is on control rather than on the motivations to commit criminal acts. Social control theory has a long history in social thought, chiefly at the macro-level, but its application at the individual level of explanation is more recent.[46]

As noted in the previous chapter, much behavior variation among cultures and societies can be accounted for by differences in such macrosocial forces as folkways, mores, customary practices, and traditions. At the individual level, such variation provides the content for much child socialization (e.g., the values parents attempt to inculcate in their children and the roles considered to be appropriate in that process). In complex modern societies the individual is likely to be confronted with many conflicting beliefs and practices.[47] The differential-association principle may be read as a statement of culture conflict; that is, as a theory of conflicting influences on socialization with regard to violation of law.

The most systematic and rigorous recent statement of social control theory has been advanced by Travis Hirschi. Hirschi's is a *social bonding* variant of social control theory, stressing the importance of the strength of the individual's bonds to persons and institutions in controlling, or preventing, delinquent behavior.[48] The basic element of the social bond is hypothesized to be *sensitivity to others*. Among those who lack sensitivity to others social bonds are weak; hence, appropriate controls over behavior are weak, with the result that the individual is free to deviate from social norms and the expectations of others. No other motivation to deviate is necessary, only the pursuit of individual interests (which is assumed to be universal).

Hirschi identifies four critical bonds: attachment, commitment, involvement, and belief. Bonds of *attachment* are formed in the process of intimate and sustained interaction. It is through such bonds that normative standards are learned and internalized in the form of the conscience, or super-ego. Similarly, *commitment* has been compared to development of the ego, in that it refers to rational choices among available alternatives. It is similar, also, to David Matza's notion that young people become involved in delinquent behavior because they "drift" between law-abiding and law-violating values, standards, and behaviors; that is, they lack commitment to conventional goals, not that they are committed to deviant goals.[49] As previously noted, modern societies place a premium on getting an education and on dedication to longterm goals, both of which require commitment by young people.

Involvement also has elements of rational choice. The nondelinquent chooses (and is influenced to choose) to involve himself or herself in conventional rather than delinquent activities. Finally, *belief* has to do with the morality of law and its observance or violation.

Social bonding theory has much in common with other concepts which attempt to explain how conforming behavior is promoted and delinquent behavior prevented. Strong social bonds to conventional persons and ideals *reinforce* the individual's *stake in conformity*.[50] Delinquent behavior jeopardizes conventional bonds: one's relationships with highly valued persons (parents and others), one's chances for success in conventional pursuits, and one's sense of integrity concerning beliefs about morality and law.

Hirschi's theory has stimulated a great deal of empirical research. Most of this research has supported the association of delinquent behavior with weak attachment to parents and weak commitment to and involvement in school. Less support has been found for the importance of beliefs in morality and law. The research also suggests that social bonding theory underestimates the importance of peers, and of learning processes such as those stressed by differential association.[51]

ECONOMIC THEORY

The final body of theory to be considered in this chapter is economic theory, macro-level variants of which were discussed in the previous chapter. Though the latter made their appearance in the nineteenth century, it was not until the late 1960s that modern economic models of individual behavior were applied to crime, and then virtually independent of traditional criminology. Gary Becker's seminal paper, "Crime and punishment: an economic approach," stimulated theoretical modeling and empirical research and set the tone for much that was to follow.[52]

Like the classical theories of the eighteenth and nineteenth centuries, modern economic models of criminal behavior assume that individuals choose rationally to allocate time and resources, and to act so as to maximize expected utility or general well-being. As was the case with classical criminological theory, individual differences that might affect such choices are largely ignored. Economic models express utility in monetary terms. By restricting choices to particular legal or illegal behavior alternatives, models "explore the way in which...time allocations change when there is a change in factors that are beyond individual control....[For example] these factors [might] include the individual's wage rate, the level of gains available in illegal activity, the individual's level of beginning wealth, the probability of criminal justice action, and the 'cost' of criminal justice sanctions."[53]

Economic models tend to be theoretically and statistically more rigorous than most theories of criminality, in that they are deductive rather than inductive. Like other scientific approaches, however, they have been hampered by the lack of appropriate data to test their models. Most economists agree that their assumptions are far too simple to reflect reality. Ann Dryden Witte's conclusion regarding this approach to the study of crime applies equally well to other theories: "It appears that economists provide a useful challenge but that the understanding of criminal behavior can now best be advanced by research which considers and incorporates the insights of several disciplines."[54]

ON BONDS AND BOUNDARIES: WHAT CAN A PARENT DO?

Most of the theories reviewed—role theory, behavior theory, social learning or cognitive theory, social bonding theory, and economic theory—share the assumption that human beings are thoughtful and socially aware. They differ in their depiction of the extent to which rationality motivates human beings, in their conception of the forces that shape human behavior, and with regard to what is important to human beings.

They differ also in other respects. Some biologists focus on particular biological anomalies or mechanisms that may trigger behavioral responses that may or may not be regarded as delinquent, thus necessarily involving the definitions and actions of others. Psychobiologists, many psychologists, and some sociologists focus on early socialization, while other sociologists focus on somewhat later life experiences. Economists employ simplifying assumptions regarding the effects of socialization on the decisions people make with regard to behavior choices.

Agreement clearly exists on some principles of individual behavior causation. Differences and similarities among disciplines provide rich materials for identifying such principles. While vast differences remain among disciplines, further agreement on fundamental principles may well be dependent on these differences, that is, on the kinds of knowledge that result only from disciplinary specialization. Even so, the welter of theories and research studies in this field often conflict and confuse. This chapter closes, therefore, with a less abstract—indeed, a very concrete and personal—case study of parental decision making and child socialization that illustrates how one sociologist responded to certain contingencies affecting parent-child interaction.

ON BOUNDARY MAINTENANCE, LABELING, AND PARENTAL DECISION MAKING

Adults—parents, teachers, neighbors, youth workers, employers, police, and others—see the behavior of children from an array of perspectives as varied as those perspectives held by adolescents themselves. Some behaviors are merely annoying. Some are perceived as threatening—to parental prerogatives, to authority in schools, in places of employment, in public places, or to the safety of persons or property. Some behaviors offend moral sensibilities. And some behaviors heighten that sense of responsibility for the moral turpitude of the young which is shared by every older generation.

Whatever their views, adult attitudes and actions vis-à-vis the young become a part of that behavior, contributing to its direction and substance at all levels of explanation. The following case study illustrates the operation of these types of social control processes.

> My wife, Kelma, and I were lunching on the back patio on a warm summer afternoon when we heard sirens signaling an in-town (as distinguished from the surrounding rural area) fire. We thought little of it, since such alarms are relatively common in the small-city and agricultural area where we live. In a matter of moments our son–age nine and one-half—and a friend came running into the yard from play, red-faced and breathless. I made no connection between the two events, since out-of-breath, red-faced boys are even more common than fire alarms.

When I stopped on the way back to my office to pick up a graduate student friend and colleague, Ray Tennyson, he greeted me with the announcement that, "I understand Pat and Mike burned down the old shack in the park!" Then I made the connection. Ray's daughters had conveyed the news. No one was hurt, and the firemen had merely stood by to watch the small dilapidated old structure burn itself out.

So, what to do? I did nothing until I returned home late in the afternoon. In response to my inquiry, Kelma said she had heard nothing about the fire over the local radio station. I told her of my conversation with Tennyson, and we agreed that I should talk with Mike. When confronted with the strange coincidence of the sirens, the fire, and his abrupt return to the yard, Mike readily admitted that he and his friend had, indeed, been responsible for the fire. His friend had brought a small quantity of gasoline and matches to the shack where the two of them proceeded, literally, to "play with fire." Things had gotten out of hand, and the boys fled. Fortunately, no one else was in the structure and no damage was done to the surrounding shrubbery.

I tried to impress on my son the serious potential of fire setting. What if someone else had come into the shack, unknown to the boys? What if a gust of wind had spread the fire to the grasses and shrubs in the area, perhaps even to nearby buildings? What if one of them had been overcome by the smoke and flames? What if the gasoline had exploded?

Mike was properly contrite.

What now? Who should be notified of the episode? To his, "I don't know," I suggested the fire department and perhaps the police. Reluctantly, he agreed to call the fire department. He made the call, explaining in spare but apparently accurate details what had happened. It was unintentional. They had only meant to make a small fire on the dirt floor of the shack. After this conversation, I spoke with the fire chief who assured me it was all right. No one had been hurt and the old building was an eyesore anyhow. The chief really didn't want to talk to the boys. He was satisfied with their explanation.

I am not certain whether it was my conservative moral upbringing or my Durkheimian sense that normative boundaries ought to be made clear to the young, but this seemed insufficient to me. So Mike and I continued our (my) quest for boundary maintenance. I suggested we call the police. Mike was unenthusiastic, but agreed to my doing so. This time I decided to take no chances. I called the police chief (out of Mike's hearing), briefly explained the situation and suggested that I would like to bring my son (and his friend, if he and his parents concurred) down to see the chief in order that the gravity of their behavior might be impressed on the boys. The chief was friendly and appreciative, but he didn't think that would be necessary. The old building had long been an unattractive nuisance and it was good riddance, so long as no one was hurt and the boys were sorry. The chief clearly was not a sociologist, so I explained that I felt it was necessary that some official notice be given the boys. The collective interest could only be served if someone other than their parents presented the message.

The chief seemed fully as reluctant as Mike, but finally agreed that if I would bring the boys down he would give them a "talking to."

I had not yet contacted the parents of the other boy. They were family friends, though not in the "best friend" category. Pat's mother didn't see the necessity of all this, but agreed that Pat should go if Mike did, and she would accompany me to the police station.

There was a bit of awkwardness as the culprits entered the station, but the chief was expecting us and proceeded quickly to the business at hand. Pat's mother and I waited outside the office while the Chief talked to the boys, eliciting the whole story. He reprimanded the boys but indicated his apprecia-tion for their forthrightness in coming forward. The fact that there were no serious consequences of the accidentally set blaze made further official action unnecessary, but they must be aware of the great potential danger to life and property from playing with matches and gasoline—danger for which they could have been held personally responsible and liable.

And so two "delinquent boys" were "brought to justice" in a small college town. An impatient sociologist at last found a way to defend the collective good. And two boys shuffled quietly out of the chief's office and into the sunshine of another summer day.

Now, let us make explicit what has heretofore been implicit in this scenario. The point of the story is not that the decisions made or actions taken were right or wrong—that doubtless would vary among different judges. The point, rather, is that decisions were made and actions taken. Each decision led to action on the part of a variety of actors—youngsters, friends, parents, officials. One can easily construct a large number of other possible scenarios *if* different decisions had been made and actions taken. The number of "what if" contingencies is, of course, limitless. "What if" a citizen, having observed the fire, had become irate, and demanded action of the police? "What if" persons had been injured—perhaps seriously—or further property damage had occurred? Would I have been willing to expose our son to the consider-ably greater risk of police and court intervention? "What if" either of the Chiefs—fire or police—had decided to "make an example" of the boys, even in this minor incident, as a warning to others? And so on. The questions have many ramifications. That the incident occurred in a small town where my wife and I were well-known citizens (though not known personally to either of the Chiefs) doubtless influenced our decision to bring the incident to their attention. Would we have made the same decision if we had lived in Chicago (as we did a short time before this incident)? Would we have acted as we did if we felt that our relationship with our son would have been damaged?

The point, of course, is that countless decisions are made—and actions taken—by countless people, acting in a variety of roles. The decisions and actions result in the screening of juvenile behavior, and of juveniles, through a variety of systems of social control. These systems may be formal and informal, official or unofficial. I might, for personal reasons, have suggested that my son discuss the matter with some other control agent, for example, his teacher or school principal. Had the property destroyed been school property, I should very likely have done so.

The importance of contingencies affecting parental decision making can perhaps be made more concretely by brief reference to another scenario involving both of our children—at a later point in time—when Mike was 14, and Susan, 18.

We were then living in another city and state, as I was on leave from Washington State University. My wife was away for the evening, and I was in my study, alternately reading and struggling with a guitar lesson. Friends of Mike had arrived boisterously early in the evening, and Sue was in her room. Some time later, I became aware that the house had become absolutely silent. Mike had said nothing about leaving, so I assumed he and his friends were still on the premises. The stillness was quite uncharacteristic, however, so I decided to investigate. I called from my study door, but received no response. It was Sue who responded to my second call, by coming to the study. What happened then was quite different from the previous scenario. Sue smiled, put an arm around my shoulders and said quietly, "Do you want them to smoke their pot somewhere else where they might get caught, or here where nothing will happen?" She explained that one of Mike's friends had acquired a "joint," and the boys were sharing it, outside, on our upper terrace.

I will never know whether it was the logic implicit in my daughter's question, the sweetness with which she delivered it, or my own conviction that the laws concerning marijuana use and possession were harsh and wrongheaded, that led me to return to my study and continue my struggle with the guitar. In any case, I did so. And three boys were allowed to enjoy the forbidden fruits of a "controlled substance," thereby testing for themselves the boundaries of socially acceptable behavior.

Again, the point is not that the decision made was right or wrong. Disagreement on what to do in this respect at that time in history (early 1970) doubtless would have been more widespread and more intense than was the case with respect to the first playing-with-fire incident. The point, rather, is that boundary maintenance is a process of decision making, and of actions which reinforce or modify, dramatize or call into question. Most important, boundary making is a process in which people's lives are affected, their values are shaped, and the social fabric is weakened or strengthened, torn or patched, restricted or extended.

NOTES

1. Cesare Lombroso, "Introduction" to Fina Lombroso Ferrara, *Criminal Man According to the Classification of Cesare Lombroso.* New York: Putnam, 1911, p. xiv. See Israel Drapkin, "Criminology: Intellectual history," pp. 547–556, in Sanford H. Kadish (ed.), *Encyclopedia of Crime and Justice.* New York: Free Press, 1983.

2. Cesare Lombroso, *The Female Offender.* New York: Appleton, 1920.

3. See Ernest A. Hooten, *Crime and the Man.* Cambridge, MA: Harvard University Press; and Ernest A. Hooten, *The American Criminal: An Anthropological Study,* Vol.1. Cambridge, MA: Harvard University Press, 1939. I.Q. as a correlate of serious official delinquency is discussed in Robert A. Gordon, "Prevalence: the rare datum in delinquency measurement and its implications for the theory of delinquency," pp. 201-84 in Malcolm W. Klein (ed.), *The Juvenile Justice System.* Beverly Hills, CA.: Sage, 1976. See, also, below, pp. 203-4.

4. William H. Sheldon, *Varieties of Delinquent Youth.* New York: Harper & Row, 1949.

5. Cf. Vicki Pollock, Sarnoff A. Mednick, and William F. Gabrielli, Jr., "Crime causation: Biological theories," pp. 308–316, in Kadish, *op. cit.,* and James Q. Wilson and Richard J. Herrnstein, *Crime and Human Nature.* New York: Simon & Schuster, 1985. Wilson and Herrnstein present an extended, and favorable, discussion of Sheldon's work and related research.

6. Research and theory concerning the relationship between physical attractiveness and human behavior, including delinquent behavior, is summarized, and new data reported, in Robert Agnew, "Appearance and delinquency," *Criminology,* Vol. 22, No. 3 (August, 1984):421–440.

7. Saleem A. Shah and Loren H. Roth, "Biological and psychophysiological factors in criminality," pp. 101–173, in Daniel Glaser (ed.), *Handbook of Criminology.* Chicago: Rand McNally, 1974, p. 153. Animal research demonstrates that causal relationships of neuro-

chemical correlates of behavior flow both ways. See Klaus Miczek, "Analgesia following defeat in an aggressive encounter: development of tolerance and changes in opioid receptors, " pp.14-29 in D. B. Kelly (ed.), *Stress-induced Analgesia*. New York Academy of Sciences, vol. 467 (1985); and Tom R. Insel, "Decreased invivo binding to brain benzodizeptone receptors during social isolation," *Psychopharmacology* 97 (1989): 142-144.

8. Eleanor E. Maccoby and Carol N. Jacklin, "Sex differences in aggression: a rejoinder and reprise," *Child Development*, 51 (1980):964–980.

9. Pollock, et al., *op. cit.*, p. 313.

10. Walter R. Gove, "The effect of age and gender on deviant behavior: a biopsychosocial perspective," pp. 115–144, in Alice S. Rossi, *Gender and the Life Course*. New York: Aldine, 1985, p. 133.

11. Alice S. Rossi, "Gender and Parenthood," pp. 161–191, in *Ibid.*, p. 179.

12. See Leonard Berkowitz and J. Macaulay, "The contagion of criminal violence, *Sociometry*, 34 (June 1971):238–260.

13. These studies are presented and discussed in greater detail in Wilson and Herrnstein, *op. cit.*, Chap.3. See also, Pollock, et al., *op. cit.*

14. *Ibid.*, p. 310.

15. See, for example, the exchange between Mednick, Gabrielli, psychologist Leon J. Kamin, and statistician Lincoln E. Moses, in *Science*, Vol. 227:983–989.

16. See Sarnoff A. Mednick and Jan Volavka, "Biology and crime," pp. 85–158, in Norval Morris and Michael Tonry (eds.), *Crime and Justice: An Annual Review of Research*, Vol. 2. Chicago: University of Chicago Press, 1980.

17. Herbert C. Quay, "Crime causation: psychological theories," pp. 330–342, in Kadish, *op. cit.*, p. 330. This section owes much to Quay's excellent discussion.

18. Quay adds "frustration-aggression theory" to this list. Like psychoanalytic theory, frustration-aggression theory lays great stress on the importance of interference with human goals, including, but by no means exclusively, libidinal drives. While a great deal of research has been done within this frame of reference, it has had limited impact on delinquency theory, in part, because so much delinquency lacks any observable aggressive character. Research has challenged some of the basic premises of frustration-aggression theory, for example, that aggression always follows frustration and that frustration can account for much, if not all, aggression. While the theory has had considerable impact on the study of aggressive behavior, it will not be discussed in this book.

19. See, for example, Seymour L. Halleck, *Psychiatry and the Dilemmas of Crime: A Study of Causes, Punishment and Treatment*. New York: Harper & Row, 1967.

20. Albert Bandura, "Model of causality in social learning theory," pp. 81–99, in Michael J. Mahoney and Arthur Freeman (eds.), *Cognition and Psychotherapy*. New York: Plenum, 1985. Elaboration of the model and evidence concerning it are presented in Albert Bandura, *Social Foundations of Thought and Action: A Social Cognitive Theory*. Englewood Cliffs, NJ: Prentice-Hall, 1986. See also, Albert Bandura, *Aggression: a Social-Learning Analysis*. Englewood Cliffs, NJ: Prentice-Hall, 1973. Bandura is the major exponent of social-cognitive theory.

21. Reprinted with permission of The Free Press, a Division of Macmillan, Inc. from *Children Who Hate* by Fritz Redl and David Wineman, Copyright© 1951 by The Free Press; copyright renewed 1979 by Fritz Redl and David Wineman, p. 22.

22. *Ibid.*, p. 50.

23. *Ibid.*, p. 57.

24. See Albert Bandura and Richard H. Walters, *Adolescent Aggression*. New York: Ronald Press, 1963.

25. *Ibid.*

26. Sensitivity to others is central to social control theory, in that it is fundamental to the creation of social bonds. See below, and Travis Hirschi, *Causes of Delinquency*. Berkeley, CA: University of California Press, 1969.

27. See Hans Eysenck, *Crime and Personality*. Boston: Houghton Mifflin, 1964; also, Gordon Trasler, *The Explanation of Criminality*. London: Routledge & Kegan Paul, 1962.

28. See David P. Farrington, "The family backgrounds of aggressive youths," in L. Hersov, M. Berger, and D. Shaffer (eds.), *Aggressive and Anti-Social Behaviour in Childhood and Adolescence.* Oxford: Pergamon, 1978.

29. See Gerald R. Patterson, "Children who steal," pp. 73–90, in Travis Hirschi and Michael Gottfredson (eds.), *Understanding Crime: Current Research and Theory.* Beverly Hills, CA: Sage, 1980. Cf. L. F. Hewitt and R. L. Jenkins, *Fundamental Patterns of Maladjustment, the Dynamics of their Origin.* Springfield, IL: State of Illinois, 1946.

30. Patterson, *op. cit.,* p. 80.

31. *Ibid.,* p. 87.

32. The theory, or principle, of differential association first appeared in the fourth edition of Sutherland's textbook. See Edwin H. Sutherland, *Principles of Criminology.* Philadelphia: Lippincott, 1939. For a more extended discussion of criticisms and misunderstandings regarding differential association, see Cressey's review of relevant literature in Edwin H. Sutherland and Donald R. Cressey, *Principles of Criminology,* 10th ed. Philadelphia: Lippincott, 1978, pp. 83–97. The work of Cressey's student, Ross L. Matsueda, supports the principle with sophisticated theoretical and empirical methods. See his "The current state of differential association theory," *Crime and Delinquency* 34 (1988): 277-306; and, with Karen Heimer, "Race, family structure, and delinquency: a test of differential association and social control theories," *American Sociological Review* 52 (1988): 826-40.

33. This sentence combines the first three propositions of Sutherland's statement of differential association. See Sutherland and Cressey, *Ibid.,* p. 80.

34. *Ibid.,* p. 81.

35. The quote is from the preamble to Sutherland's statement of differential association. See Sutherland and Cressey, *op. cit.,* p. 80.

36. See, for example, Elton F. Jackson, Charles R. Tittle, and Mary Jean Burke, "Offense-specific models of the differential association process," *Social Problems,* 33 (April, 1986): 335–356; Robert L. Burgess and Ronald L. Akers, "A differential association-reinforcement theory of criminal behavior," *Social Problems,* 14(1968):459–469; see also, Melvin L. DeFleur and Richard Quinney, "A reformulation of Sutherland's differential association theory and a strategy for empirical verification," *Journal of Research in Crime and Delinquency,* 3:1–22, 1966.

37. For a recent review of self-concept theory and research, see Viktor Gecas, "The self-concept," pp. 1–33, in Ralph H. Turner and James F. Short, Jr. (eds.), *Annual Review of Sociology,* Vol. 8. Palo Alto, CA: Annual Reviews, 1982.

38. For review of role theory, see B. J. Biddle, "Recent developments in role theory," pp. 67–92, in Ralph H. Turner and James F. Short, Jr. (eds.), *Annual Review of Sociology,* Vol. 12. Palo Alto, CA: Annual Reviews, 1986.

39. See, for example, Anthony R. Harris, "Sex and theories of deviance: toward a functional theory of deviant type-scripts," *American Sociological Review,* (1977) 42:3–16; and by the same author, regarding the influence of race among male felons, "Imprisonment and the expected value of criminal choice: a specification and test of aspects of the labelling perspective," *American Sociological Review,* (1975) 40:71–87. Regarding social types among young people, see Gary Schwartz and Don Merton, *Love and Commitment.* Beverly Hills, CA: Sage, 1980; and Herman Schwendinger and Julia Schwendinger, *Adolescent Subcultures and Delinquency.* New York: Praeger, 1985.

40. See, for example, Gary Schwartz, *Beyond Rebellion or Conformity: Youth and Authority in America.* Chicago: University of Chicago Press, 1987, p. 18.

41. Bandura, "Model of causality in social learning theory," *op cit.,* pp. 93–95. Bandura's delineation of means by which self-regulatory mechanisms may be dissociated from censurable behavior are similar to those described in Gresham M. Sykes and David Matza, "Techniques of neutralization," *American Sociological Review,* 22 (1957):664–670.

42. Daphna Oyserman and Hazel Markus, "Possible selves," *ISR Newsletter,* Institute for Social Research, University of Michigan (Spring/Summer, 1987):5–7.

43. Frank Tannenbaum, *Crime and the Community.* New York: Ginn, 1938, pp. 19–20. See also, Howard S. Becker, *Outsiders: Studies in the Sociology of Deviance.* New York: Free Press, 1963.

44. Edwin M. Lemert, *Social Pathology.* New York: McGraw-Hill, 1951, p. 76.

45. See Kai T. Erikson, "Notes on the sociology of deviance," *Social Problems*, Vol. 9 (Spring, 1962):307–314.

46. See Albert J. Reiss, Jr., "Delinquency as the failure of personal and social controls," *American Sociological Review*, 16 (1951):196–207.

47. David Matza and Gresham M. Sykes, "Juvenile delinquency and subterranean values," *American Sociological Review*, 26 (1961):712–719. See also, Thorsten Sellin, *Culture Conflict and Crime*. New York: Social Science Research Council, 1938.

48. Travis Hirschi, *Causes of Delinquency*. Berkeley, CA: University of California Press, 1969.

49. See David Matza, *Delinquency and Drift*. New York: Wiley, 1964.

50. For more extended discussion of the importance for delinquent behavior of a "stake in conformity," see Jackson Toby, "Social disorganization and a stake in conformity," *Journal of Criminal Law, Criminology, and Police Science*, 48 (May–June, 1957):12–17.

51. See Matsueda and Heimer, *op. cit.*; also Glassner and Loughlin, *op. cit.*

52. Gary S. Becker, "Crime and punishment: an economic approach," *Journal of Political Economy*, 76 (1968):169–217.

53. See Ann Dryden Witte, "Crime causation: economic theories," pp. 316–322 , in S. H. Kadish (ed.) *Encyclopedia of Crime and Justice*. New York: Free Press, 1983, p. 317. Economic models have not been applied directly to delinquent behavior among juveniles.

54. *Ibid.*, p. 322.

CHAPTER 9
EXPLORATIONS IN THEORETICAL EXTENSION AND INTEGRATION

INTRODUCTION

Must it forever be the case that disciplines "talk past each other" as they seek to explain human behavior? Despite generations of lip service to the principle of interdisciplinary research, and impressive advances by specialized disciplines, gaps between specialized bodies of knowledge remain. Exploring relationships between levels of explanation may help to bridge these gaps.

Theoretical integration means different things to different people. Integration of theories *within* a given level of explanation differs from integration of theories across levels of explanation, for the questions asked are of different orders. Levels of explanation refer to *what* is to be explained as well as to *how* it is to be explained. The relevance of each level of explanation to the other levels, and of differing explanations within a given level, is what theoretical integration is about.

WHY BOTHER?

There are practical, as well as theoretical and empirical, reasons for wanting to relate particular theories, and research inspired by those theories, to other theories and research. The advancement of knowledge and effective social policy require knowledge that transcends particular theories and levels of explanation. Toward this end, the goals of this chapter are modest and straightforward:

1. To suggest a rationale for relating theories to one another.
2. To begin to specify alternatives for simplifying assumptions of theories that ignore established knowledge.
3. To identify relationships between levels of explanation that increase their value to one another.

The Rationale.   The rationale is simple. The scholarly disciplines and the practitioners involved in juvenile justice remain by and large locked in departments, research units, and programs that, if not mutually exclusive, tend to be compartmentalized and insular. Disciplinary perspectives are guided by the questions they ask and the paradigms they employ in the search for explanation. Nevertheless, it is clear that there is much overlap among disciplines and practitioners in their interests in delinquency and delinquents. This chapter explores some of the ways in which knowledge may be advanced through relating theoretical levels of explanation to one another.

It is, in fact, common practice to cross theoretical levels in explaining juvenile delinquency, but confusion exists as to how to do it. That one cannot say everything at once forces decisions as to how to organize theory and research based within different disciplines and at different levels of explanation. Simply recognizing levels of explanation may be helpful, but it is by no means obvious how various individual-level or macro-level theories relate to one another, or to theories at other levels.

Alternatives to Simplifying Assumptions.   The second goal (specification of alternatives to simplifying assumptions) can be illustrated by the assumptions made by theories of juvenile delinquency concerning the nature of human nature. As we have seen in Chapter 8, control theories tend to assume that human nature is relatively fixed and inherently antisocial, and that the motivation to be delinquent is somehow a part of human nature. Psychoanalytic and social control theories share the view that the motivation to be delinquent is universal.[1] By contrast, theories emphasizing the influence of cultural differences, social learning theory and social cognitive processes, assume that human nature is plastic and malleable, and that delinquent behavior must be learned. Similar differences are observed in assumptions about social order, for example, the extent to which it is characterized by consensus or conflict, and by homogeneity of values versus subcultural variations on value themes.

Simplifying assumptions are sometimes little more than crutches; easy ways out of the difficult task of taking into account alternatives based on knowledge from other disciplines or research traditions. Well-established knowledge, where it exists, provides a better theoretical and empirical guide for further scientific inquiry and for social policy.

The assumption that human nature is *either* fixed and antisocial *or* malleable and developing clearly is unnecessary. The universality of self-seeking motivations and the capacity to commit delinquent and criminal acts is well established. So, too, are the shaping and modification of these motivations and capacities in the course of early socialization and later in life. Important disagreements continue to exist concerning the *extent* to which modification of basic motivations and capacities is possible and the relative importance and the consequences of different kinds of experience in bringing about such modification. Though knowledge is far from complete, it is clear that genetic characteristics of individuals both enable and limit potentialities for behavior. Human biology and social experience interact to bring about human development, as do psychological proclivities and physiological conditions.

Conversely, the full richness of macrosocial and microsocial processes cannot be understood without knowledge of the manner in which the individual compositional features of social and cultural systems affect those systems and the unfolding of events within them. If communities as well as individuals have careers in crime, for example, theoretical integration requires knowledge as to how these careers relate to the sorts of individuals who make up communities.

ASKING THE RIGHT QUESTIONS

The discovery that involvement in minor delinquencies is virtually universal has likewise led some to assume that it is unnecessary to inquire why young people commit these acts. It is only important to know why they don't do so. Increasingly, the question is being phrased as, why don't they commit *serious* delinquent behaviors, for that is the more troubling question.

Recall, also, that young people tend not to specialize in particular types of crime, and that crimes considered to be most serious (violent crimes) seem not to be very central to the lives of their perpetrators.

Clearly, then, the most relevant questions do not concern what distinguishes delinquents from nondelinquents. We need to know, rather, what the processes and mechanisms of motivation *and* control are that account for differences in behavior, and how these are influenced by cultural and social systems. As matters stand, there is sufficient ambiguity concerning the extent and nature of juvenile delinquency to warrant both questions: Why young people do, and why they do not commit delinquent behaviors. And we need to utilize all three levels of explanation in the search for answers.

THEORETICAL INTEGRATION AND GRAY AREAS OF KNOWLEDGE

Most adolescents avoid crossing the boundary between criminal and noncriminal behavior except for relatively minor infractions, but a few do not. Fewer still become repeatedly and seriously involved in criminal behavior. It is in such gray areas as the distinction between normal adolescent behaviors and those that stretch the bonds and the boundaries of control beyond the toleration levels in families and communities that knowledge from each level of explanation becomes critical. Definitions of what is considered normal behavior vary among individuals as well as communities and entire societies. They may also *change* among the definers of normal behavior as events unfold.

It is also true that those who engage in acts defined as delinquent do so only occasionally. Delinquent boys and girls spend little of their time committing delinquent acts, and most youngsters in even the highest delinquency areas spend little of their lives in this way.

What selective processes determine which boys and girls make choices to commit delinquent behavior, or have such choices made for them by others (the reactive side of question again)? Why do delinquency episodes occur when and where they happen? What kinds of occasions give rise to delinquency on the part of what kinds of youngsters? Conversely, what processes trigger conforming (conventional) behaviors and commitments? The processes, mechanisms, and kinds of life events that trigger delinquent episodes or lead to a greater commitment to deviant identities also constitute a gray area of knowledge, as yet inadequately understood.

Clues to the resolution of gaps in these gray areas of knowledge are to be found in many concepts and theories. Subcultures and group processes are important in understanding both why some individuals do and why others do not become delinquent. Why, for example, do some youngsters whose personal characteristics would seem to predict conforming behavior (e.g., those with strong bonding and nondelinquent self-concepts) become delinquent? The circumstances in which individuals engage in any type of behavior are informed by microsocial processes and knowledge of macro-level forces. Subcultures set the stage on which group processes are played out. Within such settings, micro-level and individual-level observations may inform the nature of turning points or events that influence individual behavior.

The strength of mainstream cultural norms varies, as do local community toleration levels. When either of these is weak or ambiguous, the push needed to encourage participation in lawbreaking is lessened. The ambiguity of general American norms concerning such things as cheating on income tax, making "sharp" business dealings, projecting the macho image, and using violence to settle disputes, lends support to those who would commit both property and person offenses, as David Matza and Gresham Sykes have noted.[2] In some communities "hustling" is "hard work" and a way of life.[3]

When opportunities for illegal gain exist and when community or group norms support illegal behavior, or group processes lead in that direction, legal proscriptions may lack force in *many* situations. In the absence of illegitimate opportunities and support for taking advantage of them, even weak legal proscriptions may be sufficient to insure law-abiding behavior. Similarly, microsocial principles may lead to more precise understanding of the situations or circumstances under which normative properties of groups conducive to delinquent behavior, or emotions of the moment (as in intimate interaction or participation in highly emotional crowd situations) are likely to supercede conventional norms. By studying such situations, the mechanisms by which individual decision making leads to delinquent versus nondelinquent behavior choices may be illuminated.

INTEGRATING "DOWN" TO THE INDIVIDUAL LEVEL OF EXPLANATION

Macro-level sociological theories have been criticized for ignoring both individual-level characteristics and group processes in explaining delinquency rates.[4] Social and cultural systems do not directly and inevitably cause individuals to commit crimes. They are, however, associated with "stable differences across individuals in the propensity to commit criminal or theoretically equivalent acts."[5] The very notion of *rates* of behaviors implies *probabilities*, rather than inevitable occurrence. Even clinical diagnoses of individuals are examined with an eye to the general characteristics of individuals associated with behavior patterns.

Most theoretically integrative efforts have focused on relationships between *macro*-level and *individual*-level variables associated with criminal behavior among individuals or groups. Theories now considered sociological classics draw upon psychological concepts to explain delinquent adaptations to macro-level conditions. Albert Cohen's theory of the delinquent subculture, for example, invokes the psychoanalytic mechanism of *reaction formation* to explain how a particular social structure might generate a delinquent subculture that is malicious and negativistic in character.[6] Richard Cloward and Lloyd Ohlin's opportunity structure theory emphasized the importance of *individual perceptions* of opportunities, learning structures, and role models in determining the formation of delinquent subcultures.[7]

The most far-reaching of these integrative efforts is Ronald Akers' version of social learning theory. Building on his previous work with Robert Burgess, Akers reconciles principles of general learning theory with differential-association theory. In later work, Akers and his colleagues are explicit concerning the relationship between theories designed to explain rates and their integrative effort: "While other theories delineate the structural variables (class, race, anomic conditions, breakdown in social control, etc.) that yield differential rates of deviance, social learning stresses the behavioral mechanisms by which these variables produce the behavior comprising the rates."[8]

Social structure, in this conceptual integration, provides "sets and schedules of reinforcement contingencies" and role models. These "learning environments," in turn, influence and are influenced by relationships with others such as are involved in social bonding. Each of the social bonds stressed in control theory is established or broken, strengthened or weakened, according to reinforcement, modeling, and associated cognitive processes.

Similarly, elements of opportunity structure theory can be conceptualized in terms of behaviorist principles. Differences in available legitimate and illegitimate opportunities are likely to result in differences in reinforcement for both conventional and deviant bonds and behavior.

Other investigators also have focused on translating, or operationalizing, macro-level variables as they are hypothesized to apply to individuals. Most tests of these and other macro-level theories have followed a similar logic, first operationalizing macro-level concepts into individual-level phenomena, for example, individual-level *perceptions* of social structural or cultural characteristics, followed by statistical comparison of the relationship of these and other individual-level variables to measures of delinquency. Delbert Elliott and his colleagues follow this strategy, by operationalizing macro-level strain theory in terms of hypothesized effects *on individuals*—thus treating anomie as a psychological concept (anomy, following Robert MacIver's terminology), rather than a macrosocial concept.[9] Similarly, as discussed in Chapter 7, after operationalizing opportunity structure variables in terms of individual perceptions, my colleagues and I related these perceptions to the behavior of the boys in our sample strata.

These types of conceptual integration and associated empirical tests contribute to theoretical integration by relating macrosocial concepts to individual-level theories, and by relating individual-level processes to rates of behavior that are the focus of macro-level theories. Integration of theories within or between levels of explanation is not the only means by which theoretical advancement may be achieved, however.

LEARNING FROM NEGATIVE CASES

Much can be learned by examining cases that are contrary to theoretical expectations. Four years after initially interviewing boys and girls who had been 14 and 15 years old in 1982, Peggy Giordano reinterviewed most of these young people, when they were 18 and 19.[10] While substantial support was found for social bonding (control) theory, a large number of cases could not be accounted for by the most central tenant of that theory, namely, that the lack of attachment to parents is the most important factor accounting for delinquent behavior. Giordano focuses on these "negative cases," that is young people in her sample who had low levels of attachment to parents but were not delinquent, and those who had high levels of attachment but who were delinquent.

The largest number of these negative cases were in the first category, "false positives" who would be expected to be delinquent because of their lack of attachment to parents. Several of these cases—most of them young women—manifested other forms of deviant behavior such as pregnancy or motherhood out of wedlock, bulimia, anorexia, depression, extreme loneliness, or sadness. This finding helps us to interpret gender as a categoric risk. The relatively low rates of delinquency so consistently found among girls may result in part because girls (more than boys) engage in other, theoretically equivalent, behaviors rather than delinquent behavior. Explanation of these negative cases in terms of social bonding theory requires that the *dependent variable* be extended to include these theoretically equivalent behaviors.

Some negative cases were found to support dimensions of social bonding not specified in the theory. Some nondelinquent youngsters' strong attachments to friends, for example, appeared to compensate for their lack of attachment to parents. A few respondents reported *changing friendship networks* and moving away from those that influenced them toward involvement in illegal behavior. Other low-attachment-to-parents youngsters had developed strong commitments to goals, and a stake in conformity, that motivated them to keep out of trouble. One such case, a black male who described a pattern of bitter conflict with his mother, told the interviewer, "I never take a chance. There is too much at stake. My football scholarship…and my going into the U.S. Air Force." The availability of such opportunities had established a stake in conformity for this young man.

Holistic studies demonstrate the enormous complexity of the forces shaping human behavior, and the impressive adaptability of the human species. Causal forces and sequences are embedded in a multitude of changing relationships and circumstances. Alternative interpretations of empirical observations are nearly always possible, and data necessary to test them often are lacking. Problems thus posed are both theoretical and empirical. Theories that are stated in the formal language of science and research designed to test the commonalities, as well as the differences, among alternative interpretations are rare.

Longitudinal research designs help to solve some of these problems in that they permit observations of changes in both behavior and life circumstances. While historical macro-level forces are associated with broad behavior adaptations, more immediate macrosocial influences frequently change. Individual socialization continues throughout life. The uniqueness of individual personality and selfhood are a constant challenge to generalization. Different configurations of causal forces may account for behavioral adaptations over time, for individuals, groups, and societies.

As we have seen throughout the book, a variety of strategies have developed for dealing with complexity, social change, and individual uniqueness. In spite of decades of methodological advance, however, both the identification and the measurement of theoretical variables remain crude and imprecise. Causal significance is extraordinarily difficult to determine. As life circumstances change, so may causal processes in the lives of individuals and in social and cultural systems. While historical studies typically sketch broad macrosocial forces, most lack sufficient detail to be certain that causal influences can be determined with certainty. Contemporary longitudinal studies tend to lack detail at both the macro-level and the individual level. The relatively short time span of such studies prevents specification of the role of many macrosocial influences, such as cohort and historical period effects on delinquency rates. Correspondingly, without detailed genetic, biological, psychological, and social developmental data, it is impossible to assess the influence of the vast assortment of individual-level influences known to affect behavior.

DELINQUENCY, GROUPS, AND COLLECTIVE BEHAVIOR

While the study of gang delinquency does not solve all these problems, the phenomena loosely grouped under this rubric have been studied sufficiently at each level of explanation to allow exploration of the applicability of various theoretical perspectives.

The term *gang delinquency* is appropriate for most of the groups and the behavior to be discussed in the remainder of this chapter, but the topic is broader than is implied by that appellation. As noted in Chapter 6, the number of boys and girls involved in episodes of delinquent behavior is typically very small. Particular episodes may, however, involve quite large aggregations. These episodes may also be less a product of the group and more a product of amorphous collective behavior processes, or of subcultural influences.

Research on gang delinquency addresses a variety of questions. What features of collective life among adolescents lead to delinquent behavior? What is it about delinquent behavior that accounts for its group or collective character? What group processes or mechanisms trigger delinquent episodes?

What individual characteristics are associated with gang delinquency, and how are these related to macro-level and micro-level processes?

The following discussion is necessarily tentative, only in part because the research to be discussed did not have theoretical integration as its primary purpose. The ever-changing character of gang delinquency and the elementary level of the state of knowledge at any one time preclude complete knowledge in any case.

Beginning with the Macro-level.   Boundary maintenance processes take place within existing social orders. These social orders—social and cultural systems, institutions and organizations, belief and values systems—account, we have said, for different rates of behavior. Principles of subcultural formation and maintenance discussed in Chapter 7 provide a theoretical basis for understanding the emergence of adolescent subcultures that followed upon modernizing forces. The basis for cultural differentiation occurred with the separation of families from traditional work relationships, which in turn greatly altered relationships between children and adults. While many older children continued to work side-by-side with their elders, others joined the ranks of the "dangerous classes." As the nuclear family became the special repository for moral upbringing and the schools were increasingly looked to for education and training, children were more and more separated from traditional adult worlds of extended families and work relationships centered in the family and community. The social structuring of opportunities accompanying these changes created fertile ground for differences in the nature of subcultures among the social strata. The interaction of young people with similar problems of adjustment ensured that a variety of subcultures would, indeed, emerge and be maintained.

Precisely how these processes may have been involved in translating larger social forces into adolescent subcultures—or specifically delinquent subcultures—cannot be determined by the data at hand. Concrete realities of local conditions and specific situations were critical to the form taken by youth subcultures. Among these realities, the policies and practices of local community institutions and events were and are critical.

Social types that accompany adolescent subcultures have been richly and convincingly portrayed. The fact that similar social types appear in a variety of research settings suggests that they are "grounded in the fundamental characteristics of our society."[11] In the absence of more complete information that would relate the social types to socialization in families and community institutions, however, the *mechanisms* by which global macrosocial forces are involved in the creation of social types remain unclear.

Studies of adolescent subcultures and gangs have tended to slight family experiences, and most treat experiences in community institutions as peripheral to the dynamics of group life. We know, however, that ecological processes and communities are important settings for delinquency. Moreover, while substantial agreement exists concerning general principles of learning, relating these principles to the macrosocial contexts of delinquency is a difficult and complex task.

The Chicago gang study cited in previous chapters will be drawn upon again in this chapter. That study did not investigate the operation of global macrosocial forces, such as industrialization, urbanization, and the development of capitalism. In the previous chapter, however, we saw the emergence of a drug-oriented subculture among the "Pill Poppers," including a mythology based on group experiences which served to unite the group. The importance of other macrosocial and microsocial processes in determining the nature of the youth gangs we studied became evident in the course of field observations.

THE MICROSOCIAL LEVEL OF EXPLANATION

Delinquent behavior often is precipitated by internal group processes. The dynamics of these processes are suggested by three status-related mechanisms identified in the Chicago research: (1) the reactions of gang leaders to status threats, (2) the reactions of gangs (or segments of gangs) to status threats, and (3) a utility-risk paradigm of individual decision making in situations involving the group.

Reactions of Gang Leaders to Status Threats. Attention was first drawn to the reactions of gang leaders to status threats by the sudden occurrence of "strange" behavior on the part of a strong gang leader following his return from a brief period of jail detention. Duke was a very cool leader of a tough, conflict-oriented gang of black teenagers. More socially skilled than the others, he maintained his position by cultivating nurturant relationships with other members of the gang and by negotiating with other leaders in intergang councils.

Upon his return from detention, Duke's behavior changed dramatically. The detached worker assigned to Duke's gang explained:[12]

> ...maybe it's because he's been in jail and he's trying to release a lot of energy. Maybe after a while, he'll settle down. As of yet he hasn't settled down. He is one of the real instigators in fightin'. (The worker then described Duke's behavior at a basketball game which had been scheduled with the Jr. Lords.) Duke was calling them "mother-fucker," and "The Lords ain't shit." Duke walked up to them–Duke doin' all the talkin'—instigator. Bill next to him and Harry listening. Everybody was listening but Duke, and I was having a problem trying to get Duke down there so he could get himself dressed and leave. Duke walked up and said, "You ain't shit. The Jr. Lords ain't shit. Are you a Jr.?" The boys said, "No." And he said, "A fuckin' ole Lord, I'm King Rattler." Duke walked all through all of them, "You ain't shit," trying to get a fight. "Come on Duke," I said, trying to push him down the stairs. But each time he'd get away and go over there, "You Lords ain't shit...we're Rattlers. We're Eastside Rattlers."

Even though other members of the gang supported Duke's aggressive behavior, shortly thereafter he returned to his cool ways. Our interpretation of this incident was that for a brief period Duke catered to the most broadly held normative characteristics of the group. Following reestablishment of his leadership role, and with the support of the detached worker, he was able to resume his customary mode of relating to the group. It was not until other seemingly similar cases came to our attention that we were able to discern what we believe to be the general mechanism at work.

Abstracting the basic theoretical elements of this microsocial process may facilitate exploration of its generality and possible ways of integrating different levels of explanation. A fundamental individual-level principle, we have said, is that behavior is adaptive, or problem solving, that is, reactive. The nature of adaptation or reaction clearly depends heavily on the nature of the problem to which behavior is a response. The definition of states, statuses, or situations as problematic, in turn, is in large part determined by social and cultural factors, for example, culturally or socially defined desiderata (or, conversely, things to be avoided).[13]

In the adolescent world we studied in Chicago, and apparently in many other adolescent social worlds, *status* vis-à-vis one's peers, was and is a major problem. The salience of status as a problem, and the intensity with which it is experienced vary a great deal in different situations and for the incumbents of different *roles* in the group. Solutions to status problems, in the situations we observed, were deeply embedded in normative properties and processes of the group.

Normative Properties of Groups and Reactions to Status Threat. The Chicago research suggests that the status threat mechanism applies also to group behavior. A "humbug" (gang fight) that took place at the Chicago Amphitheater involved both threats to the newly acquired adult status of a gang leader (he had just turned 21 years old) and to group identity among rival gangs. Detached workers with the gangs had arranged to take some of their boys to a professional basketball game. In the course of the evening events focused the attention of the boys on one another *as members of gangs* rather than on the basketball game.[14]

> Several elements in the incident were status threatening. One of the workers challenged the right of the gang leader's *adulthood* to buy beer (on the grounds that he was participating in a YMCA program-sponsored activity). This was an obvious "put down" of the young man in front of his own gang (the North Side Vice Kings) and degraded him in the eyes of members of another gang (the Junior Chiefs) whom he was trying to impress. The gang leader instigated a fight between the North Side Vice Kings and members of the South Side Rattlers. All of the members of the North Side Vice Kings were humiliated when their worker decided that they all must leave because of the fracas. Both their position in the gang world (because the event was witnessed by members of a rival gang) and their treatment as a bunch of "kids" in public were status threatening.
>
> When they arrived on the scene, members of two other gangs (Cherokees and Midget Vice Kings) joined in the fighting, the former against the Vice Kings just as they had succeeded in routing the Rattlers, the latter as Vice King allies. However, members of the Junior Chiefs never became involved in the fighting, despite the fact that they witnessed the entire event, beginning with the initial conflict between the worker and the gang leader. Nor did members of the Junior Vice Kings, who arrived after the fighting had been controlled, though the fights were the topic of animated discussion among them and between them and other boys.

Despite all the excitement in this incident, and a good deal of provocation which is not here detailed, the fights were short lived. All the boys, except the Vice Kings, who were most central to the incident and who experienced the greater status threats, were brought under control reasonably quickly, and they stayed to watch the basketball game. The humbug provided grist for the mill of individual and group status within the status universe of fighting gangs. In the months that followed no more humbugging between any of these gangs took place, however.

While this incident was relatively self-contained, it served to perpetuate the investment of these boys in their gang "rep." It also served the image of these boys as street warriors, whose group norms required their participation in conflict with rival gangs. Were it not for the detailed accounting of the incident available through the field research, such an interpretation would seem reasonable. It would then be necessary to discount the influence of the norms after the fights stopped, however. Why were the fights so *easily* stopped? Why did not all the boys participate in the fighting? With the exception of the Vice Kings, there were in *each* group some who never became involved.

Careful review of the incident suggests that those most centrally involved were gang leaders and boys striving for leadership, and other core members. Membership roles and personal investment in the gang are variable among individuals, and such variation influences the likelihood of individual involvement in the give and take of such an incident. It seems clear that no gang norm required fighting of *all* boys, even under extremely provocative circumstances.

Normative properties of groups doubtless influence the behavior of gang members, but that influence on most gang members appears to be tenuous and largely situational. The Chicago gangs were characterized by loose criteria of membership, frequently changing membership, and low cohesion except under circumstances that drew members together. Members of the gangs came and went for days or weeks at a time, and unless they occupied particularly strong leadership or other roles central to the group, most were hardly missed.

In the above incident, while the threat to the gang leader's status as an adult would clearly have been threatening to his status as a gang leader as well, the element of *status threat* may not have been the primary motivator for the several *group* responses noted. The basketball game might be seen as simply an opportunity to express youthful exuberance and group identity. Better decision rules for this elementary theory are needed for proper assignment of case materials. The fact that the gangs were known to be rivals, however, gives credence to the status threat interpretation.

SITUATIONAL FACTORS, GROUP SOLIDARITY, AND BEHAVIOR

The reaction of groups to situations in which group status is threatened, or in which status may be enhanced, supports observations made by others concerning the importance of the *group* to the behavior of gang members. Walter Miller and his colleagues systematically observed physically and verbally aggressive behaviors by members of one of the Boston gangs they studied.[15] The great majority of these acts were internally directed, that is, toward fellow gang members, and most served group purposes. The largest percentage (about 40 percent) of aggressive acts appeared to demonstrate personal qualities that were highly valued as criteria of group acceptance and status. An almost equally large percentage appeared to be aimed at the achievement of group solidarity or to facilitate group behavior. Other aggressive acts seemed to be oriented toward enhancing equality among group members or to insuring reciprocity within the group.

In 1966, Leon Jansyn reported that both delinquent and nondelinquent *group behavior* by the Chicago gang he observed occurred most often when group solidarity was at a low point. Group solidarity was measured by a combination of the number of members of the group hanging with the group on a given day, and the amount of time group members spent with the group. Jansyn also found that the boys' perceptions of leadership, group membership, and turf were responsive to the situation in which the group found itself.[16]

Both of these studies suggest that behavior is heavily influenced by normative properties of the group and by internal group processes (the criteria of group acceptance, group cohesion and solidarity, the value of group action, equality among group members, reciprocity within the group, and response to the group situation). The distinction between micro-level and macro-levels of explanation becomes blurred in these studies. This might itself be an indication of effective integration of these levels, but more information about entire event sequences would be required to reach that conclusion.

MICROSOCIAL AND MACROSOCIAL INFLUENCES ON INDIVIDUAL-LEVEL DECISION MAKING

Observations at the microsocial level demonstrate that individual behavioral choices are guided by probabilities of outcomes that may be valued differently by decision makers. In seeking to understand the high incidence of illegitimate parenthood among members of one gang we were studying, several facts became evident. Having sexual intercourse was highly valued by the gang members. Fathering a child out of wedlock was not a factor in determining status within the gang, and *as individuals* the boys supported quite conventional values concerning responsible fatherhood. Illegitimate parenthood was common and accepted in the local community. This combination of circumstances led to a high incidence of illegitimate parenthood among gang members, an aleatory process determined primarily by the amount of time spent at risk. Illegitimate parenthood could thus be explained independently of the boy's intentions or expectations.

Later, concern with risk-related behavior was extended to instances of serious aggression. Here, too, outcome probabilities varied, but the values associated with different outcomes were quite different for individual decision makers. The problem to be explained was the individual decision by gang boys whether or not, and in what manner, to join the action. The basic premise of this micro-level theory was that behavior is a continuing process of adjustment to elements in the situation of ongoing activities, such as those occurring on the street. We hypothesized that the decision to join the action or remain aloof from it was determined in large part by considerations of the probable consequences of that decision, and by the values associated with those consequences, as illustrated by the incident which led to the jailing of Duke, president of the King Rattlers.[17]

> The incident began with a fight between a member of the King Rattlers and another boy and his brothers, not members of the Rattlers. It culminated in the shooting of two of the non-Rattlers and a bystander. The shots were fired by the president of the King Rattlers. We do not know the circumstances which led to the altercation, but we do know that it took place in the middle of the crowded main street in King Rattler territory, and the Rattler president was a spectator. What began as a fair fight was altered when another of the non-Rattler brothers joined the fight. This led to the involvement of another Rattler, and then another brother. The detached worker with the Rattlers explained that when the third brother jumped in, other Rattlers stood back and the Rattler president "came on with the revolver." The revolver belonged to none of the Rattlers, but had been passed among them as the fight progressed. It came into the possession of the Rattler president as the fight seemed to be getting out of hand. "He jumped in the middle of the street and fired one shot up in the air, and no one responded...they started closing in on him so he fired low. He wasn't firing at any particular person...and he didn't know he shot anybody other than a woman, and he felt real bad about it. But he said that he just got excited."

The chief puzzle in this case arose from the inconsistency in the Rattler president's behavior in comparison with his customary leadership role. As noted, above, Duke was socially skilled, cool in crisis situations, and quite capable of effective and decisive action. He dressed "sharp" and "made out" with the girls. He could dance well enough to "turn out" most anyone in the neighborhood. He did not needlessly cause other boys to lose face as he led the gang. For these qualities he was rewarded with deference, both within the gang and within the neighborhood, by adults and young people alike.

Duke's behavior in this incident does not appear to be related to any implied challenge to his rank, or to any direct threat to his status. As the situation developed, there was a clear expectation that Duke would take charge, however. Duke did not "just happen" to get the gun. It was passed to him. Once it was in his hands, the likelihood that he would use it was strongly determined by the normative properties of the gang and the threat of further violence. Certainly Duke had good reason to be fearful, once he had brandished the gun and fired a warning shot. His initial actions, however, seem more clearly related to his leadership role than to concern for his physical safety.

Duke's decision-making calculus was doubtless predicated also on his perception that the probability of a worst-case outcome (that someone might be injured or killed and that Duke might be arrested) was remote. Violence was common in the community, and seldom resulted in arrest. While Duke was, in fact, arrested, he was held in detention only for a few weeks and released. The high value placed on status within the group and the relatively mild official consequences of his crime seem unlikely to have had much deterrent effect on either Duke or other members of the gang.

THE IMPORTANCE OF CULTURAL DIFFERENCES

Group processes are circumscribed by cultural differences. Differences between group and individual fighting reported by the Cambridge (England) Study in Delinquent Development are instructive in this respect. David Farrington and his associates found that the nature of aggressive incidents depended heavily on whether or not it was a group fight or simply an altercation between individuals.[18] Individual fights more often involved hostile aggression and feelings of anger, whereas group fights were more *instrumental* in character (e.g., coming to the aid of a friend or, as in the Chicago study, to gain status). Group fights occurred most frequently in pubs and streets, often in both. Compared to individual fights, they more frequently involved weapons and resulted in serious injuries. Group fighting in this study did not involve delinquent gangs, but the young men who took part in group fighting were more likely to belong to "antisocial groups." Case studies suggest that group fighting was a matter largely of lifestyle, rather than of participation in conflict gangs.

THE INDIVIDUAL LEVEL OF EXPLANATION

As previously noted, the Cambridge study also found that the most violent delinquents came from disharmonious families, characterized by harsh parental discipline and lack of parental supervision. The Chicago gang study did not study family relationships of the boys in detail.[19] Field observations clearly demonstrated differences in available role models for both boys and girls among the samples studied, however. The poolroom drug transaction described in Chapter 1 illustrates the availability of both criminal role models and opportunities. Field observations such as those reported in Chapters 5 and 7, and interview data concerning perceptions of opportunities and relationships with adults reported in Chapter 7, provide further inferential data in this respect. More direct evidence is found in observations such as the following, from one of the black gang areas:[20]

> That poolroom down there is nothing but hustlers—the worst type of people in the area—known prostitutes dressed in shorts and kind of flashy, and their pimps. There was one guy, he is a dope addict, wears his shades. He is one of the regulars. He was shooting pool, and he recognized me and spoke to me and to the fellows.
>
> The three of us started shooting a game of bank on the back table. There was a conversation that the older fellows were having on one of the front tables about some kind of robbery that they had just pulled. They had been busted. They were all teasing one of the guys that was shooting, about the fact that he was caught. The police had him chained with another guy around a lamp post. And some kind of way he got his hand out of one of the cuffs, but he still had one of the cuffs on. He couldn't get it off, and they were teasing him. Everyone in the poolroom was well aware of what was going on.

The business-as-usual nature of some types of criminal behavior in the black gang communities is further illustrated by another detached worker's report that a street dealer in marijuana in his area was enclosing a note with her new address in each bag she sold. Customers were thanked for their business and asked to continue their patronage in her new location.

Drug dealing and other forms of criminal activity in the white gang communities were more covert. The white gangs also were less visible in their communities, to younger children as well as to adults, than were the black gangs in the black communities.

Very early in the research, field observations indicated that many of the black gang boys and girls we were studying lacked social assurance and possessed fewer social skills than did the higher SES youths and other nongang members. Detached workers frequently reported that members of their gangs did not feel comfortable when outside the gang area, and that they were ill at ease in many social situations. The following excerpt from a detached worker's report is apposite, and suggests, as well, that members of the gang under observation had a low degree of mutual obligation to one another outside of the gang context.[21] The worker is describing events prior to and during the annual banquet of the YMCA of Metropolitan Chicago, a very large, dressy affair featuring a major national figure as speaker, and attended by many of the city's leaders in business and philanthropy.

> Duke wanted me to get him a date with one of the YMCA girls from the downtown office. I told him I thought maybe he'd be better anyway to take Elaine because "You've never actually taken Elaine anywhere of importance. You've taken her to the show, but she's never been to a downtown affair."
>
> Q: Is Elaine the girl who has Duke's two children?
>
> A: She has a baby girl who is a year old and one that's three. Duke's never taken her to a real nice place, and I thought it would be nice if he asked her to go. He was real excited. I had one extra ticket. I said, "Well, Duke, seeing that you and Butch get along real well, maybe Butch would go." Duke said "No, no, we don't want to take Butch because he doesn't know how to eat out in company." Then he went all the way back to the time I took them to the Prudential Building. I suggested that we go in and get a cup of coffee, but Butch said, "No, we'd better go back to the area and get a hot dog or Polish [sausage]." And Duke was all for it, too, because he didn't want to go in there either. On the "Top of the Rock" they did their sightseeing, but they didn't want to go into the little restaurant and get coffee. They didn't feel they were dressed, or something. They're real shy about going into a strange place that's real nice. Earlier in the summer I took Duke, Butch, and Harry out to Lake Meadows, and they were real shy. They didn't want to go in because they felt they weren't dressed good enough.
>
> Anyway, Duke didn't feel Butch was qualified. So I smiled and said, "Okay, how about Harry?" "Hell no. Harry hasn't got enough clothes to go."
>
> On the way to the banquet I told them approximately what was going to go on. When we got to the amphitheater, I dropped Elaine, Alice [Duke's aunt and the worker's date for the evening], and Duke and I went to park the car. Duke asked me if I would pick him up a pack of cigarettes, so I told him I would. I told him to go in and check the coats. He looked around and finally came back because he didn't know where they were supposed to go. Then I found the tables, and I put Duke and Elaine together.
>
> Q: Did Duke comment about the dinner?
>
> A: Overall, he had a real good time. Elaine complained because Duke insulted her and she couldn't eat her meat. Duke was trying to show her how to cut the meat. He said Elaine didn't know which hand to hold the knife in.

She was real hungry and she ate everything but the meat, because Duke was rapping on her so much. She felt real bad for not having eaten the meat. She didn't know whether it would have been appropriate to have Duke cut her meat or not. Duke said the meat was so tender he could cut it with his fork.

The boys' lack of social skills was advanced as a possible explanation for aggressive behavior both within the gang and in relations between gangs. In the absence of social skills, verbal aggression, body punching, wrestling, and aggressive posturing serve as the lowest common denominator for interpersonal relationships among gang members. Boys who possessed more advanced social skills were rewarded with leadership positions. In addition, the gangs provided little encouragement for the development or the exercise of skills necessary to function in such conventional settings as school, work, or marriage. Indeed, social disabilities often were exacerbated by disparaging remarks by other gang members and their refusal to discuss such matters seriously. Again, a field report is illustrative:[22]

Fuzzhead, a regular but low-status member of the Chiefs, approached the detached worker in a pool hall hangout and began to talk very seriously about his plans to get and keep a job so that he could provide for the girl he wanted to marry. The worker probed Fuzzhead and, finding him deadly in earnest, encouraged the boy in these ambitions and indicated his willingness to help him secure a steady job. In the midst of the conversation other Chiefs entered the pool hall and came over to where the worker and Fuzzhead were conversing. Upon discovering the topic of conversation they began ridiculing Fuzzhead's ambitions. Fuzzhead abruptly discontinued this discussion and despite the worker's encouraging words withdrew from the conversation.

Participation in the gang did little to prepare these boys for conventional adult roles. Being "street wise" is not an asset in most of the available low-level jobs. Toughness and physical and verbal aggression often are counterproductive on the job, as is the casual attitude toward time displayed in hanging out activities. Demands for punctuality, perseverance, and quality performance likewise are alien to gang culture. The gang context, in effect, runs counter to many of the requirements of modern civilization.

Social disabilities of this sort are not universal among gang members. The contrast between the black gang members we studied and the Mexican boys and girls studied by Ruth Horowitz and Gary Schwartz in this respect is dramatic. Schwartz notes that youth in the so-called 32d Street community "are well schooled in the subtleties of respectable behavior" and "attentive to the clues that identify a person as capable of managing to get along in conventional society...so long as those standards do not infringe on their sense of honor."[23]

SYSTEMATIC TESTING OF INDIVIDUAL GANG BOYS

Several more systematically obtained psychological measures also differentiated among our samples. Gang boys made the lowest scores on six measures of intelligence, below the scores of lower-class nongang and middle-class nongang boys, in that order. In each category, black youngsters scored lower than did their white counterparts. The tests were designed specifically so as not to be biased against lower-class and gang subjects.[24]

From the same set of testing routines, gang boys were found to differ from nongang boys on several personality factors. These tests suggested that gang boys tended to be more self-critical and self-questioning than the other boys, and to be characterized by uncertainty and poor regard for self. The tests also provided evidence that the gang boys were less decisive, more suggestible, and may have tended to daydream. They had poor immediate memory, were slower in making judgments, and they were less effective on performance tests. Whereas some of these differences may have been due simply to the testing situation, gang boys appeared to be more cautious and more easily distracted, and more concerned with how they were doing relative to their fellow gang members than were the nongang boys.

The gang appears in light of all these observations to be an arena for status achievement, maintenance, and defense. Violent exchanges within the gang and delinquent responses to status threats often occur as gang members rely on the lowest common denominator of skills and understandings that have broad appeal within the group. The greater social skills possessed by gang leaders we observed, and their generally supportive and nurturant style of leadership, further confirm the value of group membership to gang members. Ironically, boys who possess "middle-class" social skills—especially gang leaders—are often exposed to situations that involve a high risk of delinquency involvement.

Together with findings reported by other observers of gang behavior, these data suggest that gang delinquency results from a combination of the individual characteristics of the youngsters, the internal group dynamics, and external pressures.[25] Other field observers, notably Richard Brymmer and Leon Jansyn, have noted the importance of both internal group processes and relationships with the external environment in the formation of gangs and in shaping their behavior.[26]

EARLY SOCIALIZATION, NORMATIVE AMBIGUITY, AND DELINQUENT BEHAVIOR

Drawing on a proposition from role theory, namely, that socialization is a process of learning the predictability of the behavior of others, Trutz Trotha has explored the linkage between macrosocial, microsocial, and individual levels of explanation of delinquent behavior.[27] Trotha notes that responses to the behavior of others are also expected to be predictable, in order that social interaction and community life may be facilitated.

Many inner-city communities are characterized by normative ambiguity and inconsistency in the observation of conventional norms and sanctioning behavior. There is ample evidence of normative ambiguity in other segments of society, but it is among the unstable poor, and particularly among the ghetto underclass, that ambiguity with respect to delinquency is most evident. Unemployment, family dissolution, petty crime, police activity, welfare workers, and government bureaucracies are a constant presence in such areas. Law enforcement offers little protection for residents, and the bureaucracies of government and business alike seem to impede, rather than serve, the needs of such communities. Hustling becomes a way of life for many residents.[28] The result of all these factors is that predictability of human behavior and of life in general is greatly reduced.

At the individual level, inability to *tolerate ambiguity* has been found to be associated with a large number of personal characteristics, including the need for social approval, anxiety, and a negative self-concept. This research suggests that a causal relationship may exist between ambiguity intolerance and social disabilities, such as those found especially among the black gang boys we studied.[29]

Trotha attributes Walter Miller's polarities among the "focal concerns of the lower class" to the combination of reduced behavioral predictability, normative ambiguity, and inconsistency in sanctioning.[30] Concern with "trouble," for example, is pervasive, in part because law-abiding behavior is counterposed with enjoying the pleasures associated with available forms of law-violation and getting into trouble. "Toughness" and "smartness" in the rough-and-tumble of street life are necessary because the macho image of manliness makes the threat of appearing to be weak or gullible ever present. One must constantly be on guard against appearing to be weak and being victimized by others' hustles, or being "put down." "Excitement" is counterposed with boredom (as in "Where did you go?" "Out." "What did you do?" "Nothing."). Belief that luck or "fate" largely determines one's life chances is enhanced by conditions of disadvantage that are beyond one's control, and by the necessity to hustle as a means of economic survival. Universal dependency needs heighten the need for "autonomy" under such circumstances.

Trotha's focus on the predictability of behavior is relevant, as well, to another individual-level question, namely, the role of the unsocialized aggressive adolescent in the gang. Given the highly aggressive nature of much interpersonal interaction within the gang, it might be expected that such behavior would be approved, perhaps even rewarded. This clearly was not the case among the Chicago gangs discussed in this chapter. Few such cases were found among these gangs. The one gang member who most clearly fit the syndrome was in fact notorious.

This boy was a member of perhaps the most feared conflict gang in the city. His behavior was characterized by frequent outbursts of temper and assaults on others within and outside the gang, without apparent provocation. Most members of the gang regarded him as crazy and undependable. He was actively shunned by many members of the gang. He often behaved aggressively in situations in which aggression was inappropriate, by gang or other standards. His presence in the gang made the group more vulnerable to police intervention, and his low status in the gang was related to this fact. His arrest and conviction for homicide removed him from the street for several years, much to the relief of other gang members.

CONCLUSION

This chapter does little more than lay the groundwork for more formal integration of levels of explanation for collective (in this case, gang) delinquency. We have related the three levels of explanation to one another, and made some progress toward demonstrating the compatibility of several theoretical perspectives. However, we have neither integrated theories nor expressed them in the formal language necessary for testing as well as for integration.

We have found microsocial inquiry and the microsocial level of explanation to be useful in linking the macrosocial and individual levels, as well as providing valuable insights in its own right. The micro-level of explanation is the least understood and the most neglected in the research literature. Yet it bears on important and neglected issues. The micro-level may, for example, offer a way out of sociology's chronic difficulties with the concept of *norm*. It may offer a solution to our failure to explain the circumstances in which normative properties of groups become manifest, are modified, or are ignored in behavior.

The data suggest that the explanatory power of group norms has been overemphasized.[31] Groups clearly vary in normative properties, but the manner in which these properties are manifest in attitudes and in behavior also varies between and among individuals in varying group contexts and in the types of situations in which individuals and groups find themselves. This chapter suggests some of the microsocial processes and mechanisms that are involved in the translation of normative properties of groups into individual and group behavior.

Each level of explanation must stand on its own merits. For a variety of reasons, the individual and macrosocial levels doubtless will, and should, remain the primary focus of scientific attention. Some of these reasons have to do with the time, expense, and difficulty of conducting prolonged field observations, and with the problems of standardizing the results of such observations for theoretical and empirical purposes. Much work will be required before the processes and mechanisms by which delinquent outcomes are produced at each level of explanation are understood and can be formally expressed.

Harold Finestone has suggested that bridging concepts are needed between social psychological and social structural explanations, and that the *gang* is such a concept for understanding juvenile delinquency.[32] Concepts alone are insufficient to the task, however. The microsocial level of explanation, implying methods, data, and theory, may provide a means by which levels of explanation may be bridged and integrated.

NOTES

1. For a recent exposition of the psychoanalytic position, see Bruno Bettelheim, *A Good Enough Parent*. New York: Knopf, 1987.

2. Gresham M. Sykes and David Matza, "Techniques of neutralization: a theory of delinquency," *American Sociological Review,* 22 (1957):664–670.

3. Bettylou Valentine, *Hustling and Other Hard Work: Life Styles in the Ghetto.* New York: Free Press, 1978.

4. See Alex Inkeles, "Personality and social structure," pp. 249–276 in Robert K. Merton, Leonard Broom, and Leonard S. Cottrell, Jr. (eds.), *Sociology Today.* New York: Basic Books, 1959; and James F. Short, Jr., "Social structure and group process in gang delinquency," pp. 155–188, in Muzafer Sherif and Carolyn W. Sherif (eds.), *Problems of Youth: Transition to Adulthood in a Changing World.* Chicago: Aldine, 1965.

5. Gottfredson and Hirschi distinguish between crimes, as "short-term, circumscribed events that presuppose a peculiar set of necessary conditions..." and "criminality" which "refers to stable differences across individuals in the propensity to commit criminal or theoretically equivalent acts." See Michael Gottfredson and Travis Hirschi, "A propensity-event theory of crime," in *Advances in Criminological Theory*, Vol. 1, p. 4.

6. Albert K. Cohen, *Delinquent Boys: The Culture of the Gang*. Glencoe, IL: Free Press, 1955.

7. Richard A. Cloward and Lloyd E. Ohlin, *Delinquency and Opportunity: A Theory of Delinquent Gangs*. Glencoe, IL: Free Press, 1960.

8. See Ronald L. Akers, *Deviant Behavior: A Social Learning Approach*. Belmont, MA: Wadsworth, 1973 (3d ed. 1985); see also, Robert L. Burgess and Ronald L. Akers, "A differential association-reinforcement theory of criminal behavior," *Social Problems*, 14 (1966):128–147. The quote is from Ronald L. Akers, Marvin D. Krohn, Lonn Lanza-Kaduce, and Marcia Radosevich, "Social learning and deviant behavior: a specific test of a general theory," *American Sociological Review*, 44 (August, 1979):636–655, p. 637. The search for mechanisms by which variables at any given level of explanation become "translated" into criminal behavior has taken several forms. See, for example, Elton Jackson, Charles R. Tittle, and Mary Jean Burke, "Offense-specific models of the differential association process," *Social Problems*, 33 (April, 1986):335–356; Charles R. Tittle, Mary Jean Burke, and Elton F. Jackson, "Modeling Sutherland's theory of differential association: toward an empirical clarification," *Social Forces*, (1986). These studies treat age, education, race, gender, family income, employment status, number and age of children in the family, religion, church attendance, number of times arrested, perceived community interest, and perceived chance of discovery as variables characterizing individuals. One strategy for integrating macro- and individual level theory would be to convert these variables into their macro-level counterparts (age, race, gender, education, and income stratification, for example, and family *structure*, religious composition and activity of the family or community, arrest *rates*, and measure of community toleration of and concern with crime, and crime clearance *rates*) and statistically relate these measures to the delinquent behavior of individuals.

9. See Delbert S. Elliott, Suzanne S. Ageton, and Rachelle J. Canter, "An integrated theoretical perspective on delinquent behavior," *Journal of Research in Crime and Delinquency*, 16 (January, 1979):3–27; Robert M. MacIver, *The Ramparts We Guard*. New York: Macmillan, 1950. Because different questions call for different answers, perhaps it goes without saying that integration of macrosocial and individual levels of explanation by translating the former level into questions posed at the latter level is not really integration of *different levels* of explanation, though it may well constitute theoretical advance at the individual level.

10. See, for example, Peggy C. Giordano, "Confronting control theory's negative cases," in Allen Liska, Stephen Messner, and Marvin Krohn (eds.) *Theoretical Integration in the Study of Deviance and Crime: Problems and Prospects*, Albany, New York: SUNY Press, 1989; see also Peggy C. Giordano, S. A. Cernkovich, and M. D. Pugh, "Friendships and delinquency," *American Journal of Sociology*, 91 (1986):1170–1201.

11. See Herman Schwendinger and Julia Siegel Schwendinger, *Adolescent Subcultures and Delinquency*. New York: Praeger, 1985, p. 3; see also, Gary Schwartz, *Beyond Rebellion or Conformity: Youth and Authority in America*. Chicago: University of Chicago Press, 1987.

12. Adapted from Short and Strodtbeck, *op. cit.*, p. 188.

13. Some problems may, of course, be rooted in biology, or influenced by biological imperatives or limitations. Even so, such problems are likely to be mediated by macro- and perhaps microsocial definitions, perceptions, and interactive effects.

14. The field report of this incident is published in Short and Strodtbeck, *op. cit.*, pp. 203–207.

15. See Walter B. Miller, Hildred Geertz, and Henry S. G. Cutter, "Aggression in a boys' street-corner group," *Psychiatry*, 24 (November, 1961):283–298; reprinted in James F. Short, Jr. (ed.), *Gang Delinquency and Delinquent Subcultures*. New York: Harper & Row, 1968, pp. 52–78. All quotations are from p. 65.

16. Leon R. Jansyn, "Solidarity and delinquency in a street corner group," *American Sociological Review*, 31 (October, 1966):600–614. See also, Lewis Yablonsky, *The Violent Gang*. New York: Macmillan, 1962.

17. The field report of this incident is published in Short and Strodtbeck, *op. cit.*, pp. 252–254.

18. See David P. Farrington, Leonard Berkowitz, and Donald J. West, "Differences between individual and group fights," *British Journal of Social Psychology*, 20 (1981):163–171.

19. But see Ray A. Tennyson, "Family structure and delinquent behavior," pp. 57–69 in Malcolm W. Klein and Barbara G. Myerhoff (eds.), *Juvenile Gangs in Context: Theory, Research, and Action.* Englewood Cliffs, NJ: Prentice-Hall, 1967.

20. Adapted from Short and Strodtbeck, *op. cit.,* p. 108.

21. Adapted from *Ibid.,* pp. 219–220, see also, Chap. 10; and Robert A. Gordon, "Social class, social disability, and gang interaction," *American Journal of Sociology*, 73 (July, 1967):42–62.

22. *Ibid.,* p. 222.

23. See Schwartz, *op. cit.,* p. 229.

24. The measurement of intelligence and personality factors was designed by Desmond S. Cartwright. See Desmond S. Cartwright, Kenneth I. Howard, and Nicholas A. Reuterman, "Multivariate analysis of gang delinquency: IV. personality factors in gangs and clubs," *Multivariate Behavioral Research*, 15 (January, 1980):3–22. See also, Robert A. Gordon, James F. Short, Jr., Desmond S. Cartwright, and Fred L. Strodtbeck, "Values and gang delinquency: a study of street-corner groups," *American Journal of Sociology*, 69 (September, 1963):109–28; Desmond S. Cartwright, Barbara Tomson, and Hershey Schwartz (eds.), *Gang Delinquency.* Monterey, CA.: Brooks/Cole, 1975;

25. See, especially, Malcolm W. Klein and Lois Y. Crawford, "Groups, gangs, and cohesiveness," *Journal of Research in Crime and Delinquency*, 4 (January, 1967):63–75; see also, Walter B. Miller, *op. cit.;* Lewis Yablonsky, *The Violent Gang.* New York: Macmillan, 1962.

26. See Jansyn, *op. cit.;* and Richard A. Brymmer, "Toward a definition and theory of conflict gangs." Paper presented at the Annual Meeting of the Society for the Study of Social Problems, 1967 (unpublished mimeograph).

27. Trotha's point is similar to Orville J. Brim's observation that much of personality consists of "learned interpersonal relations" (quoted in Short and Strodtbeck, *op. cit.,* p. 234). See Trutz von Trotha, *Jugendliche Bandendelinquenz.* Stuttgart: Verlag, 1974. Trotha was a postdoctoral student at Washington State University in the spring of 1974. The following account is based on our many conversations during that period and subsequently, for which I am truly grateful.

28. See Valentine, *op. cit.;* see also, Elijah Anderson, *A Place on the Corner.* Chicago: University of Chicago Press, 1967; Elliot Liebow, *Talley's Corner: A Study of Negro Streetcorner Men.* Boston: Little, Brown, 1967; Ulf Hannerz, *Soulside: Inquiries into Ghetto Culture and Community.* New York: Columbia University Press, 1969; Joan Moore et al., *Homeboys: Gangs, Drugs, and Prison in the Barrios of Los Angeles.* Philadelphia: Temple University Press, 1978; and Chapter 10 of this volume.

29. See Ronald A. Farrell, "Psychological dimensions to an elaboration of deviance theory," in Liska, Messner, and Krohn, *op. cit.*

30. See Walter B. Miller, *op. cit.*

31. See Jack P. Gibbs, "Three perennial issues in the sociology of deviance," in Liska, Messner, and Krohn, *op. cit.;* see also, by Gibbs, *Norms, Deviance, and Social Control: Conceptual Matters.* New York: Elsevier-North Holland, 1981; and "Law as a means of social control," pp. 83–113, in Jack P. Gibbs (ed.), *Social Control.* Beverly Hills, CA: Sage, 1982; cf. Peter H. Rossi and Richard A. Berk, "A conceptual framework for measuring norms," pp. 77–106, in James F. Short, Jr. (ed.), *The Social Fabric: Dimensions and Issues.* Beverly Hills, CA: Sage, 1986.

32. Harold Finestone, "The delinquent and society: the Shaw and McKay tradition," pp. 23–49, in James F. Short, Jr. (ed.), *Delinquency, Crime, and Society.* Chicago: University of Chicago Press, 1976.

CHAPTER 10
DELINQUENCY
AND SOCIETY

INTRODUCTION

This final chapter sharpens the focus on relationships between delinquency (and delinquents) and the larger society, thus returning to concerns that motivated earlier chapters—coming full circle, as it were. Some of the same issues will be examined: trends and contending interests in delinquency control, for example, and local impacts of the expanded federal role in delinquency control. Much has been written on these matters and on the nature and the efficacy of programs designed to control delinquency and to reform or deter delinquents.

Whether the focus is on what happens to delinquents when they are "treated" or when they "grow up," or on delinquency rates in communities as a result of delinquency prevention activities, efforts to control delinquent behavior are implicated in its causation. Conversely, principles of learning and bonding, of macro-level and micro-level processes are relevant to control efforts and to life after delinquency, just as they are to the etiology of delinquent behavior.

We will review both the history of efforts to control delinquency and several programs designed to enhance the prospects for more productive citizenship roles of delinquents, as well as those programs that seek to create or maintain families, communities, and societies that promote law-abiding behavior. The goal of integrating levels of explanation will be pursued through analysis of social policy and practice aimed at delinquency control, and especially at its prevention.

CONTROLLING DELINQUENCY AND CONTROLLING DELINQUENTS

The major concern of most people regarding juvenile delinquency is that it be *controlled*. Control, however, means many things to many people.

For some, it means punishment, for others treatment, and for still others, prevention. Prevention is often contrasted with deterrence, though deterrence is viewed by many as the major means of achieving prevention. We must first of all, therefore, define some terms.

Social control is the general term designating attempts by some persons to influence other persons.[1] *Prevention* and *deterrence* are likewise general terms, each implying social control aims or goals.[2]

Prevention refers to efforts to influence individuals, groups, and communities so as to prevent the occurrence of delinquency. Prevention may be aimed at entire groups or populations, or at those already identified as delinquents. Prevention strategies may focus on providing positive incentives or alternatives to delinquent behavior on the part of *particular* young people, groups, or categories, or on the part of young people in general. Or prevention may focus on more effective police and community action to *guard against* crime. These distinctions are often blurred in practice, however, as many programs combine strategies aimed at both types of prevention.

Positive preventive activities are designed primarily to promote conventional behavior. Under this rubric are various types of community organization and institutional programs that provide recreational and educational opportunities for young people, or that monitor their behavior. Such programs vary greatly in scope and in the strategies they employ, and in their underlying philosophies. A variety of programs and strategies illustrate these different terms and approaches to delinquency control.

The Chicago Area Project (CAP), for example, was based on interpretations of the individual case studies and the ecological studies of crime and delinquency conducted by Clifford R. Shaw and Henry D. McKay and others.[3] The underlying philosophy of the CAP, the oldest continuously functioning community-based crime prevention program in the United States, is one of community self-help and the utilization of indigenous leadership. The goal is to improve the conditions of living for young and old alike, nondelinquent as well as delinquent.

The principle operating units of the CAP are community committees composed of residents of relatively small urban neighborhoods or communities. The CAP sought financial assistance from private and public sources outside the local areas around which community committees were organized, but control of committee activities was vested firmly in these locally constituted committees and their indigenous leaders.[4]

The CAP is committed to operating within the system; that is, the existing political and economic organization of Chicago and other cities in which they operate. Another community-based model, based on a more confrontational philosophy, was founded by Saul Alinsky. A former CAP worker, Alinsky became disillusioned with what he felt were CAP compromises with centers of political and economic power. His Industrial Areas Foundation (IAF) promoted local community interests on an even broader base than did the CAP.[5] The CAP focuses more narrowly than the IAF on crime and delinquency problems, though that focus often has led to efforts to improve a variety of community conditions.

Federally funded community programs in recent years have tended to focus still more narrowly on helping communities and individuals to *protect* themselves from crime by *reducing opportunities* for the commission of crime. A major goal of these federally funded programs—known popularly as target hardening programs—is to reduce fear of crime, as well as seeking a reduction in crime.   Unlike both the CAP and the IAF, these programs tend to ignore the causes of crime.   The following review of several police and community crime control experiments recognizes five strategies that have been used, sometimes in combination with one another:[6]

1. changes in environmental design, largely following the tenets of Oscar Newman and "Crime Prevention Through Environmental Design" (CPTED), including improvements in street lighting and changes in traffic patterns[7]
2. changes in the *development of local police* officers, mainly emphasizing decentralized tactics and foot patrols, and including specific attempts to increase the contacts between police and citizens
3. initiation and support for *community organizations,* including organizations of residents and of neighborhood proprietors
4. attempts to increase *public awareness and education* about crime and crime prevention, through media campaigns and through the distribution of community newsletters
5. *individual crime prevention efforts,* for example, engraving personal property, conducting security surveys, and block watching.

Deterrence has quite a different connotation than does prevention.   The primary focus is on apprehension and punishment of offenders in order to deter individuals and groups from engaging in crime.   A conceptual distinction often is made between *general* and *specific* deterrence.   Specific deterrence refers to efforts to prevent those who have previously engaged in unlawful behavior from doing so in the future, for example, by prompt apprehension, and by swift and certain punishment.   General deterrence is aimed at general populations.   The hope is to persuade law-abiding persons to remain so out of respect for the law or by making an example of those who broke the law.

Prevention and deterrence thus have much in common, though the means by which they are to be achieved tend to be quite different.   Deterrence focuses on the certainty, celerity, and severity of legal sanctioning.   Prevention is commonly associated with control efforts directed toward entire communities or groups (e.g., particular gangs, or communities, or particular age groups, or youngsters characterized by some condition believed to be associated with delinquent behavior).   Conversely, the goals of punishment are commonly expressed as preventing further objectionable behavior by those who have engaged in such behavior and discouraging others from engaging in such behavior.

Punishment and treatment are also quite general terms, referring to the *means* by which deterrence and prevention are to be achieved.   Treatment is generally restricted to those who have engaged in such behavior, or whose behavior is believed to be indicative of future delinquent behavior.   Examples of treatment include efforts to teach or train young people so as to make it possible for them to lead law-abiding lives (and make them want to do so).   General deterrence, therefore, is one type of delinquency prevention, though these terms are not commonly associated with one another.

What is done to control individual delinquents also impacts delinquency rates, and vice versa. Indeed, the hope of all programs has doubtless been that both would be accomplished. The results of some efforts to control delinquents, however, almost certainly have been counterproductive for delinquency control, and the converse is also true. Incapacitation of offenders, for example, clearly does not prevent many individuals from involvement in crime, either while they are incarcerated or following their release. Conversely, programs designed to prevent young people from engaging in delinquent activities have not been notably successful.

Commitment of juveniles to correctional institutions has increased in recent years, as has the average length of stay of those who are confined.[8] Evidence of the effectiveness of institutional commitment is lacking, however.[9] Indeed, rigorous evaluations of crime-prevention programs and of rehabilitation efforts within institutions or outside them have reported little success. Experimental treatment programs, a few with random assignment of eligible offenders, have yielded mixed results. Evaluations of the more rigorously designed and conducted experiments have failed to demonstrate that recidivism among those who have been subject to community treatment is thereby reduced, compared to those who have been incarcerated. Community programs are *no less successful* in this respect, however, and careful studies suggest that community programs present no greater danger to communities than do incarcerations; indeed there is evidence that community program participants commit fewer crimes than do those who are incarcerated during brief periods of release in their communities.[10]

Community treatment programs are also demonstrably less inhumane and less expensive than is incarceration. For these reasons alone many argue the superiority of community treatment and oppose incarceration for all except the most recalcitrant and intractable offenders. Beyond this, both community treatment and more broadly conceived prevention programs commonly support other goals and values, for example, helping citizens to gain a larger measure of control over their lives and their communities, promoting education and training, encouraging recreation, aiding direct economic support, and supporting family life. Some welfare programs are clearly counterproductive, as when Aid to Dependent Children programs restrict aid to female-headed families in which no adult male is present. Such programs foster and encourage breaking the law, deceit, and hustling as a survival skill.[11] Incarceration, however, either runs counter to or ignores most of these goals and values altogether, and the survival skills acquired during incarceration are ill adapted to life in conventional society.

There is much debate concerning these issues, and evidence bearing on them is by no means clear or unequivocal. Evaluation of the effects of all delinquency control programs, whether directed to individuals, groups, or communities, is extraordinarily difficult. Given the complexity of human behavior, and of explanatory forces and processes, precise attribution of behavioral effects is often not possible. The field has not been marked by rigorous experimentation, and the most rigorously conducted experiments have tended to yield the most disappointing results. It is, of course, impossible to demonstrate that changing delinquency rates are due to specific programs, given other changes in communities and the lack of precise comparability of experimental and control communities.

One thing is clear, however. No matter how successful efforts to punish, rehabilitate, or otherwise control delinquents may be, unless the macro-level and micro-level processes that produce delinquent behavior are changed, new delinquents will continue to be produced by those same processes. Given the complexities of human behavior and the vagaries of evaluating control programs, it is especially important that the latter be based on sound theoretical principles.   The course of human history in this regard is not encouraging.

THE HISTORICAL BACKGROUND

Scholars provide varying interpretations of the history of societies' attempts to control delinquents and delinquency. Most of that history has focused on the former rather than the latter. LaMar Empey, for example, describes the historical sequence in terms of the "three Rs": retribution, restraint, and rehabilitation.[12] Societies first permitted (or prescribed) direct *retribution* against offenders by those offended against. While retribution continues to be a popular reaction to some crimes, it has long since ceased to be the major rationale for crime control in modern societies. With increasing state involvement in protecting both persons and property, apprehension and punishment of offenders became a state prerogative and responsibility. State intervention also brought with it increasing emphasis on rationalization of the criminal law and the use of *restraint* rather than capital or corporal punishment of offenders. Restraint at times involved exposure to public ridicule or physical abuse of persons locked in stocks. Public execution has at times been a matter of public celebration. Restraint later became limited to imprisonment, the goals of which are well expressed in the term applied to its chief means, namely, the *penitentiary.* However, limited treatment possibilities in penitentiaries and increasing emphasis on *rehabilitation* led to more limited types of restraint in the form of probation and parole.

Other "Rs" might be added to this list, for a major emphasis in many delinquency programs during the last quarter of the twentieth century has been on *responsibility* or accountability on the part of offenders (often involving *restitution* to victims), and *reintegration* of offending juveniles into their local communities.

While changes such as these have often been justified in rhetoric and theory stressing the saving of delinquent youth, there can be little doubt that the primary rationale has been protection of persons and the property of individuals, organizations, and institutions, including the state. It would be a mistake, in addition, to think that these developments occurred in any linear or evolutionary progression. All of the "Rs" remain in place in varying degrees, in law and in practice, as well as in theory and in public and interest group attitudes and activities. Despite a retreat from rehabilitation in response to the widely shared perception that treatment programs have failed to work, rehabilitation remains a strongly supported goal among practitioners, scholars, and the general public.[13]

Concern for the civil rights of citizens and increased sensitivity to the rights and the losses of victims have led to the emergence of what has been termed the *justice model*.[14] Rooted in despair that the justice system is incapable of "doing good" without abusing the necessary power to do so and thereby creating injustice, the justice model (also referred to as the "back to justice movement") proposes that the justice system be rigidly structured so as to ensure fairness and protection against abuse. State intervention should be restricted to the minimum consistent with justice, in recognition of social and individual harms resulting from criminal victimization.

As debate concerning these matters has continued, a variety of social policies have pursued the elusive goal of delinquency control, largely in the form of strategies related to the rehabilitation of offenders, which endeavor to foster personal responsibility and to reintegrate the offenders into their communities. Empey describes these strategies as the four "Ds." It should come as no surprise (because it was the primary focus of Chapter 3) that one of the four Ds is *due process*. Due process rulings of appellate courts have attempted to preserve the preventative and the rehabilitative goals of the juvenile court while protecting against excessive intervention in people's lives, especially with regard to incarceration.

The remaining "Ds"—*diversion, decriminalization,* and *deinstitutionalization*—are all part of the same conceptual package. Consistent with labeling theory, efforts were made during the 1970s to divert from the juvenile justice system all status offenders and many juveniles who had committed minor criminal offenses. Status offenses were to be completely decriminalized, and status offenders shielded from criminal sanctions. As previously noted, one of the requirements for federal funding of these efforts was that status offenders not be held in secure facilities.

FEDERAL INITIATIVES AND LOCAL VARIATIONS

Compliance with federal initiatives, by states and in local communities, has been variable and inconsistent. Federally funded projects designed to demonstrate the efficacy of deinstitutionalization of status offenders (commonly referred to as the DSO experiments) have yielded mixed results. It has become clear that pure status offenders are rare; most offenders commit both status and criminal offenses. Solomon Kobrin and Malcolm W. Klein, the principal evaluators of the DSO experiments, also note that most DSO treatment programs have a "paternalistic stamp" that "conflicts somewhat with the liberationist thrust of the children's rights movement of which DSO is a forerunner."[15]

Local variations and inconsistencies in the rationales underlying the demonstration programs and their implementation further complicate evaluation efforts. Evidence for the effectiveness of most of the programs was lacking. Kobrin and Klein conclude that the possibility "that early offenders are not amenable to the treatments in our standard repertoire and may best be left alone" must be taken seriously and tested.[16]

INTERPRETING HISTORY AND RESEARCH EVALUATION

Shorthand descriptions of social control efforts such as the "Rs" and "Ds" oversimplify and distort. Stanley Cohen's survey of master patterns of crime control concludes that no simple description of trends is possible and no single explanatory model is adequate to comprehend them.

The history of social control has followed an uneven course. There has been less change in underlying goals, Cohen argues, than the rhetoric of delinquency and crime control suggests. The many attempts to screen, to diagnose, and to classify offenders, and to predict their future behavior have been based on the "structural principle of binary opposition: how to sort out the good from the bad, the elect from the damned, the sheep from the goats, the amenable from the nonamenable, the treatable from the nontreatable, the good risks from the bad risks, the high prediction scorers from the low prediction scorers...."[17]

It is not difficult to discern the principle of binary opposition in current concerns with identifying and selectively incarcerating "career criminals," the small proportion of offenders who commit a large proportion of all serious crimes. A major thrust of these efforts is to increase the power of the state to intervene in the lives of citizens for the purpose of preventing their involvement in criminal behavior. Despite due process concerns, the power of the state to intervene, and the scope of intervention, have increased in the evolution of the criminal and juvenile justice systems. The positivist tradition has contributed to this power, by providing the research on the basis of which classification systems are built and control strategies assigned.

Some of its most severe critics concede, however, that the goals of positivism—"understanding, kindness, compassion—might be preferable to the hidden agenda of neoclassicism" and the justice model which, by intention or inadvertence, appears to result in more people being hurt more.[18] Further, doing good and doing justice are not always—and certainly not necessarily—incompatible. "The ideology of doing good remains powerful.... [It] is the essence of a humanistic civilization to exert power and to do good at the same time."[19]

Critics of positivism and of doing good focus on their preemption and abuse by the powerful, especially in the form of state power. Yet the state has no monopoly on justice, nor is it necessary that control efforts directed at chronic delinquents and others in high-risk categories be the province solely of the criminal and juvenile justice systems. In this final chapter, I hope to convince readers that the spirit of despair that marks the back to justice movement is unwarranted, and that when criminal opportunity reduction and doing good are based on sound theoretical principles, delinquency prevention and rehabilitation programs can be both humane and successful.

THE QUEST FOR COMMUNITY

Decriminalization and diversion of status offenders and minor criminal offenders from the full panoply of the juvenile justice system were pursued with varying degrees of success and often with different priorities with respect to goals. In the state of Washington, for example, the major priority of the diversion of minor offenders from traditional juvenile court processes to locally constituted "accountability boards" was to promote *personal accountability*, though other goals were noted in the statutes.[20] The fact that such offenders appeared before boards composed of local citizens was clearly an effort to integrate (or reintegrate) offenders into their local communities.

The impulse for integration was based in large measure on the same sort of quest for community that characterized the early juvenile court movement. Like that movement, it was justified on the basis of a variety of considerations, some pragmatic and utilitarian, some humanitarian. The idealization of community was, and is, attractive to liberals and conservatives alike, because it embraces both protection of children and their control, egalitarian values as well as maintenance of the status quo. In addition, and increasingly, civil liberties, social- scientific, and cost-benefit considerations have entered into the debate. The *quest* for community remains an important part of the community context for crime and delinquency. Another aspect has to do with the delinquency *careers* of communities.

COMMUNITY CAREERS IN DELINQUENCY

Chapter 6 introduced the concept of the criminal, or delinquent, *career* to indicate the relationship among the participation in delinquent activities, the frequency of offending, the seriousness of the offenses committed, and the period (time) of active offending. Chapter 7 noted that communities, too, have careers in crime, which appear to be associated with certain ecological characteristics. Because so much crime is attributable to the young, careers in crime can be approximated as careers in delinquency, as well. The relationship between individual careers and community careers in either crime or delinquency is not clear, however.

A Study of Two Gangs. The connection between delinquent careers and community careers in delinquency is suggested by a follow-up study of two of the Chicago gangs that have been the subject of much discussion in this book.[21] The Vice Lords and the Nobles were located in very different community areas. The Vice Lords' turf initially was in Lawndale, on the west side of the city, whereas that of the Nobles was in Douglas, in the traditional "black belt" on the South Side. Henry McKay's analysis of delinquency rates demonstrated that, between 1934 and 1961 (the latter date at the midpoint of our most intense research activity with the Vice Lords and Nobles), Lawndale experienced the greatest *increase* in rates of delinquency of all 75 Chicago communities (from 0.70 of the series grand mean to 2.75 times that mean).[22]

During this same period Douglas experienced the greatest *decrease* of all Chicago communities in rates of delinquency (the grand mean index decreasing from 4.4 to 2.18). The contrast between the two communities in rates of *commitments* of delinquents from 1945 to 1962 was even more dramatic. Thus, delinquency rates in Douglas, though still high, had decreased dramatically, whereas increases in the rates in Lawndale were equally dramatic.

The Nobles' and Vice Lords' communities also differed in the relative recency of black occupancy. For several decades the great majority of Douglas residents had been black. In contrast, Lawndale had only recently, and rapidly, undergone the classic ecological pattern of invasion, followed by succession of a black population. This contrast also existed for other communities with rapidly rising rates of delinquents, compared to those in which the rates had fallen most dramatically.

Interview excerpts from a former member of the gang tells us more about the Nobles' community and its residents:[23]

The Nobles' area was secluded, about three blocks running east and west and two or three blocks running north and south. This was where most of the people grew up in that area. Their families came from the South. They had it kind of rough and they basically all stayed in the same area. The Nobles was originally a baseball team for people who were much older than we were, people that were a generation before us. I went to school with Wallace and I met a couple of other brothers.

The people around 36th and Ellis and Cottage Grove kind of hung together in groups like. They had a real close knit type of thing even before they came into what you might call a gang-like element. I came into contact with them when I was in the seventh grade. I must have been about 12 years old. I played softball pretty good. After the game we would hang out and have a little fun, you know. After awhile the group began to grow and gather in Ellis Park. A lot of girls used to be around and we would go to parties over in their neighborhood.

The Nobles used to hang around in little bunches and hit on people for money and if you got into it with one of them, as an outsider, you would have to deal with a group of them. They had some kind of closeness in growing up together. The thing about the Nobles was that a lot of people were not actually members of the Nobles, insofar as being in the club is concerned, but you wouldn't be able to distinguish between those who were members and those who were not. They were beginning to hang together. For example, if they would go into the project for a party or something and they would get into a humbug, well then they would send somebody around to 36th and Ellis, the hanging place for the whole area, the poolroom where they all hung out at.

There was a big open courtway where a lot of people hung out over there for there was a lot of drugs over there and a lot of "slick" things happening. There were a lot of people over there who were not actual members of the club but they were under the group banner thing. So the group began to expand on that level...actually when you would be dealing with Nobles as a club you would not be dealing with that mass. But when you got down to some action as an outsider you wouldn't be able to distinguish as to who.

People who lived in that area saw a lot of harsh things happen while growing up. This made them a little more violent or have a little more heart than most young people growing up. They were exposed to seeing their mommas get cut or seeing all kinds of brutality and drugs flowing right on this corner of 36th and Ellis. They saw everything there—prostitution, people getting killed, shot down, they saw all of this.

As this account suggests, the Nobles were a neighborhood play group which became a gang in the course of a variety of activities. Some of these activities were delinquent, and the loosely knit play group may well have become "solidified" as a gang in the course of conflict, as Thrasher suggested.[24] When we first became acquainted with the Nobles, 25 boys and one girl belonged to the gang. Three years later the Nobles numbered 45, and the group had become less cohesive. Some members of a related group had joined the Nobles, but older members of both groups had begun to drift away from gang life. The young woman had entered nurses' training, and many of the young men had turned their attention largely to jobs and families.

The follow-up study began in the summer of 1971, a dozen years after our first contact with the gang. By means of key informants and interviews we were able to obtain information on 19 of the original 25 Nobles, but only eight of the 20 additional members of the expanded gang. Four of these young people (14.8 percent of those on whom information was available) were dead by the summer of 1971. Nineteen of the 23 living and known Nobles were employed at this time, some 12 years after our initial contact with the group. None were incarcerated, but two of the three who were unemployed were on the streets and involved in drug abuse.

The lack of information on so many Nobles is instructive. The Nobles never completely lost their play-group orientation, despite their involvement in a good deal of delinquent behavior. As members grew up, most grew out of the gang, and most led conventional adult lives. Our key informant on the Nobles noted that when the former gang members get "into something negative," such as drugs, "they disappear because they don't want to be criticized."

By several accounts, the Vice Lords began in 1958, two years before our initial contact with the gang.[25] Unlike most gangs, plans for organizing the Vice Lords occurred not on the street, but in the Illinois State Training School for boys. Our chief informant concerning the history of the Vice Lords was the president and strongest leader of the gang. He also became our principal informant and contact with other members of the gang for the follow-up study. According to this source, the gang's first members consisted of a few boys who were at the time residents of a cottage housing the toughest boys in the state training school. They had been affiliated with different gangs on Chicago's west side. While in the training school they decided to form the Vice Lords and to make the group the toughest gang in the city.

In the latter resolve, the Vice Lords were notoriously successful. They were also aggressively expansive. At the time of our initial contact with the gang, 66 boys were identified as members of the Vice Lords. In less than two years that number had risen to 311 names constituting five branches of the Vice Lords.

This was to be only the beginning. The Vice Lords became one of the "supergangs" of the late 1960s, incorporating under the laws of the State of Illinois as a nonprofit organization claiming some 8,000 members in 26 divisions.[26] Clearly the Vice Lords were "into the political thing," as one of our informants noted. Their efforts were not limited to politics, however. The "Vice Lord Nation" initiated a variety of economic and community service enterprises, but without notable success.

The instability marking the original Vice Lords (we focused on our list of 66 members for the follow-up study) was overwhelming:[27]

Most have stayed in Chicago when they were not incarcerated outside the city. Two apparently left for California and one for Wisconsin; we lack any information on only four of the early group. Of the remaining 62 names on that roster, 12 (19.3 percent) are dead. The circumstances of death vary from the heroic (one young man was killed attempting to rescue a child from a fire) to the criminally violent, with a heavy weighting toward the latter. Twenty-seven (43.5 percent) are working, and 23 (38.1 percent) are unemployed. Of the latter, at least six (and probably ten) are regularly involved in a drug distribution network. Another ten are in prisons, as of fall, 1973 (when the roster was last checked with our informants). Nearly all of the original group have been in correctional institutions at one time or another.

Many factors doubtless contributed to the observed differences between the Nobles and the Vice Lords. There were differences in their communities, in their founding conditions, and in the supergang status of the Vice Lords, as well as in the individuals making up the gangs. The community context seems especially important, however. It is notable that Chicago's supergangs of the 1960s emerged in communities characterized by recent and rapid population turnover. Chicago's most notorious supergang, the "Black P. Stone Nation," began in the community of Woodlawn, which, like Lawndale, had recently and rapidly undergone racial transition. Other supergangs arose in communities of recently arrived immigrants from Puerto Rico and Mexico.

These communities lacked stable populations and institutions. With the help of well-meaning persons from outside their communities (in some instances including help with funding from private foundations and the federal government), the supergangs emerged as multipurpose institutions. For the most part they were unsuccessful in both business and social service enterprises. Expectations held by gang members and by those who funded their efforts or tried to help in other ways were largely unfulfilled, and there was much bitterness in the aftermath. In retrospect, there was naivete on all sides—among those who wanted to help and among the gangs' members themselves. The gangs did not possess the necessary skills for the enterprises undertaken, and there was little involvement of other community residents and institutions in the supergang programs. There was evidence, in addition, of considerable fraud in the administration of large grant funds. Programs were poorly monitored and little technical assistance was provided. Official opposition, particularly by the police, undermined some of the programs.

The political and economic structure of the largest cities of the United States, particularly those in the East and Midwest, was changing rapidly during the 1970s. William Julius Wilson demonstrates the rapidity with which poverty became urbanized during that decade. Together with demographic and structural changes in the economy, the economic downturn of the 1970s resulted in the emergence of a ghetto underclass. "Urban minorities," Wilson argues, "have been particularly vulnerable to structural economic changes, such as the shift from goods-producing to service-producing industries, the increasing polarization of the labor market into low-wage and high-wage sectors, technological innovations, and the relocation of manufacturing industries out of the central cities."[28] Black unemployment rates more than doubled between the end of World War II and the 1970s, remaining approximately twice those of whites in both good and bad economic years since the mid-1950s. The increase in numbers of the most crime-prone population (the young) in the country as a whole was especially pronounced in the inner-city and among the minority poor.

Historic and continuing patterns of prejudice and discrimination against blacks exacerbated all of these problems[29] and led to profound social dislocations. Blacks were not the only affected minority. Between 1970 and 1984, black and Hispanic families headed by women increased by 108 percent and 164 percent, respectively, compared to 63 percent for whites. Out-of-wedlock births to black teenage mothers rose to 89 percent in 1983. The pattern was similar, but the numbers smaller (a 39 percent increase), among white teenagers. The result was that nearly half of all black children under eighteen years of age were in families with less than poverty level income in 1983, and three-fourths of these families were headed by females. The impact of these changes on welfare dependency has been substantial, especially among the young.[30]

Wilson's thesis is that civil rights advances and the Great Society and affirmative action programs of the 1960s tended to favor the already advantaged among minorities. So long as affirmative action programs were aimed at blacks and women *as categories,* those who were most favored by such programs were, of course, those who were best able to take advantage of them. Those who could go to college, for example, or acquire technical skills in other ways, advanced relatively rapidly, whereas the "truly disadvantaged" remained mired in poverty, ill equipped to participate in such opportunities. Those who could also moved out of the inner-city ghettos, thereby removing from these communities the most economically successful and politically capable residents.

Wilson's analysis and prescriptions are profound and far-reaching. They call for addressing the impact of structural changes in the economy, for less reliance on public welfare and more on income transfers (e.g., family and housing allowances, child support, unemployment assistance), and for significant involvement of the private sector in programs that would expand the limited choices that ghetto underclass individuals and families have with respect to jobs and living arrangements.

The next generation of community-oriented delinquency prevention programs emerged even as problems of the ghetto underclass were becoming more apparent.

RECENT INNOVATIONS

On the face of it, James Coleman and Thomas Hoffer's *Public and Private High Schools: The Impact of Communities* would seem to have little to do with delinquency prevention.[31] The book details Coleman and Hoffer's extensive research on the performance of students in public, Catholic, and other "private" high schools, comparing academic success, school drop-out rates, continuation in college, and other matters. In sum, and oversimplifying, Catholic private school students performed better on almost all counts than did public school students. Students in other "private" schools also fared better than those in public schools on most counts. Most important, disadvantaged students—minorities and the poor—in Catholic schools did particularly well, compared to their counterparts in public and other private schools.

In seeking to explain these findings, Coleman and Hoffer draw upon the notion of functional communities. In functional communities, institutions present a consistent pattern of norms and sanctions, reinforcing one another. Perhaps most importantly, intergenerational relationships, like other relationships between segments of the community, "arise out of the social structure itself..." (p. 7). While sociological classics such as *Middletown* and *Elmtown's Youth* dwelt on the negative effects of functional communities—the stigmatizing and self-serving character of social life locked in to the existing social order—Coleman and Hoffer identify a more positive quality of such communities:

> A functional community augments the resources available to parents in their interactions with school, in their supervision of their children's behavior, and in their supervision of their children's associations, both with others their own age and with adults. The feedback that a parent receives from friends and associates, either unsolicited or in response to questions, provides extensive additional resources that aid the parent in monitoring the school and the child, and the norms that parents, as part of everyday activity, are able to...act as important aids in socializing children. (p. 7)

All parents need such resources, of course, but the truly disadvantaged have the greatest need by virtue not only of their poverty, but also because of their own lack of education, organizational skills, and self-confidence. They tend, also, to be disadvantaged in terms of "social capital," those intangible, but very real qualities consisting of "*relations* between persons." Coleman and Hoffer argue that social capital facilitates productive capacity just as physical and human capital do. Indeed, without social capital, "human capital [e.g., education and technical skills possessed by individuals] can be irrelevant to outcomes for children," as sometimes occurs when "parents are not an important part of their children's lives," when "their human capital is employed exclusively at work or elsewhere outside the home."[32]

Functional communities provide opportunities for, but do not guarantee, the development of social capital among residents. The stigmatizing and self-serving qualities of social relationships in slum communities make social capital development especially difficult. Structural differences among families also pose barriers. It is more difficult to build social capital, for example, in single-parent families than in two-parent families, and more difficult still when the single parent is a teenager.

Coleman and Hoffer suggest that the advantages achieved by students in Catholic schools can be attributed to the embeddedness of youth and their parents in the religiously based functional communities represented by these schools. They argue intergenerational functional communities are lacking in most contemporary urban communities as a result of structural changes in the family and of media influences. The problem thus posed is to promote positive relationships between the generations as a basis for functional communities in order that social capital can flourish.

Functional communities can be organized on bases other than religion. They exist in some rural areas where social isolation creates conditions favorable to their maintenance. Many of the students studied by Coleman and Hoffer were from middle-class families. Is it possible to create and maintain functional communities among the ghetto underclass, so lacking in human capital, and often in social capital as well?

Recent innovations in community delinquency prevention and rehabilitation show some promise in this regard. A major goal of some of these programs is to create and maintain a "functional extended family," while others focus on entire communities. The goal in each case, however, is essentially the same: To create a community of values in which institutions and targeted programs are mutually supportive. Ethnic and social class ties, individual needs for nurturance, boundaries regarding acceptable conduct, employment skills and opportunities, and access to the levers of community power are all recognized as of critical importance.

Among the best known of the new programs are The House of Umoja in Philadelphia and Centro Isolina Ferre in Ponce, Puerto Rico. Umoja began as a publishing house in Philadelphia.[33] When they discovered that their son was a member of a gang, Umoja's founder, Sister Falaka Fattah and her husband, David, invited the other members of the gang (about a dozen) to live in their home. Philadelphia's gang problems were the focus of much attention during Umoja's early years (the late 1960s and early 1970s). With the help of this extended family, the Fattah's brought together gang leaders and other members to work out their common problems. Former gang members then in prison were also enlisted because they were respected by the younger boys. Umoja began employment programs for former gang members and for Umoja residents.

The extended family concept was expanded to include young men referred to Umoja by the Philadelphia Juvenile Court. Umoja does not aim to organize the local community, but the program relates to other residents, schools, and business in a number of ways. Umoja provides special educational, social, and training opportunities and finds jobs for many. Through regularly held "family" meetings, the boys' problems—in school, on the jobs, and in relations with others—are aired. Successful graduates of the program are invited to share their experiences with current residents.

Sister M. Isolina Ferre, the principal founder of Centro Isolina Ferre, came to La Playa, in Ponce, Puerto Rico, after 12 years of work "during the gang wars" in Brooklyn.[34] Based on the nucleus provided by a community health center, Centro is a multipurpose communitywide organization, with broad participation by all age groups and all identifiable segments of the community. Local residents serve as youth *advocates*, representing them in court and in institutional and personal relationships throughout the community. Families serve as "family advocates" in much the same way. A variety of employment, recreational, and social programs are sponsored by Centro.

Like Umoja, Centro also receives referrals from law enforcement officials. Most juvenile court cases are apparently returned to Centro programs rather than being sent to correctional institutions.

No rigorous evaluation of Umoja and Centro has been carried out. Perceptive observers have been high in their praise of both, however, and claims have been made of high success rates according to conventional criteria.[35]

Umoja and Centro are natural experiments that grew out of the concerns of local people and their attempts to create a sense of family and community, and to minister to special problems of youth. Unlike the supergangs, which often were viewed by local residents as a threat to personal property and safety, they have been supported by their communities. They incorporate the gangs, rather than the reverse, so that community and the gangs become more acceptable to one another.

Many such programs exist in many cities throughout the country.[36] Like the CAP and the IAF, these programs emphasize local participation and control, and indigenous, rather than professional, leadership. Most rely to some extent on expertise from outside the community for consultation and training in skills relevant to program goals. They raise financial support from both public and private sources, but incentives are provided for continued funding through economic enterprise and local institutional support. Most are multipurpose, but most promote job placement and recreational opportunities for youth as a means to prevent delinquent behavior. Several have created job opportunities by initiating economic enterprises such as product manufacture and distribution, and service businesses. Most reach out to young people who have been referred by juvenile courts or have been released from incarceration, as well as those who have not yet been caught up in the justice systems.

More carefully designed community experiments in delinquency prevention have been inspired by Umoja, Centro, and other natural experiments, and on more abstract principles drawn from research and theory. A few, sponsored by the Milton S. Eisenhower Foundation, have been the object also of extensive and intensive monitoring and evaluation. Lynn Curtis, President of the Foundation and a strong advocate of these programs, notes that block watches and patrols and other "target hardening" programs "that seek to reduce opportunities for crime without addressing the causes of crime" sometimes "become public relations gimmicks designed, at best, to assuage fear." The evidence suggests, further, that "grass-roots initiatives that both address the causes of crime and reduce the opportunities for it" demonstrate both greater success and greater cost-effectiveness.[37]

LATER STUDIES OF THE ECOLOGICAL CONTEXT

Chapters 6 and 7 noted the discovery that human intervention has increasingly altered classical ecological patterns. Implications of this discovery for crime and its control are not entirely clear. While crime continues to be influenced by ecological processes, it is not possible at present to determine the extent to which market forces, as opposed to governmental policies, have brought about ecological changes. It is often not possible to disentangle these factors, since the political process brings governmental and private parties together in so many ways. This is particularly true of large-scale housing and institutional developments.[38]

It is clear, however, that some private business practices, operating within or outside the law, influence land use and demographic patterns in ways that profoundly influence crime. Population density, age and ethnic composition, and the stability of community institutions all are affected by decisions of persons doing business in communities as well as by the decisions of community residents. Such business practices as subdividing individual dwellings into apartments in order to increase rental values, further subdividing multiple dwelling units for the same purpose, "block busting" (stirring up concern about crime and "undesirable" elements coming into the community), and "red lining" (the refusing by mortgaging institutions to make loans and by insurance companies to insure property in certain areas) all contribute to crime.

COMMUNITIES AND SOCIAL CLASS AS A CATEGORIC RISK

The suggestion that first offenders, status offenders, and minor criminal offenders, might "best be left alone" by the justice system, is not unique to the DSO experiments. It has long been observed that middle-class families and middle-class communities have a greater willingness and capacity to absorb delinquent behavior than do lower-class communities. Young wrongdoers in the middle class seem often to "get away with" a great deal of behavior that would be dealt with more harshly if committed by lower-class youngsters.[39] While this often has been interpreted as evidence of the power of the affluent and powerful to influence law enforcement processes, and as evidence of a bias favoring the middle class, the matter is hardly as simple as that. Residents of middle-class areas are more likely than those in lower-class or working-class areas to have the time and the resources, for example, the funds for alternative methods of handling offenders, and the relevant organizational skills necessary to respond to offensive behavior. These resources also enhance the middle class's ability to participate in local governance and in formally organized youth serving organizations.

COMMUNITY-BASED POLICE RESEARCH AND INNOVATION

Police-community relationships also tend to be less cooperative and more antagonistic in lower-class communities than in middle- and upper-class communities. This is especially the case in communities with predominantly black residents. Complaints of police harassment and brutality, and feelings of distrust of the police come predominantly from these communities. The ecological context of relationships between police and youth gangs, noted in Chapter 3, is again relevant. Experiments to improve police-community relationships have sometimes been successful in high-crime areas, but black communities with the highest crime rates have not been targeted in such experiments.

Of all elements in the juvenile and criminal justice systems, the police have been the most open to experimentation and innovation. Under the leadership of the chiefs of several large-city departments, in collaboration with a small cadre of academic researchers, a variety of experiments in police patrol and response have been carried out.[40] While review of these is beyond the scope of this volume, proposals to change fundamentally the nature of police response to community problems have special significance for the community control of juvenile delinquency.

Known by its shorthand description as "problem-oriented policing" (POP), the proposals center around making the police a more proactive force in the community. Unlike efforts to professionalize police operations, which have focused on higher educational standards, increased control over personnel, and on police efficiency, *problem-oriented policing focuses on the substantive problems of police work*. Without abandoning the goal of rapid response to citizen complaints, POP is concerned primarily with the nature of complaints, their location, and the relationship between reported incidents, for example, the behaviors, people, and places that generate calls for police assistance.

Herman Goldstein explains that POP[41]

> ...requires, initially, that the police move well beyond the prevailing attitude that policing consists of the handling of incidents...[POP] requires developing the capacity of the police to undertake systematic inquiry; to examine each substantive problem selected for attention in all of its dimensions as that problem is experienced in the community. It requires gathering information from police files, from the minds of experienced police officers, from other agencies of government and from private sources as well. It requires conducting house-to-house surveys and talking with victims, complainants and offenders.... [POP] recognizes the broad nature of the police function and the need to look beyond just the criminal justice system—to a wide range of other alternatives; to try to design a customized response that holds the greatest potential for dealing effectively with a specific problem in a specific place under specific conditions.

POP would clearly involve the police in an even broader range of community problems and types of responses to citizen complaints than historically has been the case. Their frontline exposure to the social ills of the community provides unique opportunities for the police to identify emerging problems and to place "choices before the community" with respect to these problems, as well as to work aggressively with other agencies and the private sector in proposing solutions to identified problems. In the long run, Goldstein suggests, the police role could change dramatically, from dealing directly with crime problems to focusing primarily on supporting and strengthening community norms, and helping citizens to solve their problems. Rather than attempting to *solve* so many problems *for* the community, police would be helping them to develop and promote a sense of community. Were this to happen, Goldstein suggests, the police role might return to that "played in the past, *before citizens abdicated their responsibilities to the police,* and to a role that they never had to abandon in smaller, more homogenous communities."[42]

The implications of POP for juvenile delinquency are not entirely clear. They will depend on specific directions POP may take at the local level. Should police forces emphasize skills in mediation and community organization as well as in research methods and interpretation, as Goldstein calls for, both police and community responses to delinquency would be profoundly affected. Police might become community advocates, for example, rather than community adversaries, as is so often the case in high crime areas.

Goldstein's vision of the police role is similar in important respects to the role of the Chicago Area Project community workers and the role of community organizers and other consultants in the community-oriented programs discussed previously—that is, a vision of the police as a resource for the community, aiding local residents and working with indigenous leaders to solve community problems, with special focus on the problems of young people. The goal in each of these programs is to promote the achievement of "functional communities," that is, communities in which family life, work, religion, education, law enforcement, and other institutional areas reflect and reinforce common values.

COMMUNITIES AND INDIVIDUAL CAREERS IN CRIME

There is ample evidence that individual delinquent careers, even in high delinquency communities, can be cut short before prolonged involvement in serious crime is entrenched. It is difficult to generalize from such cases, however, because contingencies affecting individual cases are so varied and complex. The point can perhaps be illustrated by comparing the lives of two young men who lived in the same west side Chicago community, but whose careers differed greatly. One of these was the aforementioned "founder" and strongest leader of the Vice Lords. The other, when I knew him, was about to graduate from a prestigious university and was applying for admission to the best graduate schools in the United States.

There is much that we do not know about the early lives of these two young men, for example, about the quality of their family experiences. They were physically similar: tall and muscular, each with a commanding appearance. Both spent a portion of their youth in Vice Lord territory on Chicago's west side. The gang leader became embroiled with the law and a gang member at an early age; eventually he was sent to the state training school for boys.

While much remains unclear, we know that this young man so impressed leaders of various youth programs that special efforts were made to work with him in order to prevent his continued participation in crime. For a time these efforts seemed to be successful. He worked in a variety of ways with the YMCA program with which our gang research project was associated. Shortly thereafter he was recruited to another program that offered him the opportunity to attend a small, but prestigious, eastern college, located in a largely rural setting. He did so and became, for a short time, a member of the football squad.

It would be hard to imagine a greater contrast than that between the social world of Chicago's west side gangland and the social life of this elite eastern college. By his own account, the experience was dull for this young man. He did not do well in academic course work and soon became involved in selling drugs to other students. He left the college before completing his freshman year. When he returned to Chicago he picked up where he had left off, peddling drugs and playing a prominent role in the Vice Lords.

Because he was knowledgeable about the Vice Lords, John Moland and I hired this young man to assist us in contacting members and former members of the gang, and in informing us concerning those who could not be contacted. He told us that he wanted to return to college, but in Chicago rather than elsewhere. We were unaware at this time of his drug peddling activities. He readily agreed to assist us in our research, and at first he performed well. It soon became apparent, however, that the small funds available to us could not compete successfully with income derived from his drug activities. He began to lose interest in the research and after a few months we felt we could no longer depend on him.

The second young man, the university student, was a few years younger than the gang leader. Discovery that he was from Chicago and had grown up on the west side prompted me to ask him to tell his story as part of a course requirement. He reported that his uncle was a member of the Lords. I had known the uncle and several other Vice Lord members whom this young man professed to know. Other details of his story concerning the Vice Lords were also consistent with data from our research, lending credibility to his story.

Growing up in the heart of Vice Lord territory was exciting for the boy. At night, he would often sneak out of bed and on to the front porch in order to listen to the Lords "shuckin' and jivin'" on the street in front of his home. The Lords were an important part of his social world and of the community. Even nongang members would sometimes yell "Mighty, mighty Vice Lords" as they passed by. Members of the Lords were "cool," always seeming to be "in control of the situation." If his parents had not moved from the neighborhood, this young man felt certain he would have joined the gang. He "looked up to" the Lords he knew and it gave him "a sense of security" to tell his friends at school that gang members they often talked about were his uncle's friends. He was, he said, "drafted" into more than one gang, but always managed to stay unaffiliated, in part because of his own physical stature, and because the fact that his uncle was a well-known member of the Vice Lords protected him from harm at the hands of rival gangs. Having admired the Vice Lords, no other gang appealed to him.

Though he was never an active gang member, this young man was involved in a good deal of delinquent behavior. With his best friend, a slightly older boy, he stole car batteries and stripped cars of other auto parts. The practice was lucrative since a local adult fence purchased nearly everything they stole. These activities were, however, "exploratory" for the boys, and short term, rather than an intermediate phase to more serious involvement in crime. Neither the boy nor his friend was recruited or trained to steal by older boys or adults, as is the case in some neighborhoods (see Sullivan, 1984).[43] While the boys came to the attention of the police, his account makes no mention of arrest.

As he grew older much of the prestige associated with the Vice Lords "faded away" for this young man. The fact that his family moved at least twice during his early years, first out of Vice Lord territory, and then again later, helped to insulate him from the influence of gang members and from full participation in a delinquent subculture. Another important difference between the careers of these two young men arises from an apparent similarity. Both were favored by being sent to a prestigious institution of higher learning. Prior to this, however, the university student's academic promise had been recognized early in high school, and he had been sent to an eastern "prep" school.

It is not possible at this time to determine with precision the basic intelligence of these two young men. Those who knew them were impressed with their high intelligence and potential. But the university student was prevented from strong identification with a delinquent subculture, and he was removed completely from the social world of lower-class delinquents when he was a sophomore in high school. His academic success propelled him into even more opportunities.

The gang leader was firmly embedded in the gang world; he was rewarded by the gang and by others as a result of his prominence in the gang. Intervention to remove him from this world occurred only after his established lifestyle made it virtually impossible to adjust to a social world that was alien to his experience.

The university student recognized that he was "one of the lucky ones." When he returns to his old neighborhood he sees many of his former friends who "are either junkies or drunks." Others ("probably 25 percent") are dead, "mostly from violent means or drug-related crimes."

Timing clearly is important to both of these cases. So also, perhaps, is the fact that the university student was able to avoid entanglement in the juvenile justice system and the labeling experience. Yet others have been able to survive such experiences without extensive careers in crime. Shaw's "Jack-Roller" managed to live an essentially law-abiding adult life after considerable involvement in crime as a child and as a young adult, and after extensive and painful experience in both the juvenile and criminal justice systems.[44] Waln Brown's autobiographical account of a disturbed childhood, its trauma, and his delinquent behavior in a variety of institutional contexts, revealed in *The Other Side of Delinquency*, shows his eventual recovery and successful adult adjustment.[45]

THEORETICALLY BASED PRINCIPLES OF INTERVENTION

Summarizing from previous chapters: macrosocial processes—some historical, broadly cultural and structural, some national and/or local and more immediate in their influence—largely determine what is considered delinquent and the nature of the social distribution of delinquency. Macrosocial processes also constitute the social settings which frame microsocial and individual-level processes. Framing alone cannot account for enormous variations within macrosocial environments, however. Variations occur for many reasons, within and between communities and neighborhoods, ethnic groups, and even within the same family environment.[46] Microsocial processes and genetic and developmental processes, as well as the nature and strength of social bonds and external social controls, and the nature and strength of personally acquired skills, abilities, and values, shape each person's perceptions of needs, opportunities, and risks associated with behavioral choices.

Research and theory within each of these levels of explanation have attracted a great deal of attention from policymakers in and out of government, and from professionals in a variety of fields. No social policy or program is likely to comprehend or encompass knowledge from the entire range of explanations. Taken together, however, policies and programs based on sound research and theory at each level of explanation have the potential to achieve theoretical integration as a basis for primary and secondary delinquency prevention.

We bring the book to a close by making more explicit several theoretically-based principles of intervention, and by describing policies and programs that embody these principles. We hope to bring together, in principle and by illustration, the levels of explanation around which the book has been organized.

While a large and growing literature exists concerning delinquency in other times and places, this discussion will focus on urban ghettos in the United States, where the problem is the most serious and intractible. Thus, we begin, as we did in Chapter 7, with the macro-level of explanation, by returning to William J. Wilson's research on the ghetto underclass.

Wilson's policy agenda includes "economic growth and a tight labor market," supplemented by "on-the-job training and apprenticeships to elevate the skill levels of the truly disadvantaged."[47] While such a policy would do little to curb the sort of expressive delinquent acts that are virtually universal among younger adolescents, it would make theft and other forms of economic crime less attractive for young people who often engage in such activities before even attempting to secure legitimate economic employment.

Wilson also calls for federal legislation to establish inflation-adjusted Aid for Dependent Children benefits and provision of child care services and subsidies for working-poor parents. Illustrative of this type of innovative and experimental child-care program is the Center for Successful Child Development in Chicago. Better known as "The Beethoven Project" because it serves the Beethoven Elementary School catchment area in Chicago, the project is centered in six units of Chicago's Robert Taylor Homes housing project, allegedly the largest public housing project in the world. Stretched out along a two-mile section of a major expressway (which effectively isolates the housing project from the rest of the city) "Taylor Homes" consists of 28 high-rise buildings housing approximately 20,000 people. Nearly all residents are poor and black. More than 90 percent of the households receive public assistance and three-quarters are headed by women.

The Taylor Homes housing project is plagued by every poverty-related problem: high rates of drug abuse, crime, delinquency, unemployment and dependency. It has educational deficiencies that begin as early as the first grade, school drop-outs, health and nutrition problems. The goal of the Beethoven Project "is to prevent social, psychological, and physical dysfunction among...[a cohort of] children so that they will be fully prepared to enter kindergarten."[48] Like the family and community-oriented projects discussed previously, the Beethoven Project is multi-faceted. It provides a variety of health and social services aimed at both parents and children, including a "family drop-in center," which will be the project's physical base, a neurological, physiological, and psychological assessment and referral program for infants, a parent-child relationship screening and parenting education program, and a home visitation and day-care service. The most immediate targets of the project are the annual cohorts of children born between January 1, 1987 and January 1, 1992 in the designated housing units, and their mothers (who will have been identified prior to the birth of the children). There are other benefits, too, since many project personnel are themselves residents of Taylor Homes. The home visitors, who are trained specifically for this work, are residents of Taylor Homes. The project is designed to provide a "Head Start on Head Start," as a New York Times editorial proclaimed.

The project thus seeks to remedy social, physiological, and psychological deficits that result from the operation of macro-level forces affecting the lives of the target population. In a broader sense, however, the approach is experimental, with the clear expectation that lessons will be learned that can be applied on a larger scale.

If our analysis is correct, more will be required if the Beethoven Project cohort of infants and their parents are to break out of the cycle of poverty, dependency, delinquency, and other social ills. It will be important to evaluate carefully what happens to these children and their parents, and to study the impact of the project on other Taylor Homes residents. More than this, attention must be given to the maintenance of functional communities and families beyond the kindergarten years. It will be important to build on the social capital opportunities created in the course of the project if others in the larger community, as well as those who are its primary targets, are to benefit. An extended family of the kind seen in the Umoja project may not be necessary for the Beethoven cohort, but it would surely serve the interests of older children in the designated Taylor Homes units and those of other older cohorts.

Delinquency prevention and correctional programs can be evaluated, also, on the basis of their compatibility with principles of social learning and bonding, and with opportunities for achievement. Projects that are able to create and sustain functional families and communities promote both conventional learning and achievement opportunities and bonds to conventional persons and lifestyles.

That patterns of social interaction in lower-class communities are more informal than the patterns of middle-class interaction has often been noted. In addition, as Daniel Glaser observes, "subtle aspects of...social habits and skills" tend to distinguish delinquents from nondelinquents.[49] While a great deal of informal interaction characterizes all segments of society, middle-class youngsters early in life also develop an easy familiarity with formal institutions and relationships. They also have the advantages, virtually by definition, of greater accumulations of human capital in their families, in education, income, prestige, and power. Success in school comes easier, in part, because of these advantages. The "social disabilities" of many lower-class gang members, discussed in the previous chapter, reflect their disadvantages in these respects. These disabilities vary greatly among individuals and in various social settings. Jay MacLeod found that black youths were *less* delinquent and evidenced fewer social disabilities than white youths living in the same public housing project.[50] Mercer Sullivan also reports evidence that the black youngsters he studied in Brooklyn fared better in school than their Hispanic counterparts.[51] Both MacLeod and Sullivan attribute these differences, in part, to the civil rights movement and to parental influences which reinforced an ideology of achievement. The civil rights movement had little influence on the black gang boys we studied in Chicago two decades earlier. Hagedorn and Macon also describe black Milwaukee gang members as alienated from community institutions and their leaders, some of whom came to prominence during earlier civil rights struggles.[52]

Programs that seek to provide legitimate opportunities for underclass young people or other target groups must be sensitive to needs in all these respects. The complexity thus introduced at each level of explanation is a necessary condition if just and humane social control efforts are to be successful.

CONCLUSION

Most youngsters do not become seriously involved in delinquent behavior. Those who do too often become society's criminals, wards of the criminal justice system, the specter of public fears, and a major drain on the public purse. Yet, despite the best intentions of reformers and the best efforts of scholars, the combination of the uncertainty of knowledge, the continuous arrival of new "barbarians" to be socialized, and continuous social change ensure that there will always be youth problems and delinquents. Increasingly we are discovering that uncertainty is a problem in all fields of knowledge, even in the most advanced sciences and technologies. While this may be small comfort to those who suffer as a result of these uncertainties and the many flaws in social systems, we are all in the "same boat," more or less, and we must do our best to keep it aright and afloat.

The task of an informed sociology, notes Stanley Cohen, is "neither to be deceived by appearances nor to be obsessed by debunking" (p. 156). I have tried in this book to inform the reader as to what the social and behavioral sciences have to say about human behavior, and particularly what is relevant to understanding juvenile delinquency and juvenile delinquents. The last chapter suggests some implications of this knowledge, noting what has been and what might be done to alleviate problems of delinquency and of delinquents.

The task of citizens is increasingly difficult in an ever more complex and interdependent world. If this book contributes in even a small way to informing the nature of the task involved in coping with problems of juvenile delinquency, I shall feel richly rewarded.

NOTES

1. For a review of the extensive literature on social control, see Robert F. Meier, "Perspectives on the concept of social control," pp. 35–55, in Ralph H. Turner and James F. Short, Jr. (eds.), *Annual Review of Sociology*, Vol. 8, Palo Alto, CA: Annual Reviews, 1982.
2. The literature on prevention and deterrence likewise is large and complex. See, for example, Philip Cook, "Research in criminal deterrence: laying the groundwork for the second decade," pp. 211–268, in Norval Morris and Michael Tonry (eds.), *Crime and Justice*, Vol. 2. Chicago: University of Chicago Press, 1980.

3. For a general discussion of community crime-prevention programs, see Anthony Sorrentino, "Crime prevention: community programs," pp. 358–362, in S. H. Kadish (ed.), *Encyclopedia of Crime and Justice.* New York: Free Press, 1983; See also by Sorrentino, *How to Organize the Neighborhood for Delinquency Prevention,* New York: Human Sciences Press, 1979; and *Organizing Against Crime: Redeveloping the Neighborhood,* New York: Human Sciences Press, 1977.

4. For a participant-observer's account of CAP philosophy and practice see Anthony Sorrentino, *Organizing Against Crime: Redeveloping the Neighborhood.* New York: Human Sciences Press, 1977.

5. See Saul Alinsky, *Reville for Radicals.* Chicago: University of Chicago Press, 1946.

6. See Robert K. Yin, "Community crime prevention: a synthesis of eleven evaluations," pp. 294–308, in Dennis P. Rosenbaum (ed.), *Community Crime Prevention: Does it Work?* Beverly Hills, CA: Sage, 1986.

7. The reference is to the work of architect, Oscar Newman. See his *Defensible Space: Crime Prevention through Urban Design.* New York: Macmillan, 1972. See also, C. R. Jeffry, "Crime prevention: environmental and technological strategies," pp. 362–366, in Kadish, *op. cit.* See also, by Jeffry, *Crime Prevention through Environmental Design.* Beverly Hills, CA: Sage, 1977.

8. See Barry Krisberg, I. Schwartz, P. Litsky, and J. Austin, "The watershed of juvenile justice reform," *Crime and Delinquency,* 32:5–38.

9. See Alfred Blumstein, Jacqueline Cohen, Jeffry A. Roth, and Christy A. Visher (eds.), *Criminal Careers and "Career Criminals."* Washington, DC: National Academy Press, 1986; David Farrington, Lloyd Ohlin, and James Q. Wilson, *Understanding and Controlling Crime: Toward a New Research Strategy.* Report commissioned by the MacArthur Foundation. Chicago: Springer-Verlag, 1986; and Robert Martinson, "What works? Questions and answers about prison reform," *The Public Interest,* 35 (Spring, 1974):22–54.

10. See LaMar T. Empey, *American Delinquency: Its Meaning and Construction.* Homewood, IL: Dorsey, 1982; LaMar T. Empey and Steven G. Lubeck, *The Silverlake Experiment: Testing Delinquency Theory and Community Intervention.* Chicago: Aldine, 1971; and LaMar T. Empey and Maynard L. Erickson, *The Provo Experiment: Evaluating Community Control of Delinquency.* Lexington, MA: D.C. Heath, 1972.

11. See Bettylou Valentine's description of survival skills necessary for coping with governmental and corporate bureaucracies, in *Hustling and Other Hard Work: Lifestyles in the Ghetto.* New York: Free Press, 1978. Stanley Cohen argues that such apparently counterproductive programs provide "opportunities for "manipulation by (rather than of) the client," and for acquiring "the key survival skill: to know when you are being conned." See his *Visions of Social Control: Crime, Punishment and Classification.* Cambridge: Polity Press, 1985, pp. 260–261.

12. Empey, *Ibid.,* Chap. 16.

13. See Francis T. Cullen and Karen E. Gilbert, *Re-affirming Rehabilitation.* Cincinnati, OH: Anderson, 1982.

14. See Willard Gaylin and David J. Rothman, "Introduction," pp. xxi–xli, in Andrew Von Hirsch, *Doing Justice: The Choice of Punishments.* New York: Hill and Wang, 1976, *et passim.*

15. Solomon Kobrin and Malcolm W. Klein, *Community Treatment of Juvenile Offenders: The DSO Experiments.* Beverly Hills, CA: Sage, 1983, p. 318.

16. *Ibid.,* p. 319. This position is, of course, consistent with the labeling perspective. See also, Edwin M. Schur, *Radical Nonintervention: Rethinking the Delinquency Problem.* Englewood Cliffs, NJ: Prentice-Hall, 1973.

17. Cohen, *op. cit.,* p. 86.

18. *Ibid.,* p. 276. Cohen has been among the most severe critics of increasing state intervention in the lives of individuals and of the efficacy of doing so.

19. *Ibid.,* p. 214.

20. See, for example, Revised Code, State of Washington, 1977, p. 80. For a critical review of state compliance with federally mandated deinstitutionalization of status offenders, see Mary Beth Meade, "The degree of implementation of the Juvenile Justice and Delinquency

Prevention Act of 1974." Unpublished Master's thesis, Criminal Justice Program, Washington State University, 1987.

21. The following discussion is drawn largely from James F. Short, Jr. and John Moland, Jr., "Politics and youth gangs: a follow-up study," *Sociological Quarterly*, 17 (Spring, 1976):162–179.

22. Henry D. McKay, in Clifford R. Shaw and Henry D. McKay, *Juvenile Delinquency and Urban Areas*, (rev. ed.) Chicago: University of Chicago Press, 1969.

23. Adapted from Short and Moland, *op. cit.*

24. Frederic M. Thrasher, *The Gang: A Study of 1,313 gangs in Chicago*. Chicago: University of Chicago Press, 1927, see also, James F. Short, Jr., "Introduction" to the abridged edition, 1963.

25. See, for example, R. Lincoln Keiser, *The Vice Lords: Warriors of the Street*. New York: Holt, Rinehart & Winston, 1969; and David Dawley, *A Nation of Lords*. Garden City, NY: Anchor, 1973.

26. See Lawrence Sherman, *Youth Workers, Police, and the Gangs*. Unpublished Master's thesis. University of Chicago, 1970; Walter B. Miller, "Youth gangs in the urban crisis era," pp. 91–128, and James F. Short, Jr., "Gangs, politics, and the social order," pp. 129–163 in James F. Short, Jr., (ed.), *Delinquency, Crime, and Society*. Chicago: University of Chicago Press, 1976.

27. Short and Moland, *op. cit.*

28. See William Julius Wilson, *The Truly Disadvantaged: The Inner City, the Underclass, and Public Policy*. Chicago: University of Chicago Press, 1987, p. 39.

29. See Stanley Leiberson, *A Piece of the Pie: Black and White Immigrants Since 1880*. Berkeley, CA: University of California Press, 1980. Wilson notes that Hispanics have migrated to U.S. cities in greater numbers than blacks since the mid-1970s, and that this may increase ethnic hostility against Hispanics and bring about similar social dislocations to those experienced by the black ghetto underclass, *Ibid.*, p. 35. For an especially dramatic example, see Geoffrey P. Alpert and Roger J. Dunham, *Policing Multi-Ethnic Neighborhoods: The Miami Study and Findings for Law Enforcement in the United States*. New York: Greenwood Press, 1988.

30. See Wilson, *Ibid.*

31. James S. Coleman and Thomas Hoffer, *Public and Private High Schools: The Impact of Communities*. New York: Basic Books, 1987.

32. *Ibid.*, p. 221. Coleman and Hoffer note further that *trust* is a "form of social capital. A group within which there is extensive trustworthiness and extensive trust is able to accomplish much more than a comparable group without the trustworthiness and trust."

33. See Robert L. Woodson (ed.), *Youth Crime and Urban Policy: A View from the Inner City*. Washington, DC: American Enterprise Institute for Public Policy Research, 1981.

34. Sister M. Isolina Ferre, "Dispensario San Antonio, Institute of La Playa de Ponce, Puerto Rico," pp. 17–21 in *Ibid.*

35. See, for example, Lynn A. Curtis, "American violence: policy and folly," *The Annals of the American Academy of Political and Social Science* (November, 1987), p. 8; Charles E. Silberman, *Criminal Violence, Criminal Justice*. New York: Random House, 1978, p. 434.

36. See the reports from other programs in Woodson, *op. cit.*, and in Lynn A. Curtis (ed.), "Policies to prevent crime: neighborhood, family, and employment strategies," *The Annals of the American Academy of Political and Social Science* (November, 1987):494.

37. See Lynn A. Curtis, "The retreat of folly: some modest replications of inner-city success," *Annals of the American Academy of Political and Social Science* (November, 1987):71–89.

38. See, for example, Sorrentino's discussion of the (unsuccessful) efforts of residents of Chicago's Near West Side to prevent destruction of a large portion of their community for the purpose of building a Chicago campus of the University of Illinois. Sorrentino, *op. cit.*

39. See, for example, Howard L. Myerhoff and Barbara G. Meyerhoff, "Field observations of middle class 'gangs'," *Social Forces*, 42 (March, 1964):328–336.

40. The Police Foundation and the Police Executive Research Forum have played leading roles in these developments, encouraged by federal funding of experiments and innovations through the National Institute of Justice.

41. Herman Goldstein, "Comments presented to the conference on policing: state of the art III," (unpublished paper) sponsored by the National Institute of Justice, June 12, 1987, pp. 5–6; see also, Mark H. Moore and Robert C. Trojanowicz, *Corporate Strategies for Policing.* National Institute of Justice. Washington, DC: U.S.G.P.O., 1988; and Peter K. Manning, *Police Work.* Cambridge, MA: MIT Press, 1979.

42. *Ibid.*, p. 18; see also, by Geoffrey P. Alpert and Roger G. Dunham, *Policing Urban America.* Prospect Heights, IL: Waveland Press, 1988.

43. See Mercer L. Sullivan, *Youth Crime and Employment Patterns in Three Brooklyn Neighborhoods.* New York: Vera Institute of Justice, 1984.

44. See Jon Snodgrass, et al., *The Jack-Roller at Seventy: A Fifty-Year Follow-Up.* Lexington, MA: D.C. Heath, 1982.

45. See Waln Brown, *The Other Side of Delinquency.* New Brunswick, NJ: Rutgers University Press, 1983.

46. See, for example, Sullivan, *op. cit.*; Valentine, *op. cit.*; and Jay MacLeod, *Ain't No Makin' It: Leveled Aspirations in a Low-Income Neighborhood.* Boulder, CO: Westview Press, 1987, pp. 145–148 ; see also, John Hagedorn and Perry Macon, *People and Folks: Gangs, Crime, and the Underclass in a Rustbelt City.* Chicago: Lake View Press, 1988.

47. Wilson, *op. cit.*, pp. 152–153; also, Sullivan, *Ibid.*

48. Center for Successful Child Development, "Background information on the Center for Successful Child Development," Chicago: n.d.

49. Daniel Glaser, "A review of crime-causation theory and its application," pp. 203–237, in Norval Morris and Michael Tonry (eds.), *Crime and Justice,* Vol. 1. Chicago: University of Chicago Press, 1979, p. 223.

50. MacLeod, *op. cit.* pp. 129 ff.

51. Sullivan, *op. cit.*, p. 324.

52. Hagedorn and Macon, *op. cit.*, Chapter 6.

INDEX